John Mulvaney AO, CMG, whose career in history and archaeology spans nearly half a century, was the first to teach the prehistory of the Australian continent and was instrumental in fostering professional archaeology in Australia. He has written, edited or co-edited eighteen books, including *Prehistory of Australia* (with Johan Kamminga, 1999), as well as the precursors to this current work, the award-winning *'So Much That is New': Baldwin Spencer, A Biography* (with John Calaby, 1985) and *'My Dear Spencer': The Letters of F.J. Gillen to Baldwin Spencer* (1997). While foundation professor of Australian prehistory at the Australian National University's Arts Faculty, John gained fame for his promotion and public defence of Australia's heritage. Among his public offices, John was a foundation commissioner of the Australian Heritage Commission and represented Australia on World Heritage issues. In the course of his research, he has visited and investigated much of outback Australia, including many of the places mentioned in this book.

Alison Petch, an anthropologist, is on the research staff of the Pitt Rivers Museum, Oxford. With Howard Morphy and John Mulvaney, she co-edited *'My Dear Spencer'*.

Howard Morphy is Professor and Director of the Centre for Cross-Cultural Research at the Australian National University. Previously Professor of Social Anthropology at University College, London, and a curator at the Pitt Rivers Museum, he is an authority on Aboriginal art.

FROM THE FRONTIER

OUTBACK LETTERS to
BALDWIN SPENCER

JOHN MULVANEY
with ALISON PETCH and HOWARD MORPHY

ALLEN & UNWIN

First published in 2000
Copyright © Derek John Mulvaney, Howard Morphy and Alison Petch 2000

Allen & Unwin
9 Atchison Street
St Leonards NSW 2065
Australia
Phone: (61 2) 8425 0100
Fax: (61 2) 9906 2218
Email: frontdesk@allen-unwin.com.au
Web: http://www.allen-unwin.com.au

National Library of Australia
Cataloguing-in-Publication entry:

From the frontier: outback letters to Baldwin Spencer.

  Bibliography.
  Includes index.
  ISBN 1 86508 317 8

  1. Spencer, Baldwin, Sir, 1860–1929. 2. Byrne, Patrick M.,
  (1856–1932)—Correspondence. 3. Spencer, Baldwin, Sir, (1860–1929)—
  Correspondence. 4. Cowle, Ernest, (1863–1922)—Correspondence.
  5. Aborigines, Australian—Australia, Central—Social life
  and customs. 6. Anthropologists—Australia—Correspondence. 7. Australia,
  Central—History. I. Morphy, Howard. II. Mulvaney, D. J. (Derek John),
  1925– . III. Petch, Alison, 1956– .

301.0922942

Set in 10.5/14 pt Caslon by DOCUPRO, Sydney
Printed by South Wind Productions, Singapore

10 9 8 7 6 5 4 3 2 1

CONTENTS

ILLUSTRATIONS

Maps

Plates

ACRONYMS AND ABBREVIATIONS

AA	Australian Archives
AAAS	Australasian Association for the Advancement of Science
ADB	Australian Dictionary of Biography
AND	Australian National Dictionary
CW	Charlotte Waters
FJG	Francis James Gillen
HE	Horn Expedition
HEC	Horn Expedition Camp
L	letter number
M/C	Mounted Constable
M&C	Mulvaney and Calaby, 1985 (Spencer biography)
MDS	*'My Dear Spencer'* (Gillen letters)
M&M	Morton and Mulvaney, 1996 (*Exploring Central Australia*)
NLA	National Library of Australia
NT	Native Tribes of Central Australia, 1899
NT	Northern Territory
NTCA	Northern Tribes of Central Australia
OED	Oxford English Dictionary
OT	Overland Telegraph
SA	South Australia

SAM	South Australian Museum
SAPP	South Australia, Parliamentary Papers
S&G	Spencer and Gillen
Wanderings	Spencer, *Wanderings in Wild Australia*, 1928
WBS	Walter Baldwin Spencer

PREFACE

When Baldwin Spencer sailed to England in 1927, his luggage included these letters, together with those of F.J. Gillen and his other unorthodox Australian bush mates from his stimulating turn-of-the-century experiences. In London he wrote *Wanderings in Wild Australia* (1928), a semi-autobiographical work that was more personal than any of his previous books. He must have found these papers a useful *aide-mémoire*, therefore, and it is not surprising that occasional paraphrases from them turn up in his text.

Spencer embarked on a foolhardy and fatal expedition to Tierra del Fuego in 1929, leaving his invaluable archive behind, presumably in the care of his daughter, Lady Dorothy Young. Following his death, his two daughters donated these papers to the Pitt Rivers Museum, Oxford University. Back in 1885, the youthful Spencer had assisted Edward Tylor to transfer from London some 20 000 ethnographic and archaeological specimens to be exhibited in that unattractive new building. Several box files of this correspondence were shelved there in 1930 but, except for their use by Mulvaney in 1970, when preparing Spencer's biography,[1] C.E. Cowle's and P.M. Byrne's letters have remained unknown and unused.

Howard Morphy, Alison Petch and John Mulvaney previously

edited Frank Gillen's more voluminous correspondence with Spencer, which was published in 1997.[2] As Cowle's and Byrne's lively letters span the identical and vital period, frequently referring to the same persons or incidents, and because they are not reticent in voicing opinions, their correspondence provides an insight into race relations, social history and the dawn of anthropological and biological interest in central Australia.

Ernest Cowle's letters were composed under incredible difficulties of heat, frost, flies and poor lamplight, in a rude bush shack—although a thoughtful relative provided the modernity of a fountain pen. Paddy Byrne had the relative comfort of a solid Overland Telegraph building and easy access to telegraph and postal services. Less inclined than Cowle to pen his thoughts, however, he was further inhibited, tragically, when his right hand was severed in an accident. He adjusted to a crabbed, left-hand script.

Alison Petch undertook to transfer both Cowle's and Byrne's words to the computer and to check words for accuracy upon request from the Australian editors. We are grateful to the Pitt Rivers Museum authorities for granting permission to publish these letters and to museum staff Elizabeth Edwards, Malcolm Osman and Chris Morton for their help.

The late Dr John Calaby, a biologist with an unrivalled knowledge of the history of biological research in Australia, provided the data upon which most notes on fauna and flora were based in 'My Dear Spencer', the volume of Gillen's correspondence. Having performed the same service for Cowle's letters, at the time of his death in September 1998, he was collaborating with Mulvaney as a co-editor of Byrne's correspondence. Subsequently, it became necessary to draw upon Calaby's study of biological discoveries during the 1894 Horn Expedition, published in S.R. Morton and Mulvaney (eds), *Exploring Central Australia* (1996). His association with those projects was crucial.

Numerous people assisted the project in Australia, some of whom are singled out for special acknowledgement. Mrs Elizabeth Dyer, Ernest Cowle's grandniece, acting as an honorary research assistant, provided continual assistance with family history and its documentation. Other Cowle family descendants who have supplied assistance are Mr Charles Symon, Jamestown, SA, and Mrs Perdita Eldridge, Echunga, SA. Dick Kimber, the Alice Springs authority on the history of his region, answered many questions. Advice was provided by John Strehlow, London, and by David Hugo of the Strehlow Research Centre, Alice Springs. Documentation of South Australian police postings was facilitated by Dr Robert Clyne and Chief Superintendent R.J. Potts, successive secretaries of The South Australian Police Historical Society Inc. Dr R.S. Gillen was constant in his encouragement. In 1986, Howard Pearce took Mulvaney and his wife, Jean, on a memorable drive which included visits to Illamurta and Tempe Downs.

The South Australian Museum has proved an invaluable source for many enquiries and photographs. In particular, Dr Philip Jones and Ms Kate Alport have made considerable efforts to assist the editors. Thanks go also to Lorraine Macknight, Launceston; Rev. P. Scherer, Tanunda, SA; Mr R.W. Fisher, archivist, St Peter's College, Adelaide; Mrs Barbara Brummitt, Adelaide; Mrs Diana Ridley, Nedlands, WA; Emeritus Professor A.G.L. Shaw, Melbourne; Dr Luise Hercus, Pam and Colin MacDonald, Canberra; and Vern O'Brien, Darwin. The Genealogical Society of the Northern Territory and the Heraldry and Genealogy Society of Canberra provided useful information.

The staff of the Mortlock Library of the State Library of South Australia, and the State Archives of South Australia, provided courteous and helpful service. Some additional letters from Cowle to the Director of the South Australian Museum are published with the permission of that museum, while a letter to R.H. Mathews is published with the permission of the National Library of Australia. Staff of the Australian Archives in Adelaide, Canberra and Darwin provided helpful assistance. Andrew Pitt, Archivist, Northern Territory Archives Service, is acknowledged for his assistance with Patrick Byrne. David Wilkins' invaluable work on the Arrernte vocabulary used in the Spencer and Gillen correspondence (as shown in the glossary of *'My Dear Spencer'*), has been used in some of the endnotes in this volume.

Mulvaney acknowledges the facilities provided in the office of the Australian Academy of the Humanities. Extensive typing tasks were efficiently and speedily undertaken by Amanda Jacobsen. Doreen Bowdery and Jo Bushby completed the final typing stages of this project. He also pays tribute to his wife, Jean, for her patience across thirty years, during Baldwin Spencer's presence as a virtual house guest.

The staff of Allen & Unwin proved invaluable for their advice and encouragement. Colette Vella, in particular, added imagination and artistry to the project.

When transcribing the letters, care was taken to present them as they were written. Underlining is by the correspondents, while words in italics are additions made to the text. Where Cowle used a plus sign for 'and', we have transcribed it as 'and' for clarity. Some additional punctuation was thought necessary to assist clarification. Also, some additional paragraph breaks have been inserted to split up very long passages. The maps were drawn by Val Lyon, Department of Geography, Faculty of Science, The Australian National University.

The following editorial conventions have been followed: Underlining has been retained as in the original text; italics are insertions to the text made by the correspondents, either as postscripts, marginal notes or textual additions; '+' signs in the text have been replaced by the word 'and'; apostrophes and question marks have been added where necessary and minor punctuation problems have been corrected for the sake of clarity.

INTRODUCTION: CORRESPONDENTS ON A FRONTIER

This book brings together the lively letters of two correspondents to the pioneer biologist and anthropologist, Baldwin Spencer, written between 1894 and 1925. The first of the correspondents was Ernest Cowle, a bush policeman stationed at Illamurta Springs, 150 kilometres southwest of Alice Springs. The second was Paddy Byrne, a postal officer at the outpost of Charlotte Waters situated a few kilometres north of the South Australian border.

Spencer met both Cowle and Byrne on the Horn Scientific Expedition of 1894. Both men lived in remote circumstances along the Overland Telegraph Line. Their stories are shaped by extreme isolation and the harshness of their lives, and their letters provide insights into race relations, social history, and the dawn of anthropological and biological interest in central Australia.

The Overland Telegraph Line

John McDouall Stuart traversed the continent north from Adelaide in 1862. Remarkably, within a decade, Stuart's route was demarcated by a single wire strand spanning 3178 kilometres, supported on 36 000

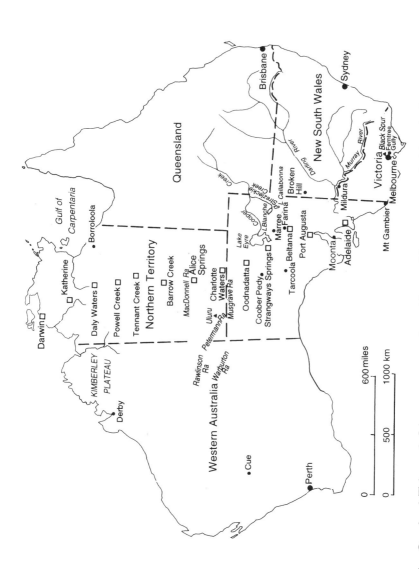

Map 1. The Overland Telegraph Line repeater stations (denoted by square symbols) and places mentioned in the text

poles. On 22 August 1872 a morse code telegraphic message was transmitted from Adelaide to Darwin. With this bold achievement, the Overland Telegraph Line ended Australia's communications isolation. Investors and politicians in booming cities like Sydney and Melbourne became expensively linked to London via this fragile wire coupled with an undersea cable through Java. This outstanding demonstration of colonial progress regrettably signalled the doom of traditional indigenous culture across a broad swathe of their land.[1]

'The Line' virtually provided an instant cross-continental frontier, constituting one of this nation's greatest technological feats. It was a heroic triumph for infant South Australia, whose colonists built and staffed the Line. Existing technology required a dozen repeater stations, approximately 250 kilometres apart, in order to boost weak signals tapped along the wire. These isolated solid stone buildings, the Centre's first European settlements, also housed repair and maintenance teams and stockmen to supervise the cattle, goats and horses upon which each community depended. Repeater stations became communications and administrative centres and lures for Aboriginal people driven from their territories by pastoral expansion. At these centres they were provided with government rations, although the extent to which, in return, Aboriginal men supplied labour and women performed domestic duties has been under-emphasised.

Improved technology soon increased the number and efficiency of telegraphic communications in either direction, and termites forced the substitution of iron for wooden poles. The basic system persisted, however, across sixty years before repeater stations became redundant. Two telegraph stations figure prominently in this volume. The central base along the Line was Alice Springs, whose stationmaster also was a legal official, a Justice of the Peace and stipendiary magistrate. The intact station complex today has major heritage value and tourist attraction. The other station is now a forlorn, deserted ruin. Charlotte Waters, just north of the present South Australian border is bypassed by road and rail. In those times it was a remote but large and important post, and, from 1890, the first settlement on the exhausting sandy haul north of the railway terminus at Oodnadatta.

The track along the Line linked natural water sources or bores, serving to funnel optimistic settlers into the interior. They moved outwards from it in every direction, depasturing herds or fossicking

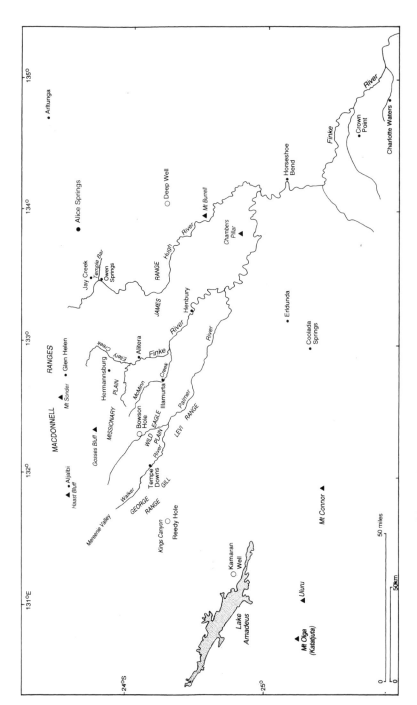

Map 2. Central Australia. Illamurta is 24°19'S, 132°41'E.

131°E 132° 133° 134° 135°

MACDONNELL RANGES

Haast Bluff ▲
▲ • Aljalbi
Mt Sonder ▲ Glen Helen •
Gosses Bluff ▲
Ellery Creek
Hermannsburg •
MISSIONARY PLAIN
Bowson Hole ○
McMinn
WILD EAGLE PLAIN
Illamurta ▲
River
Walker
Mereene Valley
Tempe Downs •
GEORGE RANGE
GILL
Kings Canyon •
Reedy Hole ○

Temple Bar
Jay Creek •
Owen Springs •
JAMES RANGE
Hugh River

Alitera •
Finke River
Henbury •
Palmer Creek
LEVI RANGE
Finke River

Eridunda •
Coolada Springs •

Alice Springs •
○ Deep Well
Mt Burrell ▲
Chambers Pillar ▲

Arltunga •

Finke River
Horseshoe Bend •

Crown Point •
Charlotte Waters •

Kamaran Well ○
Lake Amadeus
Mt Olga ▲ (Katatjuta)
▲ Uluru
Mt Connor ▲

50 miles
50km
0
0

24°S
25°

for minerals. By the mid-1880s, cattle grazed on Tempe Downs, over 200 kilometres southwest of Alice Springs, and gold was found at Arltunga and rubies (actually garnets) in the Harts Range east of Alice Springs.

The often aggressive, ambitious and individualistic pioneers were latecomers to the region. Archaeologists have established Aboriginal people's occupation through at least thirty millennia. Unfortunately their camping sites were selected near water and on grassy flats where game and edible plants concentrated, which coincided with desirable pastoral locations. The exclusion of Indigenous people from these productive areas totally disrupted their lifestyle and prevented their access to spiritually renewing ceremonial places.

Equally destructive was the involuntary process of frontier disruption following the introduction of lethal micro-organisms and epidemiological disasters, including respiratory illnesses, whooping cough and measles. This new frontier was essentially a male world (only nine white women were said to reside in Alice Springs around 1900), so Aboriginal women proved vulnerable commodities. 'Nearly every white man has his young lubra', stated an unusually honest Arltunga miner at the turn of the century. The consequence was rampant venereal disease and consequent mortality or infertility.

In this land of moving frontiers, racial violence and rugged settlers who placed a premium on alcohol, police proved essential. Yet the mounted troopers were stationed there more to defend pastoral occupation and to protect herds than to keep white communal peace. When pastoralists complained of Aboriginal cattle spearing the police proved diligent in tracking offenders. Influential Adelaide investors ensured that Tempe Downs station was protected. At considerable public expense, police posts were established successively on the Finke River and at Illamurta Springs, where the prime police duties related to hunting warriors on the Tempe Downs lease.

Baldwin Spencer and data-gathering on the frontier

Curiosity about other cultures, together with interest in human origins, and in the development of human societies and languages, has had a

long history in the European intellectual tradition. Anthropology had
its roots in the compendious encyclopedic traditions of the sixteenth
and seventeenth centuries. Out of these developed the cabinets of
curiosity in which exotic fragments of the natural and cultural world
were gathered and displayed. The origins of modern anthropology,
however, lie in the seventeenth and eighteenth centuries when explorers began to collect detailed information about non-European
societies. European intellectual and scientific discourse slowly incorporated these new facts and artefacts. In the mid-nineteenth century,
anthropology—like other disciplines—felt the impact of Darwinian
evolutionary theory and moved from a stage of ethnological description
of the diversity of human cultures to a more scientific interrogation of
the processes of human development. As European colonial rule
became established around much of the globe, information flowed
increasingly freely from colonial administrators, missionaries and trad-
ers to feed the discussions over the nature and evolution of human
societies that were engaging the members of learned societies in
Europe and America. The 'facts' about non-European societies were
ordered in sequences that demonstrated their development over time
from simple to complex, from stone to iron, from hunter to farmer,
from magical thinking to scientific thought.

In the early history of anthropology, there was a distinction
between the people who provided the facts and the theorists
who interpreted them. This continues today in the distinction between 'ethnography' (the descriptive data) and 'anthropology' (the
interpretative practice). The majority of data-gatherers remained
separate from the theorists until the latter part of the nineteenth
century, but the distinction should not be too rigidly adhered to.
Many early scientists, including such eminent figures as Banks and
Darwin, spent their time in the field on voyages of exploration.
Edward Tylor, a founder of evolutionary anthropology, spent some
years living in Central America and engaged in first-hand data-
gathering. However, the dominant model is exemplified by the
relationship between theorists such as Tylor in the metropolitan
centres and data-gatherers in remoter regions of the Empire whose
circumstances allowed them to record relevant information. This is
often described as the centre-periphery phase of anthropology. The
distinction, while capturing an aspect of the process, can also be
misleading, however.[2]

In Australia, such relationships had been well established by the second half of the nineteenth century. Alfred Howitt and Lorimer Fison, inspired by the American anthropologist Lewis Henry Morgan,[3] developed a questionnaire that they sent out to 'all sorts and conditions of people. Right Reverend Roman Catholic Dignitaries, squatters, pound keepers, government officials in all the colonies'. By 1881, Howitt was in correspondence with over fifty people 'who are more or less successfully working for me and under my direction'.[4] In order to get five replies, Howitt had had to send out 100 circulars. The very fact that so few people responded to his questionnaire suggests that, on the whole, those who did respond shared a commonality of interest with the armchair anthropologist which is underplayed in the centre-periphery model. Moreover, Howitt and Fison had themselves done pioneering fieldwork in Australia and Fiji respectively and were by no means armchair anthropologists.

Walter Baldwin Spencer (1860–1929), biology professor at Melbourne University, became a friend of Howitt's and Fison's and was certainly inspired by their work. However, even more than they, he became directly involved in the process of fieldwork. Spencer was the son of a Manchester industrialist.[5] He was educated at Manchester and Oxford and became a Fellow of Lincoln College. He became interested in anthropology during his time at Oxford when he assisted H.N. Moseley and Edward Tylor in moving, unpacking and labelling the great ethnographic collection that Lieutenant-General Lane-Fox Pitt-Rivers had given to the university. He attended the lectures of Edward Tylor who was employed by the University to lecture on the collections. His friend and Oxford classmate Henry Balfour became the first curator of these collections. Spencer's background thus linked him closely to the history of anthropology, to the cabinets of curiosity and to the theories of social Darwinism. He moved to Australia in 1887 and did not initially follow up his anthropological interests. The job of founding the Department of Biology and the excitement of natural science research left little time for that. However, things changed in 1894 when he visited central Australia as the expedition biologist of the Horn Scientific Expedition. His friend Edward Stirling was the expedition's anthropologist, but by the end of the expedition Spencer's entanglement with the subsequent history of Australian anthropology had begun.

The Horn Expedition and Frank Gillen

Scientific interest in South Australia's remote regions had been combined with the utilitarian search for mines or fresh pastures, as with
the unsuccessful Elder Expedition in 1891. In the meantime, the
director of the South Australian Museum, Edward Stirling, aroused
ethnographic interest by circulating a notice along the Overland
Telegraph Line requesting that officers collect artefacts for his
museum. He had an opportunity to accumulate them himself during
1891, when he accompanied South Australia's governor, the Earl of
Kintore, on a buggy drive south along the Line from Darwin (the
Line evidently being identified by the governor with the thin red
line of Empire).

A truly scientific enterprise was funded in 1894 by mining magnate W.A. Horn. In addition to Adelaide scientists, members were
recruited from Victoria and New South Wales. Victoria nominated
Baldwin Spencer as the biologist and photographer, while Stirling was
the anthropologist. Spencer subsequently edited and extensively contributed to the four-volumed expedition report, which described the
journey and scientific discoveries in the Finke and Palmer Rivers and
MacDonnell Ranges country.

It was on the Horn Expedition that Spencer met three men for
the first time with whom he would carry on long-term correspondence:
Ernest Cowle, Paddy Byrne and Frank Gillen. Spencer had established personal understanding and working partnerships with Byrne
and Cowle, both enlisted initially as collectors of faunal specimens,
which later broadened to other interests. Frank Gillen (1855–1912),
whom Spencer met towards the end of the expedition, stimulated
Spencer's anthropological concerns and would become his future
anthropological partner.

Frank Gillen, an Australian-born Irishman, was the senior official
along the central sections of the Line, known widely for his hospitality, an exuberant sense of humour and reckless share dealings. The
Line seemed almost a family affair when Spencer arrived. Gillen's
wife, Amelia Maud Besley, was Paddy Byrne's step-sister, two of
her brothers were officers on the Line (one at Alice Springs), and her
cousin, James Field, was later stationmaster at Tennant Creek. Gillen
and Byrne, who shared twelve years together at Charlotte Waters,

accepted Cowle as a strenuous drinking mate and forthright conver-
sationalist.

Gillen had been stationed on the Line since 1875 and was sympathetic to Aboriginal society, although largely incomprehending of its
spiritual depth. He was asked by Stirling to contribute a chapter on
the local Arrernte people and to provide information for Stirling's report
for the Horn Expedition volumes. Spencer got on well with Gillen,
spent time staying with him after the expedition was over and, when
he returned to Melbourne, they began their extended correspondence.

Spencer initially provided Gillen with advice and guidance on
writing his chapter but their correspondence quickly developed into
a scientific collaboration. Rapidly, through correspondence, Spencer
entered the process of fieldwork. At first their relationship appeared
to fit in with the established pattern in which the data-gatherer was
separated from the theorist, but Gillen's letters reveal that, from early
on, he was as much engaged in the interpretative process as Spencer.
Soon they were in the field together recording the Engwura ceremony
in 1896. In 1901, they spent a year together engaged in research in
central and northern Australia.

The results of Spencer's and Gillen's initial research were published in 1899 as *The Native Tribes of Central Australia*. This is arguably
the world's first modern anthropological monograph and its impact
was enormous. Although Spencer and Gillen wrote within a broad
evolutionary framework, the book itself was remarkably free of evolutionary theory. It provided a detailed analysis of the kinship and
social organisation of the Arrernte people, and provided unique analysis
and description of their religious and ceremonial life. It placed
the events they observed in the context of the society as a whole. The
book provided the main source for Durkheim's major theoretical
work, *The Elementary Forms of Religious Life*, which became the foun-
dational text of the functionalist anthropology that rapidly replaced
evolutionism.[6] Their work was also influential in the development of
modern anthropological field methods: long periods of theoretically
informed fieldwork and the meticulous recording of data from an
Indigenous perspective. They were among the pioneers in using
photography, film and sound recording as means of gathering data.
A sign of the uniqueness of their contribution is that their writings
continue to be used and cited as much as ever.[7] Although their
collaboration began in the form of correspondence, they subsequently

spent many months together engaged in field research in central Australia. Gillen's letters reveal the depth of the scientific collaboration between him and Spencer and the richness of their friendship.[8] The letters suggest that they knew each other as well as any two people could.

Ernest Cowle

During the years up to 1891, reprisals for cattle spearing were often brutal, the police evidently equating the life of a beast with that of an Aboriginal. When Mounted Constable W. H. Willshire was charged with murdering Aborigines on Tempe Downs in that year, he was found 'not guilty', but he was banished to the obscurity of the remote Victoria River District where he continued his notorious ways with impunity. The success of the future Gillen–Spencer anthropological partnership depended largely upon the fact that it was F.J. Gillen, the Alice Springs stationmaster, who charged Willshire, thereby gaining prestige among the Arrernte people for his brave and unprecedented action.

Henceforth, it became customary for the police to follow legal procedure and neck-chain arrested Aborigines, escort them to Alice Springs for sentencing and then lead them on to the train at Oodnadatta for incarceration in the Port Augusta prison. When Mounted Constable Ernest Cowle (1863–1922) first arrived for duty in Alice Springs, Willshire was a colleague. It was Cowle who established the new outpost at Illamurta Springs in 1893. A well-educated but reclusive member of the Adelaide establishment, Cowle conducted members of the Horn Scientific Expedition to Uluru in the following year, forging an enduring friendship with Baldwin Spencer.

Cowle was won over by Spencer's capacity for friendship, his ability to treat people as equals and to involve them in the excitement of his enterprises. Cowle's letters, unlike Gillen's, are exercises in restraint, cautiously revealing his views, acknowledging his differences of opinion but often in an uncomfortable and slightly defensive way. Perhaps he was never sure of his relationship with Spencer: his letters are tinged with feelings of rivalry towards Gillen and at times he appears jealous of the latter's close relationship with Spencer. Spencer clearly had an ability to communicate with people from very different backgrounds and make them believe that they were people of value. Precisely how he did this we can only surmise from reading between the lines of the replies since, as is the case with the Gillen correspondence, none of the letters from Spencer to Cowle have survived.

Cowle's letters are valuable on a number of different grounds. They provide a very different perspective from Gillen's on life in central Australia. Cowle valued central Australia because of its remoteness, remaining deliberately isolated at Illamurta, rigorously pursuing his task of controlling the Indigenous population, monitoring their movements, determined to reduce the predations on cattle and administering physically harsh punishments. The presence of Aborigines was almost part of Cowle's isolation.

There is no direct evidence that Cowle had anything other than a professional interest in Aborigines prior to his meeting with Spencer. The very fact that he spent so much time in their company suggests that he must have developed some form of social relationships with them, especially if it is true that—as has been suggested by T.G.H. Strehlow (see Chapter 1)—he developed a close relationship with one Aboriginal woman (a suggestion strongly denied by Cowle in his lifetime, L5.3). Most of the evidence suggests that he was a loner who avoided close involvement with his fellow human beings in general. It is precisely on account of these differences that his letters gain in value: they give a contrasting perspective to Gillen's.

Through their association with Spencer, both Cowle's and Gillen's letters are both important documents in the history of anthropology. However, in some respects they belong to different eras in the development of the discipline. Gillen's letters chart the relationship he established with Spencer that resulted in the breakdown of the old research paradigm. Cowle's letters, though rich, are similar to those written by many other 'scientific correspondents' whose careers took them to remote places: they belong to an earlier phase of anthropological history. Cowle was always the informant on the frontier passing on information to the metropolitan professor. He welcomed the correspondence with Spencer and the data collection, but saw it as a way of keeping in contact with civilisation without having to leave Illamurta.

Cowle clearly valued the intellectual excitement that his relationships with both Spencer and Gillen brought. He commented that

'if the Horn Expedition does no good to the scientists of made reputations it will have accomplished one great thing at all events, and
that is the renascence or renaissance of Science in the Norwest'
(L2.9). His letters to Spencer reveal a curious combination of admi-
ration and cynicism, as well as the self-doubt and sense of inadequacy
that may partly explain his self-imposed exile at Illamurta (L2.8).

Cowle saw Spencer and Gillen as being too sympathetic to Aborigines and towards the end of his life wrote to Spencer. 'You and I
naturally regarded certain actions of the Natives from entirely opposite
standpoints' (L5.11). Cowle's views on Aboriginal society were largely
negative and reflect a frontier ethos that required that Aboriginal
people bow to the laws of their colonial masters. He wrote apparently
without irony: 'They should be made to respect the laws of the land
that had been taken away from them.' He viewed Aborigines who had
less contact with more sympathy than those who had longer contact,
but only because they could not be expected to behave better: 'When
it is the case of an *uncivilized* one I would always be more lenient
because perhaps he might not understand white man's ways' (L4.1).
His reactions to Spencer and Gillen confirm that their position was
radical for the time and foregrounded many later debates. He accused
them of a cult of 'Spencer and Gillenism' on the native as human being
(L4.1). 'A stock phrase of the cult is "Put yourself in the Blackfellow's
place". Well suppose you and Gillen put yourselves for a while in the
"Squatters place".' Writing from the viewpoint of the indigenous
subject is precisely the perspective adopted by much 'modern' anthropology,[9] signifying the cultural relativism that has characterised
the ethical position of most social anthropologists since the turn of the
century.

Paddy Byrne

Baldwin Spencer first met Patrick Byrne (1856–1932) at the Horn
Expedition's first major stop, Charlotte Waters, where Byrne was
stationed. Irish born, Paddy had worked on the Line since 1875. When
he first met Spencer he was officer-in-charge and also doubled as
customs officer. Widely read in the sciences, Byrne was a convinced
Darwinian evolutionist, so when Spencer arrived and demonstrated his
adaptability to local mores, his inquisitiveness and his ability to share

convivial drinks, he impressed the normally taciturn and thirsty Byrne. Enthused by Spencer's expectations of finding undescribed species of fauna, Byrne exploited the opportunity to collect fauna by using the skills of local Aborigines, especially women. From this army of fieldworkers, Byrne sent a stream of preserved specimens to Melbourne over the years following. As the desert fauna was then poorly known and described, these specimens provided most of the new records and new species of mammals and reptiles resulting from the Horn expedition's stimulus.

Because Byrne's scientific reading provided an understanding of the principles of zoology and geology, his letters to Spencer contain important information concerning the specimens, their habitat and even a layman's view of evolutionary theory. While editing the expedition reports, Spencer returned briefly to Charlotte Waters in 1895, during seasonal conditions improved over those of the previous drought year. They visited an eroded hillside where Byrne had correctly identified ice striated pebbles, detritus from the Permian glaciation, hundreds of millions of years ago. This was a significant geological discovery.

Byrne was an infrequent correspondent, but his terse sentences provide scientific data and sympathetic insight into Aboriginal conditions. They convey some sense of the reality of outback isolation, of self-reliance and an outback ethos which combined thirst, rivalry, cynicism and yet warm mateship.

Byrne's essential role in Spencer's scheme of things was to collect fauna. Yet in his first letters he described the ritual known as kurdaitcha, whereby an avenger crept up on an enemy allegedly using shoes of mainly emu feathers and human hair. Spencer composed this advice into a short article under Byrne's name. As he was editor of *The Proceedings of the Royal Society of Victoria,* he found little trouble in publishing it in 1895. This was the earliest ethnographic paper to be published in the series associated with Spencer and Gillen (Appendix 5).

Byrne otherwise played little part in anthropological matters, beyond facilitating Spencer's various visits to the centre and, as customs officer, ensuring that packages and weapons sent to Melbourne moved safely and inexpensively. However, his letters reveal friendly relationships with the Southern Arrernte people, who obviously were willing to collect faunal specimens in quantity. As he held the key to the government rations store, there was a sound reason why they should do his bidding. Yet there are comments which imply that he understood and sympathised with the Aboriginal people more than Cowle, whose contempt was undisguised. His last letter to Spencer in 1925 contained sentiments unusual for their time and place: 'We take from them everything that makes life worth living, work them until they can work no longer, and then hand them over to the police, whose main endeavour is to work things as cheaply as possible, and thus please a Gov't that has neither Knowledge nor conscience' (L8.14).

The importance of the Cowle and Byrne letters

Cowle and Byrne never expected their letters to be read by any person other than Spencer, whom they respected but also held in awe. They made observations which they never would voice to each other. Their words reflect the isolation and hardships of postal and police officers and are valuable social documents. Like many other outback characters, they lived either solitary bush lives or in close proximity to often irreconcilable characters within the confines of a repeater or pastoral station. For some, alcohol provided comfort, but it fuelled aggression. Others impatiently awaited the irregular arrival of mail, newspapers and books of a quality and range which might surprise one today. It is evident that, as avid readers of informed works, Cowle and Byrne were predisposed to intellectual pursuits before Spencer met them and treated them as equals, directed their interests, and always responded to their mail with advice and relevant reading material.

In Spencer they encountered a cultured Englishman of about their own age, capable of adapting to their circumstances and personalities and enforcing their potential value as field observers. Byrne therefore expanded his zoological and geological expertise, while Cowle grudgingly and cynically answered many queries. Gillen became the major partner in their enterprise in the frontier scientific endeavour, broadening his observations and sharpening his wits until Spencer and Gillen became an inseparable and equal duo, with international recognition.

The correspondence of Cowle Byrne, together with that of Gillen, supplements and illuminates in an informal, personalised manner what scholars have read in the detached mellifluous Edwardian prose of the Spencer and Gillen classics. They frequently refer to each other, or cross reference to the same incident or people. Incidental references to race relations provide evidence for perceptions and attitudes during this colonising period. Here is well-written, raw data from an imperial frontier containing insights into social life and conditions both for indigenes and colonists.

PART I

THE COWLE CORRESPONDENCE

Letters from Mounted Constable C.E. Cowle to Baldwin Spencer, 1894–1920

1

COWLE OF ILLAMURTA

He was a great correspondent, with a keen sense of humour and power of observation, and was known to, and knew, everyone in central Australia, from Oodnadatta in the south to Powell Creek in the north. His letters, if only they could be collected, would form a valuable original source of authoritative information on the early days of central Australia.[1]

Mounted Constable Third Class Ernest Cowle (1863–1922) crossed history's threshold of significance on 13 June 1894, when he escorted the three youngest members of the Horn Scientific Expedition to central Australia from the George Gill Range to Ayers Rock and Mt Olga (as they were known). Two weeks later, Cowle delivered them safely to the main party at Glen Helen station at the appointed time.[2] This feat won him warm praise from the party and an official departmental commendation. The Horn party also ensured his scientific immortality by naming species for him that were collected *en route*—a honey ant (*Melophorus cowlei*), a wolf spider (*Lycosa cowlei*) and a small wattle tree (*Acacia cowleana*).

Posterity acknowledges Cowle only through his connection with the Horn Expedition, and from the acknowledgements in the prefaces of subsequent ethnological and biological publications by the Expedition biologist, Baldwin Spencer, and the Alice Springs Telegraph Station master, Frank Gillen. However, the fifty-one surviving letters which Cowle wrote to Spencer between 1894 and 1920 add substantial insight into their author's thoughts, deeds and character. Although such considerations did not suffice for Cowle's inclusion in the *Australian Dictionary of Biography*, this volume should redress that neglect.

Cowle's role as a bush policeman, his acts of endurance and horsemanship, his explicit racism oddly combined with humanitarian attitudes and an interest in collecting ethnographic data, his realistic and perceptive approach to environmental issues: these are all facets of the contradictory nature of this enigmatic character, who craved isolation yet enjoyed conviviality. His family status, education and Adelaide social connections promised a very different urban career. Yet from his isolated Illamurta Springs outpost, some 150 kilometres southwest of Alice Springs, he corresponded with an unusual network of scientists, family and friends, much beyond the expectations or abilities of his profession and locale. His extensive network of contacts was revealed in a passing comment (L4.1) that he received forty letters when his mail suffered a month's delay. Cowle's career sadly collapsed in only his thirty-ninth year, when this active horseman was stricken with crippling locomotor ataxia, forcing him to remain bed-ridden until his death nineteen years later.

Cowle's clearly written correspondence contributes insights and ethnological content to the Spencer and Gillen anthropological partnership. It sheds vivid light on race relations and the nature of social conditions on this remote imperial frontier at the time of this influential anthropological fieldwork. He also proved a cynical and critical observer of his anthropologist friends, whose publications transformed their 'Arunta' [Arrernte] people into the type specimens of desert nomadic 'primitive' society, with dramatic impact upon international social theory and profound influence on Australian welfare policies towards Indigenous Australians.

This correspondence further poses psychological questions concerning the motivation of this intelligent, educated man, who opted for a rough frontier existence far from kin and accustomed social and professional expectations. Cowle refers to other bush mates who also were unusual characters. How typical was Cowle of those men who expanded British imperial frontiers? Except for the potential and available company of Indigenous females, his was a male milieu, where horsemanship, prospecting and alcohol provided conversational themes.

Attitude to Aborigines

Cowle's uncompromising and authoritarian attitude to Aboriginal people is apparent. He was there to enforce the interests of pastoral landtakers. He ignored modern conventional human or civil rights by chaining captives and even flogging them. Yet it was accepted legal practice to chain prisoners until well into the twentieth century and, unlike many of his contemporaries, including fellow police, he did not shoot them; indeed, he even won praise for bringing in his neck-chained prisoners to be sentenced for crimes which they little understood. His letters may mix contempt, sardonic humour and cynicism for these people, but his outlook, criticisms and experiences reflect features of racial attitudes which still remain unresolved in white Australian society. His letters merit consideration both as expressions of those sentiments a century ago and for the reasoning behind their formulation. A reader must not take all Cowle's expressions at face value, however, for he enjoyed teasing his professorial friend, and behind his forceful and acid-dipped pen lurked a grudging paternalistic concern.

Race relations constitute a central theme in Cowle's informal correspondence, but other observations include the impact of pastoralism on that fragile environment, the introduction of European diseases and pests, and the hazards and discomforts of life for Europeans on the shifting pastoral frontier. Cowle first met Spencer only twenty-four years after construction had begun on the Overland Telegraph Line and less than fifteen years since cattle were pastured in his area, so his letters provide valuable evidence of early European impact.

These letters need to be read with an understanding of their historical and intellectual context, so it is essential to begin by tracing Cowle's family background. While modern readers may not excuse sentiments which reflected the ethos of the white pastoral frontier, Cowle should be credited with a lucid awareness possessed by few outback contemporaries.

Background and childhood

Charles Ernest Cowle was born in Launceston, Tasmania, on 2 October 1863, the second son of Charles Tobin Cowle and his wife Margaret (*née* Lewers). His father's profession was entered as 'merchant' on the birth certificate. Ernest's paternal grandfather, Thomas Pressland Cowle, formerly a shipping insurance agent, had migrated from Devon to Hobart in 1833.[3] He was well-educated and spoke several foreign languages. He soon took over a school, the Hobart Town Commercial Academy, later relocated and named the Commercial and French Academy at Pressland House. The school prospered and Cowle invested in property.

T.P. Cowle had married Mary Wigg of Norfolk, who bore him two daughters and a son, Thomas Pressland II, before they migrated to Tasmania. Ernest's father, Charles Tobin Cowle, was born on 15 May 1835, following their arrival in Hobart; there were three further children. Business interests and ill-health resulted in T.P. Cowle I returning to England with his family in 1846. The lure of gold proved too strong for the two eldest sons, so Thomas Pressland II and Charles Tobin sailed for the Victorian goldfields in 1852, their family, father included, returning to Hobart late in the following year.

After prospecting at Ballarat and Creswick, the enterprising brothers found that there were easier fortunes to be made than by prospecting. Evidently they both returned to northeastern Tasmania.

Charles Tobin Cowle possibly worked briefly as an accountant in Launceston, but he soon joined the three Lewers brothers—Alexander, Samuel and Thomas—in establishing agencies on the Victorian goldfields for the Bank of New South Wales. Bank records establish that in 1854 the Board approved 'Messrs Lewers and Cowle for the establishment of a gold purchasing Agency', at Creswick.[4]

On the day that Charles Tobin married Margaret Lewers (1836–1895) at Ballarat in 1856, his profession was registered as 'gold broker'.[5] The Lewers were descended from a French Huguenot family which settled in Devon in the sixteenth century. For services rendered to King Charles II, Colonel Henry Lewers was granted land in County Monaghan, Ireland. Succeeding generations acquired further Irish property, and it was from the village of Middleton, near the city of Armagh that, in 1853, the Lewers brothers, accompanied by their sister, migrated to assume a comfortable social position in Victorian society.[6] When Ernest Cowle justified a criticism of the Irish race by claiming Irish ancestry himself (L2.2), he therefore cited his maternal line. However, the subject of his remark, Frank Gillen, might not have considered his claim valid. While Gillen's Catholic parents came from Cavan and he was an ardent Home Ruler, Cowle's connections lay with Protestant Ulster.

The Lewers–Cowle association with the Bank of New South Wales persisted. The three Lewers brothers joined the Bank staff, becoming managers of major goldfields branches, at Creswick, Linton and Ballarat. By 1857 Cowle had returned to Launceston where he was active as a merchant and accountant. In his spare time he served as a Captain in the Launceston Volunteer Artillery Corps.[7] During those Launceston years five of their eight children were born: Florence, Eleanor, Percy, Annie and Charles Ernest; Felix, Gerald and Olive followed.

On 1 July 1865, C.T. Cowle joined the staff of the Bank of New South Wales. Until his resignation in 1878, Cowle successfully managed the Maldon bank and other branches at Kyneton, Wangaratta and Wagga Wagga.[8] Family status rose considerably from February 1878, when Cowle changed banks and was appointed to manage the Adelaide head office of the English, Scottish & Australasian Chartered Bank. Cowle's election to The Adelaide Club followed that year, while ten years later he was admitted to The Bankers' Institute of Australia.[9]

William Wardell's Gothic Revival building in King William Street was not built at the time of Cowle's promotion,[10] but when it was completed around 1883, the family lived in its upper rooms. Parental moves may have proved unsettling for young Ernest—during his first nineteen years he called nine houses home. During those twenty years of roving activity left to him, his isolated decade at remote Illamurta Springs was the closest he came to a permanent abode.

When the family settled in Adelaide, Ernest was aged fourteen. Like the sons of most South Australian landed or professional men, from 1878 Ernest and his brothers Felix and Gerald attended the Collegiate School of St Peter (St Peter's College). The sketchy details of Ernest's school activities confirm that the literacy and literary knowledge revealed in his correspondence rested on a solid scholastic experience. The prize list for 1879 credits him with sharing the senior prize for Declamation with W. Kingsmill, a future President of the Australian Senate. While he was ranked only third class in Fifth Form in 1878, the following year he achieved second class. His subjects related to the 'classical side', rather than the 'mathematical side' of the curriculum.

It is interesting that F.W. Belt was a classmate. Belt joined the 1894 Horn Expedition party which Cowle later led to Ayers Rock. St Peter's evidently contributed greatly to the education of that expedition's members. In addition to Belt, Old Boys included Charles Winnecke, Professor (Sir) Edward Stirling, and W.A. Horn, the financier of the expedition and Belt's brother-in-law.[11]

The marriage of Ernest's sister, Mary Eleanor, to Josiah Henry Symon, on 8 December 1881, was to play a significant role during Ernest's declining years. (Sir) Josiah Symon (1846–1934) was called to the South Australian Bar in 1871. He was appointed Queen's Counsel, elected to the Legislative Assembly, and briefly served as attorney-general. An outspoken architect of Federation, election to the Senate and a knighthood resulted in 1901; appointment as Commonwealth Attorney-General followed in 1904–5. Ernest Cowle therefore acquired in Symon a powerful brother-in-law, who supported him during his sad bed-ridden closing years. The Symon home, *Manoah*, set in the Adelaide Hills, offered him hospitality and support. Its superb library of some 10 000 volumes must have provided Ernest with welcome, time-consuming reading suited to his intellectual tastes.[12]

From banking to the bush

The years between Cowle's school graduation until his enlistment in the police force in 1889 remain shadowy. His apparently well-informed obituary in *The Advertiser* commented that 'after some time in the banking profession [Cowle] found an open life more to his liking'.[13] Presumably this banking phase commenced when he left school in 1880. Ernest's elder brother, Percy Alfred, had followed their father into the banking profession, so both the Cowle and Lewers family branches offered many precedents for such a career. Ernest's brothers Felix and Gerald both proceeded to Geelong Grammar. The reasons why Ernest's brothers continued to successful professional careers, while Ernest's education ceased when he was only sixteen are unknown.[14] Meanwhile, Gerald became an engineer with the General Electric Company, in New York and England.[15]

Cowle's record of his police service dates from his enlistment on 1 February 1889, when his official file listed his previous occupation as 'station manager'. Cowle's own information on that profession was meagre. He told Spencer (L4.1) that he had seen Aborigines throwing boomerangs 'about Mildura' in 1880, an incidental clue that his stint as a banker was brief. Most importantly, Cowle described stick-nest rats (L2.7) on Strezelecki Creek and wrote of Aboriginal prowess in boomerang throwing in the Cooper's Creek region (L4.1), and he mentioned Blanchewater and Montecollina stations. He cannot have visited that area following his police enlistment, as his only postings were to Alice Springs and Illamurta (erroneously called Tempe Downs on his service record).

These hints that Cowle was familiar with those areas suggested that he spent the years between his seventeenth and twenty-fifth birthdays in northern areas. The Mortlock Library's Roll of Electors for the vast District of Flinders shows Ernest Cowle's name appearing as an elector on the Rolls for December 1887, June 1889 and January 1890, as one 'who claim[s] to vote at Beltana', and was registered as a 'stockman' at Blanchewater station. That his name does not appear on the 1884 Roll (the first record before 1887) may be explained by the fact that he only qualified to vote in October 1884, when he turned twenty-one—too late in that year to be registered. As he moved to Alice Springs in 1889, he remained in the Flinders electorate, so he may not have bothered to promptly notify his change of address within that remote territory.

Blanchewater station straddled the Strezelecki Track, one of a string of stations run by those enterprising pastoralists, Sir Thomas Elder, Peter Waite and Robert Barr-Smith (Elder, Smith & Co Ltd). Both Waite and Elder held interests in Blanchewater and Beltana and, upon Elder's death in 1897, their vast holdings became the Beltana Pastoral Company. Blanchewater run, southwest of Lake Blanche, covered some 10 000 square kilometres and, during the 1880s, it was at the peak of its successful era of horse breeding when some 4000 horses produced around 1000 foals annually. Horses were supplied to Cobb & Co and other hauliers in Australia, and exported as Indian army remounts. It was said that Thomas Elder's TE brand 'came to be regarded as a guarantee of equine excellence'. Mobs of horses must have travelled frequently down the track to Beltana, so voting there by employees combined work and electoral obligations. Visitors today to this waterless region would surely echo George Farwell's wonderment that the Strezelecki 'was once a track that pulsed with a remarkable amount of life'.[16]

The Blanchewater account ledgers show that Cowle certainly was on the payroll during the years 1883–86. Evidently he supplemented his meagre wages with bounty hunting, for which the rewards were 15 shillings for a dingo scalp, 2/6 for a kangaroo and one shilling for an eaglehawk. His most lucrative payment was for eleven dingo scalps.[17]

Blanchewater homestead is a ruin today, although nearby massive posts testify to the former horseyards. Probably Peter Waite was responsible for the decision to abandon the site for a new homestead further west on Twins Creek, incorporating the run into Murnpeowie station, where a woolshed was built in 1890 and henceforth sheep, not horses, were the economic resource. These major changes may have proved unsettling for Cowle during his concluding months there, and it seems unlikely that he ever became a station manager, as he claimed in his police register.

Cowle's years of outback experience surely offered sound schooling in horsemanship and bushcraft—excellent training for his future police patrols. Years later, Baldwin Spencer reflected ruefully on the discomforts of camping with Cowle,[18] 'so hardened a bushman' that he 'thought nothing of sleeping out on the hardest ground' and showed 'tireless persistence' as a horseman. Spencer recalled that Cowle travelled 'lightly and with great rapidity'. Some of his later feats of endurance are described in his letters.

The Police Force

When a Mounted Constable (M/C) enlisted at the lowest rank of Third Class, it was customary to undertake training duties in Adelaide. Cowle was an exception, being posted immediately to Alice Springs, where a police station had been established at Heavitree Gap in 1886. Possibly Cowle's pastoral experience was sufficient, while his educational standard was considerably above that of the average recruit. Besides, an extra trooper may have been required urgently in the vast Alice Springs district. Traces of gold had been found at Arltunga and there was misplaced excitement that rubies (actually garnets) also lay in the Harts Range east of Alice Springs. More immediately, however, as pastoral expansion continued through the 1880s, influential Adelaide investors complained that Aborigines were spearing their cattle, and demanded redress.[19]

Some months after Ernest Cowle reached Alice Springs, one of the other two officers, M/C William Willshire, was sent to establish a police post on the Finke River downstream from the Hermannsburg Lutheran Mission, at Boggy Hole, nearer to the troubled pastoral territory. These were traumatic years for the Indigenous population. M/C First Class William Henry Willshire was notorious through the 1880s for his 'dispersal' policy. Robert Clyne, an historian of the Police Force, acknowledges that Willshire shot fifteen Aboriginal people; the score was considerably higher than that, however, according to oral tradition. Significantly, Clyne observed that Willshire 'had a dislike for paperwork'. In an official report in 1890, for example, Willshire stated, 'that he did not keep journals during his trip after witnesses'[20]—a gap in his records of seven months. Willshire wrote about his general experiences, however, in publications which some contemporaries considered to be sound ethnography. They combine fact with imaginative fiction, sadistic episodes and boastful self-promotion. The most quoted passage concerned his later experiences further north on Victoria River Downs, but they could apply to his Alice Springs years:[21]

> They scattered in all directions [he gloated], It's no use mincing matters—the Martini-Henry carbines . . . were talking English in the silent majesty of those great eternal rocks.

Despite its unattractive name, Willshire's Boggy Hole outpost was located on a picturesque stretch of the Finke River. It is a place sacred to Arrernte people, known to them as Alitera. Not surprisingly, the missionaries opposed the proximity of Willshire's base, for his reputation was known to them. There existed an accepted fiction that police only shot in self-defence, or when prisoners escaped, but it was difficult to disprove killings activated by 'escapes'. The euphemism for shooting was 'dispersal'. Yet even dead men told tales near Hermannsburg some time before Boggy Hole post was established. Although Willshire was not personally involved, Pastor Schwarz reported finding three dead men chained together and shot, surely neither in self-defence nor as escapees. Despite such evidence, the relevant minister in Adelaide preferred to listen to lobbyists from the Tempe Downs Pastoral Company. So the minister stoutly reprimanded the missionaries for impeding police by harbouring cattle killers, but sent two commissioners to Hermannsburg to investigate conditions. Their report in September 1890 completely exonerated the police from all wrong-doing, but did recommend shifting the police post further away. The importance of live beasts clearly outweighed the lives of Indigenous hunters.

To have upheld brutal authority is morally inexcusable, but it is worth considering that such policies were held not only by white Australians. In the same year at Wounded Knee, South Dakota, United States cavalry massacred over 200 virtually unarmed Amerindian men, women and children.[22]

Willshire remained at Boggy Hole and early in 1891 he launched a terrorist raid on Aborigines at Tempe Downs station, to the southwest. Using his native troopers to shoot two men, they cremated their bodies to conceal the evidence. It occurred so close to the station buildings that Willshire callously adjourned there for breakfast.

Such, then, was the character of Cowle's senior colleague. His other companion was M/C First Class W.G. South, another veteran of the Centre, who later gave as his considered opinion that Willshire was insane.[23] When news of the Tempe Downs incident reached Alice Springs, it proved the last straw for the Overland Telegraph stationmaster, F.J. Gillen JP, and Sub-Protector of Aborigines, who decided to investigate himself by visiting Tempe Downs and questioning the wife of one of the murdered men, now at Hermannsburg, and to charge Willshire with murder. South was entrusted with the task of obtaining witnesses and arresting Willshire.[24]

At this critical time, Alice Springs received its most distinguished visitor since the construction of the Overland Telegraph Line. South Australia's governor, the Earl of Kintore, drove into Alice Springs from Darwin. His companion on this cross-continental imperial inspection by buggy was Professor Edward Stirling, Adelaide anatomist, physician and museum director. After Stirling returned in 1894 as a member of the Horn Expedition, he and Cowle became correspondents.[25]

The governor visited the Heavitree Gap police station on 9 May 1891, meeting both Cowle and South. Possibly their visit reassured Gillen in his unprecedented decision to charge Willshire. On this occasion Stirling's diary contains a cryptic comment:[26] 'South Cowle Former going tomorrow to Tempe Downs for Wiltshire [sic] witness'. However, on 27 April the Chief Commissioner already had instructed the police inspector at Port Augusta to order Willshire's arrest. Under these circumstances, Cowle probably was warned of the consequences of 'dispersing' Aborigines—or at least of the dangers if caught.

Willshire's celebrated trial resulted in a declaration of his innocence, after sympathetic pastoralists subscribed £2000 for his defence and retained Sir John Downer QC. The real significance of this incident lay in the honour accorded Frank Gillen by Aboriginal people for initiating such action against police violence. The accrued respect was the key to the success of Gillen's anthropological collaboration with Spencer from 1894.[27]

Willshire and South were an ill-assorted pair. South confessed to finding Willshire 'eccentric' and possibly insane. Years later they both sought the South Australian post of Chief Protector of Aborigines. South was appointed in 1906, though he evidently showed little sympathy for the welfare of his charges. Yet it must have been greater than that of his rival. Ironically, the disillusioned Willshire resigned from the force to become nightwatchman at Adelaide's abattoir.[28]

Willshire's trial expedited the closure of Boggy Hole post. He never returned, being transferred to the Victoria River Downs district, where he practised mayhem with impunity. Because the Victoria was classed as an 'unsettled' district, evidently different rules applied to human lives. As Willshire's Port Augusta superior reported to the Police Commissioner:[29]

> I am decidedly opposed to M.C. Willshire going back . . . as he does not appear to get on well in the settled Districts. I would recommend he have a trial [in the north] . . . He is a most energetic and persevering [sic] Constable where the Blacks are troublesome and he thoroughly understands their manners and customs.

Double standards were justifiable, it appears, for with F.J. Gillen, JP in Alice Springs and the Hermannsburg missionaries as witnesses, treatment of Aborigines needed to be seen as just: 'troublesome' Aborigines could be dealt with more severely elsewhere.

Once Willshire learned that an alternative site was intended for Boggy Hole, he optimistically applied for that post at once.[30] Currently bored with life at Port Pirie police station where he had been posted,

he proudly gave his *curriculum vitae* as: 'stopping [Aboriginal] dep-
redations, is my special forte'. In April 1893, however, M/C Cowle
was transferred under the command of M/C First Class T. Daer, with
orders to construct a new police post. The place selected was Illamurta Springs, on the borders between the territories of Western
Arrernte, Luritja and Matuntara peoples, known to them as Ilamata.[31]

Given the current lack of mapping in this region, it is hardly
surprising that the Chief Commissioner in his Adelaide office had no
idea where to position the post on his wall map. When Daer visited
Adelaide later for medical reasons he was instructed to visit the
Commissioner's office, 'and mark the Illamurta Station on the map'.
Consequently, some five months after establishing the post, the
authorities learned where it actually was located.[32]

Illamurta Springs

Illamurta Springs is situated some 150 kilometres southwest of Alice
Springs, in the age-reddened southern foothills of the James Range,
on Ilpilla (McMinn) Creek, an intermittent tributary creek of the
Finke River system. Its great advantage to its original Indigenous
owners and to the police was provision of a moderate, though permanent, supply of water. These sedimentary rocks were laid down in
Devonian seas and water seeps from the porous Hermannsburg Sandstone.

Set among low vegetated rocky hills with a view downstream to
more level country, it is an attractive place and Ernest Cowle grew
to love it as home. Although much of the surrounding area consists
of deeply weathered and colourful rocky hills, some depth of soil
exists on the flats downstream from the spring. When Baldwin Spencer passed a day here in 1894, he referred to the welcome change
from dry, sandy country: 'for the first time we saw what might
be called black earth', he reported.[33] To judge from the surviving solid
posts and split-railing, the horse paddock was located here. The
varieties of vegetables proudly listed by Cowle, presumably also
grew nearby. By the time that the Horn Expedition rested there in
mid-1894, the vegetable garden was remarked upon as a feature. The
post was strategically placed for police to fan out and range across

the flatter country, while offering access back through the hills behind.

A crow could reach Alice Springs after flying some 125 kilometres, but a horse trod a more circuitous and difficult route through the James and MacDonnell Ranges. The picturesque abrupt cliffs and narrow boulder strewn gorges in this ancient sandstone country were not intended by nature for horses, so Cowle's complaints concerning difficulties of rapid pursuit or locating concealed warriors were very real (see, for example, L2.2, 2.16, 3.2 and 3.8). Yet it was well suited for ranging across wide areas of this recently occupied pastoral region. The first Tempe Downs homestead lay a relatively easy ride of 50 kilometres west, while Hermannsburg was about the same distance to the north, but over more difficult terrain; Glen Helen was 70 kilometres in a northerly direction, a similar distance to Henbury station to the southeast, on the Finke River.

Illamurta's spring is overgrown today. Presumably it was kept clear over the centuries by Aboriginal custodians, while Cowle referred to cleaning out the basin (L2.2). Evidence for the police presence between 1893 and 1912 consists of the ruins of two stone buildings, some high post-and-rail fencing—presumably the corner of a horse paddock—and scattered stone structural remains or fence lines. These relics cover an area approximately 350 metres by 300 metres. The most solid ruin is known as the goal, but this function seems unlikely. Routine practice was to neckchain strings of Aboriginal prisoners together and, when camped at night, to shackle them to solid tree trunks. That a goal was superfluous may be confirmed by Cowle's 1899 comment that a much sought after captive was 'chained up outside' (L3.12). Possibly this substantial stone ruin housed perishable stores, or it postdated Cowle's time. In 1902 (L5.6), Cowle referred to forty sheets of iron waiting to be carted from Henbury for use in constructing a store.

Four contemporary photographs survive of Illamurta—probably images taken by the camera which Cowle brought from Adelaide in 1898. In the background are flimsy brush sheds set against a steep hillside; some of the surviving horse paddock fence posts are visible in one view. Cowle referred to his own hut as a 'wurley', and as late as 1899, he slept 'in front of the wurley' (L3.11). A photograph of the post shows Aboriginal wurleys close by. Some insight into his rudimentary vernacular structure was provided some days later. Cowle was seated inside at tea, 'when I looked up, a snake was hanging out of the bough roof just above my head'. A further indication of the insubstantial nature of the post was contained in a letter to Spencer from James Field,[34] postmaster at Tennant Creek, when he termed it 'the Illamurta Camp'.

A significant presence at Illamurta is an abundance of Aboriginal stone artefacts, including grindstones. The permanent water would have made it a significant pre-European site, and Peter Thorley's recent excavations at the large Kulpi Mara rock shelter in the Levi Range to the west establish that people inhabited the area for some 30 000 years.[35] The many references by Cowle to Aborigines testify to their later coexistence with the police. Some were employed as trackers, but the largesse of handouts, some as official ration allowances, must have attracted people. Christmas Day in 1902, for example, provided them with a bonus—five gallons of ginger beer and three bottles of raspberry vinegar (L5.8). The most informative photograph exists in the Gillen collection in the South Australian Museum, so in all probability it dates from Gillen's period in Alice Springs. It shows an Aboriginal camp near the stone building, adjacent to the spring. If Cowle took the photograph, the substantial building was erected during his tenure.

The rapidity with which Aboriginal material culture adapted to and incorporated European advantages far beyond the zone of pastoral occupation was noted by Cowle. Following the common museological assumption that Aboriginal culture was static and that innovations derived through contact were 'contaminations', Cowle attempted to collect 'pure' cultural artefacts for Spencer's Melbourne museum. He ruefully remarked in 1898 (L3.5), that 'the ubiquitous butcher knife was there but no stone ones and I feel convinced that it is almost a thing of the past for many miles West and at least as far South as Ayers Rock'. Two years later he was near Mt Connor and obtained wood-working chisels (tula adzes)—'four or five of their curved adzes but *all* had iron tips which I am getting replaced by flints' (L4.7). The Illamurta police post probably played an important role in this diffusion of new materials. The proximity of the Aboriginal encampment to the police facilities highlights the nature of the culture contact.

Cowle's letters also shed informal and disturbing light on race relations—even during the post-Willshire years, when greater regulation of police action was attempted. They are read usefully in combination with official police records in the South Australian Archives, although files are missing there on some crucial incidents. Shocking injustices are evident in both sources, although some of Cowle's comments were intended to provoke his anthropologist friend, so he appears unduly rough and tough, because many other perceptive and humane comments suggest otherwise. He certainly discerned realistically the consequences of pastoralism both for people and country.

Being stationed with Willshire in Alice Springs must have proved an education for Cowle. A pointer to this field experience may be inferred from Willshire's letter to him in 1895 from Victoria River Downs (L2.7). Willshire sought to recommend him to headquarters as his successor in that bloodstained district. The offer was rejected (L2.8), but Willshire must have thought Cowle a suitable replacement—hardly a fine character reference under the circumstances! Against this implicit unfavourable view, Cowle's firmly stated opinion should be noted (L4.1): 'I am not advocating shooting for a moment in the so-called good old style', he assured Spencer in 1899.

Another factor was M/C Tom Daer, a veteran of the Centre since 1879. Although based chiefly at Charlotte Waters repeater station on the Overland Telegraph Line during the mid-1880s, Daer evidently patrolled with M/C Erwein Wurmbrand, who had retired before Cowle's arrival. Wurmbrand's name is linked with atrocities, including shooting the three chained men near Hermannsburg. Cowle's letters indicate his respect for Daer, unlike his later police partners, and he was deeply upset by Daer's death from diabetes in 1895 (L2.11–2.12). Daer perhaps had decided that restraint was preferable following Willshire's trial. The substitute use of the lash to punish Aboriginal cattle killers, described below, was initiated at Illamurta by Daer.

Recurring in Cowle's correspondence both with his police superiors and with Spencer are references to practical and physical aspects of official duties. Let us disregard the inhumane treatment of the Aboriginal prisoners at this point, and consider the situation as assessed by hardened police troopers. If Aboriginal offenders were captured and not 'dispersed' as under the old dispensation, there was the problem of escorting them to Alice Springs. Thereafter it was probable that they needed escorting to Port Augusta for sentence. It was tedious work to guard a line of neck-chained men at walking pace from Illamurta to the Oodnadatta railhead via Alice Springs. The police were irritated further when prominent troublemakers returned after a few months in prison and resumed their practice of spearing cattle. Insult to injury was added by the widely held belief that prisoners enjoyed their stay in gaol. In his section of the Horn Expedition report, Edward Stirling claimed that gaol proved no deterrent, and Spencer evidently agreed. T.A. Bradshaw, who succeeded Gillen at Alice Springs, reported his belief, that 'a trip to Port Augusta is regarded by most Aborigines as being more pleasure than punishment'.[36]

Whatever the improbable merits of that argument, official records indicate that the financial costs of this policy were considerable (see Appendix 4). Cowle referred to eleven Aborigines detained at the Hermannsburg mission for killing cattle (L5.6). He took ten of them to Alice Springs and Charlotte Waters, where another trooper escorted them to Port Augusta. Cowle was absent from Illamurta from 7 July to 10 August, claiming costs of £37.15.0 together with his own 6/- per diem of £7.16.0. The inclusive cost of Port Augusta and return was about £120, which the Police Commissioner agreed was 'excessive'. It was further noted that one of the prisoners was Racehorse, who already had served time.[37] Arabi, a celebrated offender, previously employed as a tracker and frequently mentioned by Cowle, was another individual whose behaviour remained unchanged after a term in prison.

While the inconvenience to the police escort was emphasised, the welfare of the prisoners was virtually ignored. In the case described, the neckchained prisoners walked for a total of twenty-five days before boarding the train at Oodnadatta, an average daily exercise of some 21 miles (34 kilometres). Bradshaw favoured a stockade at Alice Springs, because the existing policy 'is costly, ineffective, and to some extent cruel'.

Other inconveniences were involved in conducting prisoners to Alice Springs, where Gillen was the only Justice of the Peace, but had telegraph duties which required his frequent absences. Cowle made two extensive patrols during three months of 1898 and captured some cattle spearers (L3.10, 3.11). On both occasions he was delayed in Alice Springs awaiting Gillen's return. When Cowle requested the appointment of a second JP, his advice was reasonable:

> On the last occasion [August] I induced Mr Strehlow [also a JP] to go in from the Mission . . . to complete the Bench but as he could get

no mileage or fees after being absent from his home about 9 days and travelling 170 miles, I cannot well ask him to make another trip.[38]

In all these circumstances, given prevailing police attitudes to Aborigines, there remained a strong temptation to save trouble by not taking prisoners alive. Daer and Cowle experimented with an alternative, based upon Cowle's maxim (L4.7) that 'Blacks can only be ruled properly by <u>fear</u>'.

They began in November 1893, while both on patrol with four native police. Daer reported on the events officially.[39] They 'found where 3 Natives had killed a calf, tracked them up and took them to Tempe Downs, where they were whipped by the Trackers'. Inspector B.C. Besley returned this report to Daer with the marginal comment: 'This requires explanation . . . what magistrate ordered the whipping send full particulars . . . it looks like an unlawful act' (see Appendix 3).

Besley's 'please explain' was answered by Daer on 28 January 1894 in some detail:

> In explanation . . . I was 140 miles distant from the nearest Magistrate and my reason for having the offenders whipped by the Trackers was to save the Government the expense of taking them to Port Augusta . . . if the Natives were soundly thrashed by the Trackers when caught cattle killing it would have a much better effect than sending them to goal. Since the boys were whipped in November . . . no cattle to our knowledge, have been killed on Tempe Downs.

In forwarding the reports to the Commissioner of Police, Inspector Besley agreed that whipping 'is the most salutary way of punishing them but as it is illegal it is my duty to lay the matter before you'. Without moral demur, Commissioner Peterswald sought more details: 'With what was it inflicted? How many strokes? And what physical affect did it have on them?' Daer responded to these questions in March, informing Besley that twenty lashes with a horse-whip were administered; that the prisoners 'appeared a little stiff next day and very frightened . . . the moral effect seems to have been excellent'. When he received this advice in May, the Commissioner prudently forwarded it to the Chief Secretary, who returned it without comment. Six months had elapsed since the flogging.

Later that year, however, Cowle submitted a report on his latest achievement in capturing five men (including Arabi, recently returned from Port Augusta prison) for killing Hermannsburg stock.[40] 'These I flogged and cautioned', he reported. 'I was particularly careful to punish only those actually concerned in the killing and all others I fed and gave flour and tobacco to.' Daer wrote in support of these actions. This time, however, the Attorney-General intervened. 'Punishment without judicial authority can on no account be sanctioned', he ruled. On 5 October 1894, Illamurta police were so notified, as was the Barrow Creek police station.

Rules were one thing, but surreptitious practice in the bush was another. In May 1896, Cowle (L2.16) was concerned that the missionaries might 'report me for wattling the deuce out of two of their blacks', but evidently no protest was lodged. Probably like Baldwin Spencer, they accepted such practices with equanimity. Besides, he had established friendly relations with the mission staff (L2.14). This is confirmed by evidence communicated to us by John Strehlow, who has studied Hermannsburg records and the diaries of E. Eylmann who visited both Hermannsburg and Illamurta. Cowle's relations with Pastor Bognor were particularly friendly.

The lash proving illegal, Cowle devised another strategy to obviate tedious escorts. He freed prisoners, but only after some heavy handed—or worded—treatment to instil fear. Around Christmas 1897 (L3.10), his captive 'was cautioned . . . pretty severely, then I took him away with us on a walking expedition and I think he felt certain he was going to be shot'. He actually received flour and tobacco. Cowle continued with this policy, after informing offenders that 'I would have given them a hiding . . . but now we had been forced to take out Warrants or "Papers telling all about Policemen to shoot them"'. To judge from his subsequent letters, he was correct to feel 'not over confident of success'. While the death of cattle prompted drastic action, this was not so when it came to tribal killings. In recounting a payback killing (L4.5), Cowle observed: 'We do not interfere in these matters but they killed a couple of beasts . . . so I'll have to look them up soon.'

With the arrival of the Horn Expedition at Tempe Downs in June 1894, Cowle's intellectual horizons broadened. He was officially instructed to guide a party across Lake Amadeus to Ayers Rock and return them to Glen Helen. The Europeans consisted of Baldwin Spencer, J.A. Watt, a recent Sydney geology graduate, and F.W. Belt, Adelaide solicitor and W.A. Horn's brother-in-law, who recently had returned from big-game hunting in Africa. At thirty-four, Spencer was the oldest member of the quartet. Larry, one of Cowle's Aboriginal police trackers, accompanied them. Larry possibly was involved in Willshire's 1891 raid on Tempe Downs.[41]

Departing from near Kings Canyon in the George Gill Range, Cowle impressed them with his bushcraft and their traverse of the salt flats across Lake Amadeus, when they survived water scarcity. Those city dwellers were startled by Cowle's language, Belt later labelling him as the Centre's 'champion cusser'. After his return to Adelaide, Belt confided to Spencer that 'my mode of expression has become weak and insipid compared with the picturesqueness that Cowle used to infer into even the least important utterance'.[42] Gillen used the term 'language a la Cowle' [sic] with the same meaning.[43] Hard language was accompanied by hard living. Spencer later reminisced that:

> I wished . . . when sleep was not easy or comfortable, that my friend Cowle . . . had not been quite so hardened a bushman . . . because he thought nothing of sleeping out on the hardest ground, with only the thinnest of rugs . . . to enable him to travel lightly and with great rapidity.[44]

Cowle's correspondence with Spencer commenced immediately the Horn party disbanded at Alice Springs in mid-July 1894. When Cowle penned his first note and packed ant specimens for Spencer's biology department, he was unaware that his new friend was still in Alice Springs. Spencer's meeting with Frank Gillen proved so congenial that he remained behind as Gillen's guest. Although the purpose of his stay was to collect and identify fauna, ethnological interests came to dominate.

Spencer's intellectual progression from biology to anthropology is reflected in this correspondence, as faunal interests faded into relative unimportance while Cowle's responses to requests for artefacts or data on Aboriginal society dominate. Cowle responded willingly and with evident zest for the tasks requested. Sometimes he resorted to unorthodox methods, as when, far south of Illamurta, he commandeered *pitchis* (wooden dishes), but remarked regretfully 'I could only give the prisoners one each to look after', as they wended their neck-chained way to Alice Springs (L4.7). Yet he remained sceptical of the value and validity of such research: his sarcastic tribute to the first Spencer and Gillen book, '"Grimm's Fairy Tales" up to date by

S. and G.' (L3.11) set the tone. When the partners planned their 1901 route, Gillen notified Aborigines in advance of their intended visit. 'As Cowle would say', he told Spencer with good humour,[45] 'to give them time to "invent some habits and Customs"'. Cowle's frequent jibes that informants were unreliable (L4.1), or that Spencer and Gillen met with their informants in an artificial context, where they sought to please, were seriously intended, though expressed in politically incorrect phraseology from modern standards. They should consider, he contended (L3.7), 'the Black as a wild beast as well as in the shape of a Corroboree Monger'.

Cowle's anthropological perspective

Cowle initially concentrated on obtaining zoological specimens: 'Under separate covers I am sending you two tins . . . containing the Sugar Ant ('Yarumba') and small ants and embryos dug out by myself, I could not find the winged ones.' He seems to be continually running out of the spirits used to preserve specimens. However, through casual asides, his early letters show that he was aware of Aboriginal knowledge and uses of plants and animals and he was probably dependent on Aborigines for collecting most of the specimens: 'Blacks state they show up after rain' (L2.1); 'Arunta name "Inchillya", Looritja name— "Winterra"—On the authority of the *blacks* I may state it eats principally Witchitys and grubs, constructs a little nest in a crab hole with grass on top, chiefly nocturnal' (L2.15).

Gradually his letters become more anthropological in content, reflecting Spencer's own shift of emphasis. The letters also document Gillen's change of status as he shifts from being a rival provider of information to being Spencer's main collaborator. Interestingly, Cowle's references to religion become much more expansive after he has read *The Native Tribes of Central Australia* (L3.12). '<u>I believe that every water hole, Spring, Plain, Hill, Big Tree, Big Rock, Gutters and every peculiar</u> or striking feature of the Country, not even leaving out Sandhills, without any exception whatsoever is connected with some tradition' (L4.5). He goes on to discuss one of the key issues in the debate over totemism: whether people avoided eating species that they were associated with. And Cowle provides Spencer with relevant data. The ancestral animals in human form certainly did eat their own species, but the difficulty was that the ancestors also sometimes appeared in animal form. In this latter case did they still eat their own kind and if they did would this be cannibalism? Cowle's discussion is muddled but shows him trying to grasp the conceptual difficulties. Like Gillen he drew biblical parallels, but the contrast in tone is significant. To Gillen, 'the wanderings of the totems is startlingly like the wanderings of the children of Israel'; '[the sacred objects] are "sacred" in the sense perhaps that the sacramental wafer is sacred to the Roman Catholic'.[46] Cowle's analogies are less well expressed: 'These nigger yarns have many points in common with some of our biblical tales don't you think?' (L4.7). In writing to Spencer, Cowle is certainly sensitive to Spencer's views but his attempts at empathy with Aboriginal beliefs and values remain unconvincing.

Cowle was aware that ritual performances were, from an early stage, subject to and influenced by negotiations which took into account the settler population: 'I fancy emu is the object and they intend to ask Mr Parke to let them hold it at Henbury. If I were not going down I would let them hold it at Ilpilla and see the lot' (L3.1). He saw Spencer and Gillen's activities as part of this pattern and implies at times that this may influence the data they obtain. Referring with characteristic cynicism to the provisions that Spencer and Gillen gave the people they worked with, he wrote, 'Was not that an embellishment of those uncontaminated old vermin beds . . . to prolong the flour producing epoch?' (L3.8). His letters provide extensive documentation of the trade in sacred objects and other artefacts: 'I presume that you want all the churina I can get . . . and any other . . . weapons and gear, whatever that is genuine. Or is there a limit to the number of boomerangs, Woomeras, Pitchis' (L4.5). He also provides examples of the internal trade that occurred in sacred ma terials and the way it was influenced by the postcolonial context. A woman's father sold locks of hair she was keeping for her sons' initiation to 'the Crown Point Blacks for a pipe and blanket' (L3.6).

Cowle provides interesting evidence about social change, implying at various points that practices recorded by Spencer and Gillen were no longer current. 'Many thanks for the Pamphlet on initiation Ceremonies . . . especially as regards the Tualcha-mura or Potential Mother in law . . . the present system is much more rapid, certain and beneficial to the young man and one of the things he has to thank the white man for' (L3.8). The letters show an ongoing concern with the management of sexual relations. He observes a breakdown in the authority of the elders resulting in more promiscuous behaviour among the young: 'present day tribal punishments are mostly bosh as the young man is too useful as a tobacco purveyor, etc. to the older ones . . .' While he provides useful information about contexts of change his interpretations of behaviour are always in terms of individualistic motivations, showing how far removed he was from developing an anthropological understanding of the society he was living in. The high value he gives to severe punishment accords with his own police practice in which he sees beatings as an element of social control. He associates the problem of controlling cattle killing with the failure to control sexual relations: both are reduced to failures in discipline.

Cowle's letters contribute greatly to understanding the context of Aboriginal life in central Australia at the time of Spencer and Gillen's research. They reveal the limited space that Aboriginal people were allowed to fill in the postcolonial context. The letters have extraordinary pathos. Alienated from his own society, Cowle became one of the instruments for extending that society's control over the indigenous population of the Centre. He spent most of his life in central Australia exclusively in the company of Aborigines, yet very little in his letters reveals his social interactions with them and the role that they played in his life. Aboriginal people largely enter the picture in relation to his police work or occasionally as ethnographic data.

Cowle's attitude probably was tinged with jealousy, because Gillen became Spencer's chief agent, diverting his interests from fauna to Aborigines. Spencer's two first influential contacts had been Cowle and Byrne, at Charlotte Waters. They must have envied Gillen's association with 'the prof', culminating in the cross-continental expedition of 1901–2. Cowle was excited in 1896, when Spencer proposed revisiting the George Gill Range and successfully requested the Adelaide police authorities to grant him Cowle's services for a month.[47] Cowle diligently planned this diverting venture, but was frustrated when drought forced its cancellation. Consequently, Spencer spent the entire period recording ceremonies at Alice Springs, while Cowle's involvement was restricted to escorting him back to Oodnadatta via a sacred painted ceremonial site on Henbury station, so he was left with a 'dull disappointed feeling' (L3.1).

Cowle's character

Along the Overland Telegraph Line, individual personalities loomed large, for the white population constituted a small, predominantly male band. Spencer was the recipient of many confidences from lonely individuals whose mores ensured that they rarely confided in each other. Cowle's letters contain personal asides which reflect his egalitarian yet respectful friendship. Outback mateship evidently comprised convivial banter over booze, exaggerated tales of prowess, debates over Arltunga's gold potential, gambling on mining shares or betting on horse races. Spencer read many good-humoured accounts of the activities of his bush mates, including criticisms which never would be directed to them personally. Quirks and weaknesses of Cowle's character are writ large in mail from Gillen, Byrne of Charlotte Waters and James Field at Tennant Creek.[48]

Cowle's mates all found him strenuous company. Always the extrovert, his heavy drinking formed a common thread in their correspondence. Cowle seemed aware of his weakness, alternating between boastful binges and remorse. 'He bitterly regrets the collapse on the night of his arrival here', Gillen informed Spencer.[49] While Cowle was on city leave four months later, 'the Porter was flowing freely'; as Field observed, Cowle was a man who 'spent his cheque'. Upon his return from that binge, Cowle wired Gillen from Oodnadatta: 'Penniless, Sober, Sorry.' However, Gillen later noted approvingly that he 'limits his Nipping to three doses a day so that in this respect he is improving'. This relative abstention was self-imposed for one year, but Gillen correctly predicted an 'unholy orgie' at its conclusion.[50]

To what extent Cowle's alcoholic feats were bluff, to accord with the expectations or practices of his mates, cannot be assessed. It is obvious from his correspondence that his intellectual interests rose above grog and riotous living. For a man who claimed to be penniless, it is relevant that Josiah Symon acted as his financial agent in Adelaide. Late in 1898 Symon wrote to Illamurta concerning share transactions on Ernest's behalf, when his account stood at £204.16.3, a relative fortune in the bush.[51]

Moderation was not evident, however, when Cowle roused Gillen and Spencer from their sleep at Charlotte Waters in 1901. They were compelled to sample his gin 'and settled down to talk all night'; on their anthropological adventure, Cowle was 'disgusted' at their meagre whisky stocks.[52] In retrospect, Gillen attributed Cowle's later physical ills partly to 'hard-drinking'.[53] Possibly fear of the social consequences among his family contributed to his self-imposed isolation at Illamurta.

Cowle's neglect of comfort was another personality trait commented upon both by Gillen and Spencer. 'He never uses more than one blanket when camping out in the coldest weather', Gillen remarked.[54] 'It was just a peculiar form of bush side, a not uncommon form especially amongst very young men who wish to pose as hardy bushmen.' But Cowle *was* a hardy bushman, so Spencer called it 'hardihood',[55] while praising 'his tireless persistence' in chasing Aboriginal cattle killers, 'even amongst their own mountain fastnesses or in the desert country, where no white man ventured'—and this sometimes in bitter winter cold, frequently tracking and climbing on foot.

Only one image of Cowle has been traced, posed at Illamurta, probably around 1898. He stands tall and dark, boasting a moustache less luxuriant than Baldwin Spencer's, but perhaps pleased that a sagging riding boot spoiled the neatness of his image. Evidently his appearance changed according to fashion. In 1897 he was 'clean shaved and looks like a variety actor'.[56] By 1901 his beard was flecked with grey hairs; a few weeks later he looked so unkempt, that he looked 'more like a Greek bandit than a Police Officer, his belt laden with cartridges revolver and handcuffs and altogether he presents a formidable appearance'.[57] Spencer described him as like a 'brigand. His beard is uncut, he hadn't washed for some time . . . his trousers were ancient . . . and he was wearing a striped flannel jacket and a very ancient slouch hat . . . He is a beggar to talk and would have stayed up all night . . .'[58]

Cowle energetically defended white pastoralism, as a law enforcement officer. He acknowledged his duty to ensure that the Luritja people 'respect the law of the land that has been taken from them' (L4.1). Aware of Cowle's sentiments, Spencer wryly told Byrne, that once Cowle read the newly published *The Native Tribes of Central Australia*, 'I can imagine [him] using language and tearing his hair over one or two things in the introduction. At the present rate of proceedings he is rapidly leaving himself no work to do or niggers to look after.'[59]

Spencer's latter remark was prompted by the number of captives Cowle consigned to Port Augusta's prison. His arduous pursuit of cattle spearers, or lost Europeans, is chronicled both in his and Gillen's correspondence. Following Cowle's capture of two warriors who speared Charles Beattie at Glen Helen, Gillen commended his initiative and endurance to the Commissioner of Police. Consequently, just six months after his promotion to Second Class, he was awarded £10 and his police file was endorsed 'Hon. mention'.[60] Cowle's career had reached its zenith, although his most celebrated patrol occurred in the summer heat of March 1902 (L5.5). Two young Europeans were missing from Eringa station near Oodnadatta, and Cowle and his Aboriginal trackers rode some 900 kilometres through unfamiliar and waterless country. They located the bodies of Graham Wells and both riders' horses, at various locations, but the other lad's body was never found.[61]

Several character traits were highlighted during Cowle's Illamurta years, apart from his proverbial thirst. The first was his desire for seclusion, even twice declining to spend Christmas Day with the Gillen family, and avoiding the raucous Alice Springs race meeting, although his own horses were entered and ridden by Tom Daer (L2.5). Cowle craved solitude, ideally without the company of any police mate, and he created his own amusements. Obviously letter writing and reading occupied much of his leisure, his tastes ranging from the *Bulletin* to Ruskin. He was a perceptive observer of environmental changes and probably derived more interest than he admitted from experiencing Aboriginal society. It is interesting that in 1901 Gillen noted a softening in Cowle's attitude:[62] 'He no longer ridicules my ethnological work and I am grateful to notice from his conversation that he is taking an intelligent interest in the habits and customs and traditions of the natives.' The stimulation of his solitary collecting of fauna, flora or artefacts for Spencer, Edward Stirling at the South Australian Museum and others is evident in his correspondence.

Even his family associations were limited—possibly increasingly so following his mother's death in 1895. Saddened by her loss,[63] he told Edward Stirling that he was particularly affected as it was the first death 'in our circle'. After her passing, he rarely visited Adelaide, even though he had intended to do so around that time. Possibly his attachments were more with his mother than his father, who may have disapproved of Ernest's abandonment of a banking career for an obviously flamboyant bush life. The latter complained to a mutual friend that Ernest had not communicated any news of the Horn Expedition so far.[64]

Following his father's retirement, also in 1895, he invited Cowle to accompany him on a visit to their Tasmanian relatives. Cowle declined: 'I think this would be a trifle too steady', he told Spencer (L2.6). The following year he ignored invitations to visit Victorian relatives, whom he had not seen for fifteen years (L2.13). His sister, Eleanor Symon, wanted him to go to Western Australia, presumably to visit his barrister brother Felix at Cue, but he felt 'better off here'. Besides, he reflected, he felt obliged to soon visit his father in Adelaide, although 'What I mostly dread is the army of nephews and nieces and cousins . . . I . . . have to be amiable to' (L2.19). Later, when his father and sister wished him to join them on a voyage to England, he declined because it would cost him his Illamurta posting (L3.11).

It comes as something of a surprise to infer that this rugged individualist had a long-standing romantic attachment with an Adelaide woman, yet his single reference to her existence in this correspondence was oblique and was provoked only after she abandoned him to marry a more visible suitor (L5.1). In order to explain to Spencer why he regretted his decision not to purchase Tempe Downs station and stock early in 1900 when they were on the market, he commented: 'At that time though, I was thinking seriously of going down country and trying to settle and reward the misplaced affection of some damsel.'

Gillen[65] assisted in partly identifying Cowle's fiancée, when he provided her surname, Moulden, 'to whom our erratic friend was engaged for so many years'. Elsewhere Gillen reported that she broke off the engagement to marry 'a man from Burmah'. It may be assumed that it was in reference to this decision that Cowle (L4.8) wrote to Spencer in September 1900, that he had a notion to retire, but 'that is knocked on the head and now I only want to stay in the bush'.

The circumstances all point to the phantom fiancée as Ruth Moulden Moulden (1864–1931), daughter of Joseph Eldin Moulden, an Adelaide solicitor. Her brother, Beaumont Arnold Moulden, a prominent solicitor and member of the South Australian parliament, had property in the Northern Territory. Consequently, Gillen's reference to Moulden was most likely to him. Ruth Moulden Moulden met Edward Johns, a senior officer in Burma Railways, aboard ship between Adelaide and Fremantle in December 1899; they became engaged in April 1900. After this rapid courtship, she married Johns in Rangoon on 22 November 1900, having sailed from Adelaide in October. Presumably she wrote to Cowle before that date conveying the news, and this was the subject of his comment to Spencer during September 1900.[66]

Given Cowle's individualism, it is understandable that he criticised each young police trooper stationed at Illamurta. As Gillen confided to Spencer,[67] 'no man could work amiably under Cowle', as the faults always lay with the other man. After Thomas Daer died in 1895, W.B. Kean was stationed there until June 1898. Cowle disliked him from the start, for he had 'bourgeois' and superior manners (L2.13). Eighteen months later, he complained 'how sick I am of this fellow here' (L3.4). When Kean left Illamurta, Cowle unsuccessfully requested headquarters not to send a replacement, but to support him instead with two additional Aboriginal trackers.[68] When Foot Constable J.R. Barlow replaced Kean, Gillen anticipated trouble, for he was described as a 'pugnacious larrikin', and assertive characters were unwelcome at Illamurta.[69]

Barlow remained until May 1900, although Gillen reported that he was 'anxious for removal' following a few weeks in Cowle's company.[70] It took even less time for Cowle to conclude that, 'I do not care for the new man at all as a mate' (L3.10). Barlow survived for his term, however, unlike his successor F.J. Ockenden, who joined the South Australian Police in 1897 and was transferred to Illamurta on 4 July 1900; by 4 November, he had returned to Adelaide and resigned from the force.[71]

Cowle's verdict on Ockenden by 31 August was unpromising (L4.7): 'The new man is . . . terribly dull, knowing my angelic temper, you can picture him as rather a trial on the last trip, no interest in anything or his surroundings except at meal times.' Ernest's reputation suffered following Ockenden's brief posting, for it must be inferred that Cowle dispatched him south with prisoners before the end of September (L4.8). According to Cowle's version, Ockenden lodged false complaints against him in order to provide a plausible excuse for resigning from the police force, for which he later apologised (L5.3).

Some weeks earlier, South Australia's Governor received anonymous allegations concerning Cowle's immorality with Aboriginal women. The chronology absolves Ockenden, so possibly the informant was Barlow, eager to compensate for his unpleasant experience of bush mateship. The Hermannsburg mission is another possibility as complainant, although Cowle evidently established a good rapport there.

He already was on record that his camp rules allowed 'no one to sleep with lubras here black or white' (L4.1). His vehement denials of these accusations evidently satisfied both Gillen and his postal successor at Alice Springs, T.A. Bradshaw JP, who was officially asked to investigate. Cowle felt so confident that his innocence would be established that he expressed disappointment when Bradshaw asked him to ride to Alice Springs, rather than receive a probing visit from him at Illamurta.[72] Unfortunately the official files on both this and the Ockenden affair appear to be missing from the South Australian archives. The absence of any reference in the Index to Correspondence files of the Police Department possibly indicates prudent action at a high level. Was Sir Josiah Symon influential in this presumed concealment?

Demise and death

Despite these apparently satisfactory outcomes, however, there are clues which suggest something was amiss, because Cowle's health deteriorated. On 28 May 1900 (L4.5)—that is, before any allegations of misconduct—he told Spencer that 'I'm a bit twingy in the shins', reasonably attributing the cause to rheumatism. Three months later he had a severe chest complaint, subsequently 'feeling as if I had been belted all over'. Spencer and Gillen were on their transcontinental expedition during 1901, so Cowle's flow of letters decreased, making it difficult to monitor his health.

He took southern leave for some three months from October 1901. On his own report (L5.5) he 'succeeded in being a bigger crimson idiot than usual, left a legacy of offences of one sort and another behind me'. He told James Field that 'he had a very good time and spent his cheque'. Back in the saddle, in January 1903, he attributed scary dizziness and double vision to sunstroke. On foot, he was unsteady and a short climb 'distressed' him. He must have feared worse than sunstroke, however, because he wrote to his Adelaide doctor, Dr R. Humphrey Martin, a specialist in neuro-surgery. A month later Cowle diagnosed his own condition as locomotor ataxia

(*Tabes Dorsalis*), soon confirmed following a journey to Adelaide. Friends at Charlotte Waters who saw him *en route* described him 'as very shaky and looked a perfect wreck'. He never returned to the Centre.[73]

Cowle exhibited the classic symptoms of locomotor ataxia—double vision, dizziness and muscular incoordination. At that time it was thought to result from exposure and hard living producing a form of rheumatism.[74] It is now accepted that it is a progressive degeneration of the nervous system and the spinal cord, being manifestations of tertiary syphilis. Its onset frequently occurs at ages between thirty and fifty, often advancing slowly. Although usually fatal, its progress may be arrested for years.[75]

If Ernest Cowle suffered from syphilis, there are only two likely sources. Possibly he caught it on a southern binge, such as that in late 1901, when he admitted 'a legacy of offences of one sort and another'. Alternatively, there was truth in the accusations of his association with Aboriginal women. Almost forty years after Cowle's death, the anthropologist T.G.H. Strehlow recorded testimony which claimed the latter to be so. Strehlow collected kinship relationships during 1960, and Cowle's name is included in the following documentation. Whatever information Strehlow collected from his informant, Tom Wheeler Tunala, it is evident from the following that he composed the piece utilising his own knowledge.[76]

Strehlow was annotating information about a woman known as Lady Nalawuljaka, the third wife of Tom Wheeler Tunala:

> Lady Nalawuljaka (= Annalawuljaka) first lived as a young woman with a white police officer Ernest Cowle at Illamurta. She was a tall, stately women, whose face was later marred by smallpox scars. In her young days she was sometimes referred to as the Queen of Illamurta. Lady had no children from Cowle (who later had to retire to Belair, SA crippled by locomotor ataxia). She married Tom Wheeler only in her middle age. No one here today knows who Nalawuljaka's father was. There is a photo of this Lady in her old age in R.B. Plowman's book *Camel Pads*, facing p. 86.

Robert Bruce Plowman (1886–1966) worked for the Australian Inland Mission between 1913 and 1917. Based at Oodnadatta, he made three extensive patrols, each covering some 2000 miles (3000 kilometres). In 1915 and 1917 his patrols reached Hermannsburg and Tempe Downs. He wrote a series of four books during the 1920s and, although *Camel Pads* is undated, its preface is dated 1933. The credits for the photographs are so general that it is impossible to ascertain whether the photograph referred to by Strehlow was taken by Plowman. That he did take photographs is suggested by a list at the back of his journal. If it was his image, it would have been taken twelve years or more after Cowle left Illamurta, certainly making a chronological possibility for Lady to have been associated with him.[77]

The one relevant photographic image of Illamurta known to survive, in the Gillen collection at the South Australian Museum and therefore likely to date from Cowle's residence there, is a striking one. The proximity of the Aboriginal camp to the solid building which still stands there today offers striking testimony to the nature of culture contact on the frontier. Potential sexual liaisons certainly were facilitated by the settlement architecture and dressing standards.

Could Strehlow have confused the identity of the policeman? Possibly, but not likely, given his detailed grasp of people and places within the Hermannsburg region. Even so, there is no evidence that Lady suffered from venereal disease. It might be speculated that Cowle realised that he had caught syphilis by early in 1900, and that it was he who terminated his engagement. This offers an alternative explanation to his assertion in September that 'now I only want to stay in the bush'. However, given the chronology of Ruth Moulden's departure overseas, it seems more likely that she took the initiative in breaking the presumed engagement.

Dr Robert Spencer Gillen suggested to us another attractive hypothesis which accounts both for Cowle's illness and his problematic character traits. He postulates that the onset of Cowle's syphilis dated from his obscure 1880s phase, and that it was this socially distressing knowledge which led him to enlist in the mounted police, becoming a bush recluse, avoiding family and fiancée.

Locomotor Ataxia (*Tabes Dorsalis*), which may follow syphilitic infection, takes an average of fifteen years from initial infection to the development of serious symptoms. So, somewhere during the 1880s, his doctor may have partially cured his infection, but warned that secondary characteristics might follow, even resulting in tertiary symptoms. These were indeed exhibited around 1900. If Cowle cohabited with the indigenous 'Lady', evidently no offspring resulted, but this could be due to his disease-induced sterility. This scenario offers a plausible explanation for his self-inflicted isolation, his intemperance and his short temper.

There are possible echoes of this self-denying spirit in his wistful comments to Spencer in Letter 2.8:

> You, who constantly live surrounded by intellectual people and the refining influences of women would have to cage me somewhere in the back yard and if any of your acquaintances dropped across me, you would have to exhibit me as a specimen of what a Nineteenth Century Australian, debarred from these privileges and with a backward tendency, can develop into. You see, Professor, no one is more keenly alive to their imperfections than I am and yet I haven't got the stamina to get shut of them. I think it is only my memories of a few good women that have kept me from going to the dogs altogether.

Cowle survived until 19 March 1922, his death certificate attributing his demise to 'cardiac failure and locomotor ataxy'. In 1903, electrotherapy was elementary, but it was tested on Cowle. Presumably in order to stimulate degenerate nerve roots or to test the extent of nerve injury, Cowle was subjected to direct (Galvanic) current of low voltage and amperage, probably using bulky batteries. Gillen termed the process 'High Frequency Rays', while Field alarmingly reported it as 'Radium Rays'; whatever the process it must have scared the patient.[78] As recounted by Gillen, 'you lie down on a lounge and catch hold of two handles and feel nothing but if anyone touches you anywhere sparks fly from you and you feel a slight burning sensation'.

Wishful thinking on Cowle's part probably led him to anticipate improvement, for Gillen reported that following the ray treatment he 'can safely negotiate about 50 staggery yards without the nurses' assistance', but his condition was beyond cure. By late October he had left hospital and was staying with Josiah and Eleanor Symon at *Manoah*.[79]

Between 1903 and Cowle's death, details of his confined life are few. Early in 1908 he had recovered from 'this last troublesome bad turn', but a year later he was in bed, although 'looking well and bright'.[80] Always a loner, he purchased a house at Belair, where he was nursed by Kathleen Mabel Hughes for some fifteen years until he died there. The introduction in 1910 of Salvarson (the trade name of arsenic-based arsphenamine) as a remedy for syphilis, if injected into Cowle's body, may have served to prolong his life.[81] His last letters bear testimony to his many devoted friends who regularly visited him and kept him abreast of news of the Centre. The Sir Josiah Symon papers in the Australian National Library contain a few copies of letters Symon wrote him. Both were the executors of the estate of Cowle's father, who died in 1906, so most correspondence concerns its administration, particularly the finances of Ernest's youngest sister, Olive.

Ernest was in hospital at Nuriootpa in 1905, when he argued the interests of the Northern Territory to Senator Symon for the time when the Commonwealth government would assume administrative responsibility. Not only did Symon support railway construction from Oodnadatta to Pine Creek, but he argued for its priority over the successful decision to build a line to Western Australia.[82] In letters which Symon forwarded to Ernest, he followed the fortunes of various officer nephews during the Great War. From the tone of this rather slight correspondence, the two men felt a mutual respect for each other's abilities.[83]

An indication of Cowle's loyalty to Symon's political cause was reflected in some verses he penned before the Senate election on 31 May 1913.[84] Symon stood as an Independent this time because he refused to sign the Liberal Movement manifesto, but he lost his seat by a large margin.

> The Senate Elections
> One vote for Sir Josiah Symon
> The Constitution is in danger,
> And soon comes Polling day;
> Mind you vote for J.H. Symon
> On the thirty-first of May.
> Hutley's men will spout and tell you
> The Union Ticket not to split.[85]
> But be free; be independent;
> Choose the man you know most fit;
> He's not a moving picture;
> He's a man whose like there's few;
> And He's mighty level-headed,
> Though that's not the Liberals' view.
> Twelve years he's served you truly;
> Surely sufficient test.
> So mark one square for Symon,
> And leave to him the rest.

Unable to walk at all during his closing years, Cowle's debt to nurse Hughes was acknowledged in his Will. He bequeathed £800 of his £4000 estate to her.[86] Ernest's sister, Florence Anderson,[87] contacted Baldwin Spencer on behalf of Josiah Symon who sought information for 'a short account of his life', which he intended to write 'for his friends'. A search of the Symon papers and also the Symon library collection in the State Library of South Australia failed to trace such a potentially invaluable document. It is worth reflecting, however, that when Symon later donated £1500 to the Australian Inland Mission to establish the Eleanor (later Elizabeth) Symon Nursing Home which opened at Innamincka in 1928, possibly his thoughts were also with his wife's brother, Ernest, who spent his youthful years in Cooper's Creek territory (although there is no reference to Ernest Cowle in Symon's relevant papers).[88]

There is a gap in Cowle's correspondence to Spencer from 1903 to 1920, although from the surviving letters it must be inferred that there were others, and that Spencer visited him. It seems that Spencer only retained those letters from Cowle and Gillen which contained anthropological or biological reference. In his last sad letter in 1920, Cowle recalled wistfully the exciting days of their early association and reminisced about their colourful mates. He also paid tribute to his Adelaide friend, James Frederick Downer, who was a weekly visitor. Possibly they shared a bond of preferring privacy. Downer's obituarist remarked that he 'shunned publicity [and was] almost unknown to the general public'.[89] It was from Downer's North Adelaide residence that Ernest's funeral cortege left for the crematorium. At Adelaide's North Road cemetery, Ernest's ashes evidently were interred in the Symon family section. His small headstone stands in front of a larger headstone signifying that two infant daughters of Josiah and Eleanor Symon already were buried in that grave. Sir Josiah's tall monument stands next to it. Ernest Cowle indeed had been accepted as a family member.

During his long illness, Ernest's family connections were cemented with his sister Annie who, with her daughter, Jocelyn, visited him. Annie had married Edmund Bowman, builder of Martindale Hall near Clare. Amelia and Frank Gillen's children recalled that, following the death of their father in 1912, when they lived at Blackwood, on many weekends they visited their parents' friend. They hiked across the hills to Belair, where Ernest sat uncomplainingly in an invalid chair. They felt that he always was pleased to see them; another visitor recalled that Ernest had a pet parrot for company.[90] Spencer[91] paid tribute to this 'hopeless cripple [who] bore it all with the same stoical cheerfulness and indomitable courage with which he faced the dangers and hardships of his life in the Centre'.

The Advertiser carried a sympathetic tribute to Ernest Cowle, possibly written by Josiah Symon, which caught the spirit of his life.[92]

> Although he wrote no books and delivered no lectures he was regarded as an authority as is testified by the acknowledgments [in the Horn Expedition and Spencer and Gillen books].
>   He will, however, always be remembered for himself. Quick, modest, good natured, with a rare sense of humour . . . he was universally loved, and everywhere, both in the bush and out of it, he was respected, trusted and admired.

Cowle's name is indeed still remembered, if obscurely, for his name is incorporated into the scientific names of species of honey ant, wolf spider and wattle tree. A small street in Alice Springs bears his name, though few citizens would know its origin, or question why Willshire merits a more important street. Even more tenuous is the existence of a spring east of Haast Bluff, known once as Cowle Soak, because he so often camped there on his punitive patrols. Its Aboriginal name, Aljalbi (or Alalbi), is more celebrated for its role as an outlier during the 1930s of the Hermannsburg Mission, under the ministration of the Arrernte evangelist, Titus Arenkeraka (or Rengkareka).[93]

The crumbling ruins at Illamurta, now recognised as a heritage area, remain as Cowle's physical memorial, for his letters testify to his devotion to that isolated place. The numerous Aboriginal artefacts and a surviving photograph from his time there establish that it also was a significant contact place between Europeans and Indigenes. Their close proximity suggests that Cowle coexisted with Aboriginal people more easily than his critical and racially slanted comments suggest.

Cowle's abiding contribution appropriately concerns his research contribution towards documenting Aboriginal traditional culture. Despite his neck-chained prisoners and his enforcement of pastoral supremacy, which he was instructed by government to enforce, his genuine—if grudging—interest in Aboriginal culture needs to be set in context, for few contemporaries shared it. His willing donation of ethnographic specimens to the South Australian Museum and the

National Museum of Victoria represent significant collections, while biological research on native fauna was greatly assisted by his observations and collections.

Ernest Cowle's most significant memorial, however, was his facilitation of Spencer's early field expeditions and the data which he supplied to Spencer and Gillen. His support was gratefully acknowledged in their preface to *The Native Tribes of Central Australia* (1899). That book is arguably one of the crucial publications in the formative history of global anthropology and a landmark in white Australian knowledge of Indigenous Australians. Either largely ignored or selectively used for decades, today the research by Gillen, Spencer and their collaborators provides an irreplaceable resource for all Australians. Apart from their own massive assemblage and interpretation of data, their chief field agent was Ernest Cowle.

2

HOME AT ILLAMURTA

Letter 2.1

Illamurta
30th July 1894

Dear Professor,

Under separate covers I am sending you two tins as under—

1. <u>Flat sided tin</u> containing the Sugar Ant ('Yarumba') and small ants and <u>embryos</u> dug out by myself, I could not find the winged ones. Blacks state they show up after <u>rain</u>.
2. <u>Circular tin</u> containing Sugar Ant ('Ittoo-ittoonee') and four other kinds, two of which are winged and dug out of the same hole. No embryos—this ittoo-ittoone appears to be a second ant of the sugar kind and not so large although esteemed equally by the festive nigger—his congeners are a small yellow tailed ant, a large bodied ant with large callipers, a small winged ant and a large bodied winged one.[1]

I trust they will reach you safely and if you can drop me a line from Charlotte Waters[2] you might tell me which is the Western Australian one and if you want more, also any hints as to packing. Dr Stirling[3] wrote telling me you were staying behind with Mr Watt,[4] otherwise I would have posted direct to Melbourne.

How did you get on at the Alice and did Belt[5] behave himself at our highly priced hotel? There appears to be some alteration in our Mail as it was four days late and I don't know when it returns so am sending in at once to prevent missing it. If you see Keartland[6] kindly tell him I have got any amount of finch eggs if they are any use—the confounded niggers keep bringing them to me but always manage to smash any other or larger varieties. With kind regards and best wishes to Watt and yourself.

Believe me,
Yours very sincerely
C.Ernest.Cowle[7]

Send a few more bottles and some spirit if you can manage it—most of the other leaked.[8]

Letter 2.2

Illamurta
14th Nov 1894

My dear Professor,

Your very welcome letter arrived safely but I cannot say the same of the jars of spirit, one of which, and several of the smaller ones were broken. In the big jars I found a frog and a little crayfish or yabbie— was this an oversight? At all events I have put them by till I hear from you. It has been terribly dry since you were here and I saw no frogs while digging out and cleaning our Spring which was very low but will look out as much as possible when I see any tadpoles again and next mail will try and get some more of the red ants for you as I have told the lubras to locate some of their haunts. I am sending you this mail two of the small earth lizards[9] which I spoke about, they have only two legs and these seem undeveloped, they wriggle out of sight in the fine dust very speedily. I hope they are some link [sic] (On a second examination I find the larger one is growing two more legs confound him.) Re rats, I saw two the other day which you may not have got but I could not preserve them—they were coloured like the one we got from the Sandhills this side of Ayers Rock—body slightly smaller, long hind legs, on which they hopped but the female had no pouch—I have two boys out now looking for some as they say they are about here—I was awfully savage that I had no salt and that it was the hottest day up to date. At all events they were not pig footed.[10]

Everyone here highly excited over the forthcoming races and busy with their horses.[11] I don't intend going in if I can avoid it but, if you were to be there would do so and I think you would find some interesting anthropological specimens present on the Racecourse—the details of their history and private life you could obtain fully from me—Gillen[12] would not do as a cicerone as he would allow himself to be overcome with pride and prejudice which, coupled with ignorance and arrogance and a certain amount of good nature, appear to be the unfailing attributes of all that class of ill bred Irishmen. (N.B. I am of Irish extraction myself.) You know I like Gillen but also know his failings and from the little glimpses I got of him from your letter I should not be surprised if you had bottomed his character thoroughly, I wish you would let me know if it tallied with my description. I had a long letter from Keartland who, like yourself, fears the pruning knife. I am sending him two big lots of eggs which I hope will arrive undamaged although I have fears after the way your tins suffered. Winnecke[13] and the Doctor I have also heard from but Belt wants leaving in the centre of Lake Amadeus with a looking glass, he never answered my letter—I think the Photos you sent are really excellent, especially the one of Ayers Rock taken from near our Camp there, I wish it shewed that big piece of rock like a spring better. Amadeus is also nice and I recognize easily the short tail and nonchalant manner of the much anathemized Camera pack horse.[14]

Constant association with the learning and refinement of your Camp had not the humanizing influence on the native assistants that it should have had. Arrabi has certainly not been much in evidence since I met him last but 'Meenemurtyna' joined several other young men and has had rather a good time on the Peterman and Gill's Range.[15] I followed this party backwards and forwards from the camp on Trickett's Creek to Bagot's Creek on the top of Gill's Range on foot last month, saw some nice inaccessible Rockholes but had no luck as they unfortunately came across our footprints near where you were digging with Pritchard[16] and left no signs after that. I hate being bested so I am going out again in about a week.

It will take me some time to completely grasp the names of various animals you mention owing to lack of an appreciative audience with pocket books to jot down the golden utterances. 'I say Tate,[17] what did you say this was? Exaltatus or latifolia?', here Tate replies, 'latifolia', but discovers next day that it is incanis?? and so on. By the way, the member of your party that told the chief scandal mongers of Alice Spgs that Cowle travelled over a month with your Exped'n and never washed once is only to be described in the vernacular of the North West as a b-d.

Are you really serious in saying there is a chance of your coming up next year? You know we would be only too glad to see you and do anything we could for you, only I think you might lend the Camera to Gillen. One current story was that all the plates were broken between Alice and Oodnadatta and that the party was indebted to Gillen for any photos taken by the Expedition. I was down at Horse Shoe Bend last week selling a dead man's effects and saw Field[18] there, he was going down to Crown Point to meet a lady to attend to Mrs Gillen[19] so that I reckon the Pontiff[20] does not intend to let the race of Kings of Alice Spgs die out for want of direct issue.

The Garden, which you ask after, is the cynosure of all beholders, putting all joking out of the question it has been a wonderful success and without seeing it one could not picture the extraordinary growth in it. Beetroot, Cabbages, Cauliflowers, Onions, Turnips, Carrots and small stuff galore and we expect to have plenty of all kinds of melons and cucumbers also tomatoes within a month. Well, you know this part of the Colony does not go for much in the line of sensational items, so you will, I trust, excuse the jumble of this epistle and with very best wishes for a pleasant vacation and a prosperous New Year

Believe me,
Yours very sincerely
C.Ernest.Cowle

I got over a couple of gallons of Dawson's Dufftown[21] to celebrate my birthday last month—we drank more than one ounce p [sic] diem. Thanks for kind invitation to sample yours which I will avail myself of when I get the chance—one can't say how soon or how long this may be.

Letter 2.3

Illamurta
16th Nov 1894

Dear Professor,

The boys brought me in two rats or mice just now, not the long legged kind but different to the ones I saw you with so I am sending along this mail—they have thick set legs and a coarse tail—one I have gutted and one left whole as the mail leaves soon—kindly have a look at them on arrival in case they go bad—Locality Police Camp.[22]

Yours Sincerely
C.E.C.

[Note on top in Spencer's handwriting]—Ulmatum [sic—male symbol] Phascologale cristicauda—replied Jan/95]

Letter 2.4

Illamurta
22nd Dec 1894

My dear Professor,

When you were up in these parts you impressed me with your many good qualities, especially the virtue of forgiveness, but it was left to me to discover since that you were a genuine Christian—considering how impatient and untractable [sic] I was on many occasions it is awfully good of you to spare time out of your many calls on same to write such long letters to me, only one who has spent many years in the Desert like myself can fully appreciate the pleasure of hearing and being brought in contact with a high state of civilization once more, my head scorches at the memory of many things and if I have not plainly expressed myself to you it is the fault of a none too brilliant intellect at any time having become greatly corroded. I have had two days genuine work trying to get you some specimens of ants etc but had no luck at all, only finding some of those mice which we got at Bagot's Creek which I knew were no good to you, the rain still keeps off and everything is getting a very parched appearance, I am glad you asked about water—our Spgs or Soakage is running fairly well since I cleaned it out thoroughly. Bagot's Creek I visited a fortnight ago and had difficulty to get a drink for the horses, there only being the smallest possible amount of water on the surface, the Kathleen, and Reedy Hole only have the main Rock Holes just level with the surrounding country and no water escaping at all[23]—at these three places the reeds are very dense and 12 or 15 ft high. At Penny's Spgs (where Watt was snailing) there is scarcely any water at all. You seemed surprised and perhaps a little incredulous when I told you all these places run strong in the Cold weather, yet rain or no rain, they will be just the same next year—there are a fine lot of Grass trees on the East End of Wild Eagle Plain about six miles from our Camp and I am sorry you can't photograph them just now, they are all out in new bloom—some of the rods are 10 to 12 feet long and many of them have assumed most fantastic shapes.[24]

Belt has at last written and complains bitterly of his treatment by other members of the Expedition while at Alice Spgs, he says, 'You know I had no sleeves and only part of the back left in my smoking Jacket and the other Johnnies were too damned jealous to lend me anything'. The young man will not die of modesty.

Daer[25] went in to the Races on 13th and is very, very confident of success with his horses and, fond as I am of the topic, it is a relief to be done with it for a time—you see it is the great annual festival of the Country and for four months before and four months after, with many encroachments on the intervening period, forms the sole topic of interest and conversation whenever any inhabitants of the place meet. Martin[26] went in two days ago and we have not yet had Thornton up here, I read an interview in the Observer of Carr-Boyd whom you say you heard lecturing and I came to the conclusion that I only knew one greater liar.[27]

Gillen very kindly invited me in for Xmas but I had decided to stay Home this year and declined so Mrs Gillen sent me out a pudding, by the interchange of such courtesies the integrity of Gillen's Empire is kept unimpaired and alliances with outer provinces cemented.

Garden feeling effects of the hot weather but still in very fair order. I am just harvesting our little bed of onions, some of which are between 1½ to 2 lbs weight, this is not a very exciting topic to you and you may reckon it small but the importance of it on the Finke will be recognised when I tell you that the fruit of the onions is only to be purchased very rarely at from 9d to 1/6 p lb. Tomorrow I will be a sort of distributing centre and despatch Cabbages and a few of the above mentioned to Henbury[28] and Tempe Downs as Xmas offerings. Spirits safely to hand and I am glad my vermin got through—you did not tell me if the lizards were common and if you require any more 'Ill-chillyeras'.[29] We are only allowed to send 1lb parcels through the post from here and it is only through the complacency of Officials at Oodnadatta that any others reach us. Well, you know what a Country this is to collect news in so I am forced to close this, wishing you and yours health, happiness and prosperity, and Remain,

Yours very sincerely
C.Ernest.Cowle

Letter 2.5

Illamurta
18th Feb 1895

Dear Professor,

If you had only been in this Country for the last month your desire of seeing a rain here would have been gratified. I should say we had quite a foot here in the last six weeks and mail was ten days late. Daer was in at Alice Spgs and I was an orphan and kept busy dodging rain spots all night (it never ceased for four days and nights) and once, when I essayed to find some dry garments, I found myself smothered with that wretched ant, known to us as Piss-ant[30]—this little beast, evidently wiser in his generation than ourselves, foretold a damp time and shifted with his lares and penates, eggs etc into every fold of my clean clothes. I have not secured any marsupials this mail but I think I have got the Alpha and Omega of those Sugar ants complete and am sending same to you. Bottles marked Yar. are the Ayers Rock kind, and others are the 'Ittootoonee'. I got large and small winged ones in each kind and also larvae, and notice that the females of the

Ittootoonee are also red—these I dug up personally so can vouch came out of the holes of the respective kinds.[31] If this doesn't wipe out Camponotus let me know and I'll shoulder a shovel once more. I am also sending two small jars of various sized bullfrogs and frogs—there are two kinds, I feel sure, a small, dark one which sticks about the water and a larger sized one which we used to dig up in the Garden all the dry time but can't find there now. I could not separate them but I noticed that one lot of bullfrogs appeared to develop legs at a much earlier and smaller size than others. I am also sending, amongst the ants, one or two of the vermin who have infested us since the rain—I did hope to have had a real good time amongst the Marsupials but the rain kept the boys constantly going keeping the horses and Camels together—Daer being away with the others. I was awfully sorry you were not here as there were other ants especially the Bulldog which I would very much have liked to dig up and see into but he came out in too strong a force for a single man to attack and I beat a retreat[32]—I noticed a fish or two in the Creek the other day but could not catch him. I will secure one in a day or two and if they look different to the Red Banks one I will secure some for you[33]—by the way, did you get any specimens of a very small frog [drawing] (I have mistaken my vocation) he is a little bigger than above and generally appears in hundreds out of the big Sandy Creeks just before a rain. I did not notice them this year but may have mentioned them to you when we were together.

I was surprised when I got your wire a couple of days ago and could not see what it referred to at first. You said very little about E.C.S. except that he had taken all the Credit of South's cat's agility and that he had done all the Zoological work.[34] I read your letter to Daer and some of the Tempe people when they came in from the Races, transcribing some parts, so there is absolutely no fear of anything further occurring from here. Personally speaking, I am sorry that the hitch has occurred and wonder if 'that old savage' did on purpose or what, one can't imagine such a thing otherwise—Stirling has been very good to me since he went down and we write occasionally,[35] he has never asked me for anything so far beyond 'Ethnological' side lights which I cannot give him with Gillenesque assurance and finality and won't until I am certain in my mind that I am at the bottom of it and when this may be, you, who appeared to size up the niggers' intellect speedily and his capacity for replying

<u>Yes</u> to everything may guess. There will be absolutely no difficulty
about a Euro's head or skin or both and I will see to this when I get
back—our boys generally get one or two a week here.[36]

I am sending Keartland a lot of eggs this mail which I hope will
reach him in safety before he starts out on his next Expedition, at
one time the Blacks used to plague me with the little chestnut eared
finch eggs but now it's quail. I have blown over 50 and thrown away
tinfuls but they will stick to it, they are all over the place and all
sizes. Yesterday my egg man turned up with half a Billy full and after
drafting out some eggs I put the rest under the table still in a mass
in the Billy, and this morning got 5 young and now there are three
or four more cheep-cheeping so I will have to destroy the lot to be
humane.[37]

Very many thanks for the tobacco from both of us and also for
the Photos. I also received two pipes from Keartland and as I write
I puff at the joint product with much contentment. I have not yet
had time to have a good look at them, the mail turned up per
Blackboy from Doctor's Stone's [sic] yesterday, and we don't know
when it's going back, so Daer thinks I had better start at daylight
tomorrow and go to that track to meet Alice Spgs down mail in case
the regular mailman goes back via Owen Spgs from Mission,[38] this
means pretty well 50 miles tomorrow so I am a bit pushed. I quite
expected that when it did come we would have nearly a week as
usual. I know you are not interested in the Racing News but I must
tell you that Daer won four of the principal races with our horses—no
money—that hairy eared Irish shark Gillen had got most of the wagers
and refused to part—Hope you will have a decent time in Sydney
and find that rising Geologist in a clean celluloid [sic].[39] I promised
him a couple of the little 'Moloch horridus' and have had several but
have feared them going bad before arrival as he wanted them alive—
would they live secured to the bottom of a box? I know they are
hardy.[40]

You frequently write kind of tirades on the marriage state with
which I agree—marriage in itself is alright but the inevitable consequences, as Kipling puts it, are the very Devil—I am not likely to
try it at all events for years, I have formed good resolutions and when
I next visit the Cities am going slow. I am awfully glad you got to
know Pat Byrne[41] thoroughly going down—don't you think he bears
out my statement that he was the only man on the line who really

was informed on most subjects and a good fellow besides. <u>Barcoo</u> which I told you about is very prevalent at present and we all have had a touch of it lately.[42] Good night and good luck,

Yours very sincerely
C.Ernest.Cowle

Letter 2.6

Illamurta
11th April 1895

Dear Professor,

It was not forgetfulness which made me miss last mail but an utter absence of material to work on and I fear it is but little better this time. Owing to the floods I took our mail nearly to Mt Burrell and when I got back to Illamurta I heard from Gillen that you were to be at C.W.[43] on 6th Feby. I was very much annoyed at not knowing earlier as I could just as easily *have* taken the Mail to C.W., had a talk with you, and got thoroughly grounded in 'Sminthopsi' [sic] and 'Psammophilus' or rather 'Phascologale'.[44] I am posting you a skin and a salted rat which I got near Haaste's Bluff[45]—my little bottle of spirits would not take them and I tried dry salting as an experiment[46]— probably you got these at the Charlotte but the extreme length of tail and their teats being placed (drawing) like those of a cow fetched me—they are both adult females and had young ones attached which the boys lost, one has a few grey hairs in end of the tail and the other is black. I think if you wet the drysalted one she will pull into shape and you will see the udder and teats complete.[47] You did not tell me if I sent you the right kind of frogs from here, I have seen no others about yet and presume that the tadpoles and frogs in Creeks and rockholes around would be pretty nearly all similar, it is difficult for an untassialled youth to distinguish differences but if worth while I will bottle some at each camp I notice them at.

I seem to meet with better luck for Keartland than any one else and I really believe that I have got him some good eggs. Mr French[48] wrote asking me for some Polytellis Eggs[49] but I fear they have disappeared from us again—they never were plentiful about here, but if I fail in that line I will get him some others equally as rare when the Season comes again—judging by the number that have gone to Town the eggs and offspring of these wonderful birds should be as common as sparrows.

You tell me you travelled down with 'Dick', well isn't he a beauty[50]—he patronizes, lectures and advises me whenever we meet in a charming manner, and really he is quite serious in fancying himself a very shrewd business man. Yet in reality 'Dick' has been thoroughly victimized by every one he has had really close business transactions with—he came out here to try and induce me to go in with him but I reckoned Dick had lost the energy which characterized him some years ago and have an objection to getting at or being got at by my friends. He wrote me from Alice Well this mail and tells me he was ill most of the time in Town with fruit cholera, no doubt he was so greedy that he didn't wait to spit out the stones and pips.

Gillen I have not heard from lately but he is thriving from all accounts and busy over his nigger stones—as you say it is nice to be Protector of Aborigines when one is interested in the Animals— no stones—no flour etc and a hell of a lot of moral influence[51]—we get three bags a year which I distribute amongst about 30 old hags when I go out Tempe way but it is only a drop in the ocean. I was round Gosse's Range, across the saddle and close by Haaste's Bluff then along Mareena into Tempe—saw plenty of niggers and Camera spots, quite 100 in one mob all told—Pat B. tells me you were studying the nude at C.W. and has sent me 'Reef and Palm'.[52] I regret that prurience is one of the failings of an otherwise noble character.[53] I can quite picture your troubles with the 'undergrads'. I reckon you are capable of handling them though and would be sorry to be one of the ones you felt inclined to squelch. Winnecke's syndicate don't seem in any hurry to make up their minds about starting him out again—and I am sorry to hear about his liver—were you serious about this and is he really bad? He doesn't look particularly healthy. All quiet at Tempe and if things keep so, I will either take a run in to Alice and see the Pontiff or down to see Pat as I feel the want of a change and have not pouched enough yet to go slow on—I can't see where this tickles you people, as I fancy I can do it yet and will.

Pater had left the Bank and wanted me to go for a trip to Tasmania and make the acquaintance of numerous bucolic cousins but I think this would be a trifle <u>too</u> steady[54]—when I want a quiet time I think I will go on one of those excursions to the South Seas or Japan. England might be more beneficial but your tariff stiffened me. Well, good night and good luck—if I can get over some day to Melbourne you might let me take your place for a day with your Students. Thanks very much for kind wishes and invitation, it will be taken advantage of yet.

Yours very sincerely
C.Ernest.Cowle

Letter 2.7

Illamurta
16th May 1895

Dear Professor,

Yours safely to hand and I note remarks re ground vermin. You must not think it any trouble looking out for them for you, it is a pleasure as the landladies say, only I don't want to bother you with rubbish or stuff arriving in bad condition—if dry salted specimens are any good it is no trouble whatsoever to stow them but bottles run such a risk, not only travelling round with me but also on pack horses to the Bend—you see, if a Mailman finds the shape of his bags not to his liking he jumps them or waddies them to the desired shape with disastrous results. Well, with regard to <u>Haplotis M.</u> and Co. of the Jerboa species—both those came out of one hole but I am confident are not the ones that build the stick nests and which used to be plentiful about Blanchewater and Montecollina on the Strelezecki [sic] Creek.[55] Gill sent me a couple of dead Bats which seem a little larger than those occasionally around at night—if I find them presentable I will post them and he tells me he can obtain more if required.[56] I have not seen Byrne or Gillen so far although I hear the latter was close to C.W. taking Mrs Gillen and the children part of the road and that he goes down himself a little later—I believe he is timing his visit to meet Davitt, the other patriot, with whom he will join forces and together they will lecture on Home Rule from English and

Colonial Stands, I believe he intends to put the Government on a firm Financial basis and in the spare time he gets from the Bars, platform and theatres he will settle such minor details as the State-Bank, Bimetallism, Minimum Wage and assist his Brother to provide that the State shall buy all wheat grown on the Village Settlements at not less than 5/- p bushel, this and photographing Davitt the House of Commons in the old Country will about keep him from mischief of a more serious description unless he thinks of standing for N.T. District at the forthcoming Elections, in which case he will endeavour to get the Blacks enfranchised and on his return a business like canvass with the aid of Govt. Rations will be the result.[57]

Like other Nor West[58] notabilities I may visit the Southern Regions about the end of the Winter but at present am undecided in what character to appear, Blackfellow, Theologian or <u>Savant</u>—the latter I should certainly adopt if I could only keep my d-d mouth and ignorance to myself at inopportune moments, and only spread myself before the reporters—however, I believe the World is very narrow and I might run foul of a snag if I ventured very far even before them. I deeply sympathize with the trouble you are experiencing from the Treasurer Turner,[59] as you say it is manifestly unfair to bring you out, breaking up your home etc, under a specific agreement and then trying to crayfish.[60]

I received very bad news about my mother's sudden death in Melbourne this mail and seem utterly unable to realize it yet, it is the first break in our family and I was so looking forward to seeing them all once more soon, Mother's intention was to take a cottage in Melbourne and spend the rest of her life there and was over there for the purpose, luckily the Father and some of the girls were there at the sad end but after she got ill she only lived for 48 hours and the others only got over in time for the funeral.[61]

Willshire[62] wrote to me this mail and talks of leaving the Victoria River Downs Police Camp, *500 miles South of Palmerston*, and asking me to let him know if he can recommend me as a suitable man to take his place. I am replying <u>no</u> at present, under the circumstances, and am afraid if I got the position it would cause too much jealousy amongst the senior men, yet this place is getting too civilized and I scarcely think I will be a favourite with the newly arrived Missionaries.[63] If I go there later on I ought to be able to do something for my Scientific friends but would have to visit civilization first and, with that end in view, will devote all spare time to studying the <u>London Journal</u> so as not to appear outré, this journal was the favourite reading of Thornton and he left a complete file behind him, extending over many years, so that if I wade through the lot I should have a fair veneer of the language and manners of your bloated English aristocracy, so highly acceptable to Colonials of both sexes. With best wishes,

I remain,
Yours very sincerely
C.Ernest.Cowle

Letter 2.8

Illamurta
19th June 1895

Dear Professor,

Very many thanks for your kindly expressed sympathy, I do not feel it so much now that the first shock has gone off.

I have been away at Tempe for the last fortnight chiefly about head of Walker, Shag Hole and Pine Point with Coulthard and only returned yesterday with Martin.[64] By mail Martin had an offer for 500 head of Cattle on the Run and returned post haste to Tempe. I expect him back tomorrow en route for Alice Spgs to wire and if I can get my share of this mail finished in time it is most likely that I will take a run in and make obeisance to the great or rather I think the advertisement puts it Big G.[65] You know he and I are the best of friends but invariably have at least one battle royal when we meet and exchange many doubtful compliments and, after an absence from each other's vicinity of 18 months, there is bound to be an escape of pent up steam and I think the change will do me good. When coming from Tempe the other day I met Belt's friend, I mean the one he assisted in the search for that 'kind of bloody weed that grows on these ere bloody hills', and he looked very much as if the search or weed had not been a success.[66] Another acquaintance of yours has just turned up, while I am writing this, in the person of 'Arrabi'. I told you we got him employment in Police at Barrow Creek 200 miles North of Alice and thought he was out of the way for a time but here he is. We have been examining him and he reports being discharged but from my previous knowledge of the gentleman I feel certain he has shirroccoed,[67] however he will go on to Tempe till further particulars come to hand but sooner or later I fear parts of his anatomy will adorn someone's Shelves (saving presence of Missionaries).

As long as you are not too much troubled with inspecting parcels I will continue to send along anything I am not certain of, and, in accordance with this intention, I forward a 'jerboa' about <u>half size of last</u>, which appears different from 'Mitchelli' and, I think, an adult also two young ones which the blacks tried to convince me were another species.[68]

I have the names you have given me fairly correctly for Gillen's benefit but it is in ornithological nomenclature that I expect to score most heavily as I scarcely expect him to be too well up in that line, I am glad Pado is crushing well for Marsupials, what line do Squires and Field affect?[69] It was very kind of you to tell me to make your house my <u>Mecca</u> when I visit Melbourne, and I know that you really mean it, but my Sister lives there also and would never allow it and on the whole I am assured that this would be very much to your benefit,[70] You, who constantly live surrounded by intellectual people and the refining influences of women would have to cage me somewhere in the back yard and if any of your acquaintances dropped across me, you would have to exhibit me as a specimen of what a Nineteenth Century Australian, debarred from these privileges and with a backward tendency, can develop into. You see, Professor, no one is more keenly alive to their imperfections than I am and yet I haven't got the stamina to get shut of them. I think it is only my memories of a few good women that have kept me from going to the dogs altogether.

Re Northern Territory, I got a wire asking if I would like to be transferred there and that I could travel overland.[71] To which I am replying in the negative today, I note what you say in regard to the possibility of Illamurta being closed and my relegation to more salubrious spots but at present am doing fairly well here and until I have a good balance at my back and fates are propitious will remain. At least, I would like another year and as people in our line of life appear none too keen for N.T. I don't anticipate much trouble in getting there when

I desire to—besides this, unless I got <u>charge</u> of Willshire's place it would mean actual loss. I also have an enquiry from Williams (Oodnadatta) who wishes me to join him and go in for 6 or 12 mos. [months'] leave without pay and either go through to W.A. with Camels via Musgrave, Mann, and Tomkinson Ranges for ourselves or for a Syndicate which he is assured we could easily get up. This scheme I am considering carefully as one must be on the look out for a chance to rise somehow[72]—What do you think of it?

I can quite picture your restiveness re publication of the proceedings of the great Expn and look as anxiously forward to Belt's contribution to the Volume which, I am afraid, will consist of low down personalities and a gorgeous description of the immense assistance he rendered the starred members of the party. Winnecke writes in better spirits and also Profr. Keartland who seems to be having much trouble and illness in his circle—Well now, once more thanking you and with best wishes from us both.

Believe me,
Yours very sincerely
C.Ernest.Cowle

Letter 2.9

Illamurta
23rd July 1895

Dear Professor,

Your letter duly to hand and I have sent word to P.M.B. re the fawn coloured jerboa which has not turned up this way so far[73] although we have at present a regular plague of mice, they are in everything, flour, sugar, rice, etc, they were at Erldunda about six months ago and later on at Henbury so the main lot appears to be coming from the South, they seem to me just like the domestic mouse, shall I send you a specimen?[74] I went into Alice Spgs as I intended and had a fairly giddy time. Gillen may tell you, if he finds time to mention my name, that I was a little uproarious but I am giving you the facts. I was simply exhilarated—we never had a battle even, simply fair comment on subjects in general, naturally I gave him my ideas on the present one man S.A. Government and the idiocy of his (Gillen's) brother[75] in particular posing as a man of enlightened ideas and fancying Village Settlements had completely settled the labour question, and, in consequence, he believes now I am morally and politically beyond reform, we mutually plastered each other up and I won his heart completely by talking of you and the other scientists while, on his part, when talking over Native totems he said, 'You are one of the few men in the Country with sufficient intellect to take an interest in this subject without wanting to rush off and talk of lubras and horses like the other bloody fools'. I did not forget this as it was such a mouthful without a break, he really has a splendid lot of stones and I will try and get him more but these less civilized blacks are more chary of imparting any knowledge than the animals about A.G.[76] Gillen talks of how much they value these stones and of their great antiquity yet he gets these niggers round him to obtain them by any means they can, knowing full well how little the really interested natives have to say in the matter, how he reconciles this with his position as Protector of Aborigines, and his negrophile ideas in general, I can't conceive and in consequence I am beginning to think there is something in possessing a truly Roman Catholic conscience and that there may be something in the remission of sins after all. Putting all nonsense aside, he was very nice and when one is personally in contact with his bottle of Dawson, he exercises a charm over an untamed mind which is hard to realize till you experience it. If the Horn Expedition does no good to the Scientists of made reputations it will have accomplished one great thing at all events, and that is the renascence or renaissance of Science in the Nor West (provided it ever existed in the Country). All the people at A.G. who know their alphabet now seem to be going in for eggs, rats, bugs and shells etc. I saw Squires out on an unsuccessful search about Condon's [sic] lagoon.[77]

I am sorry I displayed such ignorance re the surroundings of a knowledgeable man of the present day but feel more contented now that I am aware that you do mix with the common clay occasionally and even relish it, however in view of Gillen being at present touring the other colonies I have decided to postpone my visit till the tail of that comet is swallowed in oblivion of the past.[78] I am sending Mr French a few eggs which I trust will be the ones he wanted,

I notice that even collectors of little eggs have their little animus towards one another and I fancy the black cockatoo has something to do with it.[79] French has a most exalted opinion of you and constantly tells me how good you are to him.

Horn is hanging fire properly and it must be very trying to a temperament like yours constantly kept at Concert pitch by a class of students feelingly described in your last,[80] I fancy you ought now to be metaphorically rather like a lizard's tail and apt to snap off rather short. I am off to Tempe in two days and on my return Daer will probably go over to Melbourne for a trip. The garden and hens are in great form and likewise the goats and sheep who have increased some 40 odd in the last week so I am nearly out of my mind mothering kids. I find I am reduced to scraps of paper so I must conclude, wishing you a good time and that you may survive the ordeal of Gillen who should be crushed a little since Rosebery's fall.[81]

Remain,
Yours very sincerely
Ernest.Cowle

Please remember me to Gillen if he is around.

Letter 2.10

Illamurta
5th Oct 1895

Dear Professor,

Your very interesting letter describing the visit of the Ameer [sic— Emir] of Alice Spgs to Melbourne safely arrived and I can quite picture him making an Ass of himself in each and all of the occasions you wrote about. When I meet him I will get his version and, when I let you know how he transfigures things, you will turn green with envy that your powers of <u>imagination</u> are so feeble compared to his—he will even turn those green blouses into profit and there is but little chance of our gins seeing them—as he can scarcely coerce Daer or myself into buying at his own prices no matter how those poor devils at Alice Spgs stationed under him have to ante up with the poor satisfaction of seeing their women clothed in Gillen's mistakes—I'll bet he didn't declare duty on them at all events.[82] I got a few very poor stones the other day and a nice lot of wooden ones which I have written to him about—Posing as an upright youth before both Black and White is annoying at times—for instance, I promised not to let any other Blacks know that I had been shown this Plant and in consequence could only carry away the Sticks I could jam into a pair of Pack Bags and had to leave upwards of 80 hieroglyphical sticks running from about 2 ft to 5 ft in length behind. One of these was very interesting and I believe it told of how, in the early ages, Chambers' Pillar took a long journey away to the East and then came back and settled where it now sits—I might have rigged these sticks where we rigged the Camera but I would never have got through the Blacks unseen which meant hell for my guide—I am only afraid they will find out their loss before I go there again and if so they will shift everything.[83]

Times are very busy just now, as you say, with the damned, horsethieves etc and I have only been home for three days between mails[84]—I had a trip up by Mission Stn., Ellery's Creek and the North side of the Range which I ran along to the big Glen Helen Gorge, then on to Glen Helen and across to the Palmer via Gosse's Range. I saw some strange sights in the Stockline on the North side of McDonnell and it was surprising how many foals seemed to have lost their mothers—if ever there was a forsaken piece of Country it is this part when one gets off the Pad, I had to leave two horses clean done through the stones at Shag Hole and go back and replace lost shoes before I could get them down and home. Almost immediately afterwards, I heard that several of these people were about the Finke and about a horse bearing another man's brand under the Station one [drawing][85] being taken out of the yard at Mt Burrell, shot and burnt while the Drovers were breakfasting in the Creek half a mile away—of course I started to investigate and met the Alice Spgs Police near Francis Well with the suspected offender in charge so returned home to attend to mail. Daer is still away but when he does return and things are fairly quiet, I will make a special trip out from King's Creek after Sminthopsis but you know I am not exactly a free agent here and will have to let things settle properly.

Last night Bertie, the lubra, brought me a rat, as she had been in the Sun with it all the afternoon I disembowelled him and put him in Spirits—today I have all hands searching for his Wife as I think he is a Phascologale something—he does not seem to be <u>cristicauda</u> or Dasyuroides,[86] tail too short and no crest—and much resembled a short ferret in body. Ears large and flat. If they are not successful I will pack him up tonight in the only jar I have and trust he will reach you in a fit state to examine. I was afraid to drysalt him as the sun might have made him a bit close. I would very much like to see Pat Byrne and get him to explain to me the difference between Sminthopsis, Phascologale Hapalotis, Dasyurus etc as my learning is turning dog on me properly. Which is 'hallux' Dew claw? and also what means 'crassated' scaly?[87]

Garden flourishing and I planted the Melons Mr French sent me yesterday—All the eggs I sent him got broken but I hope this mail's supply will be more lucky, I think the smashes take place before they get to the Coach at Horse-shoe Bend—I only wish I could get you more animals, so far Keartland's line seems to have been the only one I have been really successful in. I don't intend closing this till I see if the boys have any luck tonight but am not very sanguine.

No luck—I suppose my Swan is only an ugly duck, sorry I can't make him less bulky but I thought he was touched with weather.

Kindest regards
C.E.Cowle

Letter 2.11

Illamurta
5th Nov 1895

Dear Professor,

Your welcome letter to hand and I was glad the jar reached you in safety. I was always thinking that I had wasted spirits on some rubbish again—the tin on return trip got a regular smashing up—one jar in fragments and a mark on wrapper. <u>Rec'd in this State G.P.O.</u> I fancy the operators take a delight in thumping that stamp on tin. Daer talks of leaving Town about 8th inst and is, I hear, in a bad way unless some new stuff, recently discovered in England and which they have sent for, does him good, I am afraid it is only a matter of time with the old Chap.[88]

I have heard but little of Gillen's return beyond that he is rather quiet and developing temperance notions but whether this is the result of a surfeit at the Banquets in his honour or whether he considers it more consistent with his dignity I cannot say—a short sojourn in charge of his Monkey Cage at Alice Spgs should restore him to his right tone once more. I don't intend to go in at Xmas if I can help it so won't be able to administer any tonic personally. Palmer is now a knight of the cleaver at Pt Darwin and hopes by strict attention to business, tact etc to gain a fair share etc—he only lost 100 head of his sheep and goats going over.[89] Glad to hear the Horn book is at last going to the Press but evidently your labours won't be over for some time and, as you say, it is a pity a few chapters can't be added on the relation of your experiences with the other members during compilation. I have been at Home most of this month for a wonder and for once in a way quite exhausted my reading matter, finally getting down to Ruskin on 'King's Treasuries' and 'Queen's Gardens', but find he writes in a vernacular which seems almost of another age.[90]

I suppose this will reach you while in the misery of going through Exam Papers and if you are busy I will not presume to expect a letter but have the honour to inform you that I reckon our mail will only be a six weekly one for the future, I think, as there is only one train per fortnight to Oodnadatta now. Keeping very dry here and a plague of Pissants and blow flies around which take a lot of fighting. With best wishes and kindest regards,

Believe me,
Yours ever sincerely
C.Ernest.Cowle

8th
Lubra just brought me in 4 half grown Phascologales which I have packed in our old tin once more so they may be handy for distribution to your friends—if not fully developed, their teeth are—they can bite like Hell. Hope they will reach you safely, the cristicauda was very plain before I choked them.[91]
C.E.C.

Letter 2.12

Illamurta
13 Dec 1895

Dear Professor,

Your truly welcome letter to hand—thank you for sympathy re poor old Daer. I was looking forward so much to seeing him when I got back from Erldunda a couple of weeks ago but when I got to Henbury I heard he was dead—you did not see much of him as you say, so you can't know what a thoroughly good safe, reliable mate he was in all things, which means a lot in our life here, and I miss him terribly. The powers that rule our Dept. have placed me in charge, which is promotion to the extent of transferring the responsibility of the place to me, but no increase in golden pieces, however it is an especial mark of confidence. Kean from Alice Spgs is to arrive shortly and be stationed with me but I am not highly impressed with what I know of him and long for the old times and Daer.[92]

Since last writing, I have been to Erldunda and out to Reedy Hole which looks very different now to what it did when you and I were there—the waters [sic] has dried back to the big hole which the horses would not go near on account of the Reeds and there was very little at Bagot's Creek—at both places the reeds were very dense and much higher than a man on horseback. I had hopes of rounding up some blacks when I should have spelled a day and put the gang marsupial gathering but smokes are delusive affairs and on reaching there I found it was the wind that had carried the fires along the porcupine[93] and the gentle darkies evidently as far off as ever, they had been burning those high Sandhills South of the Range and it should have panned out well. By the bye, 'Lydekker's Marsupials' is not to hand.[94]

The weather has been suicidal for weeks and one would fancy a deluge was imminent by the thunder, clouds, and lightning, I was positively nervous some nights with so much steel round me—if there is no rain, the Tempe people will soon have Cattle on South side and if my duties permit I will look after the Rats and while protecting the interests of A.E. Martin endeavour to advance science one more peg. I cannot give you much information re 'Ittootoonee' as they used to go back a long way and come bundling out promiscuously—the inflated ones are much more active than Yarumbas[95]—and first shower I will dig up some more holes, the main difficulty is keeping on the line and when it's lost or getting into difficult country, the blacks guilelessly remark 'No more'. I think the rain disturbs all their arrangements but honestly I am too busy to go out now and hunt them to a finish. I am sorry Prof'r Tait thinks I have neglected him but whenever I have been in promising spots, I have not been able to delay fossil hunting and one feels chary of forwarding plants because if he happened to have got them when with H.E.E, they would be received redly [sic]. I also regret that I have been of little use to Dr Stirling in his work— the charming chaos in the Menagerie is very interesting and no doubt highly interesting to his Serene Highness Belt, the vagaries of Horn won't disturb him much as he has not been working for the unborn generations.

I really hope to spend Xmas quietly here altho' Gillen, Kelly,[96] the Missionaries and the Cook at Tempe are all desirous of my presence for that occasion. It doesn't do to make oneself too cheap, ahem! and if I had my way I would like to wire for a case of beer and slip down to old Pat Byrne whom I haven't seen for two years. It would be capital if we could manage that little Exp'n next Summer, you could bring up a Village Settler and I would supply some bare rumped niggers and that would render one member of the party at least, supremely happy—one only has to know F.J.G. and to study S.A. Politics very slightly to be convinced that there is a lot in heredity after all, I wrote to him the other day and sent him some sticks[97] civilly as I expect a plum pudding from that Quarter—Where do you intend putting in the festive season? Don't repeat the last year's experiment and take the wife and children to the Sea—perhaps though, this is a necessary relaxation for all English People as they all seem to rush off to Ramsgate, Margate or some other fashionable seaside resort periodically and have their places robbed while they are away. I had one of those intermittent shower baths today and feel thoroughly clean in body, mind and clothing. Sincerely hoping you will have a pleasant Xmas and a prosperous New Year, free from the worries of a beggarly, retrenching, promise breaking Government (Also applies to S.A. only more so).

Believe me,
Yours very sincerely
Ernest.Cowle

Letter 2.13

Illamurta
28th Jan 1896

Dear Professor,

Many thanks for 'Lydekker' who arrived safely this Mail. After last mail we had simply terrific heat until about a fortnight ago when a few welcome thundershowers put a green complexion on affairs. You, no doubt, will have heard that I did not visit Alice Spgs for the Races and Xmas, which I spent quietly here. I gave an old fellow a month's work cooking for me so that I would not be entirely alone and then Kean turned up on the 24th and with the aid of two bottles of beer, things were more typical of a Bush Xmas. Gillen sent me out a little Pudding when Martin returned and also what he calls a bottle of generous Port to wash it down—it is needless to dilate on his vivid imagination to you who can readily picture how easily he would translate cheap Colonial into the above highly named liquor. It was reported that he was to visit the Mission Station this month and I asked him to let me know the date so that I could meet him there but he changed his mind, dreading the damage to his complexion and now has the cheek to invite me in to spend a quiet whiskeyless week with him; I may have to run in on a flying trip shortly but will conduct myself very sedately. Re niggers, I believe he is something very pure—I have sent him a few stones and sticks which he says were very acceptable as they were genuine—a short time back he obtained some very choice specimens from B.K.[98] over which he went into raptures but found out later that a guileless, civilized darkie had manufactured them for the occasion[99]—he is getting on wonderfully fast and will shortly be able to teach the Blacks if not their own Customs, at least what they should have as customs—and, as you say, the beauty of the study he has taken up is that no one will refute his Statements. As usual he won some money and there is no doubt but that his Catholic Majesty looks after his own—the latest idea is that he and I should jointly own a horse next year but I feel off as the Czar is slightly too autocratic for my taste and I fancy that he would play Brer Rabbit to my Turkey Buzzard in the long Run and yet the Serpent has a wily tongue and charms very cunningly.

My assistant, Kean, is right though in his way but of the bourgeois bourgeoisy—you know the type of young man who talks of 'keeping company' with a 'young lady' etc and talks of various damned nice fellows with whom he has been intimate, Coachmen to Mr So and so and others. I sincerely trust I am not snobbish but these little items in connection with others indicating the greatness of his derivation jar one inexpressibly at times and make one almost wish for solitary state—my appointment will give me some freedom of movement once a few contingencies are settled but I don't reckon that will be much before the end of April and I have a trip to C. Waters and Gill's Range Sandhills both in view.

The complications at Home are, I suppose, settled ere this—Australia could easily be captured and all of us transferred to a Foreign Power without any of us up here being much wiser with this six weekly mail—I hope America has to come down for altho' the British race are very much inclined to be aggressive, they can retreat when convinced of error and this time I really believe they are in the right.[100] I recently have been presented with a Swan Foundation Pen and an Independent Pen, I am writing with the latter and must say that it is acting up to its name, each time you observe any alteration in the shading of the writing in this pistle [sic] you can fancy me screwing and unscrewing and breathing blessings on the maker and donor equally.[101]

That book, which is to make Horn or mar him, must have left you with but little time for pleasure for over twelve months now and I can't make out why you don't quietly pack things up and try the dignified silence rôle yourself. I fancy if you ignored Horn altogether for a time it would bring matters into better train and convince him that common courtesy is just as welcome and <u>necessary</u> at the Antipodes as it is at St. James and Hampton Court or such places as your nobility frequent.

Sisters, Aunts and Cousins unite in desiring my presence in Victoria to such an extent that I am almost afraid to go down and cross the Border for fear of only getting back in sections. I have seen none of them for fifteen years and their recollections of me are confined to visions of a pink and white youth with nice manners which he dared not cast off as his spirit tempted, having a healthy dread of a long reaching Maternal and Paternal hand—this has now lapsed and if

I could really convince myself that it is merely distance lending enchantment to the view I would risk it.

With heartiest good wishes for self and those you left behind when you went to the Mountains with Mr French.

Believe me,
Yours very Sincerely
C.Ernest

Letter 2.14

Illamurta
12th March 1896

Dear Professor,

I have to thank you very much for the Part II of the H.E.C.[102] I have not gone through it yet and only looked at the pictures which the Blacks call 'indoota' or very good and they ought to be competent critics, they recognised the Rats and lizards very quickly but the diagrams of skulls and feet seemed to puzzle them very much. What an immense amount of work you must have had getting this in order and from the Prospectus I have before me from Dr Stirling I see there are three more parts to be yet issued and pity you if you have to edit all of them as well. Who is writing the <u>Narrative</u> of the Expedition for part one, which should be highly interesting if it goes into details of the Camp very closely? I saw where Horn had read a paper in England on the Expedition which was favourably criticized and noticed where he touched on Dr Stirling.

Are you really serious about visiting Cent'l Aus'a again next Xmas? We would want to arrange a little plan beforehand and get the Comm'r[103] to <u>tell</u> me to assist you any way I could, and all would be smooth as we could use the Camels etc. I could easily arrange to be at Charlotte Waters next Xmas if you could not get further than that but my idea would be for us to go to Erldunda from Idracowra and out to Coolada Spgs from there—then on up the Palmer either straight to our Camp to replenish or on along Gill's Range, the extra distance coming in here would only be twenty miles. Why I suggest Coolada Spgs is because they are small mound Spgs in long Salt arms amongst Sandhills and small tablelands and the forms of Mus and Coy company inhabiting both should be there together.[104] I made a flying trip out that way last month just to see the Country as I had never been on that part and liked it very much and hope to be able to make a trip from close to Tricketts Creek down by Mt Ebenezer or Mt Connor to Erldunda this Winter. About 9 miles from Erldunda, on a dry canegrass and saltbush Swamp, I came across scores of those twig mound Rat nests (you told me in your June letter, that though formerly common, you did not know where they now were). I let the boys have an hour's sport burning out some of them and chasing the inhabitants which are regarded as a delicacy—there were four or five in each mound we tackled and I secured an adult male and female which I carefully salted but they got rather strong and I had to air them which let the dead men beetles get at them a bit. I have just wrapped them up in calico and addressed them for you *Hapalotis Conditor*, to make certain that they are precisely the same form as you spoke of, they did not strike me as being so Jerboaey as Mitchelli and I can get you good dry salted specimens any time if you want them.[105]

Re Phascologale Cristicauda, I see in Plate I Fig I a life size drawing, didn't I send you a lean one about three times this size? I found one of the Cats chewing a McDonnellensis the other day so they are also about here.[106]

I intend trying to go down and see Pado in May, I would have gone now only Kean has had to go to Pt Augusta again over those horse cases and won't be back till end of April. An hour or two with you or Pado with a specimen or two before us would teach me more than a lifetime of Lydekker and enable me to notice the different kinds of mus readily. I had bad luck with a splendid lot of eggs as the mice got into them while I was at Erldunda and took the lot, nearly (200) wadding and all, and my collectors not shaping well, earned a hiding but I have been enabled to send a few good kinds to French this Mail and have got niggers searching for the beloved Black Cockatoo Egg. Strange to say, this Season seems quite different to 1895 oologically—some birds which were very plentiful last year are not about at all and vice versa—last year one saw Epthian Tri-color[107] everywhere and this season I have not taken one of their eggs but those of the Blue wren were very common.

Our cats seem either utterly sick of mice or to be strict vegetarians.

There are four and every one of them eats largely of any cooked vegetable such as cabbage, carrots, beet etc. Is this natural?

I haven't heard from Palmer for ages, I think he must have been busy making small goods and Sausages for the Xmas Festivities and studying how to run those opponents out of the business.

If affairs work as arranged, I will go to Alice Spgs before next Mail day and no doubt have the pleasure of interviewing Gillen. I want to see him particularly about nigger questions and put him on a right level as regards some other items—he runs away with an idea now that no one but himself has any <u>right</u> to possess nigger Stones etc at all, utterly forgetful that he is not going in for the subject for the benefit of the Blacks themselves but entirely for self glorification. I was up at the Mission Station about a fortnight ago and found the Missionaries very kind and hospitable, I didn't see the one I object to, Strehlow, he had not arrived many weeks with a new wife and appeared to [sic] much occupied to be visible but the head man and his wife and I get on capitally and altogether this man Bogner (Revd) seems much more sensible and less narrow minded than any of those we have seen there before. I returned home along the Mission Range via Pine Point and Shag Hole and noticed one of those twig nests Rat near Pine Point—The Palmer ran from Bowson's Hole to just below the Tempe Road crossing and the Finke and Ellery's creek might get to Henbury or just past—none of the other creeks ran although there was nearly 5 inches in January and over two in about 48 hours last month—the first lot made splendid feed but the hot weather burnt up all of it in a few days and if the second lot of rain had not have come it would have been disastrous. I can notice the effect of this very plainly in the Garden here where the ends of the Pumpkin and melon vines, all tender young growths, are burnt off as if frostbitten.

I am glad Mrs Spencer's illness is a thing of the past[108]—my sister writing from Melbourne tells me that the heat there has been extraordinary, the same as in the other Colonies.

Well, as regards War—I see there is still plenty of talk and poor old Salisbury seems to be having to climb down over Armenia through the currish action of Germany, Russia and the Gillenish Irish.[109] He will no doubt prove that it is only the purest motives that have led them to help to harass England—anyhow, I hope his brother doesn't get re-elected for he appears even more pompous and assertive than the one we know and like, although we frequently dissect him in a unmaliciously affectionate manner.[110]

Don't forget to keep me posted as to your movements for the next Xmas and also as to the exact time you would be likely to have at your disposal and with the most sincere good wishes,

Believe me,
Yours affect'ly
C.Ernest.Cowle

By the way, the Blacks at Tempe report Rabbits out by King's Creek and Laurie's Creek, also West of Coolada and the Mission Blacks report them out from Haaste's Bluff. As many of these Niggers, including Arrabi and others, have been prisoners and witnesses in Port Augusta and have eaten and seen lots of Rabbits there should be no doubt about it being true—One of my trackers told me, at Coolatta [sic] Springs, that he saw a rabbit while after the horses and showed me the tracks of one on one of the Salt arms running from the Spgs. I have heard of odd ones on the Finke but fancy if Rabbits are really plentiful out there, they must be coming from the South in a line considerably West of the Finke—What do you think about it? No one asked the Blacks about it but they reported it at Tempe and again some of the Whites at the Mission spoke about it and this, coupled to what I heard and saw at Coolatta, make one think it is really true although none have appeared inside the actual boundary we work on.[111]
C.E.C.

Letter 2.15

Illamurta
17th April 1896

Dear Professor,

I was delighted with your long interesting epistle but surprised that even you could not distinguish any <u>Mus</u> on sight and felt a little easier in my mind at not being able to properly spot the one I send you under separate cover. I salted her immediately I got her but she is rather high yet. She is of the bandicooty appearance and you will observe the rudimentary pouch if you soak her in Water as I dodged

Plate 1. Mounted Constable Ernest Cowle c.1898 at Illamurta Springs, an isolated outpost some 150 kilometres southwest of Alice Springs, from where Cowle led the Horn Expedition party to Uluru. He spent ten reclusive years here.

Plate 2. Baldwin Spencer's view of the Horn Scientific Expedition crossing the dry salt bed of Lake Amadeus in 1894, Cowle leading. This feat won Cowle warm praise from the party members, official departmental commendation, and enduring friendship with Spencer.

Plate 3. The overgrown springs at Illamurta, 1986. Permanent water supply made this an important Aboriginal camping place, but when two policemen were stationed in the area from 1893, the status of the Aboriginal people changed to servants and ration seekers.

Plate 4. Ruins of a building at Illamurta, 1986. Traditionally called the prison cell, it is improbable that this building was ever used for such purposes because it is known that Aboriginal prisoners were neck-chained together and, at night, chained to a tree trunk. A broken Aboriginal grindstone, left foreground.

Plate 5. The same building photographed from the opposite side, probably c.1900. Note the proximity of the Aboriginal camp, presumably the families of the Aboriginal trackers employed by the police to aid their search for cattle spearers.

Plate 6. Neck-chained prisoners in government-issue shirts, guarded by a native policeman (left) and a uniformed mounted constable, probably at Alice Springs (undated). Such chained groups may have walked 300 kilometres or more to the Oodnadatta train, which took them to the Port Augusta prison.

Plate 7. The stock and horse yard, Illamurta, c.1898. In the centre is a drinking trough made from a hollowed tree trunk. The police buildings were behind the vegetation to the left.

Plate 8. The same area viewed in 1986, with the fence surviving. The decayed trough lay to the right of this image.

Plate 9. Mounted Constable W.H. Willshire at the police station at Boggy Hole (Alitera), an Aboriginal sacred place on the Finke River south of Hermanns-burg, c.1891. It was from here that Willshire and native troopers rode to Tempe Downs and shot Aboriginal men and cremated their remains.

Plate 10. The Lutheran evangelist Titus with his people at Aljalbi (also known as Cowle Soak), 1930. Titus, an Arrernte elder, took the Christian message from Hermannsburg to people near Haast Bluff. This was an area over which Cowle tracked cattle spearers.

Plate 11. Ernest Cowle's fiancée, Ruth Moulden Moulden, daughter of an Adelaide solicitor. After years of waiting for Cowle, she married an engineer in 1900 and lived in Burma.

Plate 12. The enigmatic Aboriginal woman Lady (with hat), probably photographed c.1915–20. Ted Strehlow knew her in the 1930s and claimed that she lived with Cowle, but the evidence for this cannot be otherwise substantiated.

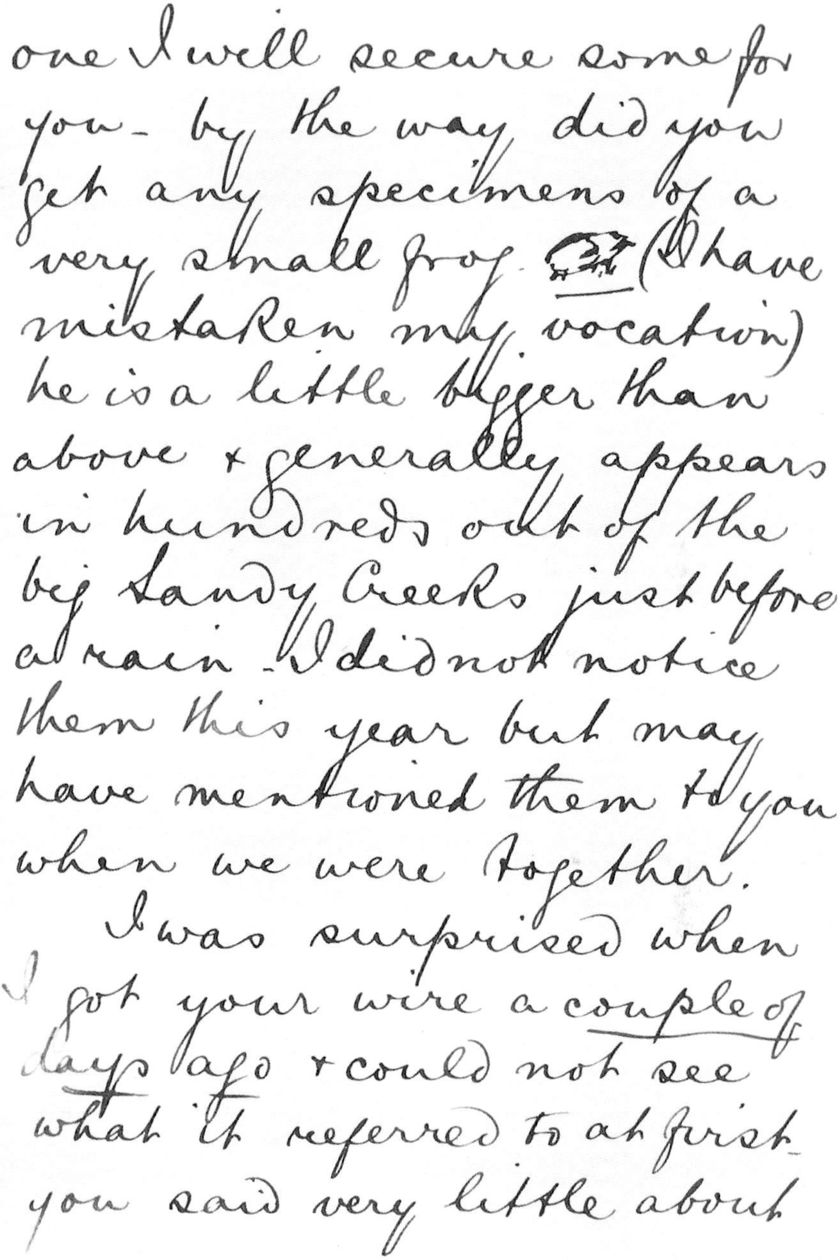

one I will secure some for
you — by the way did you
get any specimens of a
very small frog. (I have
mistaken my vocation)
he is a little bigger than
above + generally appears
in hundreds out of the
big sandy Creeks just before
a rain — I did not notice
them this year but may
have mentioned them to you
when we were together.
        I was surprised when
I got your wire a couple of
days ago + could not see
what it referred to at first
you said very little about

Plate 13. An example of Cowle's handwriting. Letter 2.5 (18 February 1895)
was illustrated by a frog sketch (line 4).

success should always be followed by
& everything give way to cash consid-
-erations. During the last month
I was out round Tempe & Gill Range,
the Country out there was looking
lovely & the blacks most of whom had
just returned from Gaol were stopping
on their own country & behaving
well so we were on the friendliest
terms, they took me to one plant
& were anxious for me to go to another
but I could not go on & although the
grass was perfect & in full seed,
water, away from the main Range
was not plentiful for the horses. I
got one stick which I will probably
send to Gillen but it is awkward
as it is nearly 2ft. long. I got it as
it is marked in squares thus,
instead of circles etc as
usual & all the natives who gave

Plate 14. Cowle's letter 4.3 (3 September 1899) with sketch of a ceremonial
decorated board which he collected on western Tempe Downs.

it in opening her up, extreme tip of tail missing—Locality between Henbury and Mt Burrell in Porcupine—Arunta name 'Inchillya', Looritcha name—'Winterra'—On the authority of <u>blacks</u> I may state that it eats principally Witchitys [sic] and grubs, constructs a little nest in a crab hole with grass on top, chiefly nocturnal—and my boys reckon that could get me some more some moonlight night in Sandhills near here by laying out some bones and watching[112]—Shall I give them a chance at it or not? Re Megadermas Gigas—which I note you did not receive many specimens of at Alice Spgs[113]—they are very plentiful in some caves near that ceremonial Stone on Henbury, if you want more; I skinned a couple but they went fairly rotten in the bags and to the best of my recollection their skin and fur seemed longer and stronger than that of some I skinned at Alice Spgs years ago. Am sending remains of one with the Rat. To recur to 'mus conditor' I don't think he is migratory at the spot I told you of, for Warburton says they have always been plentiful there.[114]

I have been in to Alice Springs and I think even Gillen will tell you that I conducted myself respectably—thanks to Mrs Gillen's kindness, he laid in one bottle of Whisky and when I finished that, I left, we had no time to get fairly discussing things in general so the atmosphere was balmy and genial and I did not get beyond telling him he was a b-d with Comfort and Prosperity and asking him if he didn't think he was a piece of costly and totally unrequired gilding to the Telegraph Station—after he had told me he could not let Field accompany me back, although he had admitted that Field had carried on everything perfectly correctly during his long absence in Ad'e [Adelaide] and Melbourne. Two or three times he started little ranting orations with outstretched hands and eyes fixed on some imaginary object in the Sky but as Field and I immediately started to converse privately together, they fell flat—he has got hold of a word or two somewhere and worries them properly—The present one is <u>Pessimism</u> and I had to listen to one or two little lecturettes on this when I had 'no get away'. Pado,[115] I believe, has at last solved the real cause of Gillen's nigger tendencies—his theory is that Gillen will shortly induce them to believe in transubstantiation and make him their High Priest and Treasurer. You know I like Gillen but, thunder!, isn't he a tremendous carmine hypocrite.

Now as to that trip of yours. I expect to see G shortly again and also Pado and get their views but I have been working out the time at your disposal and can't make it fit in with George Gill's Range (I hope to be there next week) much to my disgust—allowing you to be at C.W. for Xmas, you could not get to Reedy Hole much under ten days, at least same returning to C.W. = 20. 14 days Adel'e to C.W. and back = 34 which would make a very large hole in the time you have at disposal especially as we have allowed absolutely no time for Zoological Research and packing and unpacking the Camera. Can't you get a solid three months on the excuse of illness or something and disappear for that space of time or do you feel that your absence from the youth of Melbourne for so long a period would throw back a lot of your work almost irrecoverably? I often feel that way myself and say it honestly without egotism or any conceit whatsoever, although our lines of life are so widely separated. I can quite understand how a mug could mar *either of* our efforts in a very brief period. I will write more fully when I have seen Gillen and Pat and, at all events, if you can't get this far, I will do my utmost to get to Charlotte Waters to meet you once more.[116]

I have sent your friend French a pair of Cockatoo eggs this mail and confidently expect to hear of them arriving in fragments. I can not understand how it is that with these egg people even when a box arrives intact and unbroken, it is invariably only the <u>valuable</u> eggs that are damaged. I often muse over this.

Horn's vagaries seem to cause you all no end of trouble as S and W, in addition to yourself, hint that matters are not going smoothly. The omission of Winnecke's Map will be a more serious loss and blank than the absence of the Looritcha Castes from Stirling's Work.[117] You must be possessed of a more equable frame of mind (trained intellect, Ref—Gillen) than I have, for I am sure I would make one dash for satisfaction by giving the World a few of the facts as they are—Where does Belt come in? I suggested to Winnecke that Belt should collect the different members of the Exp'ns opinions on his brother-in-Law and publish them as an Appendix and then he might rest content with having done something stirring at all events. In reading the Zoology I notice that there were two kinds of new ants in those I sent you but I'm hanged if I can recollect the difference of C. Cowlei and C. Midas. I thought they were both alike. I will have to go digging again soon to compare—struck rock last attempt.[118] All the Blacks in the Country and many of we whites are suffering from a severe attack of Influenza or Nigger Pleurs as it is more generally called, thank goodness I am about over mine thanks to a free use of Rum. I always fancy this stimulant, if good, soars over Whiskey, I intend asking Sub-Prot'r Gillen to recommend that I be supplied with ten gallons for the Natives. I don't think I have anything further to write about this Mail so I will finish by wishing you a safe exit from the troubles of Editorship and all good thoughts.

Yours sincerely
C.Ernest.Cowle

I am keeping one P. McDonnell's [sic—McDonnellensis] in Spirits for you.
C.[119]

Letter 2.16

Illamurta
30th May 1896

Dear Professor,

Only a short letter this time for, for once I feel a bit done up—I only got home last night and have been hard at it all day answering letters and trying to finish a heavy batch of Official stuff for mail tomorrow morning. When I tell you that since the 2nd of the month I have been to Mission Station and along range via Pine Pt to Tempe and Home—off next day to Idracowra and back, off next day to Mission and out to Tempe and then off again next day to Idracowra and home you will believe that I have not had much time to spare in these short days—Reasons—a <u>rotten</u> case of using cancelled brand which will cause me to be at Alice Spgs on 10th June and a civilized beast of a Tempe nigger shaking another blackboy's lubra and turning loose amongst the cattle, he will be more trouble to get in those Ranges between the Palmer and the Finke than a dozen wild blacks as he is up to all the moves and worked those valleys running East from Palmer or Ilarra nicely—on my second trip he slipped me at the Mission Station in the night as he unfortunately was away, after wood, when we surrounded his Camp and saw us as he was coming back and cleared down the Creek. He would probably have stopped had this occurred anywhere else but I was a bit anxious as to how the

Missionaries would shape as I confidently expected them to report me for wattling the deuce out of two of their blacks for interfering with my protégée?? [sic] 'Jado', whom I had sent there with a message to the Missionaries a couple of days previous to my first visit.[120] I got the lubra and another suspected native and took them to Tempe and Martin took the lubra and saw where two beasts had been killed and only a little meat taken.

I think matters are smooth up the Finke as I was very polite to Mr Strehlow, J.P., who hates the English, I believe, as cordially as his Kaiser does and he requested me to allow him to photo my Camel and self[121]—Gillen, I missed there by a few days both times but I think he must have been telling them that my methods were sound if stringent or a large pumpkin or some tomatoes which I diplomatically took there may have caused them to think less of the wily niggers. One good turn deserves another and I will take Gillen in some stones and that is enough of aborigine for tonight. Practically speaking I dread going in to Alice Spgs as Gillen will be awful after the success of the Ministry at recent Elections—I haven't had time to look at a paper and see into things and make up a few offensive reasons to account for the defeat of virtuous members and triumph of the villainous ones, including his brother—worst of all, I believe he wins some money from me over results and I dare not dispute it for he might get his brother or Kingston to eject me Hospital Board fashion.[122] I quite agree with your remarks re the way we discuss each other and I know you thoroughly understand how well I like Gillen— I reserve to myself, in open argument, the right to pitch into him but when other people do it, I am on his side.

Kean got back here on 1st May and brought some papers and Horn's speech for me which had been missent to Alice Springs. Many thanks for the Report and also for Part Botany and Geology[123]—On my return from Alice Spgs I will send Kean to Erldunda (with orders to secure me a pair of 'Conilurus' Conditor for you) and have a few quick days at various books. A very brief epistle from Keartland this time and I was amused at your description of his multifarious appointments in the Expedition[124]—the Scientists of the Party, being all embodied in one person, certainly ought not to fall out. I think he must have been flurried and thinking of the tassels his name will bear after his return or he would not have left two lots of eggs in the chip boxes when returning empties.

Palmer writes at last and says he is not making a fortune but hopes to do well in the future—he says he is trying to work up a trade in corned beef with Java, Singapore etc., something very special sells 10lbs to the other people's one [drawing]—and has the promise of a new line of Steamers trading between Singapore and Sydney. I can't quite make out whether the Steamers are to carry his Beef or merely consume it.[125]

Re your trip, I am glad you have more time at your disposal and will hold a consultation with G and B and arrange when in at Alice Spgs. You say you want to visit G.G. Range[126] in a heavy rain—well, unfortunately this can't be fixed to order or everything could be arranged smoothly for you to miss Race Week which is chiefly notorious for the affectionateness of the Rum laden inhabitants of the District for any one with the price of a few drinks and for exhibiting a mutual friend of ours as a money grasper of a high order.[127] The rain, as a rule, comes about end of Dec'r or early in January but some years it is a minus quantity—we could be sure to be able to find a cave to keep things dry in such as camera etc and you might enjoy the pleasures of the Barcoo. When we know a little more definitely you might ask the Commissioner to ask 'M.C.C.[128] to render you any assistance he could'. While writing this Martin has come in en route for A.G. to be sworn in as a J.P. I will try and persuade him to stay tomorrow so that I can send letters to Alice Spgs where mail leaves a week later than it does with us, and now, once more thanks and good night,

Yours very affectionately
Ernest.Cowle

Martin says you can make Tempe your head quarters as long as you like. C

Letter 2.17

Illamurta
7th July 1896

Dear Professor,

Your long letter to hand last night—Re your trip. Gillen's idea was for me to meet you at C.W. and land you at Alice Spgs after which he would take you in hand and would see you back to C.W. or rather send you back as it would be impossible for him to get away for any time during the hot weather as the line would immediately feel his absence and go wrong at once. I told him you would not visit Gill's Range unless it rained and wanted to avoid the Race Week but he sat on all little objections like that in his usual lordly manner. My idea was if I could meet you at C.W. with the Camels which are all riding ones, for you to leave there or send to Alice Spgs everything that you do not require on this part of the Country so that we would not be hampered with any thing except the necessaries and travel quickly (out of Coolata if you liked) up here, get rations and on out to Gill's Range, getting back to Alice Spgs first week in December and sorrowfully bidding you good bye—the chief requirement would be some 'bouilli' as meat keeps badly at that time.[129] Flour, tea and Sugar we could get here as our loading comes up now. If it keeps <u>dry</u> the Tempe Cattle will be out about Reedy Hole and there should be 'Looritchas' there but in that same contingency you say you don't want to go near there at all.

My only fear of arrangements this far ahead is of anything eventuating between this and November to prevent my meeting you at C.W. which would be an awful mess—things are slightly unsettled just at present and I am going to Mission Station tomorrow to get a blackfellow remanded to Alice Spgs for trial and will see Gillen again then and suggest a safer plan—that is, for you to go straight to Alice Spgs by mail and then, if it rains, for me to come in and get you there in December and see you safe via Gill's Range down to C.W. *Jan'y* and Pado who would be home again then—this would prevent the possibility of your being stranded at all. I may have to take this aforesaid blackfellow down, in which case I would see you and we would know what we were doing properly, but I am not keen on going down at present at all—things are not working extra smoothly and I may be anywhere in six months and my peace of mind would be destroyed for ever if your trip was spoilt <u>through</u> me and not through my fault. Gillen was not bad this time but is whiskey starving himself and his friends to such an extent that it is getting painful and he has the cheek to say it is for our own good, luckily Martin was stopping there too and was well supplied. (G professes to be insulted if you take your own beverage.) Gillen was photographing mad and it was really hard to get a word with him—he is aggravating over Nigger questions—you tell him some little thing and he is very interested and makes all sorts of enquiries and perhaps starts talking to you on the same subject next time he sees you and calmly assures you he has worked all this out long ago—he will only see three or four 'Looritchas' at the Mission and christianity or rather associating with the disseminators of such has rendered them imbecile.

I noticed G. trying to get information from my boy and was not impressed, it was chiefly on subjects Gillen was apparently well up in and he seemed too eager to show it, for whenever the boy was in doubt he would say, 'so and so isn't it', and naturally the boy would say yes. Pado really intends going down in Sept'r and if I do, I will be back before the end of that month which would not hinder my being at C.W., in fact there is really nothing tangible to prevent my being there and able to put myself entirely at your disposal for a month or so but it is as well for us to be prepared at all points— I expect you will get the same non-committal, non- official answer from the Comm'r that H.E.C. had—people have to be so careful nowadays with this blatant Ministry but you have a friend at Court in Peter.Paul.G[illen] and he, being the echo of the Premier, can do much—Warburton has taken down a small lot of Cattle and Martin has sent down 290 head and I trust for both their sakes that they will strike a good market—I do hope we can arrange to go out Erldunda Way as it is a piece which has not been skirmished over— how would it do to go there, if there had been no rain at Gill's Range it would take about 8 days from C.W. and from there to here 4 or 5 or to Alice Spgs 7 days. Well I suppose we will all know better what we are doing in a few weeks—in any case you will require little beyond tobacco, bouilli and what little luxuries you can't do without such as <u>soap</u> etc. The main ingredients—flour and sugar, are handier to procure on the spot—Oh—bring in any case, a few pounds of good tea—All Govt tea is rotten and I can't say what ours will be like although I have written and ordered the best Assam.

I am fairly shivering with the cold so good night, with all good wishes and hoping we may soon meet.

Yours very sincerely
C.Ernest.Cowle

Letter 2.18

Illamurta
22nd Aug 1896

Dear Professor,

I was very glad to get your letter, when I last wrote to you I was hurried, worried and generally upset and could not express myself with the lucidity I wanted to and even after I had written to you I would have written again only I thought I might only make a worse muddle, let me try and do better this time. I got my nigger remanded to Alice Spgs and came home here and then found that if I did not clear again next day I would miss Gillen and no one would be available to try my animal, so I sent a boy on to Gillen post haste, burnt up my private letters and cleared myself, how I fared at Alice Spgs Gillen no doubt told you, as I asked him to explain matters and although he wanted you there Race time I think our arrangement is best and as I put it before, absolutely prevents a complete fiasco. At present 'M.C.Cowle is informed that Prof'r Spencer is visiting C.A.[130] at end of October and is <u>instructed</u> to render any assistance and to accompany him to G.G. Range'.

It still keeps dry and at present Martin has cut trenches out of Reedy Hole and Kathleen and has about 2500 cattle out there—how should this affect the Country biologically—of course, if there is rain I do not think the Cattle would be left there long and, in accordance with your instructions, I am praying fervently or blaspheming, one's just as effective as the other to a Protestant. I can't make out this year at all and the effect of rain, as you remark, is very noticeable on the fauna of this region—I have just been telling Mr French that at this time last year the Season for hawks and parrot eggs was about over, yet up to date I have only secured two eggs—even the house mice are missing. I have just been trying to secure one this last three weeks to compare with one the lubra brought in from the Sandhills without luck, to me they appear exactly alike but she has a name for each. Sometime ago I saw or caught a glimpse of a spotted cat (Dasyure) Charlotte Waters 'Chilpa',[131] Looritcha 'Coonincher', and have been offering a shirt for one. All the blacks know him but have not secured one yet and they recognize the drawing in 'Lydekker'—Jado brought me in two Rabbit bandicoots a week ago, 'Per' Lagotis I think, and a couple of days ago the boys dug out a pair by the horse yard, they bite hard and as I am probably going out Tempe way in a few days I intend to slaughter and salt them,[132] I have been feeding them on 'Yellka' and witchities and have also tried carrots and lettuce leaves but they do not appear to be thriving and as each night they turn the straw I gave them, over everything,[133] I can't say how much they eat but I must say they appear leaner than when I first boxed them.

Pado tells me he is off on 15th Sept and may run over and look at the West but perhaps the fact that our own Gold Fields are on the move may induce him to return; several of us are in a syndicate so as to be the early worms if possible, up to date my part has consisted in writing out a little cheque and I am totally in the dark as to the personnel of the Concern but I think Pado will have the engineering of the matter on his hands when he goes South—wish us luck but don't invest unless you can get in on a free pass. I have a good many sovereigns sunk in that Golconda and if this venture brings them back I'll be quite satisfied without wishing to rob my friends and the Widows and Orphans.[134]

My Camera not yet to hand and I missed an interesting subject (anthropologically or ethnologically) in a Native confinement, there were no old <u>hags</u> about, and the youthful mother seemed to have no idea of what to do, so Kean and I had to act as accoucheurs?? the child throve for about three weeks but the night before last I think the lubra slept on it and the poor little devil died. Did Gillen tell you that my prisoner took his sentence most impassively and only murmured that—'crimson lubra bin make him kill cattle'—but when he got at him in his den and unfolded a papyrus as long as himself and started to trace his descent through endless aunts, and great great grandfather's mothers he fainted away completely! Gillen was flying round with 'Sal Volatile' but I was calm as I could prove I landed him there with a full stomach, and in the event of an inquest would have pointed out that the cause of death was 'Gillen unwatered' and if his God, Kingston interfered in his Hospital Board style I should have endeavoured to wreck his autocratic Govt. on the Question even a Sub-Protector has no right to invent tortures, surpassing those of the Inquisition in general fiendishness.[135] Glad to hear that Dr Stirling's work is at last in the Press,[136] this off your mind and Mrs Spencer and the children being away in England will leave you with quite a free hand and now it rests with Providence, rain and yourself as to how we fix things finally. Let me know if you decide on trying my side of the Country first and I will try and let you know as soon as possible if there is rain. I want no more than yourself to be at Alice Spgs during Race Week and personally it makes no difference now whether I meet you at C.W. and say good bye at A.G. or vice versa. If we hit the Mission about Xmas time you would see German Style and a large lot of blacks who they feast gorgeously at that time and we might also be recipients of a shirt, trousers and hat as Bogner presented every white man there with this trousseau last year—think of that and with all good wishes and trusting Mrs Spencer and the children will have a pleasant trip.

Believe me,
Yours sincerely
C.E.C

—

Letter 2.19

Illamurta
9th Oct 1896

Dear Professor,

Whatever befalls you in this land of heat and blasphemy you will surely welcome it as a change and relief after your solid drudging of the past year; you will find Gillen 'on Aborigines' in his den very restful and soporific and can snore to your heart's desire once he gets well into the subject.

Touching Gill Range. I was out there a good deal last month, chiefly on top of it and was thoroughly disgusted with the appearance of the whole place, there appears to have been no rain there at all since you and I were there before and certainly not for the last 12 or 18 months. Reedy Hole and the Kathleen, which used to be fairly pretty little spots, are as bare as a board, all the fern and reeds eaten or trampled to pieces by the Cattle, I don't think you would even recognize Reedy Hole. Niggers being driven in from the Sandhills were slaughtering a bit, Martin and I tracked them for three days on foot and got to the old hags of the party and later in same day we saw the rest of the party carrying beef up the Range, we expected them to run into us nicely but after a long delay we found they were cooking it under that big Cliff just west of Penny Spgs and when we tried to get down to where they were, they must have heard us or two outposts who were posted 300 yards off on the Porcupine Hills to watch against interruption may have seen us—anyway the lot disappeared hurriedly when we dropped over the last ledge leaving two whole cows cooking in the fires, you will know the Spot when I tell you it was right at the 'Cycads'[137] and know how awkward a spot it was to reach from on top. I saw one rat hop out of a little cave we camped in one night and would have liked to secure him but it was dark and we dare not light a fire for fear of being seen or smelt.

In the book you are writing in collaboration with F.J.G.[138] I hope you will take cognizance of the aborigine's appetite when he has food in the bush. I calculate that the average of every man, woman, and child is 20 to 30 lbs of beef p day. This is no exaggeration, goodness only knows what the bucks actually eat because, of course, the children can't eat their allowance of the average. You see every time they wake up through the night they gorge and if it makes them sick they can start again the next moment on an empty stomach. At the same time they can do a starve with anyone. If information on the subject is of any use to you I shall be happy to give it to you when we meet.

I was greatly grieved to hear of the Commissioner's death, he was a genuine personal friend to me. I do not know anything of his successor and now also Gillen's brother has gone, he wrote me a few lines just after it occurred and the poor old chap was terribly upset.[139] I shall expect to hear from you definitely shortly after you get to Alice Spgs as to the date I am to be at Alice Spgs. Kelly will send out a boy with your letter. I don't want to be hanging round Alice Spgs longer than I can possibly avoid. On meeting with you, I will place myself under your orders and we will go where it suits you best, Kelly tells me that Comm'r Peterswald was very anxious that your trip should be a success and that he would wire me when you left Adelaide. My sister, Mrs Symon,[140] is very anxious that I should go down and go to West Aus'a but I feel that I am better off here—in any case I will have to go to Adelaide early in the year and see the Father who the girls tell me is not looking extra well—what I mostly dread is the army of nephews and nieces and cousins far and near that I will see and have to be amiable to. Very many thanks indeed for the 'Narrative', I have only glimpsed at it and will give you my candid criticism on it when I have gone through it properly. From what I saw of it I don't fancy it is exactly a true tale of what occurred, too flattering in parts and lacks luridity to a Norwest reader. The illustrations are beautiful and I think Red Bank Gorge and Glen Helen Gorge two of the best.[141] I think you had better bring a pair of thick india rubber soled tennis shoes with you (not with stitched soles) as you will find them excellent for walking on the Rocks with and in slippery places, the stitched sole ones cut too quickly.

Our gold prospects were healthy at last news but you will have heard later developments from Pado.[142] I don't think there is anything else to write about today so I will close trusting that we will soon meet and have a pleasant trip—Let me know as soon as you can from Alice Spgs as to when I am to be there and with best wishes,

Believe me,
Yours sincerely
C.Ernest.Cowle

3

PEOPLE AND ENVIRONMENT

Letter 3.1

Illamurta
9th Feb 1897

Dear Professor,

Your letter overtook me at Henbury, on the 1st of the month, as I was wearily wending my way home and I much compliment you on your clairvoyance or powers of deduction—you gauged my whereabouts to an offy gaff[1] but you are wrong in supposing that I was cursing the individuals who lured me from this Oasis—honestly, I was only conscious of a dull disappointed feeling at not having been able to do more for you and that there had not been rain, I wanted to tell you this properly before I left C.W. but when I do really feel things I am always chary of expressing them and go in for a careless style which might lead one to think I was callous of all kindly feelings. Hell, was it not hot the day I left you? I got to the Goyder with my meat rotten, in good time, shaved at daylight and on to Crown Point and pitched, scandal chiefly, with Mrs Ross till after midnight when I observed poor Miss Ross about on the snore and returned to our anty [sic] spot. Jane, at the Bend, was pretty quiet and gave me a lot of damaged hen eggs to carry me along, but the hottest day I have felt this year was the 31st.[2] I went a little past Warman's Camp[3] for dinner and pulled up at 11.30 am and tried to make another start at 3.15 but the camels would not face the sand till nearly Sundown. It was simply red hot. I heard many accounts of a wonderful barking Lizard they had for me at Henbury but it turned out to be an ordinary 'Ilchiljira'. At Idracowra I sent out some lubras to look for lizards and they turned up at Sundown with two Jam tins full of <u>scorpions</u> only, many of which got loose, so I camped nearer the buildings that night.

As regards Tempe and George Gill's Range, things are very, very bad, cattle about on the die and I believe they were going to shift them to Glen Helen but on my return home I found letters from Coulthard saying that the Blacks (who never do wrong) were killing wholesale out at Reedy Hole and not even taking the meat, also that they had killed some old blackfellow for giving me some information.[4] I could not quite make out whether there were 70 Blacks at King's Creek or 70 Cattle dead as I could not understand the blacks waiting to be counted. It is the hot weather and drought forcing the Natives in to these waters I fancy. I sent Kean and the boys out at once and would have liked to have gone myself as a lot like that should have some curios but I had to send him as he had not been away for three months. I got a few wommeras as I came home and told Nat and Kean to look out for your rat-tails and chignons etc.[5] You recollect that spear I told you of—well the niggers want me to lend it to them as it belongs to the Parinthi dance and they wish to show it to the blacks and <u>lubras</u> once more[6]—the spear forms the nucleus and is dressed with feathers and a lot of parinthee wooden churina, I think, after the style of your big 'Nurtungu'.[7] The Finke and Mission Blacks want to hold a big Ungoora[8] and are mustering 'down' for it—I fancy that 'Emu' is the object and they intend asking Mr Parke to let them hold it at Henbury.[9] If I were not going down I would let them hold it at Ilpilla and see the lot—they want me to see the Parinthie business so I will probably let them have the spear when I come back. Cranky Jack and Bad Crossing Jack are talking of what they are going to do with Nat by and bye re those sticks and I told all the blacks that I was the delinquent and would cut their combs if they went much further. B.C. Jack's long locks would be valuable for trade purposes. I saw a lubra this time and asked what she had done with her hair which I knew she was keeping for the making of a certain young man called 'Jackawarra' and she told me that it was 'too much long time' so her father sold it to the Crown Point Blacks for a pipe and blanket.[10] At all the big Ungooras they have a lot or group of those ceremonies and dances and go through that smoking process, only from what I hear on the Finke, they give the lubras an extra fumigation. I do not know the terms you have for the various ceremonies and I suppose you know the foregoing but I am just writing it in case you thought that those shows were only held on very rare occasions.[11] That is the impression you gave me when you said that the one at A.G. would probably be the last held. I enquired particularly as to who were the showmen and believe it is the Blacks, or rather old men, who have charge of the bulk of the churina which represent the object in view. Rat Rat and B.C. Jack for the Bat—Nat's father and other old men of the one they talk of now. I will try and see as much as possible of their capers and give you results from personal observation and which I can guarantee—damn hearsay —

Dr Eylmann turned up here the day before yesterday from the Mission Station and has been spending his time about there and from Finke Gorge to Ellery's Creek examining the Country[12]—He is no slouch at gathering information and his present idea is to have a look at Tempe then to Alice Spgs, Paddy's Hole, Northern Territory and then to try and go through Northern Queensland and back to his Native Land—he seems to be going in lightly for everything Fauna, Flora, Geology and anthropology and takes plenty of notes, he says he may publish an account of his observations when he goes home but that will not be for at least a year—he has <u>not</u> been working in any way with Strehlow and in fact Strehlow appears to have been just as rabbitholey with him as with everyone else for he tells me he only spoke with him five or 6 times altogether, he is not making collections as he has not means of forwarding things but has a few little odds and ends, churina etc. I asked if he noticed any differences between the Barrow Creek Natives and the Finke ones and he said that the difference is strongly marked—the Barrow Creek Natives are darker skinned and haired and that they are not nearly so Jewish in type as those about the Mission, where the hair at the tips is in many cases quite light. I believe he took samples of a good many, would you like some of the light specimens. I often wonder whether the water of the Finke has a bleaching effect. By the way, he saw our young Camel about 20 miles above Running Waters on the Finke 8 days ago and I have sent two lubras in to see if it is still there, I could not send the only boy I have left here but if I can hear of it still being there I will go myself. Mr Warburton was disappointed that we did not go round his way—he heard the Three Decker Spencer and the Ironclad Cowle were to be cruising in his vicinity.

I have at last got that well-earned promotion[13] I told you of and can now write 2nd instead of 3rd Class to my name, this carries with it a whole 6d p diem extra so, on receipt of this, I wish you would buy a long sleever[14] of the beverage I recommended for you and French. Porter Gaff (Lemonade and Stout). I hope you told him how hopeless the Season here is entomologically and oologically. I did not see an egg coming back and am wondering if the drought will delay the black Cockatoo this year. I have got bottled, an 'ilchilljera', small snake, Scorp'n, Amphibolorus maculatus, Hinulia Lesueri [sic], Varanus Eremius, Phasco'e Mac's and in a tin I have a Perag'e Lagotis with two young ones about size of Rats.[15] Hope to get something better soon. I found the garden almost a Desert much to my disappointment, nary a melon or tomato and expect none unless we get a good shower—don't forget to send me Pt Anthropology and the Recipe for Lemon Syrup without Lemons as one cannot say what the Federation Convention will say re my leave. Father wants me to go over and look at West Aus'a with him but I am off that. Kindest regards and all good wishes to you and hoping to see you soon and that Bailes climbed no red mulgahs with the team en route to O.D.[16]

Yours very Sincerely
C.Ernest.Cowle

Haven't heard from the Pontiff to date. Won't close this till last minute.

11th Field has just sent me a wire, 'Leave can't be recommended till Statistics are collected.' Don't know what Statistics are meant but I suppose I will get another wire or particulars next mail. We were stunk out by those Peragale last night—they simply filled the tin and gas oozed out to Hell. What is the reason of this or is it just heat manufacturing a deadly gas. Sorry you were not here to enjoy it.

Letter 3.2

Mission
15th March 1897

Dear Professor,

Two days before mail is due at <u>our</u> place and here I am—I was looking forward to a letter from you but must clear tomorrow—two blacks speared Beattie at New Glen Helen on night of 6th[17]—not dangerous luckily, and I am, of course, called on to arrest the articles and you can fancy my chance of success when I know their dart is Mt Jiel or Belt Range[18]—A wise lot of superiors think a man has only to walk out and get these fellows in the Street—I have a warrant, if I get near enough they will go down to Pt Augusta. I have no doubt of getting them in time for the old proverb is true that everything comes to he who waits—thank god no lubras in this affair. Beattie told these blacks to clear as they stole his flour and Sugar and threatened to shoot them—same night he was struck with two spears simultaneously, one just struck the bone 4 inches below his neck and the other went <u>right</u> through his left hand and pinned it to his breast just below the other wound. I suppose this hand and brisket bone saved his life. I have quite a jar full of Hinulia Lesueri, Fasciolata? Amphib's Mac's, Egernia, 3 Ruficaudata, one of which is lined—ocellat and some others like <u>little</u> Jew lizards only tails banded and marks on back bone placed thus (drawing)[19]—one was very gaudy—spots like crushed strawberry and ground colour greenish.

I have also a decaying Aloota, <u>ears small</u>, tail rather bare and distal end whitish, fur coarse—one decaying Con's Conditor and two of another species, smaller and with very long slender tails last 3 inches white, breast also white, came from Erldunda and boys tell me they are the other kind of nest builders but unless I see some myself this time I will swear to nothing, the Kean salted them like I told him and then shut them in an air-tight tin after they had a bit of rain—consequence ripeness and I had not got them aired when I left[20]—Wooden nosebones galore—Tempe Rain $3\frac{1}{2}$ inches at Station very patchy elsewhere—Illamurta $\frac{1}{4}$ inch drizzle, 18th Feb, $\frac{1}{4}$ in on 23rd and not quite $\frac{1}{2}$ inch drizzle on 26th. Ellery's Creek ran slightly to below Running Waters—Finke quiescent—I am writing this while waiting for the horses and would like you to tell Mr French why I am not writing to him—Have not heard from Pontiff since I saw you—I had to go after that camel calf myself and got him at Boggy Hole[21]—mutually glad to see one another—Have got G's wommera's [sic] and yours—Down unprocurable at present, Pelicans carry very little anyhow at present as I shot two but the inside of their pouch or fernambag is infested with a species of (drawing) tick.[22] Expect me when you see me and, with best wishes,

Believe me,
Your affect'e friend
Ernest Cowle

Mission people very kind and a healthier tone as regards Natives prevails at present. I spent a mauvais quart d'heure with the razor I <u>bought</u> from you before arriving last night.[23]

   A real puff in the Bulletin of 9th of Jan—complimented F.J.G. on it and asked him to send me his photos as I wished to write a few articles for Leader while I was down South—Suppose he'll snort <u>in reply</u>.[24]

Letter 3.3

Crown Point
5th Aug 1897

My dear Professor,

Only about two lines to tell you I am on my way back at last and to apologize for not writing before but I have stedfastly [sic] set my mind against all business of that kind in the City so I know you will excuse me. They humbugged me terribly all the last part of my time down South owing to the witnesses clearing from Pt Aug but we got them close to Parachilna and back in time and the result was 10 years hard. The Judge made many complimentary remarks and ordered the Sheriff to award me £10 thereby making me feel dashed un-comfortable but it will please the father.[25] I feel certain it is Gillen I have to thank for calling the attention of the authorities to my brilliancy for I had an official rem's sent to me for perusal after going from Min'r of Education to Chief Sec'y etc etc. and it stated 'I have been privately informed'. I turned loose all the time I could in between times so have left the City Vultures battening on my feathers and have left undone all that I should have done but never mind—for a time at least I was in <u>Melbourne</u> perpetually haunted by a tribe of admiring Cousins (Melbourne item from Hammerdene[26] to C.W.) Poor old Winnecke looked haggard and worried and would be all the better for a change outside somewhere. I did not see Keartland as I left the day before Calvert peoples funeral.[27] Pado is looking very well and we mutually agreed that Adelaide was a hole and Victoria the only place to go to—I stayed with him two days and got here last night—camels not very gay as they have been indulging their cannibalistic tastes on one another and in consequence are mighty lame I am taking up your M.S.S. and another registered parcel for Gillen who is sending a boy to meet me at the Bend—By the way I hear Sargeant and Jane have fallen out again, she has a black eye and is now camped on the opposite side of the Creek awaiting my arrival to put everything straight and I am now scheming to find out how I am going to sneak past[28]—I think I will tell her Mrs Ross would like her to spend a month or two with her but it won't do to tell this to Mrs C. Point who wishes to be very kindly remembered to you—and here is the mail—With all to good wishes [sic] to Mrs Spencer and yourself.

Believe me
Yours very Sincerely
C.E.Cowle

Did you get names of the long tailed white tipped rats yet?

Letter 3.4

Illamurta
20th Oct 1897

Dear Professor,

Your letter safely to hand and I regret that I still have to report dolefully on the state of the Country as far as rain is concerned. I have been up Glen Helen way for a fortnight and that is about the only portion of our district where feed is plentiful although water is getting scarce. I spoilt about 2 dozen plates through over exposure and did not discover till I got back and received your letter and some prints from Dr Grant that my plates were Ilford 'Empress' (rapid) and not 'Ordinarys' like the few I got in Melbourne, so you can guess the mess I made with exposures of two or three seconds in good lights. I ran across the Blackfellow 'Boomerang' with the abnormal shins and got a pretty fair plate but made a fearful muddle when I tried to get his shins only, I swung back the lens a bit and did not tilt the ground glass to correspond and the result was that besides being almost black I got his feet longer than his shins.[29] Many of the plates seemed to be chafed also, although I put them in pairs and <u>back</u> to <u>back</u> wrapping in black paper—should I have put the gelatine sides together?

Since then I have learned the secret of the rising and falling front to cut off or extend foreground and enclose a print or two of the lubras here to show you the latest efforts exposed, as you suggested, with shutter set for time and released as quick as can be—also 'shins'—which I have offered Gillen the Plate of if he wants it for the M. Opus. By the way he wrote to tell me he was likely to come out this way soon and, of course, relies on the use of my Camera but although that is six weeks ago I have heard nothing further and will probably miss him, Martin has just sold 400 Store Cattle to Kidman and they have gone to Ellery's Creek Gorge till the road is open, he also sold 180 to Wallis and Harding so that we have had lots of passers by and callers. Did you leave any Spirits of Wine at Sandford's Blood's Creek for vermin? I heard the fate of some there from a man a few days ago and made a notes [sic] of his words. I was putting an 'Ilchillyera' in spirits and he remarked—'Holy b-y 'Christ' is that snake juice? Bob Stuart says the b-y snakejuice that b-r left at Sandford's makes the best hot grog he ever tasted'—It must have come off something full flavoured.[30]

Glad to hear your investment in the milking line as unqualified a success as your garden.[31] I would not suggest the Export trade as I fancy there is too much swindling in the old Country. You have plenty of room and why not try a neat Kiosk facing Alma Road and a good sign-board of yourself analysing the fluid and devitalizing the bacteria on the vegetables—ought to go like anything and the returns would be quicker. As you worked up a trade, you might add 'Summer Drinks' Lemon Syrup without lemons etc. which I like very much. The Illamurta Show as you call it is rather like a bad Plum Duff at present.

Expect to be too busy to eat my Xmas Spread anywhere except here or on the wallaby somewhere,[32] things got a start on me last time and I have never caught them up again.

I don't think the yellowish rat you refer to came up about these parts—is it the fawn one that was so plentiful C.W. way? but I will examine throats of any—just now an attenuated lizard is all the ground life to be seen—The lubras had a Moloch in a box and I noticed it laid four eggs one day.[33]

I don't think there is any chance of my going to Alice Spgs in place of Kelly and in fact I would not care for it but, oh my God, how sick I am of this fellow here[34]—Gillen writes gloating over Kingston's reception on his return and still regards him as an Angelic being, only to be looked at and spoken of with deepest reverence.[35]

My sister tells me she called on Mrs Spencer but she was not at Home and that she will send my photo shortly. Please thank Mrs Spencer for her kind wishes and tell her that I am afraid civilization has seen the last of me—that beastly cold I had won't go away and causes a slight pain in my chest which I have written to Gillen about.

Frith is to be married to the much talked of Miss Bell of the Oodnadatta Pub about 17th Nov'r. Don't forget to give me your ideas of latest attempt with the Camera—toning etc—I got a lot of prints spoiled with rust in a tub the other night—Is there any means of keeping rust off a big tub for one night only? You will observe a flare spot on one print caused by a crack in dark slide which I have repaired.

Kindest regards to self and Mrs Spencer.
Yours very Sincerely
C.Ernest.Cowle

I am also sending you a serrated piece of flint picked up by Coulthard at the back of the Red Banks on Glen Helen—He says the Blacks don't know it and say they never made it—my opinion is that it is either a spear head or neck ornament from farther North or West[36]—What do you think and what tools would it be trimmed with?

Letter 3.5

Illamurta
8th Jan 1898

Dear Professor,

It is just a year today since we left the Alice together and, much as I would like you up here again, I reckon you are damned lucky to be out of the Country, or at least the Western portion of it, this year. I fancy all the ground vermin must be dead, one never sees the track of any species of rat and even snakes are missing. The higher mammals such as Sheep, Cattle and horses are rapidly following suit. I hear eleven horses are dead out of the Missionary teams at Horse Shoe Bend—things are serious here, at the Mission, Henbury and at Tempe although Martin wrote that he had a third of an inch in December.

I had a long trip about and on top of the Gill Range in November, and secured you a few nose bones and hair girdles, the blacks had very little except these and stone adzes which I could not carry, the ubiquitous butcher knife was there but no stone ones and I feel convinced that it is almost a thing of the past for many miles West and at least as far South as Ayers Rock.[37] As soon as I got back I set sail for Alice Spgs but, as I had to go on to Paddy's Hole, I had but little time with the Gillen, not even time to quarrel as he devoted most of the conversation we did have [to] a dissertation on Kingston's many good qualities. He (the Pontiff) looked very well but complained as usual of overwork—I interrogated him as to the duplex system and he told me he had it all at his fingers' ends but was not so confident when I asked him why Todd sent up Griffiths and Johns while he and Kiernan were already on the Ground.[38]

I told you I had a job getting back and, after the mail left, I took a walking tour through from here to the Mission via Palm Creek to start the Blacks back to their own haunts, I should say it was not more than about 32 miles, but I found the Bed of the Finke pretty heavy from Palm Creek up, carrying a waterbag and some tucker in my fly round my shoulders.[39]

I quite agree with your remarks as to his *G's* knowledge of blacks and I think he would make a most excellent Protector down below[40]— He, and the Missionaries, I do not regard as a blessing to either Native or Caucasian Population in the Country and I leave it to your own unbiased judgement to say whether the aged and infirm have really done any better from the presence of either party. I had a lively interview at the Mission when I got there but Bogner and I are first rate friends again and trouble, I think, comes from Strehlow. I objected strongly to being held out as a threat to the uncivilized blacks while the Christian ones were being allowed to do as they liked—you should see the state of affairs there and without being prejudiced, honestly they only hear of the things that are done by the Natives who do not happen to be persona grata with the scholars—the others they rig out and shield in every way and, when anything does occur, they pretend not to know who has done it—fancy psalm singing all day and then dancing all night with the others in the Creek.[41]

I have not heard from Byrne for some time and cannot understand why he does not write to French or you, by the way, can you instil into the mind of this respected gentleman that Pado and I live only a trifle over 200 miles apart and that it is much easier to communicate with him from Adelaide generally than from here—writing for a Bower bird he says 'if you can't get time to skin, send one down in Spirits, I think Byrne has plenty' as if Pado and I played in each other's yards daily.[42]

12th Jan Today I packed up four poor skins for Mr French and hope he will get one good one out of them and the Bird of Paradise into his possession and in the same box I am sending two large 'Tiliqua' for you, gutted and dressed with arsenical soap they appear to have dried well and should be stuffable without losing colour. I wish you would let me know how they get down, the large one was a male and the lesser a female. Kean had wasted the spirits when I got back but I expect two gallons by Marsh next month[43]—he is bringing Rations for Tempe. I can't say when I will get another chance at Boomerang who runs about the Darwent and Belt Range but when I do, rest assured that I will get him in two or three positions. I fancied that his legs would astonish you, there is nothing wrong with the Print and I often told you of his legs before when you expressed a desire to have his shin bones—hunt the Missionaries and Protector and perhaps you will and perhaps G. might get you an order from Kingston for his Skeleton in toto. Gillen was pleased to say that I focused alright after trying me with his camera but we had no time for lessons in anything else. I sent him the plates of Boomerang and some others that he asked for so that he could print and tone some himself, haven't heard or seen results. I had to lay my Camera up, could not spare horseflesh to carry it this last trip or two and did not care to risk having to leave it and the packbags hung up indefinitely in a mulgah while we walked home—must try and take it next time though— Dr Grant sends me a lot of prints that he takes, with details on the back, but, of course, he scarcely understands the sort of place we live in, postal disabilities etc and that we have not a druggists within 5 or 600 miles to get 'Rodinal' hydrochinone etc from. I have an exposure meter and have also made a note of your hints.

Had a very quiet Xmas this year but not so bad if the horse feed worry was away—the boys got a lot of ducks from the Finke and I really spread myself in the manufacture of the pudding. I do not think there was another mob of natives in the North so well satisfied with themselves and their lot for the time being as ours. Mrs G.'s pudding to come and one from my sister sampled today—The Post mistress at Mt Lofty told the sister she could send up to 11 lbs, result C.E.C. Dr to E.H.S.

Parcel paid Wells 3/- Bend Sargeant 3/- = 6/-. Wells has rose price to 6d p lb. Honest Ted has done the same. Happy New Year.

Yrs truly
E Sargeant

This is from Charlotte Waters.[44]

Kean is just back from Erldunda and tells me Parke is going to put 500 Cattle at Ilpilla (you know a mile from here) and this means that I will have to take our horses somewhere if it holds out—Coolata Sp on Erldunda or Glen Helen are only places I can think of at present but I might get a Soakage down at Roger's Pass.[45]

Glad your garden is still flourishing, ours is a shadow of itself and everything stunted—tomatoes spotted and melons burst when half ripe—fancy us being glad to buy as the passing Afghan to sell—Potatoes @ 3 p lb and Onions @ 6d—low rates owing to so many going bad on the Vendor but it will give you an idea of what the vaunted Oasis has come to.

This will reach you in the midst of the Federation Fuss and I believe the clan will be very strongly represented in your City about even Felix and his wife are coming over from West Aus'a.[46] I hope Mrs Spencer and the children had a really nice time at Sorrento and that the publication of the Book of the Century will enable both you and Gillen to devote a *little time to your wives.*[47] *Mrs G. looked haggard and tired. Please thank Mrs Spencer for her kind enquiries after me. I am right as ever and the spell here for the last three weeks has completely set me up. Most sincerely wishing that you all will have many pleasant, prosperous New Years and at least seven of Plenty with the phenomenal Cow.*

Believe me,
Yours very affectionately
Ernest.Cowle

Letter 3.6

Illamurta
25th Feb 1898

Dear Professor,

Mail here last night nine days late and leaves tomorrow, so only a line to thank you for the 'Beetle' and Paper—Heat here January damnable 110 to 121 = good rains all round the Stations but nothing here beyond drizzles, we had about an inch in ten days falling so slowly that it never ran six feet away from the iron roof and nothing sprang up but flies, flies, flies. Camels in a very bad state and I fancy some will lose eyes altogether. Beautiful feed at Running Waters, Finke ran from top end past Henbury and further down in patches. Blacks still bad at Tempe among Cattle—(there is something lovable about them is there not?) following Cattle wherever they are taken—latest stand was at the Ilarra, just over the big hole—'Arrabi' is one of the worst. Camera did not look well when unwrapped and I fancy the weather has affected plates—air ball bung etc—I enclose Racehorse F.16 Exposure as p your instructions, also Kean on old 'Ahzul'—Am sending for Acetate of Lead and Glauber's Salts to make combined toning and fixing bath as this 'Austral' Sun Paper would not tone with the borax and chloride of gold and faded out almost completely in the hypo, the detail in Keans is good. Please tell French I am not writing this mail. Racehorse and Jado egg hunting on the Finke—did you get the two 'Tiliqua Occip' I sent you care of French. Exposure for Kean F.16 and as directed. I hope Mrs Spencer and the little ones had a good time at the Seaside. Good wishes to you all.

Yours very Sincerely
C.E.Cowle

Letter 3.7

Illamurta
17th Apl 1898

Dear Professor,

Very glad indeed to get your letter, we were not allowed an extra fortnight like the Alice Spgs people and it was about eight weeks since we had heard anything from the South. Pado, I can no more make out than yourself, I get a line about one mail in three, I fancy he is terrifically tired of the euphoniously christened 'Stinkpot' Kiernan, whose nose old Jilly pulled scientifically some time back. Ross gone South for a spell and will probably return with a wife and governess.

You must be delighted with the finish of the 'Black Work' you have been engaged on but I think you should have seen the Black as a real wild beast as well as in the shape of a Corroboree Monger and knowing your common sense, I feel convinced you would have thought there was also something 'hatable' about the Aus'n Native as well as loveable—you often used to tell me that I only saw the worst side of the blacks, perhaps I do, but in your brief experience of them did you ever come across a sign of genuine gratitude or feel convinced that any goodness of yours to them could not be wiped out in a second by a word or two from another black—also in your researches into their distant origin, did you ever come across anything represent'g our 'thank you'. I speak sourly just now. Last January we found some killing wholesale and one got 'hurt' seriously in the leg[48]—Well, I thought this would be a lesson to the others so did not proceed against the one we had caught, and who had already been in gaol, but gave him and the lubras flour, tea and Sugar. Well, when I was out there last week I saw these at the Station alright but, happening to go over the Undia [sic—Undiara?] Country twice, I found that when they thought I would not return, they had skipped over there and were as busy as ever with the Cattle—Unfortunately I lost their tracks in rain but came on another mob who killed three and one was damaged. You also say—You wonder they do not kill more—'Damnation' what more can they want when each mob kills enough to gorge on each day and, if the beast is not fat enough, leaves it untouched and kills another—this was alright, and there may have been some excuse on account of the drought, but what can their supporters put forward now when Tempe has had over 8 inches of rain—and feed everywhere, and all kinds of bush tucker plentiful— No, Professor, I do not like severe measures myself, unless driven to it, but I reckon these blacks want one real drastic lesson in the same way that Strikes etc should be treated, and taught that, if they have the protection of our laws, they also <u>must</u> conform to the others.

Our share of the rain was about 5 inches and fell too steadily to leave much water in Creeks but the feed is lovely and vermin in the shape of caterpillars and flies a regular plague, I got an awful soaking out on Laurie's Creek for 2 days and another along the Levi Range some days later. Water fairly ran out of the tops of our boots and, as everything in our swags was soaked, we had to build a fire and dry ourselves as we could, even my diary and record of Natives, in the middle of my blankets was wet, me furious of course at the tracks getting washed out when we were so close on them, when we might have kept dry in a cave. I have not seen any rats yet but I think they should show up and I should not be surprised if 'Spathopterus Alexandrae' returned. Most of the small birds are plentiful but I have not seen a quail yet.[49]

Did you not see 'Albani'? It seemed quite strange to get your letter and needless to say refreshing to get one which did not run to a paragraph or two on her merits or demerits. I have tried to please the hearts of the egg people this time but there are a lot under my bed going stink rapidly, when one has only a few hours to do a big mail in, eggs are certainly de trôp. I never heard from Verb Sap[50] if he could do anything with the Bower birds I sent or if you got the Tiliqua and nosebones. Haven't seen the Pontiff but expect to before long. I reckoned to get some blacks this bush trip and go in but failed as I told you—I must go out to Tempe again at once. Martin will probably shift all the Tempe Cattle to Glen Helen to try and give them a show but I am afraid a few others will follow them and make things hot—Just now Martin is up there trying to send a mob of stores to Town, fair feed there all the Season. Parke's people in difficulties and I think Joe Breaden[51] is up in the Bank's interests. Mission Station keeping its even tenor of muddle, one or two yarns but I can't relate them at present. Garden starting to look very promising—hope yours is the [sic—missing word, same?]. You should take a spell, old man, or you will be ill. Kindest regards to Mrs Spencer and yourself.

Yours very Sincerely
C.E.Cowle

Letter 3.8

Illamurta
24th June 1898

Dear Professor,

I do hope and trust that the almighty Pontiff found time to put my message in one of his letters to you, otherwise you must be thinking me most ungrateful for not answering yours. Well, to go back to the start—shortly after sending you my last hurried line, I wended my way to Tempe and in a very few hours cut tracks of some poor creatures after cattle, followed these for four days to point of Mt Levi Range when, as we were only about six hours behind them judging by their fires, I took to them on foot but soon discovered that they had just taken a scoot round and come back to where they had started from to get a good view of the Country and see if they were still being pursued and of course saw our footmarks and bolted, after a few days fruitless fooling, trying to track them on those hard Peterman flats, I struck for the Ilarra and Wild Eagle Plain which was the only other place where there were Cattle and, of <u>course</u>, soon had their tracks again, I sent the horses to Tempe and early next morning sniped this lot (3) on the top of Mt Shady—took them to Tempe and left them and returned to Wild Eagle and Horse Plains as we had seen tracks of another mob after Cattle. Next morning early we saw where they had been after Cattle which, unfortunately for us on that occasion got away after being speared and, as I learnt later, they were on one of the high points that morning and saw us tracking them when they went to see where more Cattle were. I again abandoned the horses (you can imagine what a handicap they are in those narrow plains where the points of the Ranges command such an extent of country) and followed them for two days in the centre of the Range between the two plains then across Wild Eagle to Nth side and along it East. I reckon they must have been getting pretty hollow by that time for they shot out on plain and ran a beast up a very rough Creek and killed it and I made pretty sure of them for, at next Camp, I found they had only gone an hour or two and felt confident that, loaded with beef inside and out, they would not go far but, as usual, while trying to keep their tracks down the side of a range we were seen and when we rushed the Camp only found the meat, and after a long chase in the hills we only managed to get one out of the four near Bosun's Hole Plain—this left us with over 25 miles to walk back to Tempe and I can assure you that on these cold nights there is not much pleasure in camping blackfellow fashion without blankets and just a little fire on each side. I find that the fire either toasts you or that you wake up with unfailing regularity each hour when it dies out and sometimes you cannot even light the fire for fear of being seen.

You say, I always see the worst side of the blacks and I hardly think you judge fairly—these four were Station blacks and all well treated and generally getting odd jobs about the place with no excuse at all to go out to Wild Eagle, and only did so because Martin and Coulthard were at Glen Helen and they did not expect me to be out again so soon, and relied on their tracks being obliterated before anyone saw them. The force of example of the 'whites killing' does not apply at Tempe because, thank God, so far that place has been immune in that respect from the absence of travellers.

I took the niggers to Alice Spgs, where they were sentenced to six months and sent Kean down with them, did not see much of Gillen as I was only there forty eight hours and raced home here and on down the road to attend at Horse Shoe Bend as Dep'y Ret'g Officer over the Federal business[52]—had to wait there two days and as the place had been recently ennobled with a licence to sell Wine and Spirits etc, things were very mixed, then on to C.W. and back home via Erldunda. Mrs Sargeant has gone to Town and has a deed of separation with her husband, he to allow her 15/- p week as long as she remains <u>chaste</u> and, unless people have a very depraved taste in Cities, I should say he would have to pay alimony for many years. Pado was bright and cheerful, more so than I have seen him for a long time. I said, 'Spencer is wondering 'what's up' and tells me you have 'not written for ages', to which he replied, 'Well, to tell you the truth, old man, there is absolutely nothing to write about and, although he very kindly writes to me, I reckon I would only bore him.' I don't know whether this was the whole truth but at any rate he seldom writes to us up here now and perhaps in your case is a bit ashamed to after his neglect. I hoped to see the Ross' who were due from Town but they were all detained with influenza at Oodnadatta.

Many thanks for the Pamphlet on Initiation Ceremonies which was very interesting,[53] especially as regards the <u>Tualcha-mura</u> or Potential Mother in law.[54] Was not that an embellishment of those uncontaminated old vermin beds, 'Rat-Rat', 'Cranky' and Bad Crossing Jack's, to prolong the flour producing epoch? At all events the present system is very much more rapid, certain and beneficial to the young man and one of the things he has to thank the white man for but I suppose you and your collaborateur would avoid that description as it is too near actual facts and hardly romantic enough—Putting all nonsense aside though, old man, I think the amount of work you have done is simply stupendous and, to the interested people, will be of most absorbing interest and value. (Don't see that it will actually benefit the Aruntas much though) and I hope it is properly and beneficially recognized but don't, for goodness sake, tell Gillen I have said so, you have fairly spoilt that man and he goes about with his brisket out and a comb on him like a Langshan Rooster and, unless he gets a P.C. ship [sic] at least, will be disappointed—I told him I could guarantee him one subscriber and he snappishly said, 'We don't want subscribers all we want is <u>Kudos</u>' (did you teach him this latter word?, his silence when I asked him appeared to me as if it were so). We only had time for a skirmish or two, chiefly on the conduct of aboriginal warfare, he is inclined to be most philanthropic at the Govt and other people's expense but his own pocket is another affair—he amused me when I said he never spent anything on them—he got most indignant and said, 'Why, don't you know, it has cost me <u>over £100 for Photographing Material in the last few years.</u>'—He was very much taken with my Camera and offered me his and a horse, he wanted £7.10 for an exchange but we did not deal although the Native question at present keeps mine idle.

I read your critique on Roth's work[55] and also that of the 'Bulletin' of 25th Dec 1897 (in case you missed it). I thought the idea of Circumcision being a kind of <u>mimicry</u>, pretty absurd—and the regulation of Classes by <u>Food</u>—Very very German 'The God of the Belly'. Before I forget, I want to ask you a question—There is a rumour current that a lubra at the Mission gave birth to two abortions with <u>tails</u> (dead), presumably this is the result of allowing the dog to have intercourse with her and is supposed to be frequently done by old women—what I want to know is, whether, granting such intercourse has taken place, could the woman conceive?[56]

I expect, by the time you get this far, you will reckon that Pado was right but I can't help it, I feel in good spirits thanks to Kean telling me he would not return if possible and on account of the glorious Season.[57] Besides the good rains I told you of before, we have had light showers every month and when I came home the other day the garden was a picture and Cauliflowers etc bursting all round. Tempe people shifting more Cattle to Glen Helen and many of the Gill blacks have in consequence gone over to Mareena, so I suppose they will give us trouble there now instead of visiting their more outlying properties to the South. I expect you heard the Parke's were in the Bank's hands for a bit and that the working man is now a little less independent on £1 and 25/- p week in lieu of 30/- and 35/-. I think Parkes affairs will straighten shortly. I expect you have fathomed our mail arrangements by this time and learnt that it takes us two months now to get a reply instead of six weeks and that it is supposed to be an advantage for us—Wells appears able to do just as he likes with Todd and everyone else seems to conspire to allow him to make £300 or so a year by running a mail with less than half the horses he really should have[58]— Of course you saw that yourself—War news etc is antique when we get it and when, like myself, we miss a mail or two and papers, we get fearfully behind times. (I have been reading Feb and March papers since I got back to try and get a grip of things.) French says you, he and someone else are just off for a holiday which I hope was an enjoyable one, and that he attended to the provender satisfactorily. I am asking him what you people consider an outfit on these occasions—glad his last eggs arrived safely for the first time and hope to send him a few black Cockatoos this mail. I am enclosing <u>two</u> in Keartland's lot for your friend Dr Ryan and telling K to hand them to you.[59] Please remember me very kindly to Mrs Spencer and trusting you are all well and safely over the Measles.

Believe me,
Yours Sincerely
C.E.C

Letter 3.9

Illamurta
7th Aug 1898

My dear Professor,

You are a true Briton to write when you had no letter from me and when you were in trouble over Mrs Spencer's illness which I am heartily glad you tell me is over. I understood from your last that it was something very mild, you told me it was about half a measle but it must have grown much worse. I think I wrote you nearly everything that was going in my last, and would not have attempted anything this mail had I not wished to call your attention to the idiotic things papers will publish on Ethnology and am referring to an article by W.H. Hardy in Observer of 23rd July—this man is blacksmith or something at the Arltunga Cyanide Plant and you will see the depth he has gone if you trouble to look at the article[60]—I suppose he poses as an authority now and this is the sort of damned rubbish that people read and believe—he can scarcely be ignorant that you and Gillen have really gone into the subject and are publishing a book on it, for Gillen was out there in the beginning of the year and no doubt blasted on his trumpet or he is not the man you and I know. If this Hardy is the man I think he is, I fancy he got most of his information from the young lubras which he mentions several times.

I saw Dr Eylmann again at the Mission last month and he really is a close and inquisitive observer—talking over blacks adding hair to their own to lengthen it, he told me that he had really seen them doing it somewhere above Tennant's Creek although he was convinced that it did not take place down here and also that the stuff used as cement was beeswax of a kind—he intends visiting Arltunga and then riding down the road to about Hergott, selling his horses and getting back to Germany[61]—he, of course, cannot take specimens home but he draws capitally and has a great number of sketches—those of various birds heads and feathers being excellent and very recognizable even uncoloured. I was sorry I could not see a little more of him but I had to go on a wild goose chase round Glen Helen searching for Arabi and three others who were supposed to be about Mareena Bluff, but whose tracks I did not find till I had run down the Walker to within a dozen miles of Tempe, and found where they ate a calf. I left the horses at Tempe, and put in four days on foot on those hills, bounding Horse and Wild Eagle Plains, and saw six of their camps step by step. Returned to Tempe for horses and more food and followed them on to another bullock, in and out of hills and finally left them going towards Mission, in those Hills dividing Wild Eagle Plain and Mission Plain. I must get this lot by hook or crook and am off again in three or four days but anticipated trouble for, besides Arabi, there is another ex Barrow Creek tracker and the others are semi-civilized. All the others against whom I have warrants are temporarily scared back and if I could snap this lot might remain in back country and in that case, with the exception of two or three who really do know better, I would get the warrants withdrawn. I do wish they would steady off again and that you were coming up this year. I feel certain this tribe has some divisions because of the rows lately over one or two having wrong lubras and I cannot get time to sit down amongst them and really worry at it.

There is a new man here in place of Kean but I can tell you but little of him so far, he is not impressive although full of ideas and suggestions which he is not slow at airing and I will probably be able to dilate on him in my next—According to his own account he has been a terribly wild young man in his time and tremenjiously [sic] successful with fair women etc. I would like you to meet this type if they only would not be subdued by your presence.[62]

The Ross' got up to Crown Point after a rough time at Oodnadatta, influenza etc, and I hear now that Mrs Ross is very bad with rheumatism. Martin shifting nearly all their stock to Glen Helen—strange to say, in spite of many rains, there has been no water near the Station for more than twelve months. At Ooreyechikna Spgs in Mareena where I got water last year in the drought, I could not fill waterbags, another lot of Spgs at the head of the Walker were quite dry although usually at this time of the year they run freely and make a big waterhole but, as regards this part of the Country, I should say from appearances that there had been none of the rains there this year and for quite two years previous.

I was pleased the publishers gave you all the pictures you asked for and hope the next three months will pass rapidly and land you in the long vacation and a well deserved rest. I am not writing to French this time as there is nothing in his line to chronicle—hawk eggs should be about but my huntsman is not extra spry at present owing to an old spear wound in the thigh breaking out all round. Kindest regards and good wishes to you and yours.

Yours very sincerely
C.Ernest Cowle

Glad Pado wrote again, he missed me this time.

Letter 3.10

Illamurta
1st Sep 1898

Dear Professor,

Very glad to get your letter a couple of days ago, just after my return from a long spin round Tempe Downs. I had the new man with me and went zigzagging about without any luck for about ten days and, as a last hope of seeing blacks, I went to Laurie's Creek, West of your beloved Gill Range and got seven, four of which are now outside and I intend taking them in to Alice Springs on Monday for trial but I am afraid we may be delayed there for the noble dispenser of Justice is, I believe, down the road with his wife. This gang, I was rather pleased to find, did not attempt to clear out beyond a temporary aberration on the part of three of the younger members, although they had a most excellent chance of getting away because they saw us some distance off—I scarcely felt happy and comfortable the night we got them because I had a feeling that they had, to an extent, been deceived but I hope I made matters clear generally that I had not broken my word. You see last Xmas we had one of this gang and cautioned him pretty <u>severely</u>, then I took him away with us on a walking expedition and I think he felt certain he was going to be shot but instead of that I gave him some flour and tobacco and sent him to his Country and told him to tell his friends that if they ran away when we appeared they would be shot and that they were to stop, after we growled at them they would be our mates till they went wrong again and get tucker and tobacco whenever we saw them—twice members of this party got away since this occurred but 'Wurnwinta' was not with them, on this occasion he was and I believe kept them steady, I made the boys explain that, if they had stopped on the previous occasions I would have given them a hiding and finished growling but that now that we had been forced to take out <u>Warrants</u> or 'Papers telling all about Policemen to shoot them'.[63] I would have to take them to Mr Gillen and probably gaol—presented 'Wurnwinta' with a blanket, Shirt and tucker. After seeing Martin at Tempe Downs, I decided to let three more go as an experiment, one was an old man and the other two young men of that impressionable age when 6 mo's [months] in Pt Augusta would finish their education as thorough scoundrels, they were not on the warrants although we had two cases against them and went away with some flour and unscathed with various messages and instructions as to how to act on our appearance in future, I am not over confident of success but I would like to get these blacks into the present condition of those at Glen Helen Station. The four we have here, Peetalla, 'Purnka', 'Chuperoo' and 'Toolinya' have had a long innings since 1896 but have kept out of the road since the drought broke up and I cannot feel so bitter towards them as I do to the more civilized ones such as Arabi and Coy, who are still in the ranges between here and Shag Hole. Racehorse was here a day or two ago with some emu eggs as a midwinter offering.

It is getting pretty difficult to locate the blacks on Tempe now for the reason that nearly all the Cattle have been shifted to Glen Helen and so few remain that the wily aboriginal finds it pays better to stick to legitimate game on the Ranges. I have been a bit prolix on this subject I fear but you have some idea of the surrounding circumstances and I think you are scarcely always fair to me, I mean, I think you believe I am harsh when in reality nothing would please me better than to be able to go about and them come up to me at once instead of clearing and they would do this were they not perfectly aware that I know what they have been doing the few days previously. I do not care for the new man at all as a mate and your idea is most erroneous that I desire to live alone for I would always employ a cook—I can't always be with another man patrolling and one slip or mistake on his part might undo the fruits of a good deal of my endeavours to instil confidence in fair play amongst these Natives whom so few people understand or get a grip over.

Sorry to hear of French's smash again, one has to be careful about enquiries, you know P.M.B. is a trifle 'difficile' and if he gets worried with enquiries from the authorities, may get snaky and you also know how, by his courtesy, many little parcels over the statute weight of one pound reach C.W. and here.[64] I was very much amused at French's list of articles for that trip, notably Insectibane[65] and Fire Kindlers, I presume each member carried his own soap.

Glad to hear of the progress of the Book and know it will be as accurate as possible for such a work, especially as you have had the editing and correcting part of it to do, I have considerably more confidence in you in this direction than in the Pontiff and when you are away from his magnetic influence more dispassionate and the term Gillenized remains in abeyance for the present. I only hope the old fellow will be back when I get into Alice Spgs so that we can have a day's talk for once in a way, I would not be in such a desperate hurry to get back this time.

Your exemplary conduct for the last two years certainly deserves a fitting recognition from Mrs Spencer and I trust that even if you do not manage to get as far as this you may be able to accomplish that Lake Eyre trip. The locality is doubtful to me but I fancy the Blacks stretching over towards the Cooper are much more intelligent than C.A. specimens but to get them undiluted you would want to get well back from the Stations. I saw most of the Gladstoniana in Martin's Illustrated Papers and thought it bad taste, I mean the different pictures of the Widow etc. in a privacy but I suppose in historical events like this the public's craving for detail must be satisfied.[66]

Pretty busy just now getting ready to start for Alice Spgs so you must excuse me, I was very pleased to get your assurance that Mrs Spencer was well again.

With the best wishes to you all,
Believe me
Yours very sincerely
C.Ernest.Cowle

Letter 3.11

Illamurta
18th March 1899

My dear Professor,

I am delighted to hear from you again and that you are back safely from the old Country.[67] I intended writing a line of welcome to you last time but unexpectedly received word from the Missionaries that my friends had come in there after the gins I left and that they had managed to secure three, so that I had to bustle round and start in earlier than I expected. 'Arabi' once more escaped, although the Mission boys had hold of him. On arrival at Alice Spgs we had to wait about a week for a second Justice and, when they were convicted, I sent Barlow on down with them, a nice batch of six, making sixteen in less than twelve months which surely should convince people that this playing with Blacks is all rot, you have a fair idea (when away from Gillen) of what it is like to have to capture them and I would never despair of moderating your views a little but a man who will get up on a Public Platform and calmly state that a blackfellow <u>occasionally</u> kills a beast because he is 'hungry', and that he doesn't appreciate the offence because the whites kill his euros and kangaroos, is beyond all hope and either criminally ignorant of the real state of affairs or wilfully perverting for some purpose or another. (I don't think I have written to you since I saw him on his return from Town have I?)

This last gang have been busy all last year and especially so since November and knew apparently that we could not go out on account of the boys being laid up with measles, and had killed three beasts and a calf in three days at Gilbert Spgs and then gone back into the

Hills towards Shag Hole to manufacture a new lot of spears and it was while thus occupied that we came on them, I know the wood they use for the body now because there was practically a plantation for miles at this particular spot, very crooked and tough it is but generally of the same size throughout, I destroyed 27 new spears besides several unfinished ones which was not a bad outfit for only six blacks and one young fellow, was it? I fancy they have no totem connected with cattle and no restrictions and that it doesn't matter a damn whether their fathers or mothers or great uncles kill the beast, it is common property and bulky, hence their desire for it.

Gillen was more retiring and modest than I expected, after his Command Interview at Govt. House and his successful debut as a lecturer but had altered his views on the Great Work a little, spoke of pecuniary profits now and I succeeded in getting him properly riled several times.[68] Please accept my most sincere thanks for the book which has just come to hand, late mail as usual will prevent my reading it yet but I will review it in my next. I do not think the illustrations are as well got up and finished as I expected, what do you think of them. I must write and congratulate Gillen on 'Grimm's Fairy Tales' up to date by S. and G. He takes anything about the book so seriously—Anyone who has said anything in its favour is 'One of the Leading Scientists of the World, old man', all others—Carmine Idiots.

Of course you heard of Beattie's fate, about half a mile from the H.E.E. Camp where I left you on Red Banks Creek, a cold blooded murder by one of the semi-civilized natives.[69] I was very sorry to miss Gillen at the Alice this time and am afraid I won't see him now before he goes down, if ever again, once we get so widely separated. The Alice itself was just awful, especially the Police Camp, and no doubt one does miss Kelly and his wife there; no matter what people may have said about <u>her</u>, she was always kind and hospitable, even to extremes. But oh, the difference now, untidiness and un couthness brought to a fine art doesn't half describe it, the woman is generally <u>barefooted</u> and talks vulgarly and incessantly, squints, shrews and oh hang it that's enough, I don't suppose you are likely to be there after Gillen leaves unless you come up to work out this Looritcha mob.[70]

A man called Price Maurice[71] has been up round here lately and picked up some marvellous information from the blacks, he is a chum of old Winnecke's, has money and is his own master, not a bad fellow away from strong drinks and the subject of blacks and what they tell him—he started down by Gill Range and L. Amadeus to look for Gibson's remains but turned back and I suppose is in Town now,[72] I was a bit annoyed because he was securing every Churina stone he could get hold of and several places took stones that I had not interfered with, to please you and G. I fancy he collared my sugar ant stones which I wanted as a parting gift to Gillen and arranged with the owners to purchase honestly but told them to wait till I told them to come down with them as my movements were uncertain[73]—You recollect I had these once and gave them back to them. P.M.'s modus is to entice a nigger to show him things (generally some scoundrel), and give him a shirt and collar the boodle—I told him that, they seldom belonged to the shower and that the trouble came afterwards. I hope when this reaches you, you will have settled down a bit and not feel the irksomeness so much— did the business that took you home, turn out in your favour and do you know a J.F. Jervis-Smith F.R.S.[74]—he wants Native things for the Millard Laboratory, Oxford but I am not in the business. My sister, Mrs Symon, her husband, five children and probably my Father and other sister leave for a six month's tour of Europe, America and Japan, in Prinz Regent Luitpold on 2nd Ap'l and I had serious thoughts of taking down those last lot of blacks and joining in. I spent a good many hours on pros and cons but I reckoned I could not expect to get back here if I left and starting on new ground on an empty exchequer is not in my line.

Snakes have been giving me fits lately and shaken up my nerves considerably, I have had no less than four very narrow squeaks in the last month. One night, lying on my blanket in front of the wurley, I felt something against my leg and took no notice as I thought it was one of the dog's tails—after a bit I raised my head and you can guess how I felt when I saw a good sized snake coming over my thigh and towards my face. I sang out to Barlow to get a light and then kept perfectly still—He was a long time fumbling with matches and rubbing his eyes and it seemed an eternity to me, luckily snake had come off my breast and gone just round my head and away for I don't think I could have stood the brute on my face and would have moved and probably got a nip—two nights ago, while at tea, I noticed the Cat very excited and when I looked up, a snake was hanging out of the bough roof just above my head and presumably was going to use me as a ladder—Got him about an hour later.[75] Please remember me to Mr French and tell him I regret I cannot make birds lay without rain which still avoids our camp. With kindest regards to Mrs Spencer and the children, whom I hope you found well and all good wishes for yourself.

Yours very affect'ely
C.Ernest.Cowle

Letter 3.12

Illamurta
15th Apl 1899

My dear Professor,

I got home (to stop) four days ago for the first time since last mail day so you will know that I have not yet been able to read the Book, which wants time to enable me to grasp those systems etc, even admirably put as they are. I got through the introduction, in which I see you perpetuate the same story about the cattle killing which Gillen disclaimed and said he had been mis-reported on. Then I got on to the 'Urabunna' tribe and was very much interested. I suppose this is the Tribe you were anxious to get to Lake Eyre to enquire further after.[76] The idea of the Totems being divided between the two classes is ingenious and, were it not for the sort of promiscuity of the marriage system, ought to be as effective as others in preventing marriages of those too closely related. I note the remarks as to jealousy not being noticeable among them as one man's 'Nupa' is 'Piraungaru' to certain others[77]—surely, though, in some cases (I mean in the present day), it must lead to ructions where a Black-fellow gets over fond, not affectionately perhaps of one of his Piraungaru who is someone else's 'Nupa'. Of course, from personal observation of blacks I see that some of them resent very strongly any interference with their women, be it by a white man or a black, even if of the proper relationship while others are apparently indifferent. The book does not want reading, it should be studied which takes time. I see the Illustrations are excellent, when I looked at them first by a smoky glassed lamp without cutting the leaves, I thought them bad, the spear throwing and boomerang throwing and Triff and Lottie side and full face look like Gillen and the Anschutz at loggerheads *though*.[78]

Measles have thinned out the Blacks round about considerably, Mission Station about 18 since the middle of February, Tempe two, Erldunda one and about enough at Henbury and Idracowra to make it up to 30 for my district and I presume we rejoice thereat on different grounds. I have our mutual friend Arabi chained up outside at last,[79] he cunningly saved his bacon when he found he was cornered—we could not get a shot while we were galloping in the scrub at foot of the range as both hands were occupied in steering our horses and I reckoned he had once more escaped but we headed him off the gorge and he dare not tackle the range which would have exposed him too much so he walked back to us—when we first saw him he was carrying half a wallaby, cooked, in his hand and the hind legs of a calf on his head—the calf probably in case that occasional hunger seized him. I expect I will have to take him in to Alice Spgs as soon as mail goes and then on down, I will try and get rid of him at Charlotte Waters or Oodnadatta if I can manage it. Barlow is not back yet from the last gang and I don't know when he will be as he did not write.

I have been down to Erldunda, out of Tempe twice and up to the Mission and back since I last wrote you, so you will see that when I say I have been busy it is a fact; the night I returned from Erldunda, Martin came and reported that he had been attacked by one of the blacks that had come back from Gaol in January at a little Spgs called Mt Shady and had to shoot him in self defence—so I had to see if Strehlow would hold an enquiry or not—Martin had taken this blackfellow as his others were either away or down with measles.[80] I do hope this will give us a rest from Cattle killing and that I can do some photographing etc. I am getting awfully tired of being at their tails so constantly (Blacks) but like the outside life—Three of the George Gill Gang camped here last night returning from Gaol and were profuse in their protestations of how they were going to sit down and I suppose they will till the Cattle come back from

Glen Helen directly (there are only about 500 on Tempe this last 12 months).

I did not get as far as 'Magic' in your book but is it not astonishing how firmly the *belief* of what some blackfellow can do, is engrafted in them all. A certain lubra died a bit to the North here recently (probably of measles) but they had the idea that she had been speared in the head by Mission Blacks, 'perhaps might him bin walk too close long corroboree' no sign of a wound anywhere but the <u>Blacks</u> had <u>closed</u> that up and she was alright for a week after leaving the Mission and then took ill and died. I tried to see if she had ever been near the Corroboree place but she had not. Old Larry whom you will remember, is fully believed to possess all these magical powers and to be able to make the dead live and is to give me ocular demonstration of it (our boys are thoroughly convinced of his ability which one would not Credit after the time they have been with the whites and it shows that tradition dies hard), by letting me kill a 'Possum' and if <u>it</u> recovers after <u>my</u> treatment and his I will give him a bag of flour. I want to see how the old dog will shuffle out of it. They cannot understand the measles yet but I expect will discover it to be the work of someone before long—They know whites get it and perhaps that will confuse them for a time but I'll back their inventive faculties to be equal to the occasion.

I get scraps from Byrne occasionally and hope to see him in a few days, he is like me, pretty tired of it but want of dollars and dread of the future keeps him anchored.

I suppose you are settled down to routine work now and almost miss the magnum op. but receiving congratulations on its success will occupy you a bit—Gillen, I hear wears a nose bone now and never speculates in any shares without first rubbing his belly with his sacred churina—I hope I get in, in time to see him.

Yours very sincerely
C.Ernest Cowle

Please remember me very kindly to Mrs Spencer whom I trust is in good health and yourself likewise.
CEC

Letter 3.13

Charlotte Waters
10th May 1899

Dear Professor,

I was lucky enough to meet your eminent collaborateur at Alice Springs and to be present at the small social tendered to him by a few of his intimates, of course flattering remarks were the only ones admitted and his receptivity was great, at times he was a little inclined to let himself go and rave on 'Basil Thompson'. 'Andrew Laing' [sic], the 'Times' etc, but we did not thoroughly succeed in penetrating the mask of modesty in which he has wrapped himself since his lecturing tour—God alone knows where it will end for he has now tasted publicity and although he disclaims all notion of again lecturing, fancy, he has a large stock of phrases carefully rounded off and waiting only the hint of an invitation to launch them on the enlightened Public. Living alone has done him a lot of good[81] and he is now more human and rational and far more like an Alatunga of the Alcheringa than a white man degraded by contact with the blacks, he takes the 'Observations' at irregular intervals[82] now. I went out again from the Bend and met him on his way down and he trapped me beautifully over the election of his Political Idol C.C.K.[83]—When I fell in, his language was like that of Robert Cran and totally unworthy of him, quite subdued me because I was so completely had and instead of his having to give me a bottle of whisky, found I owed him one. Voting was not brisk at Horse Shoe Bend and the air was heavy with the flavour of rum and onions but I believe the old members will be returned and the Bend Electors showed their common sense in almost unanimously rejecting Extension of Franchise for Legis'e Council.

Arriving here on Sunday night, I again met the Pontiff and Bradshaw[84] and have spent the last couple of days in amiable discussion. Pado has not been in his best form and his very natural grief at Gillen's departure has robbed me of an ally that I firmly relied on several times and firmly convinced the Pontiff that he had overwhelmed me completely. Bradshaw, who seems a nice fellow, left yesterday after we had all pushed his trap a hundred yards or so towards the Boundary line[85] and G left this morning amidst a perfect volley of curses and invocations to the Holy Trinity from Bob Cran after breaking the buggy pole as a preliminary. I would like to be present at the 1900 Meeting for Advancement of Science[86]—If you advertise fully the fact the F.J.G. is to be a Vice President it should be a great draw and many people no doubt will forego the Paris Exposition Trip to hear him speak. Pado joins in kindest regards.

Yours Sincerely
C.E.Cowle

You are as hopeless as Gillen on Blacks. I read your letter to him and he punctuated it with 'Quite Correct', 'I agree entirely' etc. May the Bulletin give you your desserts.

4

AFTER GILLEN

Letter 4.1

Illamurta
10th June 1899

My dear Professor,

Yours of 17th Ap'l, which I see you posted at Carlton on 10th May,
reached me tonight. The mail was four days late and, as it will go
back on its usual day, I have only a little over 24 hours to answer
something over forty letters, some of which must go by the board.
I had already read the Bulletin Critique[1]—got it at the Bend on my
way back after writing to you from Charlotte Waters. I did not like
his remarks on the <u>Style</u> at all, for I knew you were writing purely
for the Scientific World and not the Bulletin readers who rather run
to twaddle by Harry Stockdale and others in 'Aboriginalities' etc, but
I would much have liked to have seen the writer whom Gillen told
me was a very able man, tackle it on <u>facts</u>[2]—He ought to know as
much on that subject as the authorities you quote, at all events,
for even you will admit that all Australian Aborigines customs are not
similar although perhaps they may have much in common. Take the

instance of the Boomerang returning to the thrower, which you mention. I have no doubt that most scientific people are firmly convinced that all aborigines have the power but, as you say, they do not do so in this Country at all. As a boy, in Victoria I saw them bringing it back frequently in 1876, on the Murray about Mildura in 1880 and also some of the Cooper's Creek Blacks were very expert, I will certainly enquire into the evolution of it from the straight stick but on the Cooper they used both.[3] Another thing is, what became of all the stone axes that they had on the Finke in years gone by?—I can't get hold of them although I know they used them not so long ago and I know they used to get them somewhere near that Warman's Camp where you and I photographed that lubra.

The part that rankles in one is the growth of the new cult of 'Spencer and Gillenism', so to say, on the Native as a <u>human being</u>. I do not talk of their traditions or rites because I firmly believe you went deeper into them and more correctly than anyone ever will again, but do you honestly think you and Gillen saw any Natives as ordinary beings—wherever either of you met them, were they not always on their good behaviour (outside tribal rites etc mind), with the perfect confidence that they would be rewarded with tobacco or flour etc? Did you see, from <u>personal observation</u>, if they were sensuous, cruel or immoral? You seem to have a sympathy with scoundrelism of the 'Arabi' type and look on them as heroes for leading the others astray—Such Blacks I cannot have any sympathy for, but when it is a case of an <u>uncivilized</u> one I would always be lenient because perhaps he might not understand the white man's ways. Any one reading about Arunta Blacks might easily be led to believe that they only wanted wings and haloes (vide F.J.G's last report and lectures to Luritcha Blacks when being sentenced) but he knows perfectly well that it is on account of so many people about those more settled Stations and <u>Fear</u> that was properly installed into them that keeps them from cattle killing—It is not so many years ago since they <u>were worse than even these Luritchas have been and they were not cured by gaol</u>. You must bear in mind that there was no Protector about Alice Spgs and most people in the Country had some good reason to keep the Native subdued. I am not advocating shooting, for a moment, in the so called good old style, but they should be made to respect the law of the Land that has been taken from them, and it would be better for them—as for whites killing their emus and kangaroos etc, Alice Spgs is the only place where this is done, one might say and the carcase is nearly always given to the Blacks but, if it has been <u>skinned</u>, in most cases the Blacks won't trouble to cook the carcases because, thanks to the advent of the White man, they are not hungry, you saw an instance of this at Crown Point. A stock phrase of the cult is 'Put yourself in the Blackfellow's Place'. Well, suppose you and Gillen put yourselves for a while in the 'Squatter's Place'. You rent the Country and if the Government does not prevent the blacks destroying your property wholesale, do you not think you would feel inclined to do so. I don't know you well enough to positively swear what you would do but I am certain the blood of Gillen's ancestors would rise and that of his coloured brethren fall in his case and he would cry out pretty loudly.

By the way, Field and I had each a wager with Gillen before he left Alice Spgs—He bet us each that neither you nor he would reap a penny profit from the great work in five years.[4] I pondered over this a good deal and have now come to the conclusion that <u>Lang</u>, Tylor, Frazer and Coy must have been very, very expensive. I wish you would tell him this. I'll advertize it here.

I am perhaps bitter on the Native question again tonight—My two best boys ran away a few days ago, <u>Nat</u> after being with me four years and <u>Jack</u> six years, of course there was a woman in it. Nat, I considered old enough to have a lubra of his own and told him whenever he got a right one he could have her and live with her but as the one he wanted had gone down below the Goyder, he said leave her—he knew the rules of the Camp, that I allowed no one to sleep with lubras here, black or white, as I know from dearly bought experience that a young blackfellow with a lubra is utterly useless for our work and yet I found he was sneaking and camping with one here which he had told me was a wrong one for him—I hunted her off the place, the [sic] banged him round and a little later he said he wanted to go too. I thought he wanted to go at once and caught hold of him and said, 'Alright, I'll let you go but I'll straighten you up first'. This was because he knew thoroughly well that I had impressed on them all that I would let them go at any time if they told me but that, if I had punished any of them and they wanted to go, <u>then</u> they must wait till I got someone to replace them—He told me he would wait till I got another boy and I explained thoroughly to him, quietly and dispassionately, why he had been punished and that I had looked on him to set the others an example and he said I had always told him straight and that he knew I would have told him to take this lubra altogether if he had told me that her relations now would overlook the consanguinity (not extra close). I thought he was really convinced of his error and intended letting him stay here about a month and then letting him go away altogether if he so desired when he was cool.

I don't know if I have made this clear to you that they are perfectly at liberty to have intercourse when they play together because then they cannot go to extremes as they can when sleeping together for I may assure [you] that the young native, away from the tribal control, with a lubra of his own is immoral in the extreme. I considered Nat quite old enough to have a lubra but he preferred to deceive me although he knew my promise was as sacred as my word, that a transgressor would be punished and I felt that if I had overlooked his offence, my influence over them would be gone—he would either think that I was frightened to do it or that he was invaluable and you will see that it would have had a bad effect on the other ones. So much for his case.

The other boy, Jack, is not yet circumcised and ran away from his friends when they wished to perform the ceremony, he was spelling from 1st March to about 12th May and being found in full rations by us during that time—came back here of his own accord on that date and then ran away with Nat—the pair of them reached the Mission Station that afternoon—got a lubra to go up to the Station and get these gins to come down to the Creek quick and told them I was camped there and wanted them—the gin Jack was after, he had followed out from Alice Spgs to the Mission when she came out with Mrs Myers[5] (who was confined that night) and the pair then made into the Ranges and over A.G. way. You see these semi-civilized boys talk together—ours have been in there too much this last twelve months and seen the slackness of discipline at other places and that, if a boy got a job at the Police there or Telegraph, he could keep any gin he had managed to get, you see it is a gain to the tribe in one way and reprisals don't occur as they used to—the old men cannot straighten up these boys as they used to and it is only out back where you see the young fellows keeping to their correct camps till their wives are handed to them. It is bitterly cold and late and I won't have to write tomorrow. I feel half inclined to throw this in the fire but on one or two occasions you have been pleased to say that our blacks are properly treated and that is why I have told you so much tonight. I know that if I have been strict at times with the boys, that

I look after them in sickness and feed them on a scale and style different to anywhere else, expect them to come to me when anything is wrong and rely on fair play but deceit is innate in them somehow— if I had given Nat a good hiding when he came up as I should have done and then said, 'Now go away if you want to', it would have been alright and the others would have further understood that I would keep my word about allowing no boy to leave in <u>anger</u>. You can understand how if that was allowed, every time one checked or had to speak sharply to a black he would want to go and in a place like this we would be stranded, they are the first that ever served me in this way at all events and I will bring them back sooner or later. This is probably the last time I will worry you on the subject of blacks as beings—My next will be on them as Dreamers.

I hope now to have a little quietness till Snider and Co returns and, if I get Nat and Jack back, I will go down the Sandhill way to Erldunda— Get fairly pure Native that way if I can come on a lot—there are a good few somewhere about E of Ayers Rock I fancy and it is only odd ones that visit Tempe.[6] Racehorse's lubra 'Coomba' died the other day—much to Coulthard and my sorrow, and Coulthard tells me that Racehorse cried like a white man over it—he was to come to me for consolation after a trip out somewhere. I like him and nearly all the Glen blacks who have behaved splendidly while the Cattle have been up there, now they are all being brought back to Tempe but I must go up and take them some good conduct rewards soon. I tried hard to get a photo of an aged couple here the other day but I am afraid I failed—They were agreeable in every way but very unsteady on their pins and I could <u>not</u> get them to stand in one position while I pulled out the dark slide, anyway I'll develop them after mail goes. Have you seen G. yet? I am anxious to get at the papers and see what he has been up to—I got one slip where he has been giving his opinion on the Mineral Wealth of Cent'l Australia and the Railway etc.[7] Please thank Mrs Spencer for her kind enquiries and tell her I am well, and believe yourself that I get hell from rheumatics occasionally. With kindest regards to you both.

Believe me,
Yours very affect'ly
C.Ernest.Cowle

Letter 4.2

Illamurta
9th July 1899

My dear Professor,

Thanks to the Charlotte Waters mail having been left behind at Oodnadatta in mistake we are practically letterless and paperless this time and this is only a short screed to heartily congratulate you on the 'Magnum Opus' which I have carefully read since last writing to you—Criticising such a work is out of the question and no one could do it unless he practically traversed over the whole ground again and then compared the results—the amount of information of a hidden character which you have got together is simply stupendous and I only wish you could get up and do the Western tribes as thoroughly—the myths relating to 'Inapertwa'[8] are especially interesting but I cannot get that right about not eating the 'Totem' or only sparingly—they did it apparently in Alcheringa times and my questions have led me to believe that they still do. I tried an old Kangaroo man of 'Undiarra'[9] and he seemed surprised at the idea of not doing so but I will watch closely, when I see old fellows together, if I can get their right totems and see how they shape, I also note the fact of the totem name originating from where the mother 'conceives' the child—Do they not, in some cases, take also or claim the totem of their actual birthplace in addition. P. 584. I see I am quoted as the authority of saying the 'Amera' might be used as a 'musical instrument'. This is the first I have heard of it. I know I took several in to G. and perhaps Nat may have told him of it but as there are only boys here now I cannot enquire at present.

I intend going over the whole book again shortly and am more convinced than ever that the conditions of tribe as regards severity of punishment for tribal offences is very lax nowadays. Barlow is at present away after those boys. I heard they were about Owen Spgs way and sent him in. I heard a fortnight nearly ago, that he had got them and some others killing a beast near Owen Spgs but nothing further and do not know if he has taken them down or not. Can't understand his not sending me some word unless he has and that boy levanted as well. You see the lubras that have been here, they have got pretty sweet on and want to exercise sole rights of proprietorship without any title whatsoever—the parties interested, of course, do not object, although they are offending against all tribal canons, because they are <u>Police boys</u> and they look to them to screen their offences as a reward for their complacency. I have tried to guard against this by not allowing any of them to consider such and such a lubra as his sole property in opposition to the other trackers but found out recently that it was what had occurred and that there had been internal dissensions over the matter. Don't want to have to deal afresh but will have to if I don't get matters straight—present day tribal punishments are mostly bosh as the young man is too useful as a tobacco purveyor etc. to the older ones and it is generally the gin who suffers.

I am sorry I missed the papers as I expected to see some <u>Gillen,</u> I must write to him as soon as I see him settled at Moonta whither I see, Chance, who used to be at Alice Springs has just been moved to—something over drink I fancy.[10] Racehorse called last week to inform me that evil influences had been at work and the cause of his lubra's death.[11] I fancy he wished me to act as the avenging party but I think I convinced him that it was not evil spirits that were responsible for the measles and told him how she should have been cured and how so many white people died from same thing—this may save some other unfortunate on whom suspicion might fall but, as his Mother and another tribal father also pegged out, I am sceptical especially if the suspected party possesses a desirable lubra to replace either of the missing ones— Coulthard still at Glen Helen getting the remainder of the Cattle together and Tempe quiet—Is it the lull preceding another outbreak? I trust not—With kindest regards to Mrs Spencer and yourself.

Yours Sincerely
C.Ernest Cowle

Bitterly cold up here—no rain. I fancy temperature lower some mornings than when you were up.

Letter 4.3

Illamurta
3rd Sep 1899

Dear Professor,

It is so long since I heard of or from you that I thought you had forgotten me. I can understand the quantity of work you must be getting through, removing all the articles from National Library to the Museum, and must congratulate you on the appointment as Director, provided it is not a purely honorary appointment which Governments are so fond of rewarding deserving people with—latterly some of my preconceived notions have received a very severe shock and I now think success should always be followed by and everything give way to Cash Considerations.[12] During the last month I was out round Tempe and Gill Range. The Country out there was looking lovely and the blacks, most of whom had just returned from Gaol, were stopping on their own country and behaving well so we were on the friendliest terms, they took me to one plant and were anxious for me to go to another but I could not go on and although the grass was perfect and in full seed, water, away from the main Range was not plentiful for the horses. I got one stick which I will probably send to Gillen but it is awkward as it is nearly 2 ft long, I got it as it is marked in squares [drawing] thus, instead of circles etc as usual and all the natives who gave it to me could tell me, was that it represents lubras sitting down and had been stolen from other blacks very much further west when they were children.[13] I think their marriage system could be more easily got a start on amongst the more civilized blacks about Oodnadatta as I think the Natives there are chiefly Luritcha or closely allied—All the less civilized ones that return from gaol to Gill Range come back from there via Alberga and complety [sic] West of Finke and Erldunda which they would not be likely to do if they had not much in common and would probably prefer the civilized road. I have had a long letter from Gillen who appears to be settling down and beginning to like his new surroundings in spite of occasional hankerings after the old unrestraint of Alice Springs, and, at Alice Springs, I fancy they rather miss the old regime. I have not been in since the new Governor arrived there.

We expect Henbury people up every day to take away some of the Tempe Cattle and Martin hopes to get them all away from Tempe before January which will make things a lot easier for us. I do not think the Blacks will follow the Cattle there. I hope Mrs Spencer yourself and the little ones are well and with all good wishes.

Remain,
Yours Sincerely
C.Ernest.Cowle

Letter 4.4

Illamurta
13th Ap'l 1900

My dear Professor,

No letter from you but I suppose you are still up to your eyes in Exams etc. The Pontiff wrote at length on this occasion and fairly gloats over his Melbourne triumphs,[14] I think I told you that he no longer dates events from any period but that, and every remark, is prefaced, 'Before I was or After I was President etc etc etc.' We have actually had rain at last, although none of the big Creeks ran properly, it was soaking and every promise of a splendid season—feed in abundance everywhere and a royal time for blacks for there are simply millions of 'Illpierer' and 'Uttnirringhita'.[15] Caterpillars everywhere and they can and do get bushels in an hour or two. The 'Illpierer' is on the grass and herbage only, from an inch and a half to $2\frac{1}{2}$ inches long and about as thick as a blue lead pencil. Colours vary, the one in front of me [drawing with notes] ground [species] colour from green to brownish black—belly cream. 'Incharlka'[16] also a ground species [drawing with notes]. Spots are black with pink centre and the bottom stripe is white, belly and general ground colour green.

'Uttnurringhita' infest Eremophila Paisleyi and some of the other Eremophilas which it strips completely and one kind of the eremophila, the Finke blacks call the Uttnirringhita bush on account of the caterpillars liking for it—Size something like that of the others [drawing with notes].

The circles are orange and there is an ill defined yellow stripe of spots underneath, then the same little yellow spots on brown or greenish black ground under belly with a greenish yellow stripe between the legs from head to tail. These grubs or Caterpillars must grow very rapidly and I presume the eggs of the two former must be laid in the ground and the last one on the Eremophilas, but I cannot make out how they retain their fertility through such long droughts and it is only a good rain which seems to release them. I have churina of first two and also got some pieces of stone representing the bark which those Alcheringa women used in the old days and also some of the foreskins which are represented by little hollow pipes.

I was up the Peterman just before the rain and found the blacks busy—speared five one day[17]—I did not get the ring-leading gaolbirds so I let those we did capture on Range go—Since that I have been down to Erldunda and saw an interesting Rat Spot away to the South about 25 miles, two parallel rows of stones for a long distance and one row near the Rockholes, our old guide explained that the single Row was the spectators watching the others dancing and had names for some of the stones—a devil of a mob must have gone into the ground at this spot and I reckon the hoary old frauds that placed those stones there must have perspired freely while they were thus salting the ground for their credulous descendants. I got two beautiful Snake stones from Mareena. They show the striation, naturally representing the marks on the Snake. I have sent for some Flour and Sugar and can make a rise in churina directly. On my return from Erldunda I went into the Finke and got 'Jado', who used to be my egg hunter, and a boy for killing a calf and at present he is chained up and I expect we will take him to Mission for trial in a day or two, this confounded wretch I let off at Xmas for same offence and he keeps coming here and getting Rations and physic for his child's eyes which in reality they <u>throw</u> away and only want to find out whether I am at home or where I am likely to be so that they can go in at the calves without their tracks being seen.

Pado talks of going for a trip home to the old Country in Sept'r or October and I think is souring considerably of late like myself from uncongenial companionship. The Bogner's [sic] went down a fortnight ago and I do not know if they will come back, other local matters quiet.[18] I wish you would send back the letter from R.H. Matthews [sic] which I sent for your opinion, I have another long one this time in which he asks questions enough to run into a small volume but I must tell him I have not got any time.[19] As a matter of fact I have not yet read the papers of the mail before this and don't see much chance of doing so for a bit—You see, when one is home there is cooking etc to attend to besides other little jobs.

Under separate cover I am sending you my four little beloved Lollitcha 'Churina' which I told you of before—I could not find out what the little stone in the paper meant for it does not belong to the other churina but was in a nigger's bundle carefully wrapped up. Gillen might have got the ones I send you but I always am sceptical of his collections destinations nowadays and I reckon your Institutions were slow that they did not supply someone like myself with a ton or so of flour to purchase these sort of things with while they were plentiful and before every Tom, Dick and Harry got hold of them. I have to go carefully to preserve their confidence and prevent people who know they will trade these things with me taking advantage of them and spoiling matters by yapping and telling lubras and others about them, the whole secret lies in not appearing grasping and stifling covetous thoughts when viewing objects <u>later</u> they will be offered to you. Ross is at Oodnadatta and getting on alright and Kelly writes regularly from Adelaide and sends me his bible, the 'Bulletin', and the 'Australasian'. I wish if you have any prints of pictures you took on the Horn Exp'n or going down with me, you would send him a few, he has often asked me to try and get him some of the views and been very good to me. I know it is a vicarious sort of way of repaying his kindness, by trading on someone else's, but it is the only way I can do it—His address is:

A.Kelly
c/o Police Station
Two Wells
S.A.

It is a pity you are not up here just at present and me with a little time on hand so that we could go and view the plants which the Blacks want to show me, I don't trouble to go as I told you and more especially because I am afraid of other people getting the trackers who might be with me at the time to take them to the repositories when I might be away somewhere.

There is a yarn about a party of 5 whites and an Afghan[20] who started 8 or 9 months ago from West Aust'a being attacked by Blacks in Rawlinson Ranges and a man and many Camels being killed. All I heard was that the party had turned up at Oodnadatta and were going to report to the Police there and that the Afghan had gone off his head and tried to shoot the leader of the Expedition and been shot dead by one of the others[21]—if there is any truth in the yarn, I suppose details will have been in the papers but I hope I don't have to go after the Blacks. For I do not see how the right offenders can be identified, knowing how they would probably put the blame onto innocent ones; anyway I think the occurrence took place on Western Australian ground. I can equip myself here for a three weeks or a month's trip alright but beyond that with present appliances I could not do much good and would require more transport like our Army in S. Africa. I hear Belt joined the second S.A. Contingent over there.[22] Well I must shut up, I reckon I weary you when I get scratching along—I hope this finds you well and that Mrs Spencer will return from England in the best of health and spirits.

Yours very sincerely
C.Ernest.Cowle

I saw the pictures in both Leader and Australasian. G. looked quite a noble Roman amongst the other Scientists and as scanty haired as any of them if that is an indication of brains.
E.

Letter 4.5

Illamurta
28th May 1900

My dear Spencer,

Yours of Ap'l 11th turned up about three weeks ago, evidently crossing one of mine, I could not possibly reply and in a line to K, asked him to tell you so—on this occasion I am taking time by the wool.[23] I told you I was going to the Mission to get Jado and boy tried—the boy got a whipping and Jado was sentenced to 6 months. I brought him here and shod up a lot of horses and started away South to try and get him some companions but had an unsuccessful trip. We did not see a sign of any tracks till we got over 100 miles from here, about 50 miles West of Goyder (Coolida) Springs and a bit S.E. of what I took to be Mt Connor—the ones I wanted had been about here and boxed with a lot of others from further South, we tracked them to one or two dry claypans and then had to give it up and make back for water, I would have liked to have gone on as they were evidently making a young man (the trackers pointed out where they had been tossing him up etc) but I had never been in that part of the Country before and feared the water they might make to might be impracticable for already thirsty horses—as it was, at one place we carried water out of a gorge for over two hours and the only other waters were Native Wells in ground something like that at Kamran's Well[24]—we lost a day at each of a couple of them, cleaning them out, and found they made about 10 gallons p hour or say 1 to 1½ horses, rather slow you can guess, with twelve head to water—saw three other wells we did not use and no doubt there are plenty of others scattered about if one had a good guide—don't seem to be any good waters about the scattered Ranges—the most eventful occurrence was when we tried to cut off a corner by crossing an apparently safe arm of a lake, all went well till we reached the far side and I was just congratulating myself when all the horses went down flop—the saddle ones struggled back onto safe ground with the loose ones but the heavy packs anchored the others, took off everything and got out two—Your friend 'Manfred' would not make an effort and I felt inclined to shoot the pig, we had to clear his legs out of briny (oh so salt) mud and then roll him over and over with the surcingles, even when he reached good ground, he would not trust himself to stand up for a good bit.

As soon as I got home I started Barlow off down with Jado and since that, I have been here, reading up the accumulated papers and doing odd jobs, nursing a smart twinge or two of rheumatics etc. We had two or three nice showers since I wrote you and all the Country could not well look better although the rain was a trifle late. Martin has got nearly all his Cattle off Tempe and onto Henbury and is trying to sell the horses and station now for very little. Just before we went to the Mission, eleven blacks, including 'Meenamurtyna', came over to Tempe one night from Ayers Rock way and speared an old man, left him rather bristly with 8 spears in him.[25] (I believe he was sleeping with two others whom they first woke up), they also wanted 'Arabi' but the devil looks after his own, for I told you he had gone out George Gill Range way. The reason was that these two had killed one of their mates close to Tempe a couple of years ago. We do not interfere in these matters but they killed a couple of beasts as they were going, back on Tricketts Creek plain, so I'll have to look them up soon.

I note your remarks re Cassias and Eremophilas etc and I am sending you some of the Palm seeds ('Livistonia Mar') and some of the seeds of that 'Tecoma Australis', at least that is what I think you call it, the thing that the last joint of the spears is made of with a pithy centre and grows near Rocks the clusters of flowers are large and pretty, creamy coloured with brownish centre, flowers about size of Eremophila. I will get Cycads first chance and also others. I am sending you a specimen of a poisonous creeper which appears to attach itself to the prickly Tribulus and wish you would give me its name. I have not seen it growing here myself but the Missionaries attribute the death of a lot of their sheep to it just after the rain.[26]

I have not got anything in the nigger line lately or since I wrote to you, too good a season I reckon at present, I had the old fellows up here for a day or two and tried to get some information from them but their yarns are a bit incoherent to us and they do not seem able to tell you <u>why</u> things were always done. I will probably copy out my notes soon and send them to you. <u>I believe that every water hole, Spring, Plain, Hill, Big Tree, Big Rock, Gutters and every peculiar</u> or striking feature in the Country, not even leaving out Sandhills, *without any exception whatsoever* is connected with some tradition and that, if one had the right blacks at that place, they could account for its presence there[27]—you may recollect when we left Idracowra and camped before photoing Chambers Pillar with the telephoto— we went on next day and came to a box watercourse (caused by blood escaping from a Snake woman's teats) a lot of jumbly little hills (Crows that came from Jay etc), we had dinner at two little Hills ron a creek (the breasts thrown away) and so on endlessly, almost to account for two bright stars in the sky—You, of course, know the sort of thing. It seems to me that Alcheringa blacks of, say, <u>Kangaroo totem</u>, these fed on Kangaroos—Now the difficulty comes in that these kangaroo totem men sometimes assumed the actual shape of Kangaroos (see Undeara notes *of mine*), Snakes or Emus etc. likewise, and it is difficult to tell when they are feeding on their ordinary totemic food or eating each other cannibalistically. I am not using the totemic names as you do in your work like Erlia (Emu) men, Achilpa (Wild Cat men), but I think you will see what I mean. The Erlia Men or men of Emu totem lived principally on <u>Emus</u>, this does not come in always for I have a churina of blue crane totem and this one and others travelled with Mulgah seed men and fed on Mulgah seed. I think I told you about the set of circumcisional articles I got—

Pooras—Peni
Illknaguirta—Testicles
Ill-ying-a-pooler—Foreskins
Lallira—Stone knife
Im-itch-er-iknilla—Gum tree bark
Stone Nanja—of Twantinna
ilknurritcha of the grass seed totem

These are just sufficiently like the articles they are supposed to represent to be recognizable—The stone knife is [drawing] flat like that and the stone, representing the piece of gum tree bark, is not unlike the shape a burnt flake often assumes. In this case it was a woman of the Lizard Totem that was burning the articles off a lot of Ullakupera totem not far from where you and I saw Walter Parke after leaving 'Undeara',[28] and it was a grass seed Totem man who showed them the Lallira and gave them some. This man came from between Doctor Stone's and Mt Burrell, varies a little from the Alice Spgs version, but I suppose each lot differ a bit—It is your friend 'Ungutnika' that looks after these and brought them to me. When the old fellows were here before I just wrapped a piece of Paper on each stick as—kangaroos from 'Undeara', Kangaroo from Attitara—Kangaroo from Idracowra and so on, to see if there was any humbug about the churina they had fetched but the three who came this time never failed in the slightest degree in re-identifying them which is a rum thing when one cannot see any differences in a probably perfectly plain stick with considerable grease on it. I may send you an untoned print of a photo I made of them—the individual pictures were failures—I fancy the heat spoilt some of my plates or the gelatine on them during the summer.

Whooping cough very bad at Mission and I know six little ones died there recently and a lot of old blacks have a sort of cold. I can't keep them here and they will not look after themselves unless under your immediate eye—My own keep well and I often try and explain the theory of germs to them but I fear they look on me as a Munchausen[29] and ascribe disease to evil influence of others although they reckon I pulled them through the measles and kept them from any deaths which occurred at nearly every other place. War still dragging on in spite of Roberts' presence, I do so hope Mafeking gets saved in time.[30] Pado writes occasionally and is well but a bit down just now over shares, like myself. I put every penny into them and if I had sold out on the top prices, could have stood behind about £2000—now not a quarter of it.[31] Never mind, they may go up again. Gillen wrote me a long letter by same mail as yours and I think likes Moonta in reality and is taking a leading part in local affairs by the aid of a Magic Lantern and a glib tongue.[32] I reckon his successor at Alice Spgs is not much liked and for some reason has his knife into Gillen on every occasion. I have not been there since poor old Gillen left and don't often hear any news of the place—things very mixed at the Police Camp there. Well, I suppose you will be pretty full of me before you get this far so I'll hope you are well and shut up. May add more after mail. I hope Mrs Spencer and Miss Dorothy get out safely and a pleasant trip.

Yours Sincerely
C.Ernest.Cowle

Over Over [for continuation of letter on inside page]

7th June 1900 Your letter came yesterday, so I'll add a bit to this long screed. Glad the churina got to you safely. They are not 'Illoota' as you seem to say.[33] They are 'Loollitcha', this is a bush something like an Acacia only with smaller dark green leaves and grows a little purple fruit [drawing] of nice flavour and glutinous if I recollect aright, blacks are very fond of it but I have never seen it South of Glen Helen Gorge and it ripens about Ap'l or May. I will send a specimen when I go that way.[34]

I see what you say about Native Collections and agree with you as to the best place for their final resting spots. I hope you did not think I meant anything personal in my remarks, I wrote pretty stiffly to the Pontiff when I heard he had sold parts of his for such a big sum,[35] not because he made money out of them if he felt that way, but on account of his saying always that they should not be taken from the blacks and that he was only getting them purely in the interests of science and all the while holding out both his hands and a carpet bag for everything he could get, I know when he said the trustees had wired to him, I replied, 'Why don't you say Spencer wired and repay one good turn by advising the Adelaide people to buy his now.' (Spencer's) and that if he had straight out at the start that he might make something out of them it would have been alright see. I also see that you have sent Ross £20 for me to lay out—this should be ample for a good bit although I did not mean you to do that when I wrote. I meant it was a pity you had not done it ages ago before the blacks parted with so many things to Tom, Dick and Harry as they have done and that a lot could have been got cheaply at the start before the more civilized ones taught them to put a higher price on things. I told you in a previous part of this that the market was slack at present owing to a good Season but can only say I'll do what I can—the guileless native, though, when he really knows one is in the market, shapes somewhat thus—1st, several churina, all blacks liberally rewarded. 2nd visit—about half a dozen turn up with perhaps a couple of churina and when it comes to payment each produces a good sized sack and can't understand that there is a limit to flour and the purchasing power of each ancestor. Consequent disappointment. I presume you want all the churina I can get both wooden and stone, and any other nigger weapons and gear whatever that is genuine. Or is there a limit to the number of boomerangs, Woomeras, Pitchis etc?—I was collecting a few things myself but will knock off and get Ross to send me about £10 worth of stuff and leave the balance in his hands for cartage etc till we see how we get on. Anyhow, don't send any more money because I could have financed the concern and settled easily enough with you.

Grubs Illpierer, Uttnirringhita, 'Uncharlka'—are only obtainable now in unrecognizable cooked forms, apparently keep well, will send Attnyum-eeta[36] (Witchety proper) by and bye. And will see if there is an Utnirringhita bush in flower round about Camp before mail day.

Thanks for sending prints to Kelly. I have some spirits. I still hear from old Winnecke regularly, I do not think he has missed more than one mail since 1894. Papers seem full of bubonic and the Appeal Clause in the Commonwealth Bill. My talented brother-in-law, Symon, seems to be in hot water all round and of course is right—His advocacy and support of Kingston, in spite of the bitter feeling between the pair of them, will please the Gillen immensely and draw us very close together.[37] No more just now, old man, I'm a bit twingy in the shins—With best wishes.

Yours Sincerely
C.Ernest.Cowle

Shall I write out the notes on Churina I got here and see if you can connect them with any others—one, I think, relates to the origin of the Finke River.

Letter 4.6

Illamurta
8th July 1900

Dear Professor,

Just a line to congratulate you on the F.R.S. and the Fellowship of the Ant'l Soc'y which you richly deserved. How is it that the Pontiff did not get some letters such as K.C.B.[38] etc. I thought it was a certainty with Kingston at Home to advocate his claims. I have posted you seeds of two of the Philotus'—it is difficult to get properly ripe ones for they shed the lower ones before the tip is mature, also a kind of daisy which grows in the bed of seldom running sandy creeks and is rather pretty and a very free flowerer,[39] I got some of the Palm Kernels (Zant'a and Thorntonii) but I found they were all too old and have told blacks to bring me more for the inside of these was rotten. Re Native Peach or quondong (Santalum), note that the kernels of these are carried by the Blacks and used as an unguent for the hair and head. I found a bag full in an old nigger's kit last month, they soften a bit when kept and when squeezed are like thin putty. I often wondered what they cracked up the peach stones for as I knew they did not do it for eating and fancied that it was done in play by children.[40]

A new man came in place of Barlow a few days ago but I cannot give you an opinion on him yet as he has not had time to develop his various madnesses—hasn't been in the Bush before and, on first impressions, is decidedly commonplace and I fear from what I have noted, far from energetic—hope he will be a success and find a few more 'aspirates' in time.[41]

Ross advises me that rations ought to get here about end of the month. I was mixed a bit over the cheque. He told me you had sent him £20 and told him to send me some Flour etc and you telling me you had told him to do this and to draw on him for cartage made me think the £20 was on this account—he has explained that the cheque was for moles and rats and everything is alright now. I got three ancient Emu Churina during the month—markings very indistinct, I saw a very old Stick in Martin's possession which I am anxious to get from him as it is not of much value to the person he is getting things for in England. But Tempe is Yorkshire and a queer nut in a deal.[42] The churina is of the 'Nyee roo' which is a little bird, either 'melanodryas bicolor' or one of the Cuckoo Shrikes, I will ask details before I go on with my attempt to get it. So far I have Eagle Hawk, Kangaroo from Idracowra, Carpet Snake from Erldunda uncharlka grub, Illpierer Grub, Dove, Little Hawk, Carpet Snake from Main Camp, Wild Dog from Irrecowler, Mulgah Seed, Blue Crane, 'Goanna' from Ippia, Kangaroo from Attitara; Kangaroo from Undeara, Witchity grub (the one they get underground).[43] Emu from Horse Plain, Inncharlka from Deception Creek and others from Glen way that I have not yet got details of, nor of the stone Emu, and Snake from Mareena.[44] Am just finishing mail—so I must shut up. With best wishes

C.E.C.

The sticks I have been enumerating are not <u>Museum</u> a/c—but mine, and will go to you first chance and you can do as you like with them only you must give the Pontiff a little divvy out of the duplicate ones or he will reckon I have deserted him.[45]

Letter 4.7

Illamurta
31st Aug 1900

My dear Professor,

Under separate cover I <u>have</u> posted you a bundle of notes on Churina, whether you will read them or not is another question. I tried to avoid the Native redundancy as much as possible but altered nothing else—you know how they go into details and irrevelancies crop up, the why and the wherefore of which, one cannot well get to the bottom of and all I can say is that these notes are the result of many long hours of questioning in an evil atmosphere and ought at least to enable you to label the churina into their right totems—

Yesterday I got a group of 7 Sticks, genuinely antique and relating to the 'Tukinjerra' totem—<u>Amphibolurus Maculatus</u> for certain.[46] They are the Churina of a brother and Sister, the yamsticks they each carried are narrower = 4, an abnormally shaped old boomerang [drawing], the lizard meat [drawing], two other heavy old boomerangs, the ribs they used to throw away = 3 more. The last three belonged to the male Spirit and I believe there are three similar churina belonging to his Sister which I want to complete—The seller was the reincarnated man, now old and blind and led here and he promised to sell me two good white stones which represent the navels of these same two 'Alcheringa'. I am anxious to see what they are like—these sticks are all about 2 ft 9 or 3 feet—Some of those in the notes are longer and it is difficult to get boxes long enough for them. These nigger yarns have many points in common with some of our biblical tales don't you think?

Since last writing to you, I have been down Erldunda way and came back by Coolida Spgs then East of Mt Connor and by the Kernot Range home, we saw two or three scattered lots of blacks and got two that we wanted, you know the lot I was after down that way last April that I told you were making a young man of a youthful cattle killer— The latter is still at large with his brother and another connection and not yet allowed to go in the vicinity of the lubras, they keep them apart much longer in the West I fancy and it was amusing to note how careful they were to warn each other by smokes before approaching a well that they might meet at and camps about a quarter of a mile off—I did a war dance at one camp but got no loot except an odd girdle or two of human hair, one of the domestic cat gone wild (much esteemed),[47] and a couple of pitchis, there were any quantity of the latter and I could have fully stocked you if I could have carried them home but I could only give the prisoners one each to look after, I also got four or five of their curved adzes but all had iron tips which I am getting replaced with flints.[48] I hope your 'petition' is a success, the funds should be forthcoming if the Anthropological lights are in earnest.[49]

Thanks for information re the 'Dodder'—Maiden of Sydney said some of the species were injurious to plants but not known as hurtful to stock, it was sent to me from the Mission Station where it was plentiful just after the rain and they reported it as killing about 60 Sheep and some horses, I never saw it here nor actually growing.[50] I think I wrote you last mail about the Acacia or Wattle at Gosse's Range which I won't forget. I see nice Eremophilas occasionally but I am hanged if I can see them seeding and flowering at the same time and the foliage of most of them is too much alike for me to discriminate. I have been busy as usual and get little or no time for reading even the papers somehow, but I have glimpsed at those N.S. Wales outrages by the 'Governors', can't understand them being at large so long in such settled Districts and can only put it down to too many people being on the trail and humbugging up tracks, I do not fancy our best C.A. trackers would get on well in such parts for there would be much to confuse them, although in the Bush where it is simply nigger, they are wonderful.[51] I cannot stand the semi-civilized black—blacks can only be ruled properly by fear and once this wholesome respect is blunted, as in the case of knowing gentlemen like those under review, they can be properly bad—it is not harshness that controls the outer barbarian, so much as thoughts of what the white man really can perform, should he decide to be severe, that makes the ignorant native much more amenable to discipline and common sense, familiarity and civilization teaches him to despise the white man's ideas of punishment after trial and capture instead of 'revenge', sudden and effective at the point of a spear or rifle.

The new man is improving a little but is terribly dull, knowing my angelic temper, you can picture him as rather a trial on the last trip, no interest in anything or his surroundings except at meal times and by the end of the trip, he almost knew his own quart pot from mine and what pack it and his swag belonged to—the pot was a mere detail but he is a syrup man and once I had sugared my tea, I did not care for another quarter of a pound being dumped in to it—I used to tell him to go to Hell out of the road pretty frequently for no matter how often a thing was done in front of him, he did not seem to grasp an idea of it, sort of man I can't realize the density of and moved always as if half asleep. I think he would develop into a man too lazy even to keep his pipe alight unaided, if he got a show but he is going to develope [sic] some energy or have a sorry time.[52] I think I told you of the colds prevalent amongst the Blacks, they cannot shake them off and I have been off colour for a couple of weeks myself—not exactly like infantile whooping cough but when one of the paroxysms comes on you have a strangled feeling, salivate a lot and each inhalation of breath sounds like a foghorn or whistle and you are distressed and exhausted for a few minutes afterwards— Don't run away with the idea that I am ill for I reckon I am getting alright but from my own experiences I can now understand why the boys seemed so half witted to me on the trip before last.

I hope Mrs Spencer and the daughter were blooming when they returned and that she will raise no objections to your projected trip in common fair play. Please remember me kindly to her. Kelly's address is:

Two Wells
South Australia

Alec McKeod was out from Owen Spgs to inspect Tempe Downs for Kidman Bros.[53] but I did not see him going back nor hear if there is likelihood of a trade, failing that, I may go in for half of it myself with another man who would look after it. I expect Martin in a day or two to go in to A.G. with the Blacks, we have not been in since the Pontiff left and personally I don't anticipate a particularly enjoyable time for I fancy G's successor is a bit amorphous and vaseling [sic].

With best wishes,
Believe me,
Yours very Sincerely
C.Ernest.Cowle

Letter 4.8

Illamurta
30th Sep 1900

Dear Professor,

Yours to hand and I am very glad that the Petition was satisfactory in getting your leave and only hope the monetary part is satisfactorily settled—it is one thing for Scientific people to sign their names and another to put their hands in their pockets[54] but probably they imagine that the 'kudos' should simply repay you for the trifling outlay that a year's work in the Back Blocks[55] where locomotion and everything else is so cheap entails upon you—Gillen wrote me pretty fully on the subject and I have replied in kind and suggesting Sly Grog Selling as a means of raising the wind. I was in at Alice Spgs a fortnight ago and found the place very different to the old times and the Telegraph Station much drier except for the surreptitious bottles in various of the Quadrangular rooms[56]—The Police Camp ménage was ghastly and I was very glad to get home again even although I found all hands as bad as ever with colds and have suffered a relapse myself. No sense of taste or smell whatsoever and just a feeling as if I had been belted all over—Gabriel sent me some stuff for the boys but says the epidemic will not go away till the hot weather comes and that one can do little or nothing. I sent Ockenden down with the Blacks and may not be writing to you next mail as I will in all probability be down the road over the Elections to escort my vote and Sargeant's from the Bend to Charlotte Waters. I note your remarks re Seeds and am glad they are coming on alright, I can't yet get good conditioned 'Cycads'. I have my eye on a shrub in Ilpilla paddock, the seeds were not ripe when I was there a few days ago nor did I catch it in bloom this year but I always intended getting the name of it from someone for Ilpilla Paddock is the only place I have seen it—hundreds of blue balls like pincushions and very striking[57]—Will canter down and see it if a horse comes in today in time.

I think we burnt that big porcupine bush in the Palmer Gorge or Blacks did, for it is no more.[58] I note the sarcastic tinge of your remarks on the subject of the Camera at that and other spots but you must recollect that I prided myself on keeping appointments with Blacks, Whites or Brindles and arrived up to Time and you will admit that there was not much time afforded to be spent anywhere—you people arranged the affairs without knowing distances and had I been con-sulted I would have allowed margins—however, if I am still here and you can get a look round, we will try and do better next time.[59] Should Bower birds in Spirits have the abdomen lanced and entrails extracted or not? I can get them and put them in one of the nigger cases. French has always been asking for them but I could not send him any by mail. They are always plentiful here about Xmas, and a curse in the garden on the Tomatoes, but they get shattered a lot with the gun if a big one and are rather too cunning for the little one. I have seen no Polytellis Alexandrae since 1896 and I do not think they are in the country anywhere at present—they are rather an enigma but may appear at any time again. I got a long enough box at last and packed up for you goods as p enclosed list. I must try and get a second box filled somehow to balance it so that these independent carriers will take it away for me.

I pick up a boomerang whenever I see one but pitchis are awkward, they take up so much room and weigh nothing[60]—hope you got my long bundle of notes. Got several Churina on my way back from Alice Spgs as two old bucks met me on the road—they swore they had not manufactured them to sell and as two had hair strings on them and evidently had been used, perhaps they were telling me the truth but they are newish, they are to bring me more by and bye and I will get details.[61] I cannot get old 'Chinna-puppa' from Mareena Bluff so as to get the particulars of my two cherished Snake Stones which are about 14 and 18 inches respectively.

Martin is trying to get rid of Tempe, he has moved all the cattle off and the place is under offer to Kidman with the plant and horses at about £800, I think. I was a fool not to snap it when I had a chance and now it has slipped me—you see I had a notion of giving up the Bush and settling but that is knocked on the head and now I only want to stay in the Bush.[62] Martin is a real good fellow but he will never make a do out there for he always requires assistance and is what one looking on, is forced to reckon a pottering messer, he never seems to tackle a job and go through with it straight out. Please thank Mrs Spencer for kind enquiries, I hear Chappie and her Sister go to Miss Chambers' school. Mus Domesticus is very thick just now again, their latest game is to root up every melon, pumpkin and cucumber seed you put in and I don't know how to block them. Tried phosphorous paste last night but did not go down to the garden till after breakfast, seeds gone again but crows had taken all the bread so I could not say if the mice had also a feed—found two dead crows this afternoon at all events.

Good luck and good wishes to you both.
Yours Sincerely
C.Ernest.Cowle

5

BUSH ETHNOGRAPHY

Letter 5.1

Illamurta
23rd Nov 1900

My dear Professor,

I have yours of 11th Sep and 21st October to reply to; when last mail left I was down the road over Elections as I surmised I would be. I spent the best part of two days at C.W. and had a good time, John and William Bailes were there bound for Adelaide and old Jelly was in from the Bore,[1] the Bailes did very well out of this last contract and John has not altered much since you saw him, while at C.W. I posted you some seeds of everlasting and some of that other Bush that I am anxious to get the name of and think it would look well cultivated. Who are Knight Bro's of Bendigo? they have been writing to the Mission for Palm seeds.[2]

Old Syme came out of his shell over the Funds for your Expedition, I was very glad to hear, but still, I think the scientists who were so anxious for the work to be done, ought to have contributed some of the Cash.[3] (I noted the objection that results would have had to go to them though.) I suppose Gillen sent you a letter I saw, signed 'Cropless Farmer' which I expect riled him a bit,[4] especially being called a 'Postmaster of a small Town at a big Salary'. Whoever it was that penned this, must have some knowledge of the Pontiff, for he appears certain that he won't be out of Pocket over it and I agree with him in that respect—It is a pity you could not get old George Hablett but old Chance is about as handy a man as you could have dropped across and a good cook[5]—what's more, he will not worry you too much before sunrise which will suit F.J.G. I never knew whether you really objected to my earliness or not, for you always seemed to get up so readily and cheerfully—About spirits—you ought to have accepted the claret for your Friends' sake—take plenty of that 'medicinal brandy' instead of that limited supply, but keep it entirely under <u>your own immediate control</u> (not meant for G.) I am speaking seriously now and travelling day after day, if hot or cold, one or two nips of good liquor has a wonderfully beneficial and tonic effect. I know you consider the daylight 'nip' most reprehensible but it is the one of the day to restore and enliven the nerves dulled with slumber and should be a generous one. I can picture your saying 'Fancy Cowle talking seriously on a subject like this', but honestly, except when in Company or playing the fool, I hardly ever take more than three nobblers in the day. No matter what Kitchener[6] or anyone else says about men being better without it, there are times when it is invaluable as proved in Hospitals and, if you have not got it, God help you, if you supply its place with what you will obtain in most places North in its stead.

Kidman Bros got Tempe Downs Stock and Coulthard has the Country. He has sold the Mt Burrell place to old Hayes.[7] Martin will probably go down soon and take a trip home, he says he will come back and try and get a little place lower down country (am afraid he will fritter away his capital if he does though). I hoped Kidman might not close at the end of his option and that Louie Bloomfield and I might have got the place for, in that case, I could have still remained here but the Kidmans knew too well what a good thing it was.[8] Martin offered me Tempe, with all rations, plant and about 400 horses of one sort and another a few months back, for a little over £<u>800</u>. At this time though, I was thinking seriously of going down country and trying to settle and reward the misplaced affection of some damsel, so declined.[9] Shares were at a good figure and the Money would have been no trouble at all.

Subsequent events (affections transferred elsewhere), robbed me of my only reason for desiring to leave Bush and then Cash was not so plentiful but still tried to get place and found it under offer to Kidman. Have been kicking myself ever since. Suppose Kidman will remove stock now that there has been rain down at C.W. and should get over £1000 for the first 100 head. Tempe has been sacrificed through the regular arrival of budgets of English Magazines and papers and the policy of always 'Going to do' instead of 'Doing'. Do you understand what I mean? Had a most awful storm here on the 3rd, it only lasted about a quarter of an hour but unroofed the hut, ruined the garden, smashed nearly all the big trees and left the place looking as if a bush fire had passed over it, killed 10 kids, stunned others and drowned or killed 20 chicks and 4 hens. The hail was the biggest I have ever seen and bruised the bark of trees as if shot from a gun.

My companion is not coming back and has resigned, he got down below and tried all sorts of ways to get out of going back to the Bush and at last reckoned he could not live with me—(I would not have let him in any case). Have not seen the correspondence but suppose I'll get it next mail. What annoys me though is that new people coming up this way are not informed what sort of a place it is and come from Town believing Illamurta is a village—when they arrive they want to leave at once and this last article, I think, used to do his utmost to get me to report him so that he might get near a Pub again. I wouldn't do that for his Father's sake but told him he must alter or cook for himself—this hut was erected chiefly for me and at my expense and did not cost H.M.G't one penny for iron or anything else so I think I am entitled to the occupation of it.

Re poor old Todd,[10] the loyalty you speak of amongst his officers is very pretty and touching but that is exactly the bane of our Civil Service all over the Colonies. Retirement should be compulsory at a certain age if not earlier and no loophole whatever, such as 'Unless considered beneficial to State to be allowed to remain longer'. This simply means, if popular and influential in most cases, and the States go on paying high salaries to useless figureheads who ought to have saved enough to have comfort to the end of their days, instead of this they are let hang on to their places as long as they can be wheeled to them and their compensation goes on mounting up and up while some poor subordinate is doing all the work at a pittance and the Public, if they inquired, would be told, 'Oh, the head of the Dep't is simply indispensable and we have no one we could promote to his position' and so on.

<u>Churina</u> Am trying to get a 2nd box filled—have about 50 of one sort and another in addition to the list I sent you of the closed case. Expect camels about middle of the month but they are damned independent and won't trouble to take a case or two often, because they say one or two camels loaded delays them so much as if all were and there's something in it.[11] Several of the Stone Churina I got last month are good and also big—'Utnurringhita' Grub, 'Uncharlka' Grub, 'Possum', 'Euro', and Kangaroo, very old in most cases but can't get much information except that 'they bin all day sit down at such and such a place and by and by bin go long a ground there'. One wants to see a big Waterhole or cave or some other feature and to have, just at the moment, the nigger associated with that spot and ask how that tree or rock or so forth got there and then you would get the Tradition—you know how little the others know of the tradition of groups not intermixed with them or closely associated. Four old Pigs came from Owen Spgs with a dozen sticks last night (of course mail time and cost me four hours this morning for no results except one snag).

One Churina represents a <u>boy</u>, one of a lot of boys of the Alcheringa times with <u>no totem</u>. Just a Boy as Uncle Remus would say—the other boys rambled round away to Glory but this one went into the ground near Mt Giles—from where they started, his name is 'Kookitcha' now <u>reincarnated</u> as a <u>lubra</u>, 'Yabbayer', her totem I think is 'Bark' which the boys at this spot played with and threw at one another. Her mother conceived her at this place and the child was a <u>female</u>, what interests me is that the only Alcheringa that went into the ground here was a male and I did not know the <u>sex</u> could be transferred in this manner. I fancied the old people would have got out of the fix in some other way.

Let me know what you think of this and if you have come across similar cases. My best intermediary is away but there is no doubt about the foregoing—when my boy returns from his spell I will try and get this old fellow, the churina and him together and see if I can get anything more but the getting the 3 together will be difficult.[12]

Must shut up—I hope to see you on the road somewhere and discuss matters. Please wish Mrs Spencer and the little ones all good luck and their heart's desire and may they have a Royal time at the New Year in France and yourself the same amongst the <u>poor</u> Blacks.[13]

Yours sincerely
C.E.C.

Letter 5.2

Horseshoe Bend
29th Dec 1900

Dear Professor,

I sent you two cases by Camels on 13th Dec'r, hope they reach you in time to open before starting up. No time to write to you, came here post haste immediately mail got up on account of one man killing another in Sargeant's store by a blow with a rifle—had Xmas dinner under a tree this side of Crown Point en route for P.M. Byrne and self got here last night and Inquest today[14]—no forms or anything but work and heat—details in my next. Am nearly done up. Regards.

C.E.C.

Letter 5.3

Illamurta
17th Feb 1901

My dear Professor,

Yours of scattered dates from 16th to end of January safely to hand and by this time I hope you have got the Cases safely. Martin was under the impression that his one had gone to you in error but his is still at Tempe Downs because the Afghans did not wait for Coulthard to come home, he is a bit disappointed because he wanted to fix it up for the old Country. I wrote you a few hurried lines from Bend advising you of the boxes and giving you news of Pado and self—well after that, I had to go back to look for and bury Comack who was

reported as dead out East of the Govt Well—fortunately he was only
nine miles out and the hot weather had left the body dry so that it
was not such an unpleasant job as I anticipated. Neither crows nor
wild dogs had disturbed the body, after about five weeks' opportunity,
so you may imagine that there is not a great amount of fauna in the
vicinity of yours and Pado's hunting ground at present.

Did I tell you that the man I had here with me put in a very
venomous report about me, to avoid having to go back to the Bush and
wrote and asked me to forgive him for anything he said about me, he
had to resign and I did not see the report till I asked for it[15]—the fool
practically pointed out that I did not want him to cook or do things
not connected with Police for me but to do things for himself and as
he liked and the reality was that I had <u>struck</u> at waiting on and being
a servant practically to such a loafer—all this is mere detail. About the
same time, some [sic] sent an <u>Anonymous</u> Letter to Lord Tennyson
stating that it was commonly reported, on the best authority, that I kept
several aboriginal Native mistresses, to my disgrace and the scandal
and detriment of the young troopers, stationed under me. I had done
this for years to the injury and degradation of all concerned. I had
powerful friends but undoubtedly in the interests of morality I should
be removed to settled Districts and civilizing influences and any of
the young troopers who had been stationed under me could convict
me if they chose.[16] His Excellency had promised to assist the helpless
Natives and this was a chance to redeem that promise—Tennyson, with
the customary gentlemanly instincts of a man ennobled through the
accident of having had a talented father, put this before the Cabinet
and Comm'r of Police and Bradshaw was to hold an enquiry[17]—As he
could not well come out, I went in and saw him and I think he was
satisfied of the malicious falsity of the charges—Personally I would
have much preferred his coming out and seeing things for himself and
making the very fullest enquiries but if people in my position are to
be subjected to such things on the strength of anonymous letters, then
the game is not worth the candle for instead of a charge being proved
against a man as in ordinary justice one has to <u>disprove</u> them and
half truths are always worse to combat than either straight out lies or
whole facts.

Both Pado and I know the Maurice who called on you, he is the
son of the late Price Maurice, one of our wealthiest absentee owners
of Station Property, Maurice is a splendid fellow, a first class bushman

with a fancy for exploring outside spots with a few camels and a blackfellow or two whom he systematically spoils, BUT he is cursed with the demon of Drink and when in its vicinity, seems able to exert no self control and makes a perfect beast of himself—I can quite understand the vinous smell as I have been <u>there</u> when he has been that way.[18]

Your remarks re the Bush bringing out the better qualities are flattering to the out back people—Personally I believe that the bush dweller, I mean the one with a real love for the Bush, get[s] perhaps <u>too</u> self reliant and from a constant habit of doing things for himself a certain irritability, when others are doing these things in his company and either seeming to be sleeping over the job or slumming it. You see there are not many of us with a real love for the Bush and so many of the so called bushmen one comes across nowadays only look to it for its monetary advantages and are wholly praying to get away from it. Pado and myself were talking over Bush life when we last met and in spite of some hard times and experiences in it and often cursing it, we were quite agreed that it would be a regular heart wrench to suddenly sever connection with it.

Well now, we have had the rain at last, and it has put me clean out of all chances of writing for, for the last four days, everything has been dripping like a sieve, for that last storm left a legacy of little holes etc in the iron which does not lay as close as formerly—We had about $2\frac{1}{2}$ inches, Tempe 2.15 and Henbury 1.64 up to yesterday morning, I do hope this has been general all over the Country more especially for the sake of your expedition than anything else. I only stopped two days at Alice Spgs, it was in a most desolate condition and the Police Camp as 'hospitable' as ever—Bradshaw was very nice and produced some whisky—I am sorry to hear his brother died there the day after I left. I think you will be well out of the Commonwealth celebrations—certainly Sydney seems to have done things well but as you say, the wealthy people have had all the cream of the expenses and the bulk of the people got on the Pageant.

Glad to say the Pontiff was in such good form when you saw him, I do not think I can write to him this time but may see you on the road up—I am off tomorrow for the Bend to meet the up mail for I am instructed that Census papers are coming by this intermediate one. Probably Brookes may be going down over the Craig-Wilson case and this may mean that we will be doing the whole district and after that

I reckon on Federal Elections so there is every chance of my happening up with your menagerie.[19] So, with that end in view, will try and arrange to work the lower end myself. All sorts of rumours are current as to how you are coming up—First I heard Raggett was bringing you to Alice Spgs.[20] Then that you were coming p Camels and from A.G. with horses—none of you tell me any details—I will not have time to go through this scrawl so you must take it as it is, I can clear up any of it's failings if we meet which I devoutly trust is coming off.

Kindest regards and best wishes,
Yours very Sincerely
C.E.Cowle

If this reaches you in Melbourne, please remember me to Mrs Spencer, when does she go to England.

Letter 5.4

Illamurta
14th Apl 1901
11 p.m.

My dear Professor,[21]

I rode through from Henbury the night before last so as to get a day to answer my mail in, and on arrival, I found three ancients waiting for me with about a score of good genuine Churina of the Yam and Emu Totems. 'Yam' are always liberally scored and marked. Naturally I cursed some, but devoted all yesterday morning to trying to get the history relating to the sticks—you may recollect our conversation at C.W. on Blackfellows in Alcheringa times apparently existing without any totem proper at the same time as those interchangeable people and G's pooh-poohing the idea, and as these churina now in hand, bear on the subject, I want you to enquire carefully as you go along and see what you can make of it. The Pontiff may drop on something and then will declare he was aware of it all along which is rilesome. I think his idea was that the blacks did not care to tell the totem but that is not so as they would not hesitate to tell me if they knew for one moment—My theory is that perhaps these were exceptionally talented people and were superior to the ordinary double carcased people but their full performances have been lost in the distant ages. Whenever it is <u>Blackfellow</u> only, he seems to have been very powerful and if he had a <u>totem</u> it would not have been forgotten but retained in their memories for the glorification of that Section, don't you think. The reincarnation of the Blackfellow <u>is</u> associated with a totem which he probably obtained through his mother. Also do not forget to enquire re the change of Sex in reincarnation and if you have time, let me know how they account for it. This is all in case I do not happen to see you near Alice Spgs and talk things over quietly when you are both more sober than at C.W. Kindest regards and best wishes to you both as well as to Chance and hoping the eggs were fresh when they reached you.

Yours Sincerely
Rossa [sic]

Be careful and do not spoil my <u>market</u> 'Verb Sap'.
Many more Churina promised me when I am ready.
Wooden—from 15 inches to 3 or 4 ft.
Erlia—Emu

9.1	Choora-tarka	Male	Panunga[22]
9.2	Indoor-innika	Female	Panunga } Sisters
9.3	Kayer-yinyikka	Female	Panunga }
9.4	Toor-pa	Male	Bultharra[23]
9.5	Kurn-koonika	Female	Panunga
9.6	Mye-oong-onya	Male	Apungata R.C.[24]
9.7	Carpulla	Male	Apungata R.C.
9.8	Lay-tcher-inya	Male	Panunga
9.9	Irree-lannana	Male	Panunga
9.10	Lerree-irrika	Male	Papungata R.C.
9.11	Ooltarrika	Male	Apungata R.C.

Emu totem from 'Inmurtoolitcha' near the Hugh Yard. In the Alcheringa, these and many others started from Ooraterra between Temple Bar and the Jay,[25] they had many churina and had some on their heads—They crossed the Jay Creek and got to Turkillara and stopped there and showed their Churina and quabara to the Emu men there and then on to Indooritcha the other side of Hugh Yard and made many more Corroborees—(the above and some others wne [sic] then to Inmurtoolicha), the others went on West to Quarta-tooma and near here there was an old man called Maka-coorna.

A Blackfellow (no totem at all)—this old man heard the noise of the Emu men jabbering and stood up and looked out and saw a big dust—the old man had a stone axe. The old man Maka-coorna called to the Emu men by putting his hand to his mouth and making a noise like an Emu and then he saw the big mob coming up and they all had churina on their heads—when they came close up, the old man tried to round them up and to kill them—'Maka-coorna' had no totem—he lived on 'Inmoota' (the herb in Creeks after rain like Cress) his re-incarnation who was the father of 'Looltcha' who is mother of a lubra here was of the Raritcha Rat totem (probably Bettongia) Looltcha is of the Ice totem. The Emu mob spread out their wings and charged at Maka-coorna who jumped onto a stone and a gumtree marks the spot—As they passed the stone Makacoorna jumped down and killed one of the Emu men with his axe this Emu man was lagging behind—The others ran on and got into a big cave and Makacoorna gathered many bushes and porcupine and closed the opening of the cave and lit the bushes and the porcupine and waited—By and by, after a bit, he opened a hole in the bushes and he saw two of the Emu men dead and he looked further and saw the others running away out of 'Apowara' (Belt Range) Emu centre—He left them and came back to the two smoked Emus and cleaned off their feathers and took off their churina and cleaned out their guts and made a fire and put in the Emu's [sic] and cooked them and while they were cooking he eat [sic] the guts and then he took out the Emu meat and cut it up and smashed up the bones and eat the marrow and when he was gutfull he lay down and went into the ground.

Finis A waterhole marks this spot (and various other things show that the occurrence really took place for do they not remain there as silent witnesses to this day). Informant 'Oolperinya' of the Emu totem assisted by Illpulter alias old man Crow and Lattchea of the Yam totem.

Letter 5.5

Illamurta
12th April 1902

My dear Professor,

I see you have once more returned to civilization and this is only a short letter to congratulate you on getting back alright, the scare headlines about stranded explorers, malarial fever etc made us think you really were having a risky time, I suppose it was a case of 'save us from our friends' or was it a scheme of the Pontiff's to work up some excitement.[26] I never heard of you after you left Tennant's Creek nor did I ever receive any letter from either of you, I wrote once and after that I heard you were likely to be back in Melbourne about the end of the year. You know I went down about the end of October and succeeded in being a bigger crimson idiot than usual, left a legacy of offences of one sort and another behind me, with my golden pieces but had the satisfaction of spending the cheque personally instead of reading week after week of how this or that mine had been badly managed and ore reserves over-estimated etc etc. I only ran over to Melbourne for about three days so I did not see much. Like a fool, I went up to the Museum just for an hour the day I left and had a look at the aboriginal impedimenta, I think they are capitally arranged and that numbering system makes it easy to recognize the individual articles at a glance and see its locality etc in the descriptive part at once.[27] There was absolutely nothing on in Adelaide except Rickards and a circus at the end[28]—Oh, there was a Mayoral reception on the Victoria Park to which I somehow got inveigled and whereat I got hustled and prodded from head to heel and wedged in the centre of a moist, perspiring crowd of female voters or ratepayers—it was their corroboree and someone was providing the Flour and Bacca on the nod and <u>Hell</u>.

I came out of Town limping with awful corns on the sole of my right foot from the effects of my general restlessness and the asphalt, then got orders to wait at Ood'a till next train to take a man called Burke up to Alice Spgs for trial—Finished that job and came here to get fresh horses and off down to Eringa to search for two young fellows. I expect you will have seen in the papers that I found the white boy and all the horses dead in various spots[29]—this was about 60 miles up the Goyder and it is not a nice country biologically or otherwise in a season like the present. I got home nearly three weeks ago and was delighted that I only lost my own special, private horse through some poisonous weed, I spelled three days at the Goyder Well with two sore eyed men for company, innumerable flies, hot weather and the only literature was the 'Confessions of Maria Monk'.[30] If I only had been possessed of some paper I might have written a brilliant essay on 'How to be happy and a Policeman'. It is a bad season again after that glorious rain of twelve months ago, how fortunate you were in striking it—This letter is all about myself but I have got out of touch with you and when you get time you must write and give me a little idea of what you are doing. Please remember me very kindly to Mrs Spencer and with all good wishes to you both, besides the hope that your recent work will benefit you not only in the well earned kudos but also in Shekels.

Believe me,
Yours very sincerely
C.Ernest.Cowle

Letter 5.6

Illamurta
20th Sep 1902

Dear Professor,

Yours of 8th July reached me last mail also letters from Gillen and Chance, the really first authentic news I had had of any of you since I saw you at Alice Spgs. I followed most of your ramblings in the Leader till I went to Adelaide though—of course I can understand how busy you have been since your return, preparing for the lectures which I am pleased to hear were so successful. The money from Gillen's was apparently, after all, devoted to the Aborigines but the price of admission should be higher especially as the interest of the Public is excited with the idea of seeing pictures more or less indecent.[31] You may have noticed various telegrams and reports of the starving condition of Blacks in the Interior, well, certainly it is an awful season for feed and water but I am quite convinced that it is a mistake, this distribution of rations in a regular manner—from what I can see it has the effect of encouraging Natives in to centres where game is very scarce and the natural foods almost entirely absent, they get a pittance of flour and hang on, too lazy to hunt as long as this is a certainty, and spend the day in talking etc whereas if they remained in their own Country in little groups they would be fat[32]— you notice the difference travelling for the condition of many is astonishing even on Tempe where there are no longer any cattle for them to trouble—our insolvent State will find the trouble increase instead of diminishing because more and more will go to centres each year whenever things tighten and it bears out my argument all along, that on the Stations it is <u>not</u> the whites who keep the Blacks at head quarters but the Blacks who will congregate in their vicinity once they have got a taste of various articles.

Tempe Downs is not troubled with Blacks at all now, except by the few Station ones and ex working boys. Coulthard has given them the Station and shifted to a well on the Palmer about 18 miles from here and near the junction of the Walker and that Creek, only employing an old fellow and his lubras to shepherd goats and three young boys, two of whom are from Glen Helen way and his trouble is to keep these others away from this one spot so that they will not go through his goats in his absence with his man or cadge the tucker that he gives to his workers.[33] These sneak in in spite of his precautions and are off again to their soakages where whatever they get to eat, keeps them really in <u>show</u> condition, I could hardly credit the beef they have on them, while the sheep and goats are so poor—here, I have had to kill over 60 lambs last month to try and keep their mothers alive and if it does not rain soon I will be compelled to fry chops in Castor oil or neatsfoot for I have a little of that left. The garden has been excellent all the year but there are various caterpillars beginning to show up and something wrong with the onions which I do not like the look of —

Re Churinga. I understand how those notes you have cover more than you have, but I have told you, in my last letter, that I had a case waiting here which the Afghans would not take in February and I have nearly got another and hope to get them both away in November. I have been here alone since the end of April and hope I am likely to be left so, lately I have been cutting timber with the intention of putting up a place to keep stores in, the Govt has given me 40 sheets of iron as I offered to put up the place free of any cost to them and I am now waiting till I can borrow the Henbury donkeys to drag in the stuff. If I get this wurley up it will be a godsend for with rations, papers, clothes and other rubbish gathered in last 9 or 10 years my shanty is simply crowded. Have done a great deal of travelling this year. In July the Missionaries wrote me that they had secured 11 Blacks for cattle killing on their Station so

I escorted them to Alice Spgs and then to Charlotte Waters where I handed them over to Williams, Pado was looking very well and to my sorrow, he would not join me in whisky even with the seductions of lemons added, I hope he sticks to his resolution—Bennett of Barrow's Creek travelled down with me and we just missed Scott on the road[34] (see Appendix 4). Alice Spgs is getting a queer place now, no less than nine women in it and at time of my visit they were all on friendly terms and 'my dearing' one another. Progressive Euchre Parties, Margerison's soap and cheap perfume pervaded the township and a lawn tennis club is talked of. Bradshaw is <u>not</u> a bad fellow to my fancy. Mrs Brookes was in Adelaide and her husband's ménage was characterized by a total absence of restraint which was charming—Oh, I received a letter from Jim Field and also a watch I presented you with, I could not understand why you returned it until I set it going, <u>then</u> I found out, it's vagaries are rather startling and in the vernacular, it is a <u>b--r</u>. Chance is happy at the Diamantina,[35] I did begin to think, from his silence, that you or Gillen had him planted and were going to use him as a diagram to illustrate tribal markings etc.

<u>25th</u> Mail got here today and Pado says he has just heard poor old Winnecke is dead,[36] the old chap seemed to have gone off a lot when I saw him in Adelaide and presented a frowsy, unkempt appearance, don't know whether business was bad or if it was illness but he was a totally different man to the Winnecke I had known so long. I enjoyed your description of your journey from Borrooloola very much, the Queensland Govt evidently know their duty as regards liquors and no doubt have had experience of other explorers and parliamentary parties.[37] I noted your remarks about Democracy and think you are right, what surprises me is the way people advocate gigantic Schemes as if we had unlimited millions to work on instead of being in a state of practical insolvency—for instance flooding Lake Eyre. Now, has the University come out of the financial troubles? I hope the State came to the rescue although someones neglect was 'criminal'. You must pine for the privacy of Hammerdale but you are close to your work and if Mrs Spencer is satisfied I suppose you will have to be.[38] Are the Un'y Residences any way commodious? I hear of various Churina that are to be got but I am <u>standing off</u> for a while. I have often told you that too many gentlemen escort probably one or two sticks and how each produces either a 50 lb bag or the leg of

a No.7 pair of moles and expects them to have a bloated appearance on his departure, by showing them that I am not keen I will get the articles easier directly if they are worth securing. No more tonight, this is terribly scratchy and disjointed but it is close and muggy and insectivorous round the lamps. Kindest regards to Mrs Spencer and trusting you are having a bit of a rest. With all good wishes for yourself and the Book.[39]

Believe me,
Yours very sincerely
C.E. Cowle

P.S. Isn't it surprising how these German Missionaries breed—they are good neighbours though and we get on excellently now that they have realized that the aborigine has a few failings, it is a pity that they cannot learn that christianizing them is all rot, drop it and confine themselves to feeding them and teaching them handicrafts.

Letter 5.7

Illamurta
25th Nov 1902

My dear Professor,

Only a short letter to acknowledge yours of 23rd ult'o and to wish you the usual compliments customary amongst civilized people at this time of the year. I have cased up and addressed to you all churina etc. on hand and camels should be along in about <u>ten days</u> and take them away, I cannot find the list of the box I packed before I went to Town last year and fancy I posted it to you. List of smaller case is enclosed and I hope to hear of safe arrival soon—Let me know by the return mail, <u>without fail</u>, up to how far I gave you notes at Alice Spgs and what I posted you afterwards. I got the Sugar Ant Stones the other day and they are very old—do you not think that originally all the Churina were Stone and have been gradually replaced with wooden ones as they wore out? I observe you have been pretty busy lecturing but it should come easy now even if monotonous. Gillen wrote me quite a nice letter this time, I am wondering what is up. No rain here although various places round about got more or less, Tempe about 1½ inches (stopped altogether 13 miles West of here), Henbury 60 pts, Idracowra Bend and Charlotte nil, while Eringa Station had over 2 inches. Arltunga 2½ and Alice Spgs Undoolya from an inch upwards—haven't heard what the Missionaries got if any—Been busy most of the month putting up a storeroom with an old chap I gave a job to and am now renovating the other wurley so as to be comfortable but just about when I get things fixed I expect I will be moved. Terribly hot this Summer, don't suppose the Races affected you much unless Mrs Spencer persuaded you to take her to the Cup.[40] Will write you properly soon—curse Xmas mails old man. Once more wishing you and yours many happy and prosperous New Years.

Yours very sincerely
C. Ernest.Cowle

Don't forget to let me know last numbers or letters to notes I gave you at A.G.

Other box has all other Churina of which you have notes and others.

Smaller box
1 Shield
1 Pitchi
 # }
1 } Stone Churina
 # } Blackfellow and Lubra
2 }
 # }   *# Jerboa rat?* [41]
3 } Wooden Churina   *3*
 # } Rat   *# Perameles Obesula?* [42]
4 }   *4*
U.1   *Stone Churina*   *Kangaroo*
J [or could be T] 1.x   *"   "*   *Fire*
E 1.2 and 3   *Stone Churina grassseed*
L. 1.2.3 and 4 X   *Stone Sugar Ant*
1 p'r Kurdaitcha Boots
Various Nosebones
11 Spear Throwers
1 Wooden Churina Snake   *}*
1 ...   *... Lubra } Laurie's Creek no details*

2 Stone	*... Green Snake Mareena Bluff no details*
3 Wooden	*... Boys } West of Gill Range*
1 ...	*... Lubra } No details*
2 Belly Bands–1 Rat tails	
2 wooden and 2 bone Poison sticks with down attached	

Letter 5.8

Illamurta
21st Jan 1903

Dear Professor,

Yours to hand and many thanks for good wishes. We got very patch [sic] rains here between end of Nov'r and middle of December, totalled about 2½ inches just here, and feed came on capitally but it has been murderously hot ever since (till today which is cool and windy) and feed dried up rapidly, a lot of that smoky weather you and I had in Jan 1897. Xmas passed off quietly. Coulthard was here and the old chap that I keep to look after things while I am away, camels arrived a week beforehand with a nice selection of fixings from sisters, liquid and otherwise, my two kegs of wine etc, garden yielded Rockmelons, tomatoes and carrots and the boys got 15 large fat wild ducks. I don't think many blacks fared better than ours on that day for I got old Dave to make them 5 Galls ginger beer and gave them three bottles of raspberry vinegar.[43] We drank everyone's health and cursed the flies and I thought of you and old Gillen more than once. At the New Year I started for Erldunda and on the 1st day I believe I got a sunstroke or was affected by the heat. Got dizzy and seemed to be riding down Hill. Slightly uneven ground, appeared to be all holes and gutters and a few bushes dense scrub, if I used my eyes fully, all objects were duplicated but it was alright if I closed one or lowered my eyelids, as it got towards dusk I could see Desert Oaks, natural size, ahead of me and a miniature reproduction of some trees near me, and at night, two moons, two fires etc. and was very shaky on my feet. I felt rather scared and wondered if I would wake up blind but was better in the morning and after a day's spell at Erldunda, pretty well got over the dizziness and eye trouble but my legs are still anyone else's but my own and frequently when I go to walk, I reel and tack like a drunken man and have difficulty in standing up on my feet—appetite and condition good and I have been living well so I do not think it can be anything else but the Sun. I walked about a mile to look at a Bower Bird's nest this morning (didn't know it was so far) and got very distressed climbing up the little rough range to get to it. I am going for a trip to the Mission at end of the week to see if the shaking up will pass it off and have written to a Doctor in Adelaide for stuff.

Niggers pretty quiet as far as I know and a rare crop of Yellka [sic] is assured[44]—Great rains over Alice Spgs way and Pado tells me that tribes of shark faced individuals are flocking to Arltunga as representatives of little 20/- syndicates. I fancy things are exaggerated for S.A. smokes big for very little fire[45]—these people hardly realize Central Austa till they get two bung eyes and strike the simoon[46] of the Desert in the shape of one of Honest E.H. Sargeant's Price lists at Horseshoe Bend in a duststorm. Am standing out myself p force of lack of cash for one reason and distrust of the damned hole for another. Tarcoola[47] was going to be another Kalgoorlie and Mt Morgan combined until I shot £250 into it and that collapsed it. Blast it (C. French revised). Notice Maurice has been having a good time in Adelaide and his niggers naming articles in the collection he has given the Museum, how does it fit in when they are Musgrave blacks and many of the articles come from Finke and elsewhere? What becomes of Aboriginals when fee simple [sic] of the land, Trans'l Railway, is handed over to Syndicators? Are they to be allowed to run the show under their own laws as at present or do they become absolute property of the Concessionaires as Products Mineral or otherwise? Would like to see the terms relating to them but I rather fancy the concocters of the scheme have overlooked the Aboriginal question altogether and wonder that no stringent provision has been made for their protection, certainly if the line does go through it will eternally damn a great many of them, male and female, with civilization.[48] Will go into balance of those Notes next letter. I am glad you had a holiday even if that tramp did score his Xmas fittings at your expense. No letter from Gillen this time, he wired at Xmas. Good luck and prosperity to you all in the present year is the sincere wish of

Yours very Sincerely
C.E.C

Letter 5.9

Illamurta
17th Feb 1903

Dear Professor,

Notes herewith, I am still damnably shaky, and am afraid it is Loco-motor Ataxia[49] and not Sunstroke that has overtaken me—ought to know by next mail when I get word from Dr Marten.[50] I am doing as little writing as possible so excuse brevity, hope cases reached you safely, I know Camels got to Oodnadatta but I did not hear from Manfield.[51] With all good wishes.

Yours Sincerely
C.Ernest.Cowle

Letter 5.10

Miss Hand's Private Hospital
Hutt St, Adelaide
17th June 1903

Dear Professor,

It was not until I received your letter last week, that I recollected that I had not answered your former one and I must ask you to overlook my carelessness. Well, you will see from the heading of this that I am still here and I cannot say definitely how things are going, for condition is very like Sharemarket and fluctuates in a damned annoying manner, sometimes I fancy I am getting nice and firm in my legs and just about then, I get a set back in the shape of some awful rheumatic twinges which keep me in bed where I get terribly stiff and am debarred by my surroundings from the relief of a good torrent of blasphemy. The City seems to be cursed with a perpetual drizzle and to know absolutely nothing regarding its definite inten-tions. I sometimes feel inclined to get a few gallons of physic and clear back to the old N. West and its dry climate where I feel sure I would recover more rapidly if it is to be and in the other case, peg out, amongst kindred spirits, Pado wants me to go up to him[52] and

Marsh wants me to go to Oodnadatta but I will give the Doctors every opportunity first, I am putting on condition and everyone tells me how well I look and considering that I weigh about 12 stone, it is hard to realize that I am at all queer—latterly my legs have been massaged for about half an hour night and morning and it has had the effect of making me sleep considerably more than before, I almost doze[d] off during the operation, if ever you are troubled with insomnia after all your worries I would advise you to try it.

Latterly I have waded through the 'Living Races of Mankind' by Hutchinson Lydekker and Coy and noted various of your Photos in the Aus'n types[53]—the Illustrations struck me as being good but not representative as they were mostly of good specimens of their race and chosen on that account and the Letterpress was poor and the same in the 'Living Animals of the World'. I thought this latter would be a complete Natural History but found it was only the best known varieties of species that were illustrated.

A week ago, I went to the last day of the Races on the old Course near here and although it was a bleak dreary day, I thoroughly enjoyed the excitement and change. Kelly went with me and we patronized the Derby stand so that I could avoid meeting a lot of Women who would have asked me the same old questions till I was mad.[54] Martin left here about a fortnight ago, having been forced to remain considerably longer on account of nasty cold which gave us all a turn, then he went and stayed at John McKay's and got diarrhoea or something and is at present at S.A. Club, think he goes up to Gillen soon. Heard from Gillen yesterday and from Field a few days back. Jim was in great form as they had had most bountiful rains and there was a good chance of he and Scott, disposing of their Country and Stock[55]—Byrne writes regularly and as you can imagine, is particularly caustic concerning the experts he has seen passing and read the accounts of since the Boom, he meets very few of them personally for his 'aloofness' is superb. Geology Brown[56] has been to see me a couple of times and, of course, when any of these Norwesters are in Town I see a good deal of them. Just now there is Frith from Oodnadatta, Williams, the mail Contractor from Alice Spgs, Elliot from Horseshoe Bend and one or two others, which to a certain extent unsettles me and makes me hanker for the old Mulgahs and Ordivician outliers—am afraid, from the line my successor wrote me en route this time, he will not care for the Bush and I am much afraid my things will go to rack and ruin[57]—the fool does not know what a chance

I have given him and how I willingly would give all I possess to be back there again in his place. People here cannot understand my craving for the Bush again and I am quite convinced that they really think I am not in my proper senses.

I note that Stirling is back and I hope you saw him on the return jaunt, I expect I shall see him before long, would like to have a stroll through his Museum with him—Poor old Winnecke, from what I can learn, was quite queer at the end and his wife had either left him or could not live with him, think she was a nurse and a sort of distant connection of his—How long is Mrs Spencer to be at home in England?, I note you get up to the Black Spur whenever you get a chance, is it a 'buggy' sort of a spot in addition to the giant Ferns,[58] I think I have seen many illustrations of it in Vic'n papers—I must shut up, this is very jerky; as the Lord Mayor of Adelaide gave his annual Ball yesterday thereby bringing much of my relations to the City, I have been frequently interrupted by callers relating their doings and adventures. Kelly and Mrs Kelly asked to be kindly remembered to you and with all good wishes from myself to you and yours.

Believe me,
Yours very Sincerely
C.Ernest.Cowle

Hope when you next write to hear that Proofs are all corrected.

Letter 5.11

Belair
26th May 1920

Dear Professor,

I was so pleased to have your long, interesting letter of 5th just as I planned to write and tell you so I went down to it for six days with a bad attack of pains, have managed to avoid bed at undue seasons for about a week now, and tobacco once more begins to taste less like pollard or some other 'Ersatz'—I read in the 'Bulletin' that you were retiring to England after your 33 years out here, then in the A'sian[59] that you had bought a property out Sassafras? or Healesville way and intended living there.[60] I have been trying to think how long it is since you called here for a few minutes en route to Mrs Gillen's and thence to Dr Stirling's, I know I expected to see you again on one of your trips to England, as it was reported you were coming to South Aus'a for some days en route. I think you are mistaken about <u>Xmas 1895</u>, you spent Xmas 1896 at Alice Spgs, I went in there a few days later and called you to the Charlotte in the early part of <u>1897</u>—we had a belated Xmas dinner [of] a very fine Domestic turkey at Old Crown Point on <u>18th January</u> as p extracts from my diary enclosed.

Your letter brought old memories and regrets flooding over me once more—I had a very bad attack of pains during February, Miss Hughes ascribed it chiefly to <u>worry</u>[61]—The fact was that Thorold Grant[62] wrote to me about some information Fitz (who used to manage 'Undoolya') had given him concerning Bob Coulthard and I finding traces of Gibson (lost by Giles in 1876) out west of Tempe Downs, it was not accurate and like so many of Fitz's stories, it needed cutting in half and censoring, I got turning up old diaries, or rooting round I came across a ration bag I had. I had tossed a lot of letters into when I was leaving Illamurta 17 and 18 years ago and when I fully expected I would be returning there fit and well again in a few months, they were principally letters from yourself and Gillen, with a few from Winnecke, Keartland and others and they <u>just got me down</u>—After all the Bush was my <u>home</u>—I <u>loved</u> it in spite of its hardships and exactions in many respects. I was always happy enough there and after a little spell in civilization I was glad to get back to it.

I have received many kindnesses since my enforced existence among the more civilized of the human race, but I have also observed the petty jealousies, hypocrisy and general artificiality, that it is comprised of in many instances, to a degree that has been a revelation to my simple belief—As for Religion, one has only to live in a narrow little community such as this, and note the constant quarrelling among the 'professing' christians and Church pillars, to be convinced that where there was none of it, the men were no worse as men or fellow beings, and that the beliefs of the Aboriginals which there is so much anxiety to Missionize out of the remainder of them, had their good points and might well be left in peace.

Of course you and I naturally regarded certain actions of the Natives from entirely opposite stand points, but although my methods might be considered harsh, I tried to be absolutely just in my dealings, to take no unfair advantage and to give him the benefit of the doubt if there was a possible one, and I endeavoured to convince him that my word was to be absolutely trusted no matter how inconvenient to myself it might be sometimes, and I do flatter myself that I succeeded to a considerable extent, for they would show me places or things quite satisfied that they were inviolate, except in their own terms, I never exploited them for my personal benefit.

The Administration at the top end, both in the matter of the Natives and generally, does not appear to have been an unqualified success and the breath of suspicion hangs over those recently in authority there and their satellites, were we behind the times in C.A. or just respectful of our opportunities I wonder[63]—you are right in saying I would probably know few of the inhabitants of the old hunting grounds if I revisited them now, fully 150 I met more or less intimately have died, many others left the North and settled elsewhere. I still correspond with those that are left whom I was pally with and whenever they come to Town they invariably come to see me. Coulthard sold Tempe Downs and lives mostly in Adelaide, he often runs up to put in the day, Mrs Gillen was here lately also Dr John or Jack,[64] Field who is now postmaster at Glenelg and enjoying much better health, was here on Sunday—Martin sort of dropped out, he is at present Chief Clerk on the Murray Locks construction work at Blanchetown—Have not seen Mrs Ross for ages, they live down on the plain between here and the City, Ross was over Wells etc in the Centre but gave it up, he has just run up to the Stuart's Range Opal Fields but did not stay long or do anything profitable, Ruby Ross (the little girl in the print you sent me) has children now bigger than she was in 1897 and young Alec who did well at the Wolfram Field,[65] has just discovered that there as [sic] better 'get rich quick' schemes than going into business with Town smarties. Kelly's wife died some three years ago, he is super-annuated now and lives with his daughter in one of the suburbs below us and comes along now and then.[66]

As for my actual self, I bob along somehow thanks to Miss Hughes who has been with me 13 years and is invaluable in every respect, she studies my interests financially etc just as though they were her own—I have not been able to walk now for something over two years, I get into my chair at the foot of my bed with Miss Hughes assistance, and sit in it for an hour in the morning, then back onto the bed, in the afternoon she usually wheels me along the road for an hour—occasionally my friends, the McTaggarts,[67] come along, load me into their motor car and take me for a run, generally to the City where I love to watch the kaleidoscopic scene after the monotony of this Show, I used generally to lose some of the hide off my hips in being embarked or discharged from the motor, but they have now got one with wider doors, I could go out frequently were it not for the dread of bowel complications.

I lost one nephew at the War[68] but the others are alright and my especial friend Fred Downer,[69] one of Elder Smith and Co Directors who went to the London Board while the War was on, returned on Xmas eve, he comes to tea every Friday night and runs up in between, sort of saves me from utter stagnation, this locality is not humorous, it takes its politics, religion and other matters too stolidly and there is little satisfaction in pulling its leg. Do not suppose I will see the Prince,[70] too big a crowd, if I went down in a car everyone would be standing up, I can't, I would be like the pistil of a half opened lily—suppose you are in the thick of it in Melbourne at this moment.

You do not tell me how you fill in your time now that you do not have the grind of lectures, nor the size of your Estate, nor of any particular hobby on it, I hope you soon will and with all good wishes. Believe me never forgetful of friends and their kindnesses to this irresponsible, who has no longer as good a capacity for strong drink as of yore.

Your affect friend
C.Ernest Cowle

1897

Jan 1 Left Alice Spgs at 8.15 am with Nat and . . . [word illegible] 'Ahzecl', 'Avondale' 'Tennant' and 'Strike'—dinner at Running Waters and camped at Boggy Hole—Water very salt 28 miles[71]

2nd and 3rd

4th   Police Camp for dinner—saw Mr and Mrs Kelly and Mrs Chance[72] —after dinner Kelly drove me to A.G. where I saw Professor, Mr and Mrs Gillen, Squires, Jagoe, Medworth, Hablett, Gleeson, Crick[73]—Later on Oliver and Smith with whom I fraternized and got very squiffy. Chance passed at teatime from Bond Spgs and Jack Besley came from Township tight at 8 pm

5   at Telegraph Station all day and 'sorry' saw Grant, my camera pictures framed—

7   Up to Alice Spgs with Camels after dinner paid Gunter £2/14/-
     South £3.13.9 Met Pep who also stayed at Alice Spgs[74]

8   Left at 10.30 a.m., stopped for 10 minutes at Police Camp. Dinner
     at gate and on to near Rat Holes—Camel calf very troublesome

9   M Clure Spgs

10   Red Ochre and to 'Undiarra'—Hazy all day. most peculiar spot on
     Sun at 6 pm Professor photographing and also Sun Spot[75]

11th 12th 13th 14th 15th—

16th Jan photoed Mulgah Scrub—porcupine and Crown Point had
     dinner and a clean up at Afghan Hole—Saw 4 teams at Pigeon
     Well (Hunt, Talbot and Coy) and on to Crown—saw Pado, Field,
     Mrs and Miss Ross. Stokes also Mrs Woolcock of the Cyanide
     Plant 19 miles [by side of paragraph–Tiliqua occipitalis][76]

17th Self Professor and Pado up to Crown Point Stores left for
     Idracowra Woolcock and party for Arltunga—Ross home at tea
     time

18th Ross and Field to Cattle Camp and returned at 4 pm—Self,
     Professor and Pado up to the Crown for Photos etc. Ballingale
     turned up 5 pm _Xmas Spread_ in the evening killed a bullock—
     Teams all left

19th Ross out to Cattle Self Professor and Pado left at 9.40 am—

20th—

21st—

22nd Started out with Byrne and Prof Spencer in buggy for Anderson
     Range but turned back after going 6 miles—Professor was
     unwell very dusty and a few drops of rain and saw Cowan going
     Aringa [sic] way

PART II

THE BYRNE CORRESPONDENCE

Letters from P.M. Byrne to Baldwin Spencer, 1894–1925

6

PADO BYRNE OF CHARLOTTE WATERS

Catherine Byrne (née Hayes) was nineteen when her son, Patrick Michael, was born in Limerick, Ireland, on 2 October 1856.[1] Nobody could have predicted that Patrick (Pado to his 'outback' mates) would spend half a century at Charlotte Waters, a remote Overland Telegraph repeater station on the hot gibber plains, 6 kilometres north of the South Australian border. His life and times were associated with significant events in Australian history, particularly his links with the pioneer anthropologists Spencer and Gillen, the subjects of this correspondence. Near the end of both their lives, Sir Baldwin Spencer, biologist and anthropologist, paid tribute to Byrne: for 'his generosity and long friendship I am deeply indebted for invaluable help in my Zoological work'.[2]

Catherine Byrne was widowed within a few years so, following her husband Michael's death, she migrated to Melbourne some time before 1864. There was a family tradition that her son was aged twelve before he left Ireland, so possibly he was cared for by kin until his mother was able to look after him. The same tradition has Catherine meeting her second husband, John Besley, on a ship. Besley was an Oxford-born Catholic schoolteacher who migrated in 1851, so they could not have met on his migrant vessel. In 1865 Besley left Melbourne employment to take charge of St Rose Catholic School at Kapunda, SA. At the time of their marriage in Adelaide on 30 October 1865, Catherine's place of residence was recorded as Adelaide, so possibly they both chanced to be passengers on a voyage from Melbourne.[3]

John Besley (1832–1916) and Catherine Byrne (1837–1892) had six sons and three daughters, so their children's step-brother, Patrick, was considerably older than his siblings. The family left Kapunda in 1869, when John Besley commenced teaching at Mt Gambier's Catholic school, where he remained for most of his life. Possibly this move provided the opportunity for Patrick Michael to rejoin his mother. It is interesting to reflect that 1869 was also the year when Amelia Maud Besley (1869–1928) was born. In 1891 she was to marry a long-time friend and colleague of her step-brother Patrick Byrne, Frank Gillen, the Alice Springs telegraph stationmaster soon to become Baldwin Spencer's anthropological partner.

The Besley family made their mark in the South Australian postal service. Apart from Patrick, Jack and Dick Besley served on the Overland Telegraph, while three other brothers worked in the Mt Gambier post office. James Field, a first cousin from Mt Gambier, became a prominent Overland Telegraph identity, hosting Spencer and Gillen at Tennant Creek during their 1901 expedition. A minor correspondent of Spencer's, Field made significant ethnographic collections for Victoria's museum. For good measure, John's brother, Bryan C. Besley, served as Inspector of Police at Port Augusta, thereby becoming closely involved in the careers of both Gillen and Ernest Cowle.[4] Byrne's mother had died before he met Spencer, so omission of family news is understandable in their correspondence. He rarely took southern leave, yet this remarkable kinship network must have kept him in contact with his family.

Patrick Michael's educational background is unknown but, as his stepfather was a popular teacher and musician, he may have guided his reading. Byrne's correspondence reveals a man with broad interests who evidently passed much of his isolated life in reading. His letters contain three accurate quotations from poetry, his geological knowledge was impressive (although possibly gained in the field), and he felt challenged to read books on zoology and chemistry. His observations reveal close newspaper reading with an interest in politics. When Spencer and Gillen spent some time with him at Charlotte Waters in 1901, Gillen's diary recorded:[5] 'we finish the day with a discussion on Literature on which Pado talks well and interestingly'.

Although Byrne was renowned for the infrequency of his letters, they were the product of a taciturn, cynical, well-read and literate author.

Top End telegraphist

Pado Byrne was just sixteen years old when he joined the South Australian postal service. His first post was far from home, for he was appointed as a messenger at the Southport Overland Telegraph station, across Darwin harbour, 42 kilometres south of Palmerston (later Darwin). He commenced duty in September 1873, on a weekly wage of one pound.[6] Southport was a raw settlement, a consequence of the Overland Telegraph construction. Only surveyed four years before Byrne's arrival, it was destined soon to become a ghost town, because Darwin became the telegraph terminus and from 1886, the Darwin–Pine Creek railway bypassed it. A century later plentiful broken glass defines both its location and the thirst of its frontiersmen. Pado Byrne's thirst was a topic for discussion in the Centre in later years even among hardened drinkers.

These were rousing times for a youth. A gold rush funnelled through Southport in 1872, when optimistic miners combed the region to Pine Creek, though most soon dispersed, disillusioned. Upon the year of his arrival, the non-indigenous population of the entire Northern Territory was said to be 961,[7] so although Southport was the gateway to the swampy goldfields track, its residents were few.

The official record of Byrne's postal career is unduly sketchy, although his later years may be supplemented from the South Australian Blue Book, when individual appointments were listed and included in parliamentary papers. His promotion to operator (telegraphist) dated from 1 April 1875, at an annual salary of £100. By this date he must have transferred to the Darwin telegraph terminal, where he remained until July 1877. For three months he then left the service for reasons unstated. Thereafter he was stationed in Central Australia, presumably always at Charlotte Waters.

His correspondence refers often to mining prospects or shares, together with a grasp of geological field evidence, even to stating his intention to go prospecting to Western Australia or other central regions. Life in Southport must have proved influential in encouraging this interest, so it is possible that his departure from the service in

1877 allowed him a foray around the Pine Creek goldfields in search of a quick fortune. Relevantly, his absence from 4 July to 15 October coincided with the Dry season.[8]

Byrne's life and times in Darwin may be glimpsed through fragments reported in the infant *Northern Territory Times*. That paper busily recorded court cases involving Byrne on at least four occasions between 1875 and 1877. His appearances, mainly as a witness, hint at social life and race relations on this minor imperial frontier.

The first incident occurred when Byrne and a mate were playing billiards and they witnessed a brawl close by, presumably involving grog.[9] He was directly involved in the next incident, when he and others were running along a track at night to escape a December thunderstorm. They were opposite an Aboriginal camp when a spear was hurled by Corimbelee, a Larrakia man. The spear passed through Byrne's shirt sleeve and grazed his stomach. While still running, he broke off the shaft and shouted a warning: 'look out, spears and niggers'. Corimbelee was charged but because of the darkness the offender could not be positively identified, so the case was dismissed.[10] It provides a rewarding indication that justice sometimes was administered in the white man's court.

The next vignette was provided at an 1876 race meeting. When two persons obstructed the track as horses were about to race, mounted trooper W. Stretton ordered them off, his action provoking remarks 'more expressive than polite'. As a consequence, 'P.M. Byrne [was] charged with unlawfully disturbing P.T. Stretton in the execution of his duty'. Byrne had been knocked by Stretton's horse, so he grasped the bridle until Stretton struck him, allegedly with the back of his hand. Confronted by claims and counter claims, the magistrate dismissed the case. To have been on the track and argumentative, however, Byrne must have been intoxicated.[11]

Four months later, Byrne was back in court as a witness in an embezzlement case. He had purchased some goods from a salesman for £2–14–6, but evidently the latter pocketed the money rather than putting it in his employer's till. Perhaps the magistrate was concerned over the veracity of Byrne's evidence, because this case also was dismissed.[12] Whatever the merits of Byrne as a witness, or the extent of his imbibing, he proved a model citizen at Charlotte Waters, where he served as resident Justice of the Peace.

After Byrne resumed telegraphic duties from October 1877, his record sheet vaguely lists him as a telegraphist 'on the Port Darwin Line', at a commencing salary of £120 p.a., rising to £160 by 1883, when he again resigned. It must have been a brief break because his employment entry continues without explanation. Mineral prospecting pervaded the era and the 1880s were a period of optimistic prospecting activities in central Australia, soon resulting in gold discoveries at Arltunga and 'rubies' (garnets) in the Eastern MacDonnell Ranges. Other possible incentives further north were the discovery of tin in 1881 and copper in 1884, so Byrne may have briefly sought a fortune from the rocks.[13]

It is probable that Byrne remained permanently at Charlotte Waters until 1908, where he was the stationmaster from at least the mid-1890s, and possibly following Gillen's departure from there to Alice Springs in 1889. As explained later, changing circumstances rendered Byrne too senior for this diminished station, so he was transferred down the track in 1909 to Hergott Springs (Marree). One year there proved enough. He resigned and returned to Charlotte Waters under other employment capacities until about 1930.

Charlotte Waters telegraph station

All Byrne's surviving correspondence reproduced here was written at Charlotte Waters, so it is appropriate to set that remote place into historical and geographical context. A chain of freshwater lagoons was discovered in January 1871 during surveys for the route of the Overland Telegraph. This was Duffield Creek, an ephemeral tributary of the Finke River some 15 kilometres to the east. The location was given the unlikely name of Charlotte Waters in honour of Lady Charlotte Bacon, whose son was a storekeeper on that sector of the Line. Thus were Indigenous names abandoned for such mundane reasons along the Line. Lady Charlotte's memory was more frequently honoured, however, by dry watercourses than by waters.

According to Gillen's rendering, the Southern Arrernte name was Alknulurilirra, but Luise Hercus was informed by Edie Strangways and Mick McLean, both born around the 1890s, that the name of the 'proper Charlotte Waters waterhole' was Adnyultultera. More reliable holes in nearby tree-lined Coglin Creek and around its junction with the Finke were known to Aborigines as Abmakilya and Akiltya, also called McKenzie's Waterhole, where there was a stockyard. These were important places where people congregated. The nearby plains were known to people as Anhemara Ilkurkanha ('feeding about, the grubs cleared the plain'). This area was an Emu Ritual Centre.[14]

These water supplies were strategically placed for the location of a repeater station, before the long dry haul north. The function of the station was to amplify weak signals and transmit them automatically at full strength along the single galvanised iron wire to the next station in either direction. It was 271 kilometres (168 miles) from The Peake repeater station to the south and 373 kilometres (232 miles) further to Alice Springs. By the 1890s the railhead was at Oodnadatta, 216 kilometres (135 miles) south. An 1874 proclamation reserved an area of 25 square miles around the station. A bore was sunk later about 2 kilometres north of the station adjacent to the track.

By 1872, a complex of buildings was constructed using white sandstone rubble obtained 12 kilometres distant and timber sawn and milled at a waterhole on the Finke. An impressive establishment resulted. When F.J. Gillen and Byrne were both resident there during the 1880s, there was an eight-room stone dwelling with a galvanised iron roof, a 9000 gallon stone and cement tank in the courtyard (designed to withstand a never-eventuating Aboriginal attack), another 25 000 gallon stone tank, a cartshed and blacksmith shop, harness room and stockyard. An 1883 inventory listed 528 sheep, 100 cattle, 150 goats, thirty-two horses and two camels (then escaped), whose food supply must have denuded the already fragile environment. The goat population numbered about 400 in 1901. Add to this the impact upon the environment of innumerable Afghan Camel trains and the passing stock which watered at the bore, so that environmental changes were rapid. Then in 1895, Byrne (L7.6) reported the arrival of rabbits in the region.[15]

Photographic images of Charlotte Waters station may exaggerate its appearance of size and solidity, because the buildings rose starkly on a flat, barren landscape, ensuring that they were visible like a shimmering mirage from great distances. This treeless plain was hardly an attractive place for a European to call home, despite its appeal to the original inhabitants. Baldwin Spencer[16] remarked on the surrounding 'great open, stony plain without a sign of human habitation', and the pervading 'feeling of desolation'. Gillen, who served there for twelve years, revisited it during 1901 and reflected that:[17]

> Some early resident named Charlotte Waters Station 'Bleak House' and he named it well; looking south . . . I know no drearier aspect . . . looking out on the surroundings . . . with its total absence of any sort of attractive scenery without or social life within I marvel how I could have spent 12 years here happily.

William Littlejohn, based there as a policeman in the early 1930s, remembered the sheer discomfort during the hot weather.[18]

> It was impossible to sleep inside . . . in the summer . . . we used to put our beds outside . . . about 100 yards away. The closer you got to that building the hotter it got.

Doris Bradshaw arrived at Charlotte Waters with her parents in 1899, *en route* to Alice Springs where her father succeeded Gillen as stationmaster.[19] This eight-year-old girl recalled that 'it seemed to me that we had arrived at the end of the world. The aspect was truly dismaying'. When night fell, their host Patrick Byrne, announced that he was moving 'farther out' to sleep. Perhaps it was the heat, or that he charitably made room for the travellers inside. As Doris remembered the occasion, his blunt explanation echoed down the years: 'The place is becoming overrun by women.'

Throughout his correspondence, Byrne refers frequently to Aboriginal people and provides their names for animal species. It is obvious that although Spencer credited Byrne with collecting varied faunal specimens, it was the Aboriginal people—particularly females—who brought them to him. It is equally evident that Byrne maintained good relations with them and that he was less contemptuous of their society than was Ernest Cowle. There are two possible explanations for this relationship.

Years before Gillen's association with Spencer from 1894, he became interested in Aboriginal society. He was in charge of Charlotte Waters when he was contacted by the Victorian squatter, E.M. Curr, whose compendious *The Australian Race* was published in 1886. Gillen supplied Curr with a vocabulary of about 130 words from the local Southern Arrernte language.[20] Gillen also was a Justice of the Peace, a position to which Byrne succeeded,[21] so it is possible that Gillen's sympathetic attitude to Aborigines influenced his future step-brother-in-law.

Another factor motivating Byrne's relationship with Indigenous people is more materialistic, in that he controlled the system of rationing (rewards or punishments) at the station. Possibly it was due to Gillen's pressure that in 1885 the South Australian Aboriginal Protector established a government ration depot there.[22] The main Aboriginal camp was at Illunga (or Akiltya), Finke Well, on the Finke River over 15 kilometres to the northeast, but as rations were stored at the station, Byrne was well placed to provide incentives for those who brought ethnographic items or animal specimens in exchange for rations. In addition, Baldwin Spencer was unusually generous with his own financial contributions for distributions of rewards in kind, which passed through Byrne's hands.

By the time Spencer arrived at Charlotte Waters in 1894 as a member of the Horn Expedition, it was a busy place. In addition to the two staff telegraphists, two maintenance linemen were based there, together with a labourer, a cook and three Aborigines employed to maintain the plant and stock.[23] Unfortunately the South Australian Blue Book, an annual parliamentary paper, was compiled erratically, so that details of individual postings, dates of final employment and other data sometimes were omitted, or in other years entries were contradictory. Byrne's name is absent during the years 1889–95, even though he was stationed there. He appears in most lists until 1901. Gillen wrote to Spencer during 1897,[24] adding 'did I tell you . . . that Byrne had recd substantial promotion?'. This must refer to his appointment from 1 July 1896 on a salary of £180, plus 'quarters, rations etc. and 25 percent allowance on salary'.[25]

From at least 1895, both Byrne and B.J. Giles, the telegraph operator, held a second official post, that of Customs Officer, for which each received £12 annually. Although they collected duties on goods travelling north, their main function was to inspect stock travelling south for cattle tick (*Boophilus microplus*), responsible for tick-fever ('redwater disease'). As quarantine restrictions were lifted in 1900, and interstate customs duties abolished at Federation, their posts became redundant. In the year following the end of quarantine, 7200 cattle passed southwards through Charlotte Waters.[26]

Once the Commonwealth Postmaster-General became responsible for the postal service, Byrne's name annually appeared in the *Government Gazette*, between the first published staff list in 1903 and 1908. Evidence for one daily chore at Charlotte Waters has been preserved. Staff methodically entered meteorological observations in specially supplied books: those surviving cover the years 1900–7.[27] Whether they were put to practical use is not known, but they give purpose to the rain gauge and related meteorological equipment which stands prominently in Spencer's photographs of the bare landscape.

Because of the diminishing role of Charlotte Waters station, Byrne's seniority evidently became a problem. Leaving the telegraphist, H.O. Kearnan, in charge, Byrne was transferred on 1 January 1909 to Hergott Springs (now Marree). From 1886, the Strangways Springs repeater station closed, and one at Hergott Springs was substituted.[28] Although this transfer meant no demotion and Overland Telegraph work remained similar, it evidently did not satisfy Byrne. Although the relevant official record was not found, he must have resigned at the end of the year. Whether he diverted for a prospecting foray to Western Australia or the area west of Uluru later made famous by Lasseter is impossible to say. His letters refer to the golden prospects out there for those able to read the geological signs.

Bore caretaker

Whatever the possibilities, Byrne must have returned to Charlotte Waters, because the records locate him there as a Justice of the Peace between 1910 and 1919. What other role he played there cannot be determined before 1914, from which time he was employed at the bore as 'caretaker and pumper'. As this bore was soon to determine his future, it is relevant to describe it.

Apart from rainwater collected from the roof and stored in a large concrete underground tank, there were four sources of water. In this region they fluctuated; water was abundant at times in Coglin Creek or the Finke River, but at times these were dry. A well had been sunk on the Finke at what was an important Aboriginal living area, Illunga. By 1914 Finke Well was near collapse, so it was re-timbered.[29] The crucial water supply was the artesian bore, about 2 kilometres north of the station, alongside the Alice Springs track. It had been sunk by John Bailes, the ubiquitous bore contractor across the Centre, and fed two 10 000 gallon tanks. Frank Gillen was sufficiently interested in 1901 to record some details of the bore. It was sunk in 1898 to a depth of 1474 feet, the water rising to within 160 feet of the surface, from which it was pumped for watering stock. Its temperature was 80°F, so it was considerably cooler than the ambient summer temperatures.[30]

The latter was one of the few virtues of this 'very hard' water. When analysed in 1920 it received a lukewarm report:[31] 'not suitable for drinking purposes, but would probably be palatable to stock. It is quite unsuitable without treatment for use in steam boilers or for domestic purposes.'

While operating the massive pumping machinery on 25 May 1915, Byrne received a serious injury when his sleeve caught in the cogs. His right hand was severed, requiring later amputation between his wrist and elbow. Writing in a new spidery left-handed script, he sought compensation from the government. He laconically described his traumatic experiences before the Commonwealth medical officer treated his injury:[32]

> As the journey from Charlotte Waters to Oodnadatta occupied nearly four days, the arm was in rather a bad condition on arrival, and is healing slowly—It will probably be some weeks before the wound has closed.
>
> I respectfully ask if I am entitled to compensation, and if so, will you please accept this as an application for such.

Just how serious his accident was, and its impact upon the tiny Oodnadatta hospital, was recounted by the hospital sister:[33]

> As we have only one ward and that was occupied by a lady and her baby, I was obliged to turn my sitting room into a ward and operating room. Doctor Abbott amputated the arm below the elbow. As the accident happened four days before the arm was in a shocking condition . . .

On 27 August, by which time resilient Pado's wound had healed, Byrne again wrote to the department resigning as bore caretaker because it proved impossible even for this hardy individual to operate the machinery one-handed. The cautious department sought opinions concerning his condition, to which Oodnadatta's postmaster responded that Byrne 'had an exceedingly bad time'. The department relented, on 29 September offering him £100 in compensation. Upon his agreement that no further claims would be lodged, they paid him a month later. That sum only equalled the doctor's fee for treating Byrne, a bill paid grudgingly despite a file comment that it was 'a try on' by the doctor.[34]

Storekeeper

Aged almost sixty years, Byrne was undaunted by his misfortune and had no intention of leaving Charlotte Waters. In December 1915, the Northern Territory Administrator agreed to the lease of five acres of the Telegraph reserve to 'Mr P.M. Byrne (formerly an officer of this Department) for the purpose of establishing a storekeeping business' for a yearly rental of ten shillings per acre.[35]

Byrne persisted with his business for at least twelve years. A visitor in 1918 praised his 'determination' in running his 'small store'.[36] The Northern Territory electoral roll for the Alice Springs subdivision listed him as 'storekeeper' in the rolls for 1922 and 1928, but his name was absent from the 1930 roll.

By the end of the 1920s Charlotte Waters was sinking into obscurity, so his trade must have become minimal. Technological progress resulted in the closure of the repeater station in 1930, the place reverting to a non-official post office maintained by the wife of a now-resident policeman. Even more significant, however, was the extension of the railway to Alice Springs from Oodnadatta between 1927 and 1929. The line ran some 15 kilometres west of Charlotte Waters, so pastoralists now left or collected their mailbags at the new Finke Siding further north. Stock and goods were transported by train. Motor transport was also burgeoning, spelling the end of the era of Afghan camel trains. Consequently, pastoralists, drovers and travellers mostly avoided the long dry route to Charlotte Waters, so the bore water facilities and Byrne's store lost their importance.[37] Sacrificed to progress was Byrne's attachment to that place, symbolising a change in lifeways from the harsh conditions of the first generation of European frontiersmen. Lifestyles for most country travellers were improving; only those of the Indigenous inhabitants worsened.

Changes also affected policing in the region. Since 1893, no police had been based at Charlotte Waters. Now, the Alice Well police station was closed. Instead of building a station at Finke, on the railway route, the government saved money—if not police convenience—by transferring police to the telegraph complex. Common sense prevailed in 1938, when a police station was established at Finke and the telegraph station was abandoned. If Byrne had not left by September 1930, he may have soon departed once constable Littlejohn and his wife took up residence.[38]

Pado Byrne vanished, but he did not travel far. Apparently he moved south to Oodnadatta where, on 31 January 1932, he died from 'heat apoplexy'.[39] Indeed, the day was extremely hot. By chance, Skipper Partridge, a conscientious member of the Australian Inland Mission, drove into Oodnadatta that night. He experienced a deserted township:[40]

> the entire population . . . was at the dam for that day the temperature had reached 53°C. One old man, Pat Byrne, had died, and the men of the town had had great difficulty digging his grave in the iron hard and burning hot ground.

The correspondent

Of the twenty-nine surviving letters written by Byrne to Spencer, all but two belong to the period 1894–99. These two date from 1921 and 1925, so it must be presumed that some are lost, particularly as they corresponded concerning the visit by Spencer and Gillen on their 1901 expedition. When at Charlotte Waters they were joined by two local Southern Arrernte men, Erlikilyika and Purunda. Although this arrangement required correspondence, like much other business, it was arranged via telegraphic messages. Readers must form their own impression of Byrne's character, but what follows are some insights by his contemporaries.

That Byrne was self-reliant and capable of enduring severe discomfort in difficult living conditions, heat and physical pain is evident. When Skipper Partridge met him during 1918,[41] he was intrigued to observe Byrne's 'determination to stay in this remote place even though he was well educated and widely travelled'. While the former is proven by Byrne's letters, the extent of his travels may reflect the ability of bushmen to spin yarns to city visitors. Unless he travelled more than can be established, his adult experience was limited to the environs of the Overland Telegraph.

The critical depth of Byrne's geological reading and fieldwork is impressive, while he appreciated his newfound enthusiasm for zoological collecting, and avidly read what Spencer supplied. Probably resulting from his mineralogical interests, when Gillen visited him in 1898,[42] he was 'now studying chemistry'. His knowledge of literature and international affairs was extensive. A political conservative and a republican, he shocked the left-inclined Gillen by voting for Josiah Symon, Cowle's brother-in-law, in the first federal election.[43] His opinions were strongly anti-British and frankly expressed and yet his leanings and prejudices made him closer to Spencer in politics than was Gillen. The latter painted a colourful pen-picture of his friend while he and Spencer enjoyed his hospitality:[44]

> Talked all day Old Pado's pessimism more pronounced than ever. His tirades against the British and their incompetence in the conduct of the Boer War transcend anything I have ever heard . . . the whole British Pharmacopea would not unload Pado's liver of its . . . bile but nevertheless it is a great delight for us to be with him.

Other visitors also appreciated his hospitality and willingness to assist them. Spencer clearly was a major beneficiary. So was Winnecke. During the Horn Expedition, when members stayed at Charlotte Waters, Byrne lent Winnecke his own camel when they were in short supply. Winnecke subsequently acknowledged 'my indebtedness to Mr Byrne for frequent favors'.[45] The German scientist and ethnographer Erhard Eylmann lodged at Charlotte Waters more than once during the late 1890s, and expressed gratitude for Byrne's 'hospitality' while he studied the Aborigines.[46] When the missionary R.B. Plowman called at Charlotte Waters in 1916,[47] he sought Byrne's advice: 'Had long talk with Mr Byrne at his store before going on to Crown Point.' Ernest Cowle, ill in Adelaide but before the full extent of his physical disabilities was known, reported that 'Pado wants me to go up to him' to recuperate.[48]

Pado Byrne, with his fixed opinions and cynical attitudes, may not always have proved easy company. 'He's an awfully touchy beggar', Gillen wrote.[49] In another contact, he noted 'Pado . . . firing volleys of pessimistic criticism on men and things generally'. Cowle cautioned Spencer not to complain if parcels arrived via Charlotte Waters in a poor condition, because as customs officer Byrne let overweight packages pass.[50] 'P.M.B. is a trifle "difficile" and if he gets worried with enquiries from the authorities, may get snaky'. It was standard practice to criticise Byrne, also, for his infrequent letter writing, Spencer was fortunate to receive as many confidences as he did, Gillen concluded. 'Byrne was always an erratic correspondent', Gillen assured Spencer,[51] 'he rarely writes to any of his relatives and sometimes my Wife writes him half a dozen letters before she receives a reply'.

Like so many lonely, isolated men of his time, Byrne drank heavily; evidently his southern vacations resulted in a 'spree'.[52] 'Is it not a pity that he cannot drink in moderation', Jim Field observed to Spencer.[53] Yet a few months later Byrne attempted to reform, though Cowle evidently doubted his success. 'Pado was looking very well', Cowle reported in typically sarcastic vein,[54] 'and to my sorrow, he would not join me in whisky even with the seduction of lemons added, I hope he sticks to his resolution'. Two of Gillen's daughters remembered Byrne when interviewed in 1971. They commented upon his excessive resort to alcohol, but emphasised that he was 'highly respected' despite his addiction.[55] Devout Catholics, the sisters made no reference to the religious status of their step-uncle. They must have known, however, that he favoured atheism, as his letters reveal. Born into a Catholic Irish milieu, with a mother and stepfather who were pillars of the Mt Gambier church, Pado passed his life far from the ministrations of the clergy, accepting the tenets of evolutionary science.

It is in his relationship with Aboriginal people that Byrne merits honour. The Overland Telegraph Line suddenly spanned the world of Indigenous Australians, rapidly facilitating its colonisation by Europeans. Pado Byrne belonged to that first generation, but as a public servant rather than a land taker, or their agent the police. It is worth noting that his letters refer frequently to Aboriginal people, but without the harshness or contempt which characterised Cowle. As the custodian of the ration store, of course, he could influence them more subtly than gun-toting pastoralists or policemen. Modern revisionists may cite him as an agent of colonial supremacy, but that is to ignore the context of his activities. His final letter to Spencer in 1925 summarised concepts which remain central problems today in race relations and indicate his understanding. Byrne's correspondence reveals considerable and friendly interaction with the Southern Arrernte; at one stage 150 people were claimed to be on the lookout for zoological specimens. It also included his rendering of Aboriginal words, including the names of sixteen animal species. This suggests some interest in the vocabulary, possibly a flow-on from Gillen's work for Curr around 1880.

Nowhere did Byrne claim that he personally collected any of the stream of preserved zoological specimens laboriously sent to Melbourne, although Spencer so credited him. While he failed to identify his collectors, he made it clear that Aborigines were his agents. His emphasis upon the importance of women in the search is exceptional for this male-dominated era, particularly if his attitude to women was really that attributed to him by Doris Bradshaw.

Dick Kimber is familiar with the Charlotte Waters area and he has talked to old people about their memories of the telegraph station times. Although they did not know Byrne well personally, they recalled him as the one-armed man, and 'chuckled' over their memories. 'I think they remembered him with a kind of fond regard', Kimber wrote,[56] 'simply because he had been for so long at the Charlotte, and at times must obviously had the responsibility of giving out rations, and otherwise being involved in the well-being of the people'. That Pado was remembered half a century after his death by Indigenous people contrasts with his impression on white Australians, for he is buried in an unmarked grave at Oodnadatta, long forgotten.

Byrne should be credited with initiating a proposal which has contemporary relevance when reconciliation is sought between Indigenous and other Australians. When Spencer and Gillen were far advanced in their preparations for their 1901–2 cross-continental expedition, Byrne telegraphed Gillen at Moonta.[57] He recommended that they take 'a first class black boy who will go right through with us'. They left Charlotte Waters, therefore, with two Southern Arrernte men. Following current colonial ways, they referred to them as 'boys'. Byrne's 'first class boy' was born around 1865. Europeans know him as Jim Kite, or Kyte, but his real name was a variant of Erlikilyika. The other man was Purunda or Parunda (Warwick).

On the expedition they both proved invaluable, as a reading of *Gillen's Diary* establishes. They rounded up the horses, drove the wagon team, provided game, and reliably travelled long distances to collect or deliver mail at repeater stations. Parunda specialised in constructing bough shelters. More importantly, Erlikilyika spoke both Arrernte and Kaytej languages, so he proved his worth as they pushed northwards beyond the range of Gillen's linguistic comprehension. Gillen nicknamed him 'The Subdued', a term suggesting his quiet manner and reliability. He also may rate as the first anthropologist of his own people. Spencer praised his assistance in recording oral traditions during their long stay at Barrow Creek.

'Though he could not write a word, he always had a paper and pencil . . . on which he made marks', Spencer remarked approvingly. The marks noted the sequence of stories and places recounted by the informant, which he evidently used when he repeated the stories to Spencer to assist his note taking. He also was sensitive to sacred activities conducted by informants, absenting himself on at least one occasion. Parunda startled the camp one night when he used his revolver to drive away an assumed predatory 'kurdaitcha', an Aboriginal executioner.

Both men accompanied the party until they reached Borroloola, well over 1500 kilometres from home. While Spencer and Gillen were marooned there for weeks awaiting a boat, their assistants set out on their return journey after two weeks in this unfamiliar and disturbing tidal river landscape. Tinned foods had been secreted for them in hollow trees between Borroloola and the Overland Telegraph and, each armed with a revolver, they departed on horseback, with a packhorse. They safely negotiated the route and four months later returned their mounts and impedimenta to Byrne. 'Their only remuneration', a grateful Spencer acknowledged, 'consisted of clothing, abundant food and tobacco'. Their saga deserves greater praise than Spencer's who, in his final book, even confused their identities. The episode surely established that a mutual trust existed between Byrne and the men he sent with his anthropological friends.[58]

On their expedition, Erlikilyika drew a number of sketches which are reproduced in *Gillen's Journal*. Following his return, if not before, he developed a facility for carving small figures and tobacco pipes from gypsum, obtainable some 3 kilometres west of the station. Some of his sculpted figures are held by the South Australian Museum.

By a curious chance, an Australian visitor to London in 1920 was observed smoking one of these pipes. A porcelain manufacturer expressed interest in utilising this kaolin-like substance. As a result, the Home and Territories Department soon requested samples from Charlotte Waters. A parcel arrived in Melbourne of 'Kao-lin' white stone 'as used for carving by Aboriginal Kyte'. A surveyor was then sent to investigate the deposit. In his report he noted that in the telegraph station was 'a vase 1 foot in height and 6 inches across the top, artistically carved by Aboriginal Jim Kyte from one piece of kaolin'. Regrettably for commerce, however, laboratory analysis concluded that the source had 'no value as a pottery material'. Yet this 'first class boy', Erlikilyika, whose products burgeoned during Byrne's residence, may have owed much to Byrne's encouragement.[59]

The cultural heritage of a place destroyed

In 1945, during that lack-lustre period before the terms 'heritage' or 'conservation' entered the jargon of Australian cultural value systems, the Commonwealth postal service sold the deserted buildings at Charlotte Waters to the even more remote Andado Station. The roofing iron and timbers were then removed and the unprotected walls left to nature's assault. They had virtually collapsed by 1947, when the stone rubble was taken to construct New Crown Station. Sadly, the site became an archaeological relic, with most surviving traces being sub-surface. Even so, the place is deeply significant for National Estate and Northern Territory registration and protection. The issue was expressed succinctly by David Carment,[60] that the ruins 'are of significance for much the same reasons as the more substantial evidence of the other surviving [telegraph] stations'.

Despite its desolation, this place has great potential for archaeological investigation associated with the sites around Finke Well area and along Coglin Creek, where Aboriginal people concentrated, and the bore, where travelling stockmen and Afghan camel teams must have camped. It is to be hoped that no further unsupervised disturbance is permitted within this complex.

The station's association with events and people of national historical and cultural importance should be recognised, not least for its association with P.M. Byrne. In the first place, it was a major repeater station on the Overland Telegraph Line for sixty years. Only the stations at Alice Springs and Barrow Creek also contained eight rooms.[61] It played a crucial role in the transport and communications system with central Australia throughout that period. Afghan camel trains came this way, and from here in August 1872 Ernest Giles set out on his expedition to Lake Amadeus.

Its great cultural importance, however, is its link with Byrne, Spencer and Gillen. F.J. Gillen spent twelve years there, and his first anthropological research, the vocabulary in Curr's *The Australian Race*, resulted from his residence there. Then the Horn Exploring Expedition arrived at Charlotte Waters, which served as a temporary base.

It was an association of considerable scientific importance, which involved Byrne in significant fauna collecting. During this expedition, Baldwin Spencer met Gillen, then at Alice Springs. The series of books which followed their anthropological collaboration rate among the most influential books in the history of ideas written by Australians. Through their work, the Arrernte people became (misleadingly) the 'type' of 'desert' hunter-gatherer society, prominent in the works of such social theorists as Durkheim, Freud and James Frazer.

P.M. Byrne was the first inland informant and collector for Baldwin Spencer's future work. It is not recognised that Byrne's Kurdaitcha paper, rewritten and published under Byrne's name by Spencer in 1895, was actually the first publication in the series of anthropological works by Spencer and Gillen which followed.

In the history of ethnographic fieldwork, Charlotte Waters is a landmark in the use of new technology. It was here during late March and early April 1901 that Spencer and Gillen took movie film of Aboriginal activities, including ceremonial dances, and recorded sound on bulky wax cylinders. Their film and cylinders were then sent south from Charlotte Waters.[62]

Byrne is significant also as Spencer's major supplier of faunal specimens. A gecko (*Diplodactylus byrnei*) and a dasyurid marsupial (*Dasyuroides byrnei*) testify to Spencer's gratitude for Byrne's collaboration. John Calaby summarised Byrne's role as follows:[63]

> He collected the specimens that provided most of the new records and new species of mammals and reptiles; and his correspondence with Spencer and wide reading gave him the grasp of zoology and evolution.

Future Aboriginal Australians, however, may respect Charlotte Waters as the territory of two Indigenous men who accompanied Spencer and Gillen across Australia. That they returned in good order testified to their reliability and initiative, characteristics too often denied by critical white Australians. Both Spencer and Gillen remarked upon Erlikilyika's ability to record material from informants.[64] He also won fame as one of the first Aboriginal artists to adapt his art to European taste and utility. So the endeavours of Byrne and the Aboriginal associates of Spencer and Gillen render the remote ruins at Charlotte Waters a place which all Australians should respect. They were associated with events which have been under-rated, but which bulk large in Australian cultural and scientific history.

Byrne's mates, Frank Gillen and Ernest Cowle, merit the concluding reflections, when they separately wrote to Spencer conveying a sense of their sincere friendship with Pado.

In 1897, Gillen reassured Spencer:[65] 'I don't think there is any man living whose friendship he values as highly as he does yours. He feels and knows that you understand him.'

'I am awfully glad that you got to know Pat Byrne thoroughly', Cowle told Spencer,[66] '. . . don't you think he bears out my statement that he was the only man on the line who really was informed on most subjects and a good fellow besides'.

7

CORRESPONDENCE 1894–95

Letter 7.1

Charlotte Waters
10th Sept'r 1894[1]

Dear Sir,

Since the receipt of your letter, I have been collecting information about the Urtathurta, but with some difficulty owing to the custom of using them having been so long discontinued.[2] Only two of the old men, now alive, have worn the shoes, and the last instance of their use occurred more than twenty years ago.[3] The younger men only know of the custom from the elders of the tribe, and in a few years it will be quite forgotten. The wearing of the Urtathurta and going 'Coordeitcha lumah', (Coordeitcha—bad or evil spirit, lumah—to walk), appears to have been the medium for a form of vendetta. It did not supersede the 'Adninga', or war party, which was always dispatched to avenge the death of a native supposed to have been killed by spells, or to recover a lubra that had been stolen.[4]

When any native threatened the life of a member of a different tribe, the threatened native could await his enemy's attack, or take the initiative himself. If he decided on the latter course, the doctor was consulted and a Coordeitcha lumah arranged. In either case the attacking native was called 'Coordeitcha'. A doctor always accompanied the Coordeitcha, and both were similarly attired.

The headdress worn consisted of a bunch of feathers in front, and a bundle of Green leaves behind. As a disguise the face was blackened with charcoal, the whiskers tied back behind the neck, and a broad white stripe drawn from the top of the forehead down the nose to the bottom of the chin, a similar stripe extending across the breast from shoulder to shoulder. A girdle, made of hair cut from the head of a blackfellow after death, was worn round the waist, and the legs, from ankle to knee, were covered with ordinary hair string. This covering was to protect the legs from snakebite. In the girdle, which next to the Urtathurta appears to have been the most important article, the doctor carried a live lizard.

On leaving his camp, the Coordeitcha walked in front followed, at a short distance, by the doctor; both armed with spears and carrying the urtathurta. When hidden from the view of their tribe they put on the Urtathurta and proceeded towards the hostile Camp. The Coordeitcha always led the way, and every precaution was taken to prevent their advance being seen. On arriving at the Camp the Coordeitcha crept forward alone and (if successful) speared his enemy dead. The doctor then came up and inserted the head of the lizard he carried in his belt into the wound. The lizard was supposed to drink up the blood and so remove evidence of the manner in which the deed had been done.[5] Sometimes the wound was seared to prevent it being recognised as a Spear wound. Almost invariably the attack was made at night, and, when successful, the Coordeitcha and doctor started back at once, halting some distance from their Camp to remove and conceal the Urtathurta before going in.

If, by chance, the tracks of the Coordeitcha were seen they were avoided, and the adjacent Camps merely kept on the alert. But if the Coordeitcha himself was seen in the vicinity of a camp, he was at once attacked and Killed. The doctor who accompanied him was in all cases allowed to return uninjured to his tribe.

When the body of a man murdered by a Coordeitcha was discovered no attempt was made to track the murderer, but the doctor immediately appointed a relative of the murdered man's, or, failing a relative, one of the same class—a coomarra if he was a Coomarra etc—to avenge him. This was done by going as a Coordeitcha in a similar manner to that described.

If the Coordeitcha was unable to find the man he wanted to spear he Killed a blackfellow belonging to the same tribe. This, however, rarely occurred.

Immediately a Coordeitcha was seen near a Camp the man who detected him informed the others by saying 'Oodnurrah Pitchimi', (Oodnurrah—a wild dog. Pitchimi—is coming). He did not mention the word 'Coordeitcha', but his meaning was understood, and preparations were made for an attack on the Oodnurrah. In this connection, one of the head men of the tribe informed me that, when a blackfellow reported 'Oodnurrah Pitchimi', the doctors could appoint a Coordeitcha who had the power to accost the other Coordeitcha and Compel him to return to his Camp. I have been unable to fully corroborate this, but it seems possible that, when the custom prevailed to an abnormal extent, such a course was adopted to prevent excessive bloodshed.

This is all the information I can gather. As I have said, the Custom has completely died out, and the Urtathurta are only made to supply orders from the whites, or perhaps to illustrate the deeds of other days, when the old men play the Gascon[6] before the half admiring, half sceptical Younger Generation.

Yours faithfully
P.M. Byrne

The girdle of dead blackfellow's hair worn by the Coordeitcha was, no doubt, *supposed to Connect the wearer, in some way, with the spirit of the dead man.*

Letter 7.2

Bleak House[7]
Charlotte Waters
5th Oct'r '94

Dear Sir,

I was glad to hear that the Amperta is probably new to Science,[8] and regret that the spider turned out such an unmitigated fraud. The old Professor will be delighted with the latter result as, presuming that the beast is occasionally flatulent, he undoubtedly scored.[9]

Giles desires to thank you for supplying the name of his lizard, and appears relieved at getting such a formidable customer safely off his hands. For my part I am not surprised that the unfortunate reptile wilted and recklessly shed his tail, under such a diabolical appellation.[10]

I believe the baleful effects of the scientific mania are beginning to be felt at the Alice. Gillen's apparel consists principally of nitrate of Silver and Court plaster.[11] Field[12] is saturated with Arsenic, and as I have just sent them some recipes for preserving, the Chief ingredient in which is perchloride of mercury,[13] I am looking forward with cheerful anticipation to an inquest or two in the near future.

I am sending you five ampertas packed in two parcels by this mail. Unfortunately the blacks had two of them on hand for some time before I obtained possession and, like a humpbacked acquaintance of ours, 'They smell most awful vile'. The natives say the Males are living in holes apart from the females at present, and that they do not return until the young are able to run about. However, I don't think they are far away, and I hope to get you some soon.

Still no rain and this place looks if possible more arid and desolate than when you saw it. Next *month* our waters will be dry, and then the 'winter of our discontent' will begin in earnest.

With kind regards.
I am,
Yours sincerely
P.M. Byrne
Professor W Baldwin Spencer

P.S. If you can spare a copy each of Ayer's Rock and Mt. Olga I should like very much to get them.[14]
PMB

Letter 7.3

Charlotte Waters
19th Nov'r '94

Dear Sir,

I am glad the rats were of Some interest. When sending them I thought they were larger than the sketch you showed me, but as they agreed so well in other respects I concluded that the[y] belonged to the same species, and that the difference in size was attributable to the luxuriance of the feed about here. I hope to get you some males, and a female Notoryctes before long, but I am afraid the young of the latter are now fairly Grown.[15]

I have been trying to get information from the Natives that might shed some light on the reason for the stoutness of the rats' tails, but without result. Isn't it possible that some lizard Ancestor of theirs affected a Caudal appendage like N. Platyurus and that the peculiarity has survived in a modified form?[16]

The waters here are nearly dry, and all the stock have been shifted to the Finke so that there is even less life than usual about. I don't know what we will do if no rain falls before March, as the stock are existing on dust and recollections now.

Many thanks for Hudson's book which you so Kindly sent me.[17] At present I am suffering from bad eyes, so that I have not been able to do more than dip into it but I can see that I have a treat in store.

I will send something by next mail if possible, and if not, when rain falls!

With kind regards.
I am,
Yours faithfully
P.M. Byrne
Prof W Baldwin Spencer

Letter 7.4

Charlotte Waters
16th Dec'r '94

Dear Sir,

I am sending you, by this mail, a female of P. Cristicaudata with young ones,[18] a brush tailed rat,[19] and a family of lizards. The latter are fairly plentiful about here, but, as they belong to a genus that I have never seen off the tablelands, you may possibly have missed them.

So far I have been unable to get either adult males of the P.C or females of the Notoryctes, but <u>when rain falls</u> I think I can promise you some, as there are about 150 natives at our well on the Finke and they are all enlisted in the Service.[20] One of the boys saw a mole a few days ago, but it was too quick for him Altho' he had a spade and dug nearly four feet into the sand after it. Of course it was a beauty—almost pure white and very large. 'Twas ever thus from Childhoods hour'![21]

I am sorry that my Pedigree of the fat tailed rat is unsatisfactory, and humbly apologise to the unknown Amphibian, who is supposed to stand in loco parentis, for trying to supplant him. Still the peculiarity is hard to account for. The blacks say the beasts do not hibernate, and if the fat tails are provided against a time when food is scarce they should be loose and flabby now. In summer I believe the rats move about during the day and night—especially the night, but in winter they do all their hunting in the daytime and retire to their holes at dusk.

I have nearly got thro' Hudson and think *him* a Charming writer and a Keen Observer of birds. Some of his Puma and tender hearted Gaucho stories are—very affecting. His remarks about the antics of birds certainly seem to point out flaws in Darwin's theory, and his observations on the instinct of fear also appears to Clash with the generally accepted idea. But I hardly think he represents Darwin's views quite fairly, and, altogether, he disposes of them in too glib and summary a manner. Even if sexual selection has not been the cause of the brilliant Coloration and Ornaments on birds I think it has come in to play in modifying the higher Animals, and it certainly seems to apply to man. Tho [sic] whether it has tended to raise him either Physically or mentally seems to be an open question, as, despite our hoard of accumulated Knowledge, the Race which produced a Socrates over twenty Centuries ago, and boasts of a Talmage today can hardly be said to have made great strides.[22] What sort of selection would marrying for money be considered—Natural, or Unnatural? Natural I suppose, as money should help the possessors in the struggle for existence!

After all, I think, climate and food cause more change in Animals and man than Natural and Sexual Selection Combined and the way Australians and other colonists diverge from the Parent type in a couple of Generations seems to be a proof.

All our Prospectors have returned from the West unsuccessful, but

I don't think they worked very hard or knew very much about their business. The inexperienced man of one party brought in what he thought were specimens of Cobalt and Galena but they turned out to be Manganese and Micaceous hematite! None of the rocks I have seen Contain fossils, and they are similar in Character to those of the main McDonnells except that the Granite is less Gneissic and is finer grained—This reminds me—Have you a specimen of the peridotite known as Kimberlite in your museum, and if so, could you get me a small Chip.[23]

I am glad the lizards and other Animals are turning out so well and hope you will be able to illustrate them as fully as you desire. I don't know what getting up a book usually costs but £800 seems a fairly liberal Amount.[24]

Still no sign of rain here, and I hardly expect any before next year. I shall be alone with the Chinaman at Xmas and intend spending the day in cursing the N. West, its climate, inhabitants etc., and only wish I had Cowle here to give me his able assistance.[25]

Wishing you a Happy New Year.
I am,
Yours Sincerely
P.M. Byrne
Professor W Baldwin Spencer

P.S. Your telegram to Cowle arrived too late for mail so I sent it on by a traveller on the 15th and he should get it about the 22nd Inst.
P.M.B

Letter 7.5

Charlotte Waters
15th March '95

Dear Professor,

I was sorry to hear that you had such an unpleasant trip to Oodnadatta, and sympathise with you over the monotony of the train ride. Old Jimmy must have been in a mild state of excitement when 'dem hausses' were trying to get into the trap, and I can picture the look of Stoic resignation on your face during the Proceedings.[26]

Palmer's defection is inexplicable. When in ordinary form he can keep going for a week, and with the recently discovered North East to draw upon he should have reached Adelaide babbling like a rather profane brook. No doubt 'that snake' is largely responsible, as when free from its malign influence I believe he nearly paralysed some old and respectable citizens with his 'Gulf' yarns.[27]

Winnecke's birds have been exercising the minds of the whole Railway and Telegraph Depts for some time, and everybody is glad that they are handed over at last. I have said nothing to Gillen about yours—it isn't safe![28]

When Horn hears from you I hardly think he will persist in his intention of publishing everything at home. It would be childish to sacrifice a book that is likely to attract more attention than any published for the last ten years to a petty feeling of pique. Not to speak of the injustice to those who have worked hard to make it a success.[29]

I am glad to be able to send you a mole with two young by this mail, and as Harry and a couple of Gins are out hunting exclusively for moles and the female of Antechinomys I expect to have a good bag for next Post. I am also sending Antechinomys and what I take to be Sminthopsis Crassicaudata (ahem!).[30]

Four or five old ladies are going to Oodnatchurra next month, and as I have been assiduous in my attentions to them and prodigal with tobacco, I hope for a reward in the shape of some Bandicoots and Ant-eaters. From what Harry tells me, I think P. leucura will probably be found in that neighbourhood.[31]

I hope the Photos—especially the Studies of the Nude—turned out well.[32] If they have, no doubt they will prove one of the greatest attractions in Winnecke's little museum!

In your next letter Kindly describe the feet of Antechinomys. I think I have discovered some pads that don't exist!

Parties are still going West but in nearly every instance they are poorly equipped and badly led so I don't think they will be very successful. Gold there undoubtedly is in the Western Country, but it will be difficult to find out and the Party searching should have a man like Watt at its head,[33] and consist of four or five old miners with a dozen camels and rations for six or nine months. As things are going

I think the Western Australians will discover Gold in South Australia while our wretched little Parties are wandering aimlessly about the Country.

Michael Doolan has just brought in a nicely marked snake which I will bottle, and send along with the other beasts.[34] This is the fifth since yesterday morning, but the others were rather big, and in deference to the wishes of the other inhabitants I did not attempt to preserve them. It's astonishing what a prejudice people about here have against preserved snakes since your visit!

Still very hot and dusty, with the Cheerful Mosquito rather more in evidence than usual. Shouldn't be surprised if we had a big rain before long especially as Sir C. is not very anxious about the weather reports and seems to think the wet season over.[35]

No news worth recording from here. Kind regards from all.

Yours Sincerely
P.M. Byrne
Professor W. Baldwin Spencer

Letter 7.6

Charlotte Waters
18th April '95

Dear Professor,

Your fears were only too well founded, as I was completely taken in over the Young of Notoryctes. The little lumps in the Pouch struck me as being rather formless, but I never dreamt that they were simply fattened teats. It was lucky you made an examination before imparting any more information to the Students, and I have no doubt you envied Palmer his gift of Picturesque language when you discovered that I was mistaken. I am very sorry that I disappointed you, and will remember in future that I have to deal with something more protean than the stolid quartzyte and reliable Mica Schist.[36] I tho't [sic] I had made such a haul too!

I am glad the lizards turned out well, and will try and get some like your specimen when it arrives. It should have reached me by last mail, but I suppose the Postal Authorities have sent it via Port Darwin by way of a change.

That claypan dweller has not been secured as yet altho' the Youngsters have been on the war path every day. They are going to the Nine Mile tomorrow and they will probably drop across him there.

Many thanks for the honor you have done me in naming the Phascologale and Diplodactylus. I hope the unfortunate beasts won't inherit the bad luck attached to the cognomen, as the burden of their first names is a sufficiently heavy infliction.[37]

What you say about C. damæus is Curious, but how is it that when a beast is found in Australia Similar to one in another part of the world, People always wonder how it got here? Even you don't ask how the lizard got to Persia and India![38]

The Photos are first rate, especially those of the Adminga and the Finke. The venuses are delighted with their Portraits and promise to get you unlimited rats.[39] I notice tho' that they appear to stop at the promise as they haven't made a start to collect yet. Female collectors seem to want age before they are a success![40] Giles was very pleased with his copies and sends his thanks and Kind regards. But I am afraid he looks on that snake in the light of a success, as he talks of preserving another in a similar manner and Sending it to the Museum!

It is difficult to understand Horn's idea in having the book edited at home. He surely must know that the members of the Expedition are better qualified to do the work than any outsider could possibly be.[41]

Stirling's personal deficiency in Native lore does not surprise me as I tho't from the first that he relied on his professional brother at A.G. for all information. Still, if Gillen has supplied the notes, some interesting Chapters could, surely, be written which, with the accompanying photos, would add to the value of the book.[42]

The Gins caught a fine mole yesterday. His fur was a bright Golden colour on the back and merged gradually into a rich orange over the less exposed parts. It literally shone when he was first brought in but immersion in the Spirit appears to have dimmed it sadly.[43] This is the only find made lately altho' the Gins have been looking continually for Ampertas and the female of P. byrnei.[44] The latter seems to be as difficult to obtain as the Male Amperta, and I am inclined to think that the Natives are right in saying that the sexes of these two species live apart at times. During the summer I must try and find out something more about the habits of Phascologale.

Both P. cristicauda and P byrnei are <u>fossorial</u>[45] and live in holes which they line with Grass, but Sminthopsis, according to the Natives, Generally occupies holes made by other beasts or takes advantage of natural crevices.

I have heard nothing of Gillen lately so cannot say how your letter has affected him. But if you have aspersed the memory of Grattan I can quite understand the Home Ruler being shocked into silence. Any other form of attack might arouse his ire, but Grattan is sacred. He will fight you about O'Connell. In fact he generally produces O'Connell in an argument and his opponent finds that it is necessary to prove Daniel an unmitigated scoundrel or admit himself wrong about—say free education![46]

I am afraid you do not properly appreciate the worthy Brian's father.[47] He believes in Progressive taxation and the building of an Overland railway on the land Grant system. As progressive taxation means the gradual introduction of the single tax, the railway will be paid for with land which the Government will eventually tax to its rental value, so that the railway will cost the colony nothing! From a South Australian point of view this seems thoroughly sound.[48] Of course the English Syndicate that builds the railway, and people incapable of broad and Statesmanlike views may regard the matter differently. It must have cost Winnecke a big effort to sacrifice those bits about the Obnoxious members and, as he will find a vent for his feelings somewhere,[49] I fully expect to hear of an unfortunate bird fancier coming to an untimely end.[50] I would like to see him and Cowle together in an office for a week—especially if they had been regaled on b–s and salt beef for a fortnight previously.

I can quite imagine how dreary the never-ending round of lectures and demonstrations must be, but I think on the whole you need not envy me *my* bugs and Philosophising at C.W. If anything is calculated to drive a man mad I should say a lengthened residence anywhere between Crown Point and Oodnadatta would do it, and, if you want to Kill him outright, give him about five years at Strangways Springs!

The rabbits are beginning to make themselves felt. They have reached Henbury on the Finke, and at Koppadeitchika, fourteen miles east of here, they are very thick. I am sorry for the poor misguided animals and will mercifully shoot as many of them as possible before the next drought sets in.[51]

No sign of rain yet, but when it comes I hope to have some

success in the Mole line, and if I advise a female with young you may feel tolerably *certain* that the young are fairly well developed!

Yours Ever Sincerely
P.M. Byrne
<u>Professor W. Baldwin Spencer</u>

19th
Lubra just brought in female of P. Byrnei, but it shows no trace of a pouch at present—at least not to my vision. Expect more Gins in tomorrow.

    Received spirits from Winnecke. You need not have sent them as I had over a gallon on hand.
<u>*PMB*</u>

The Gin found the female rat in among some iron poles stacked near Station.[52] *One of the males I sent you had a burrow under the same lot of poles, but as I had them shifted two or three hundred yards, recently, and restacked, the female was probably in the hollow of one of the poles.*

    Just got a specimen of what I take to be Antechinomys laniger.[53] *By some means or other she got into a wire covered box containing M. horridus and could not get out. Mail won't leave here for a couple of hours so something else may turn up before its departure.*
P.M.B

Letter 7.7

Charlotte Waters
24th May 1895

Dear Professor,
    While sympathising with your disappointment over the embryos, I am glad that the mole proved to be of some value, and gave you the opportunity—so dear to all scientists—of 'rolling over' a brother in the Craft! Did you discover any traces of the embryos in the interior of the beast or had they already been born? When your paper on the reproductive organs is ready I should very much like to see it, as I am curious about this uncanny beast, which smuggles its young into the world in such a mysterious manner.[54] The microscope work you describe must be very interesting and if I knew a little about the subject I think

I would like it.[55] As it is I rather favor brilliant generalisation than minute and accurate research!

I fancy the specimen of P. byrnei must have come from Tom Hanley[56] as he is the only man I know who donates anything to the bottle and old junk emporium which does duty as a museum at the Malodorous Port. In all probability the specimen was sent him from here. The animal that I think is P. leucura has so far eluded capture, but as the old men still maintain that there is a beast with a white tail, having a brownish tip, and resembling P. lagotis, it may yet turn up. The boys also describe a yellow beast, smaller than P. Cristicauda with large head, medium ears, feet resembling those of P. Crist, and a short incrassated tail. A Gin came in a few days ago who saw several of them about twenty five miles North East of here, so I started a party off at once to search, and they will probably be back before the mail leaves. In any case the ultimate Capture of the beast is a certainty as the Gins are confident they can get it.[57]

Your letter should bring Horn to his senses, and if he doesn't gratefully accept your offer he is an idiot.[58] Brown's report on the N.T. will boom Public interest in the Geological work,[59] and these Swedish collectors are Coming down the Line and no doubt sending home Specimens and reports.[60] So, if William Austin doesnt make up his mind soon, he will be to some extent forestalled, and may have to be content with the common C.M.G.[61]

'Restive' should describe Tate's condition exactly.[62] He is a regular old war horse, and, as you say, the duel *between him and Horn* would be worth listening to—

Gillen left the Alice on the 19th, but as it has been raining ever Since he will have a very rough and unpleasant trip and I do not expect him here under a fortnight.[63] When he arrives I will have a chat with him about his Anthropological work, and urge your recommendation. Still it will be rough on the unfortunate 'General' reader of the book if he has nothing of a lighter vein to relieve pages strewn with Ceramodactylus damæus, Tiliqua occipitalis and other flowers of the Biologist's playful fancy.[64]

I see Smoky Magarey and a Gentleman [illegible word] Worsnop have been spreading themselves on the Native Question.[65] The latter thinks their rock pictures represent some stupendous mystery and hopes the symbols may some day be deciphered! Now, the World is badly in want of a new religion. Theosophy is about played out, and

Plate 15. The staff of Charlotte Waters Overland Telegraph station in the late 1880s. Paddy Byrne is seated (right) and Frank Gillen (left). They spent twelve years together there.

Plate 16. Isolation personified. Paddy Byrne standing by the rain gauge set on the flat and featureless plain. The station was obliged to keep detailed meteorological records.

Plate 17. Charlotte Waters station c.1900, 216 kilometres north of Oodnadatta and 373 kilometres from Alice Springs. It had eight rooms and sandstone rubble walls. In addition to large underground water tanks, the station had a battery of tanks (right) to collect rainwater.

Plate 18. Rear view of the same building (right) showing that it was constructed around a courtyard that could be fortified from Aboriginal attack. The forge is the building left foreground.

Plate 19. Baldwin Spencer's sketch of the Charlotte Waters complex.
The buggy shed (left), the forge (right) and the rear of the station (centre).
Note how the telegraph line across the heat-shimmering plain
dominated his vision.

Plate 20. Charlotte Waters today. This heritage building was demolished in
1946–47 and the roof iron and stone carted elsewhere. Note the tanks which
are the sole visible testimony to the orientation of the building.

Plate 21. The massive bore machinery 2 kilometres north of Charlotte Waters. Byrne's right hand was severed here in 1915 and he survived without medical attention for four days. His compensation cheque was for the same amount as the doctor's bill.

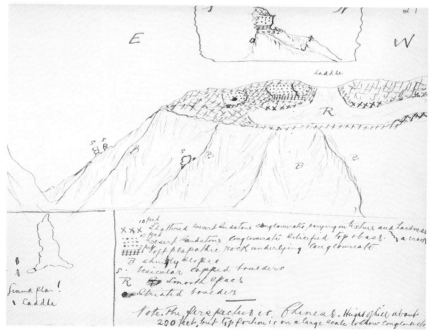

Plate 22. Byrne as field geologist, letter 8.5: his sketch of the hillside section, the dot near the surface indicating the presence of striated pebbles, scratched during ice movement in the Permian glaciation.

Plate 23. Spencer's image of the Overland Telegraph Line south of Tennant Creek, 1901. This monotonous track was the lifeline from Oodnadatta to Darwin.

Plate 24. The 1901 expedition 'staff', probably at Barrow Creek. Spencer seated (right) and Gillen left. Mounted Constable Chance stands in the centre, Parunda at left and Erlikilyiaka right. The kneeling figure is probably Tungalla, their chief Kaytej informant.

Plate 25. Paddy Byrne (right) at Charlotte Waters with
Southern Arrernte men, c.1890.

Plate 26. Aboriginal cameleers and the same Southern Arrernte men, c.1890.
This photograph was taken by H.Y.L. ('Geology') Brown, the government
geologist who surveyed the entire Northern Territory over some years.
The camels were probably his.

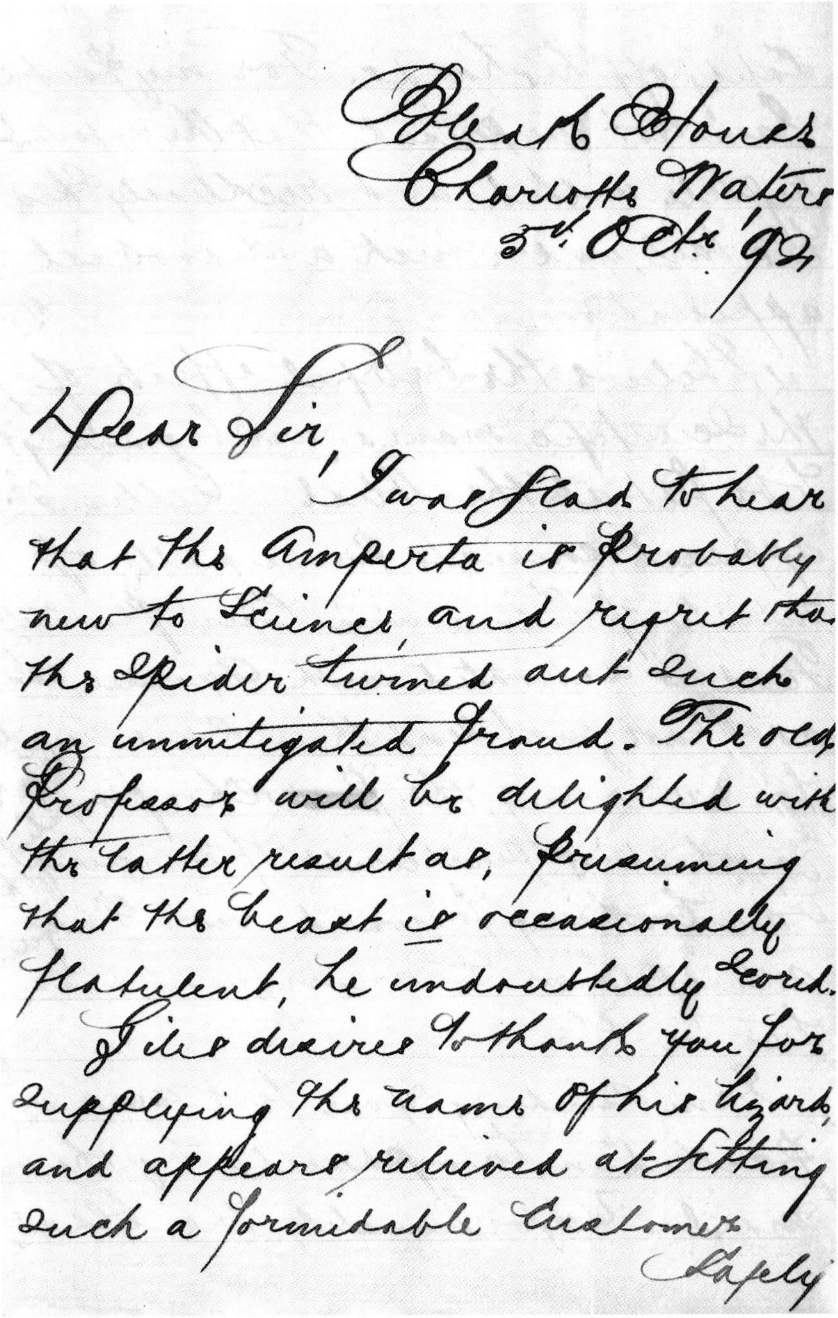

Bleak House
Charlotte Waters
5th Octr '94

Dear Sir,
I was glad to hear
that the Amperta is probably
new to Science, and regret that
the Spider turned out such
an unmitigated fraud. The old
Professor will be delighted with
the latter result as, presuming
that the beast is occasionally
flatulent, he undoubtedly scored.
Spencer desires to thank you for
supplying the name of his lizard,
and appears relieved at settling
such a formidable customer
safely

Plate 27. Byrne's letter 7.2 to Spencer in 1894, in which he appropriately refers to Charlotte Waters stations as 'Bleak House'.

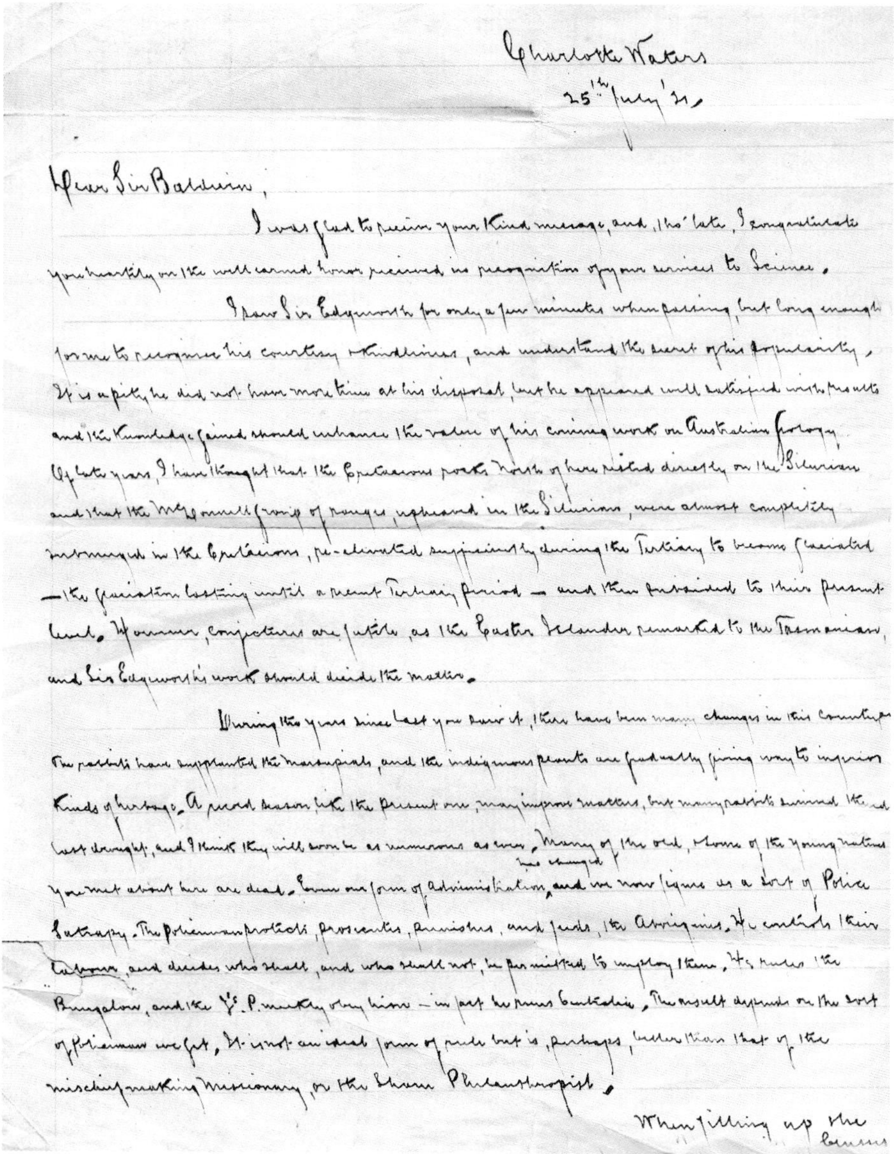

Charlotte Waters
25th July '21.

Dear Sir Baldwin,

I was glad to receive your kind message, and, tho' late, I congratulate you heartily on the well earned honor received in recognition of your services to Science.

I saw Sir Edgeworth for only a few minutes when passing, but long enough for me to recognise his courtesy & kindliness, and understand the secret of his popularity. It is a pity he did not have more time at his disposal, but he appeared well satisfied with results and the knowledge gained should enhance the value of his coming work on Australian Geology. Of late years, I have thought that the Cretaceous rocks North of here rested directly on the Silurian and that the McDonnell group of ranges, upheaved in the Silurian, were almost completely submerged in the Cretaceous, re-elevated sufficiently during the Tertiary to become glaciated — the glaciation lasting until a recent Tertiary period — and then subsided to their present level. However, conjectures are futile, as the Easter Islander remarked to the Tasmanian, and Sir Edgeworth's work should decide the matter.

During the years since last you saw it, there have been many changes in this Country. The rabbits have supplanted the marsupials, and the indigenous plants are gradually giving way to inferior kinds of herbage. A good season like the present one, may improve matters, but many rabbits survived the last drought, and I think they will soon be as numerous as ever. Many of the old, & some of the young natives you met about here are dead. Even our form of administration has changed, and we now figure as a sort of Police Satrapy. The Policeman protects, prosecutes, punishes, and feeds, the Aborigines. He controls their labour, and decides who shall, and who shall not, be permitted to employ them. He rules the Bungalow, and the J's. P. meekly obey him — in fact he runs Centralia. The result depends on the sort of Policeman we get. It is not an ideal form of rule but is, perhaps, better than that of the mischief making Missionary, or the Sham Philanthropist.

When filling up the Census

Plate 28. Because Byrne's right hand had been amputated, he had to write this 1921 letter (8.13) with his left hand.

want of cash will soon compel Booth to retire.[66] So I think if one were to decipher these rock pictures and start a religion compounded of a mixture of Theosophy and Boothism with a few Native high Priests, of the Mahatma description, living in the vicinity of the Rawlinson Ranges, to form a background, there might be money in it. A conjuror would be required, but if a third rate female trickster can deceive an Australian Judge, one should be able to educate a nigger to gull the ordinary Public in a very short space of time. The Programme might be varied by having mass Prayer Meetings enlivened with occasional jigs and Plantation breakdowns by the Elect. I think there is the Germ of Success in the idea and I'll consult Cowle when we meet.

I am sending you, by this mail, a female of Antechinomys which appears to have six teats, and a Sminthopsis with a long fattened tail which does not agree with any of the described species.[67] I am also sending four moles, two of which are for French.[68] The lizard family must have had a free fight as their tails have undergone considerable repairs—These and the two single specimens are the only small lizards I have been able to get—Diplodactylus isn't around, but I think I have secured Apus Australiensis.[69]

There will be a big field day here when Gillen arrives and I intend adopting extreme Tory views for the occasion. The result is doubtful, as it is difficult to corner a man who trots out Niall of the Nine Hostages, and Firnachta Oig Fleadhach, on the slightest provocation.[70] Possibly we may unite and devote our Combined energies to the Characters of our friends!

The rain is still pouring steadily, and I can't see the paddock thro' the window as I write. When it clears up I should be able to bag a few moles as their tracks are very thick in the vicinity of our Well.

With Kind regards.
Yours Ever Sincerely
P.M. Byrne
Professor W.B. Spencer

P.S. What is the small, slender-tailed rat resembling Sminthopsis, and is the small rodent the ordinary house mouse?

Letter 7.8

Charlotte Waters
26th June '95

Dear Professor,

I was glad to hear that all the matter for the book was so nearly in readiness, and hope you will be able to publish in Melbourne. Horn should be content when it is in the Printer's Possession, and I expect you too will be relieved when it is off your hands.[71]

I quite agree with what you say about Horn. No one should grudge him any honor he may get, as he has done good work in bringing a comparatively unknown part of the World under the notice of Scientists. It is to be hoped that they won't create a new order and make him a Knight Commander of the Most Distinguished Order of the Marsupial, because he happens to be a full Pouched Australian!

Your intention with regard to the full description of Notoryctes is Christian, and I charitably suppose that Stirling would have acted likewise had the Positions been reversed.[72]

Many thanks for 'Darwinism', which I thoroughly enjoyed.[73] Wallace is a wonderful man, and he makes out a strong case for Natural Selection as the Preponderating Cause in the Production of Species, but I can't follow him everywhere he leads. His view, that the extra vitality of Moles during the Pairing season is *sometimes* applied to the Production of Colours and Ornaments, which are useless in the Struggle for exis-tence, is difficult to understand when one considers that the extra vitality is Presumably Supplied and required for the reproduction of the Species. Then his theory of the Origin of Spines does not appear so reasonable as that the Spiny plants have adapted themselves to the barren, and arid Places which, as a rule, they inhabit—In fact, Animals that live in deserts seem to have been modified so that they can live on these plants, and the Camel prefers the Prickly Acacias to plenty of unprotected shrubs. Again, his idea that Man made his first appearance near the happy hunting grounds of the Mahatmas, in a yellow condition, which became darker when he approached the Equator, and lighter when he went towards the North Pole, does not explain how the Fuegians and Australians came by their sable hides. What do you think of his views re the effects of Climate and environment? And are you a believer in *the* heredity of acquired Characters?[74]

Gillen was far from well while here, and as he has not yet recovered he will probably abandon his trip North and start for the 'big Smoke' at once.[75] During his stay he took several Photos including some good ones of the 'Rain Dance', and initiated me into the mysteries of developing and fixing. I thought the work rather uninteresting and Monotonous, but as he enlivened the time by paying eloquent tribute to the Commanding Genius of the 'Nation builders', as he calls the Colonial Statesmen to distinguish them from the ordinary sort known in Europe and elsewhere, I managed to sit the proceedings out.

I am sending you four moles, a male and female Cristicauda, female byrnei, Male and female Antechinomys, Assorted Sminthopsis, and a Jerboa like rodent with a tufted tail. What is the latter? If of any interest I can get you more as they are plentiful here now.[76]

As it has been raining at intervals during the last fortnight and I have four old Gins out I fully expect some more moles shortly, the Cristicaudas and byrneis have gone North West according to the blacks, but Sminthopsis are very numerous just at present. The jerboa like rodents are coming from the Eastward and they almost amount to a plague here—I am sorry the Cristicaudas have lost some of their hair, but the lubras brought them in a long way crammed into a small bottle which I had to break to extract them. I notice that they seem to vary nearly as much in length and thickness of tail as the Sminthopsis. Would byrnei be considered a Specialised form probably derived from P. Cristicauda?[77]

You need not be afraid of my tiring as I am really beginning to take an interest in these Confounded beasts, and only regret that there is not a greater variety of them about.

I am keeping a look out for the Claypan Animal, likewise the Yellow crassicauda and leucura.

Cowle has not turned up, and as rumour says that he has had his hair Cut, he may possibly wait until he can appear in his normal Condition.

I have abandoned the trip West for the Present, as cannot get anyone worth having to accompany me. We are having glorious weather, not too cold, with occasional Showers of rain. Up to the present, nine inches has been registered, and the grass is waving like a wheat field over that beautiful vista to the S.W.!

With kind regards—
Yours Ever Sincerely
P.M. Byrne
<u>Professor W.B. Spencer</u>

Ceramodactylus damæus Genus Arabia/Persia[78] *[in Spencer's handwriting]*

Letter 7.9

Charlotte Waters
21st July '95

Dear Professor,

Gillen will be here tomorrow on his way to the 'big Smoke', and as he may not stay long I am packing up the beasts, and will send them by him.

I am glad you dignify my remarks anent 'Darwinism' as Criticisms, but, taking into consideration those 90 students, and other little matters you have on hand, I'll let you off the discussion! Still I think Wallace's 'Origin of Spines' theory won't stand, as in this country, at least, the thorniest acacias grow Chiefly on the Stony rises where there is little moisture or Soil, and the less Spiny Kinds on the deeper alluvial Ground near Creeks.[79]

The preliminary accounts you speak of will be very interesting, and the proofs of plates will be a great assistance in getting specimens of the lizards you want. H. maculatus and the blue and red fellow, should carry off the honors so far as color goes, but I daresay some of the more delicately marked species will also look very well.[80]

Your name for the new Sminthopsis is really a Pretty and appropriate one. I am glad he has proved distinct from the remainder of S. Crassicauda and I will try my best to get you another specimen.[81]

I suppose Dasyuroides byrnei is Phascologale of that ilk rechristened? For God's sake don't put him in Sarcophilus or my friends will make remarks![82]

I hear they have seven or eight moles at Crown Point, some

preserved in spirits and some with the intestines taken out and the body sun-dried. The latter, of Course, will be of little value. Should I hear from Grout about them I will act as you desire, but I think there is little fear of their going outside the Colony, and I can get you plenty here.[83]

Your story about the Baron is delicious. What a study their faces must have made (especially the lady's) when he excused himself so admirably! [See Appendix 6, 9 July 1895]

I have not written to French lately and am afraid to do so until I can get him some beetles and eggs. If you see him you can gladden his heart by telling him that McKay at Barrow Ck has a beetle, about six inches long by two broad, for him.[84]

I will keep a sharp look out for Varanus Gilleni and V. eremius. Your tin contains four notoryctes, Antechinomys, H Cervinus (more due?) an assorted lot of Sminthopsis and some lizards. The latter are principally old friends, but there are one or two I am not sure about.[85]

The Niggers are not yet back from Oodnatchurra where they are on the lookout for Leucrura [sic], the Isabelline Kangaroo, and the fawn-colored beast resembling P cristicauda, which I mentioned in my last letter. They are also on the look out for Chæropus and the claypan beast.[86]

Judging from Lydekker's description, ('The Pigfooted Bandicoot is a free drinker, but never attacks mice'!) Chæropus must be somewhat of a bad Character, and probably keeps to the thick mulga Country where he can indulge in his orgies unobserved.[87]

Granting rain there can be no doubt that the winter is the best time for getting Notoryctes, and, judging from the quickness with which they appear on the surface after a light shower, I question whether they ever burrow so deeply as at first supposed. Immediately a shower falls the moles shift from the creeks to the bordering sandhills, keeping under cover as much as possible, as they are preyed upon by the Jackaroos—magpie like birds, with a rich note—and Crows.[88]

I note what you say about the breeding times and will Keep the blacks mole hunting exclusively between Dec'r and Feb'y so as to get those d–d embryos if possible.

By the by, while I think of it, I want a supply of tins at once as I am reduced to one. If you can send half a dozen <u>by rail</u>, care of

Hewish Oodnadatta,[89] I will get him to forward them by next mail. The Gins rub the hair off the larger beasts forcing them into bottles.

<u>22nd</u>

Gillen just arrived, looking like a two year old, and loaded with totem stones and vermin. He has a phascologale resembling Calura, and a beast looking like the offspring of a Hapalotis that had gone astray with Cristicauda.[90] The Cimmerian darkness of his political views is more pronounced than ever, and he nearly had a fit when I told him that the Conservatives had an absolute majority in the House of Commons!

He has several moles which he obtained from Crown Point, and he brought me a letter from there asking how many moles you wanted at the price you quoted. They do not say how many they have. Please let me know when you receive this whether you still wish to purchase and how many you want. I fancy from what Gillen tells me that the C Point people have about a dozen altogether.

The Gins brought in two more moles this morning which I am sending on with the others, and as the weather is unsettled looking I will probably get some more soon—Don't forget the tins as the Oodnatchurra Contingent will probably have some rats when they come in.

Yours Ever Sincerely
P.M. Byrne
<u>Professor W Baldwin Spencer</u>

Letter 7.10

Charlotte Waters
2nd Aug '95

Dear Professor,

The Gins just arr'd with a consignment, and I have about ten minutes to pack up, and write you.

The tin Contains several Cristicauda with young in various stages, Sminthopsis resembling S larapinta, and Chæropus with young. Owing to the Gins only having one tin they threw away a Chæropus and another beast called E'wurra, which I have been trying to get for some time.[91] I told them to bring everything in whether rotten or not, but I suppose the odor was too much for them—tho' I know you will fail to understand this!

Cowle wrote me about H. Cervinus. The beast arrived about the beginning of June, and is still in the Sandy Country but in diminished numbers. It makes holes like P Cristicauda and not temporary nests or shelters under stones. Whither it is travelling I can't say, but will try and find out.[92]

P Cristicauda, Sminthopsis (Ar'tillah), Chæropus (Tobyah) and probably D byrnei bred in June and July this year. H. Cervinus (Oola'biah) bred in April or May, but I fancy the breeding times may vary in accordance with the Seasons.

I got a note from Crown Point offering any number of Moles, up to twenty at your price, but I am waiting to hear from you before replying—I also heard that several moles had been found at the Alice Well, and altogether they appear to be exceptionally numerous this year.

I expect Gillen is spreading Socialistic views and Sedition Generally, amongst the bucolic inhabitants of Clare, prior to disporting himself in your metropolis. You should have him with you soon.[93]

!More ampertas and another Chæropus just arrived, but they must wait until next mail as the driver is calling 'All aboard'—

Yours Ever Sincerely
P.M Byrne
Professor W Baldwin Spencer

I am sending a small lizard which the blacks say attains a length of six or seven inches when mature.

Letter 7.11

Charlotte Waters
6th Sept'r '95

Dear Professor,

The Consignment of Moles from Crown Point arrived Yesterday. They were all in good condition, and as the owner was willing to take £1 each for twenty, I thought it better to take that number than give fifteen pounds for ten. Still it is a fearful price to pay for the little beasts, and I'm sorry I could not secure a monopoly of them.[94]

A few days before your letter arrived I had a mole alive for about twenty four hours, but he was very weak when brought in, and seemed unable to burrow to any depth in the tub of sand I put him in—He ate one witchetty, and once or twice, when everything was quiet, he elevated his head and tail slightly and made a slight chirping noise which he repeated two or three times, running forward a few steps between each Cry. I fancy that fear has a good deal to do with their dying so quickly in captivity, as they are very nervous little Animals and the slightest sound disturbs them and starts them burrowing. When holding them scratch incessantly [sic]—I will try and get another alive and put the head in Muller's as you describe, and I have also given some of the fluid to the Crown Point People and asked them to do likewise.[95]

You must be heartily sick of Horn, his Photos and everything connected with him. Surely the man isn't in his right senses.

As you surmise, the Winneckian woes are pretty widely known. He must have imparted them to someone in Strict Confidence as everybody coming from Adelaide tells me that Horn has 'Gone through' Winnecke.[96]

The Baron's talent for blundering seems to improve with age. What will he be capable of when he is eighty!

I suppose Gillen has been with you ere this, and Converted some of the benighted Melbournites to his Home Rule and Socialistic views. What a time he will have among the Anthropologists! Cowle writes me in an awestruck strain of the probable effect of his visit on them, and I have been wondering whether he will offer to perform the rite of Circumcision on Howitt—just to show him how it is done! I sympathise with you in the removal troubles and would suggest distributing a few snakes in the rooms where the painters and hangers are at work.[97] If that won't shift them you can surrender hope!

I have noticed the increased size and fecundity of the cristicaudas, and the crassicaudas also seem to carry more young.

Re crassicauda, I think the larger and more scaly tailed varieties live principally on the stony tablelands, and the small smoother-tailed ones on the soft ground near the Creeks, and in the Sandhills.[98]

Cervinus is becoming scarce, but I managed to get a couple of Specimens and am on the look out for more.[99]

By this mail I am sending five tins of beasts. One contains the moles from Crown Point and the others have Tubaija (u is correct) Ur-peela, E-wurra, Cristicauda, Antechinomys, Sminthopsis, Cervinus and one Mole. In Ur-peela I think I have new species of Peragale. The blacks told me some time ago that there was a beast called Ur-peela, with a white crested tail and long ears like the Oogarta (P. lagotis) but never attaining more than half the size of the latter. The specimens I am sending seem darker than lagotis and the ears and head appear smaller in proportion. When first I looked at them I thought they had four incisors in the lower jaw the last one is so nearly divided. Is lagotis similar in this respect? The brownish beast (*E. wurra*), I can't locate as he seem[s] too small for Macrura and the color doesn't quite agree with that of Aurata. Anyhow, thanks to the efforts of the blacks in spilling the spirits, they are fine, full scented beasts, and a little opoponox would be handy when you interview them. Should they be of interest I will send the blacks out after some more with a good strong vessel filled with spirits. Three Tubaijas are in good condition tho' the lubras have 'killed' them rather too much.

The Ur-peelas and E-wurras live exclusively in the Sandhills, and the specimens I am sending were got about forty miles North East of here.[100]

D byrnei is like Joey B,[101] sly—devilish sly, and I have not been able to get a solitary specimen altho I have had the lubras continually on the look out. At present, at all events, they seems to be scarcer even than Tobijas [sic], and from what the blacks say they are never numerous.

When the hot weather sets in I should be able to get you some more specimens of the Smooth-skinned lizards, and that Claypan beast. If you could send me a proof plate of each of the lizards required it would be a great help, as the blacks would know exactly what to look for.

Do you want a pair of Urtathurta? The blacks are manufacturing a pair for French, also a stone axe, but I'm afraid they won't be finished in time for this mail.[102] I will send them to him next post, and should any of his enemies come to a mysterious and violent end you will know that he has been 'Coordeitcha lumah'!

Yours Ever Sincerely
P.M. Byrne
Professor W Baldwin Spencer

Letter 7.12

Charlotte Waters
10th Oct'r '95

Dear Professor,
Your proof of the Mammalian Article, descriptions of new species, and
plates arrived safely. Very many thanks for them.

The plates were a surprise as I never dreamt that they could turn
out this class of work so well in Melbourne. They are incom parably
superior to Lydekker's or any others that I have seen. Macdonnelensis,
Psammophilus and Cristicauda are beautifully done, and Dasyuroides,
with a whole plate to himself, looks splendid.[103] It is a thousand pities
that Horn did not decide to have the whole work published in
Melbourne, and if his days are embittered by Engravers, and his nights
haunted by Printers devils, the punishment will only be just. I wonder
how the 'Old Warhorse' is feeling about the matter. 'Nursing his wrath
to keep it warm', I expect!

With his banquets, political discussions, Scientific lectures and
Green and red rumped trams, Gillen's trip to Melbourne must have
been a wild whirl of excitement and enjoyment. I had a hearty laugh
over your description of his adventures and sympathise deeply with
the feelings which you must *have* experienced when he gave vent to
some particularly bloodthirsty and villainous assertion—and appealed
to you for support!

Since his return to Adelaide he has been plunging into Mining,
and sending excited telegrams asking me to join him in all sorts of
speculations. I think they must have had him in hand praying for rain,
or something of that sort, before he went to Melbourne and that his
nature is now wildly trying to regain its original Cussedness! He will
be full of news when he returns, and I expect to have a pleasant day
or two with him before we start Quarrelling.

There will be no difficulty in getting you a decent specimen of
Ur-peela when rain falls, but at Present the Country to the Eastward
is very dry, and the Gins cannot go out.

Speaking of the habits of Ugartah and Ur-peela, the natives say
that while the Ugartah invariably occupies the inner extremity of his
burrow, the Urpeela, during the cold weather, lies within a foot or so
of the entrance of his, and only uses the inner Chamber during the

Summer. This peculiarity is taken advantage of by the Natives who spring on the surface of the Ground, behind the Ur-peela, breaking it in and cutting off his retreat to the inner Chamber. He is thus compelled to rush out thro' the entrance, where a native is waiting to give him his quietus. The Ugartah cannot be captured in this manner, and has to be dug right out. Both species are nocturnal in their habits.[104]

Sic transit leucura! I'm afraid I must have unwittingly supplied the Guileless native with the idea of that black tip to the tail!

The E-wurra and Tubaija are almost identical in their habits, and build similar nests of grass and twigs in shallow oval hollows scooped in the Ground. They are captured in the same way. Viz by placing one foot on the nest, pinning the animal and then pulling him out with the hand.

By this post I am sending you males and females of byrnei which were found in burrows, about two miles from the Station, female Antechinomys, larapintas, including female with Young, Notoryctes, and a skin which I got from the Crown Point People as handsel when I paid them your cheque.[105] The skin is that of a young animal, and is about one third larger when the beast is mature. I suppose it is Geoffreyi.[106]

There are no native cats here, and very few on the Finke South of Crown Point, but farther up they are more numerous. I will try and get some.

Referring to Cristicauda and byrnei, several old Gins, including the best hunters, inform me that both these species prey largely on Mus and Stapalotis. The younger blacks cannot corroborate this, but I am inclined to think that there is something in it—especially as you say that their dentition approaches that of Dasyurus.[107]

You do not say what you tho't of the condition of the Moles. Were they all right?

I have given up the idea of going out to the Musgraves as, if I were to go, the time during which I was away would be deducted from my leave. And as I have been nearly six years without a trip South, I feel that a visit to the land of Gaiety Girls and Green and red rumped trams would do me more good than prowling about the Western desert with a blackboy.[108]

Summer is setting in rapidly and the waters are drying at Such a rate that if it does not rain before December I am afraid we will have to invoke the assistance of the Pious of N.S.W., whose corroboree appears to be more effective than that of our own rainmakers.

Whether we get good rains or not we are sure to have a few thunderstorms and I will have the niggers on the look out for notoryctes and lizards.

The postage you speak of isn't worth mentioning. I seldom have such a consignment as that by last mail and it only amounts to a few shillings in twelve months! Besides I am rapidly amassing a fortune dealing in W.A. shares and if the luck continues you may see me blocking the way in Collins St about the middle of next year.

Yours Ever Sincerely
P.M. Byrne
<u>Professor W Baldwin Spencer</u>

Letter 7.13

Charlotte Waters
11th October '95

Dear Professor,

The North Mail, and Gillen with your letter, have just arrived so that I haven't time for more than a hurried scrawl. Gillen is looking splendid and evidently bursting with news and information of all sorts! He says he hasn't given himself away to Stirling, and doesn't intend to give that gentleman any more of his notes or photos—for publication at all events.[109]

Re the Coordeitcha. If you think it is worth publishing you can lick it into shape for a short article as you suggest. The description, so far as it goes, is, I think, correct.[110]

I have a pair of Compasses which will do for measuring so you need not send any.

The Gins will soon start out for a Second Expedition to the eastward and I hope to get a good many specimens of Urpeela and Ewurra with the Chance of Something new.

I hope you will come up again before long. We would all be

delighted to see you, and if you let me know in time, I think I can manage to transport you from O.D. to here and back.[111]

Yours Ever Sincerely
P.M. Byrne
Professor W Baldwin Spencer

Letter 7.14

Charlotte Waters
14th Nov'r '95

Dear Professor,

By last mail I sent a short scrawl saying that you could do what you liked with the Urtathurta notes, but apparently it has not reached. As I put it in the Road bag at the last moment it may have been crushed out of recognition like some of Cowle's egg parcels! So I wired you as desired.

You must be having a fearful time of it with the University Exam's [sic], Horn Book and other work, and I wonder how on earth you stand the strain. By George, the thought of what it must be almost makes my hair stand on end, and I recognize that one has something to be thankful for even on a retired and breezy tableland.

I am glad that Horn has at last given evidence of his existence—or rather that of his Pocket's—and hope his emergence from the shell will be permanent. The near prospect of the book's appearance may stimulate him a little, and no doubt the financial prosperity of the W.A. Octagon Syndicate will tend to put him in a better mood.

Our folks seem to have been nearly as demonstrative in welcoming the descendant of Edward III as your people were in recepting [sic] the offspring of the Sieur De Brisci [sic], and I suppose the recepted were both about equally wearied of the tomfoolery.[112] Syme will have to whip up the fierce democracy.[113]

Gillen stoutly asserted that he had not given anything more to Stirling, but I hae ma doots. Probably the Privilege of disembowelling some unfortunate devil of a Patient was dangled as a bait—and the Pontiff is only human![114]

He was rather subdued while here and only defended the 'Nation Builder' in a negative sort of fashion,[115] by saying that the other

Parliaments were worse! Once or twice he quoted a few paragraphs from the 'Advertiser', and finished up with a peroration from 'Speeches from the Dock' but he eschewed Argument. Said I didn't understand the subject! I fancy, tho', that it is beginning to dawn upon him that the Gifts of Street Corner oratory, and Supreme Self confidence, so plentiful amongst our Politicians, would be better for the addition of a little capacity.

I'm very much afraid that he thinks of invading Parliament, and only hope that the Lord will keep him out of the Treasury. If he ever gets there it will be all over with us.[116]

The latest 'bold and comprehensive scheme' is the opening up of a Stock route from Oodnadatta via the Musgrave Ranges to W.A. The Gentleman charged with the performance of the work is Mr. S. Hübbe of Ornithorhynchus and Franco-Prussian War fame so Carr-Boyd will have to look to his laurels.[117]

The weather savours of the nether regions just at present, and our waters are drying rapidly. I'm very much afraid that we are in for another drought—the fourth in five years! The worst of it is our drinking water is not particularly nice now, and it won't, like wine, improve with age.

Owing to the outside waters all being dry the tin is not a very interesting one this time, but if Jupiter P[118] will only spread himself a little I hope to get plenty of Notoryctes and Urpeela this summer. The rodents I am sending are called Inda-lara and they are similar in their habits to H. Cervinus. I am trying to get the lizard which the doctor carries in his Girdle when accompanying the Coordeitcha. It is called Ina-Kowina.

Poor Daer died rather suddenly in Adelaide from diabetes just as he was thinking of starting back to Illamurta. We will all miss him very much as he was an old identity and a thorough good fellow.[119]

Giles has left for West'n Australia, where he has received an appointment in the Tel Dept so that I am all alone in my glory.[120] I suppose they will send someone in his place if the Colony doesn't file its schedule at the end of the Present Quarter.

Wishing you a Merry Xmas and a Happy New Year.

Yours Ever Sincerely
P.M. Byrne
Professor W Baldwin Spencer.

15th Nov'r '95
Niggers returned without Ina-Kowina but I will get him eventually. I am sending you an Erwulla (Bullroarer) belonging to the Pultara class.[121]
P.M.B

Letter 7.15

Charlotte Waters
20th Dec'r '95

Dear Professor,

Your letter with catalogue, lizard plates and the Kurdaitcha notes received, but not the notes on Notoryctes.

Many thanks for the catalogue which I can see gives much fuller descriptions than Lydekker, tho it is rather technical in places, and I will have to trust to inspiration for the meaning of some of the terms used.[122]

The plates are splendid and the blacks were delighted when they saw them. They identified everything at once, and, during the next week, brought me in Varanus Gilleni (A-punna), V Eremius (Er-punda), A Maculatus (Arta'KoKila), D Winneckei (Pungalitnina) and they are now prowling round after C. damæus which should be findable in this hot weather.[123]

I quite agree with what you say in the Kurdaitcha notes about the natives being able to track the Kurdaitcha if they chose. In fact I am very sceptical about most of their professions and beliefs and feel tolerably certain that their most cherished secrets and belongings can be Purchased for bacca—Provided that the deal can be made Privately.[124]

While Gillen was here I had a chat with him about the Kurdaitcha lumah, and he was of opinion that the idea was never carried out, but existed solely in the imagination of the blacks, and he also thot [sic] that the lizard mentioned by them was not a reptile, but a stone 'called the Lizard'. As to the first, I think the description Given me by the old men was too Circumstantial to be purely imaginary, and the blacks stoutly maintain that the custom was in vogue until some years ago. Gillen made enquiries amongst them and found that a lizard, and not a stone, was used. Since then the old men have informed me that three kinds of lizards are used. When I heard that more than one kind of lizard was carried I thot it probable that there was one for each class but the old men say 'No'. The lizard which was most frequently used was called Oolam'ella and resembles E. Whitei, and after that the Inakowina (H bynoei?), and a slender longitudinally-striped lizard found on the Finke—I am sending you the Oo-lam'ella and Ina-kowina.[125]

I am glad that you are gradually bringing Horn round to your own way of thinking about the book, but you must be getting tired of eternally stirring him up. When it is finished and he sees how well the work is done I think he will be rather ashamed of his simulated indifference. Anyhow, he should be. And if he is at all wise he will drop the introductory Chapter.[126]

Your Mission to Adelaide must have been a Particularly delicate one, and I should like to have been an unseen witness of the Machiavellian manner in which you satisfied the Amour Propre of both Parties, and yet maintained Peace, when you and Tate met Winnecke![127]

Since writing you we have had a very heavy thunderstorm which filled all the waterholes and made the country for three or four miles around the Station look nice and green. Unfortunately it did not extend as far as the Finke, and I was utterly disgusted when the Gins, I had started out after moles, returned with the news that there had been no rain. The time was so favorable for getting them with young that it was especially disappointing.

If no luck this season we must have a big try for them when you come up next year. We will also—rain permitting—go out to the eastward of the Finke into the Ur-peela and E-wurra Country after P leucura and that yellow fat-tailed rat that I have been looking for so long. If leucura is anywhere in the vicinity, he is in the sandhills to the Eastward.

I'm not altogether certain that the Summer is the best season for collecting. No doubt reptiles and insects are then more numerous, but judging from this year's results, Winter appears to be the best time for beasts: tho possibly the aversion the blacks have to overexerting themselves in the hot weather has something to do with the case.

Our Goldfields are still under a cloud and the few on them with sufficient energy to go anywhere are off to the West.[128] Tennants Creek has not yet been tried owing to the Gov't not having come forward with an offer to put people on the ground free, find them in everything, and give them three pounds a week while prospecting. The money so advanced to be paid back in yearly instalments extending over five hundred years!

Still, South Australians won't part with their 'Glorious birthright' to an English Syndicate, and I suppose things will be at a standstill until a Royal Commission—at a cost of several thousand pounds—is appointed to report on matters and then, probably, a railway will be constructed to bring the Finke sand to Adelaide for building purposes. Nation building, possibly!

I am still in W.A. Mines but think I will come out all right when they get rain next year; that is, unless those confounded Yankees and Turks cause a Panic in the English money market. Johnathan and john's affair is absurd. War would mean ruin to both, as America would lose her fleet and her commerce, and her coastal towns would be battered, while England would lose Canada, and possibly India if Russia tho't the opportunity favorable,[129] At all events, they should show more consideration for holders of W.A. stock and not get dancing around and frightening people when they really mean nothing.

I shall have a very quiet Xmas all to myself, but it will be a much pleasanter one than I expected. Before the rain the Country looked wretched and our water supply had rather more bouquet and taste than was necessary, now there is a coat of green over that noble expanse to the S.W. and I am getting the boat ready to launch.

There are hundreds of turkeys and ducks about the Billabongs so we are all certain of a good dinner at any rate, and the blacks, with the assistance of your tobacco, and an indigestible duff which I have made for them annually, should hold high revel. With Best Wishes for the New Year.

I am
Yours Ever Sincerely
P.M. Byrne
<u>Professor W Baldwin Spencer</u>

NB I want some more tins, and about a dozen of those glass tubes for claypan beasts.[130]

8

THE MAIL 1896–1925

Letter 8.1

Charlotte Waters
6th Feb'y '96

Dear Professor,

Your letter with tins and copies of Kurdaitcha notes to hand [see Appendix 5]. You need not have gone to the trouble of sending me the latter, as I don't want any for distribution amongst the long suffering Population of the NW!

I am glad so much of the Horn Work is off your hands, and expect you will have nearly all of it in Print when this reaches you. As the Octagon Syndicate appears to be flourishing, Horn should be in an amiable mood, and no doubt he will eventually give way to you altogether. He seems to have the quality of Passive resistance well developed tho'!

The war scare appears to have subsided, or else the Newspaper liars inventive powers have failed, but it has woke England out of her lethargy and I think She will pay more attention to her army in future. The manner in which, of late years, she has deferred to Germany has made the Germans look upon England as a sort of little Germany, and it is just as well that they should be disabused of the idea, I fancy the vaunted triple alliance has seen the best of its days,[1] as Austria is only held together by the Present Emperor, Italy is hopelessly insolvent and it is more than doubtful whether Bavaria and the other German states relish the high handed rule of the talkative William— England in alliance either with the United States or Russia could laugh at the 'Machine-like' army, which if History speaks truly, was just as machine-like at Jena, and yet came to grief.[2]

Jamison [sic] committed the greatest of all sins—he failed! Had he been successful I think Rhodes would have annexed the Transvaal nolens volens.[3]

I can hardly believe that Cleveland intended a quarrel with England.[4] He has always seemed a fair and upright man, but no doubt there are some bad eggs amongst his Party, and they must have fanned the flames for Purposes of their own. Still neither Nation seems to have taken the matter seriously and I think Uncle Sam would fall into line with his Kin if the combination of 'God and the German Sword' got meandering around the Union Jack. I was amused at the way the Continental Powers backed up England during the row— wouldn't they have liked to see her embroiled with America!

I agree with most of what you say about W.A. but think there are many good mines there, and that there will be a mild boom when rain falls. This South African embroglio will also benefit W.A. eventually, as the English investor will prefer ventures in a Colony under the Control of England to those which are at the mercy of the Boers. And after all the Western Country is not such a desert as represented. An old friend of mine writes that a Great Part of it is infinitely superior to the interior of South Australia, and that the Hampton Plains near Coolgardie, are splendidly grassed and husked. The water difficulty is the great drawback.[5]

The stick I sent you is an Er-wulla or bullroarer, used in the Initiation Ceremonies, and carried by the Initiate while isolated during his recovery from the rite. Each class makes its own Erwulla in a manner peculiar to the Class, and uses it in the initiation of its members, but the Erwullas of all classes can be looked at by any man after he has been initiated. Boys and lubras are not allowed to see the Erwulla and severe penalties are supposed to be inflicted should they offend against this rule. As a matter of fact nearly all the lubras and boys see them sub rosa, and the same lubras and boys, if of similar classes, tho' afraid to look at each other if anyone is about, not infrequently 'Sin by two and two'—under the Acacias. As one would naturally expect, infidelity is the Crime most heavily Punished, but death is rarely inflicted in any of the tribes for this offence, tho' the lubras are sometimes badly mutilated.

I have only seen portions of the Rain 'Ungwobarah' and have never paid much attention to the matter, but I will try and get some information from the old men.

Scott of Tennants Ck passed here a few days ago with a half caste boy who is thoroughly versed in the sign language of the T.K. tribe. Gillen had him in his sanctum nearly every day while at Alice Springs so you should have a great budget by this mail.[6] The fact that in the T.K. tribe a lubra is only allowed to use sign language while communicating with the other blacks for some months after the death of her husband, and that the boys are similarly interdicted while recovering from the Initiation, seems to explain why the Sign language is so largely used in this tribe.[7]

I have had a pair of Troras (the sticks for beating time) made, but they are rather rough and I will wait until the boy who made French's comes in before sending any.

Again, I have only lizards to send you as the Country is too dry for the blacks to go out, and I am afraid the bag will continue small until Winter or rain Comes. Among the lizards is C. damæus which I had some difficulty in getting as only two old women Knew the beast and they had a job to find a name for him—He is called Jilyarrra, and is said to be exclusively nocturnal in his habits. I think during the hot weather he must be so, as, tho' Winneckei and other lizards were captured during the day, I could only get damæus by supplying the Gins with lanterns and sending them out at night. He is a very pretty beast, before going into the spirits, being a delicate shade of reddish brown down the sides of the back and head, and the white markings show out very distinctly. The figured specimen hardly does him justice.[8]

Directly rain falls I must start the Gins out after Urpeela and other beasts as I believe the Crown People have communicated with the British Museum Authorities who desire to purchase an all round Collection from Central Aust—I do not think they will get much outside Moles, but they might drop across Urpeela and Ewurra.[9]

When you come up we will be better able to decide which is the best direction to go in search of new beasts—Gillen should have no difficulty in Getting down unless his magisterial duties interfere, or the break up of the Paid Patriot Party causes him to commit suicide.

We had a fearful spell of hot weather during January. For nearly three weeks it averaged 110, sometimes going up to 116 or 17, and I began to fear that the advent of General Booth had banished Old Nick to central Australia—During the last few days it has been cooler and as the boat is now launched on the waterhole, Yelept Atnooralooralirra, I go for a row between those majestic Coolabahs on the banks and admire the Scenery generally.

Still, I think I would prefer a stream that 'stole by lawns and grassy plots, and slid by hazel covers' to the Goat pondy waters you wot of, and even you would, I think, get tired of seeing Mt. Frank malevolently blinking at you thro' the haze.[10]

With kindest regards.
Yours Ever Sincerely
P.M. Byrne

P.S. I enclose a Memo from Gillen.

P.P.S Had to detain a parcel for Cowle by last mail as the Contractors objected to carry P.P. Parcels there being no Parcel Post route up the Finke— I will try and send it on.

Letter 8.2

Charlotte Waters
29th Feb'y '96

Dear Professor,

As Ross from Crown Point is going to Oodnadatta tomorrow I am sending you a Consignment of beasts and this note by him.[11]

I was very sorry to hear of your home trouble, and hope that all is now quite well again. With this anxiety added to the Colossal amount of work you have on hand, I can well understand your feeling jaded, and only wish that you could take a run up here during the Winter months when the trip would really do you good.[12]

I don't think I quite realised what the work of editing was until I had a look thro' the bulky volume you sent. It is really a splendid work in every way, and must make a big stir in the scientific world.[13] Speaking of it, Winnecke, in a recent letter, says regretfully, 'Owing to Spencer's indomitable energy, Horn is going to have another show for the Knighthood!'

I see that he (Horn) is rather in evidence at Home of late, especially at the Colonial Institute where he caused the August Sides of the Members to shake with his jokes about CA—I wonder if he gave them that description of a camel which so tickled the S.A. Public, or confined himself to the humorous experience he had between Oodnadatta and HS Bend![14]

We had a nice rain on the 21st which, altho' it did not put any water in the Creek, has made the place look nice and green. I started the Gins out to the Finke immediately it fell, but they were unable to get any moles. I am now sending them to Oodnatchurra, and if the waterhole there has been filled they will be able to get Urpeela and Ewurra with any other beasts that may be misguided enough to live in that vicinity.

As some crabholes on the tableland had been filled I searched them for bivalves this morning and I succeeded in getting two varieties—one a reddish brown in color and the other colorless and transparent with the lines of growth few and rather faintly marked. So far I have not been able to get any with the dorsal line serrated as in your sketch, but I will keep a look out for them—Apus are to be had in millions, and I got one univalve which is in the bottle with other specimens.[15]

I am still solus here so you can imagine how quiet things are. Gillen, I never hear from, and Field tells me he is working like a Trojan, night and day, at his Ethnological notes. Rumour has it that recently he got up in his Sleep and adjourned to the washhouse from which there presently came a sound of chanting accompanied with vigorous stamping of feet; and on the astonished Night Operator going to see what was the matter, he found the Pontiff, artistically decorated with Day and Martin [sic], and with fancy patterns in Postage Stamp selvage bestowed over his ample person, corroboreeing away like an Aroondah warrior![16]

The blacks had a rain corroboree here a fortnight ago, and I saw several of the morning dances. They take place about an hour before sunrise, and have a vivid effect on one in the dim halflight. Some of the headdresses are very elaborate, and the different chants with the corresponding dances remove the monotony so common in their other corroborees.

When you come up we will get them to go through the Series.[17]

With Kind Regards,
Yours Sincerely
P.M. Byrne
Professor W Baldwin Spencer

Letter 8.3

Charlotte Waters
30th April '96

Dear Professor,

I am glad the last collection proved of Some interest—I was very doubtful about it, but tho't the Eulimnadia did not quite agree with any of the Species described in the Horn work. I have since tried to get some *more* of them, but without success, and I am inclined to think the species is a short lived one. Those I found were in small, rather deep, crabholes which had a good deal of vegetation growing in them, but, even in these crabholes they were much less numerous than the Estheria, and in the shallow, muddy claypans and billabongs they were altogether absent. By this mail I am sending you what appears to be the Permanent species of Estheria (?)—They were obtained in the tank live while carting water from the big billabong. They are very thick thro' the umbones.[18]

I shall not be greatly disappointed with the Geology as I didn't expect much. The only Geological effusion of Tate's I have seen is his Inaugural address to the Society for the Advancement of Science and that was simply all padding, and very poor Padding at that.[19]

I can see that Horn has been at it again, when you speak of his feeble jokes! He surely isn't going to resuscitate that labored one about the Camel, and inflict it on an unsuspecting Public under a Scientific Cloak?

I am sorry the trouble is not over with Winnecke, but am certain he would not do anything he tho't dishonourable. The only thing is, would he in a fit of spleen persuade himself that a Course was right, which in his Cooler moments he would Condemn.

Many thanks for the Banjo's verses,[20] several of which I have not read. He writes spiritedly and knows the bush—that is the bush of fences and shearing sheds, but as a Poet I think he comes behind Victor Daly,[21] Lawson and one or two others[22]—not to speak of our big gun Stephens.[23] Still I suppose he is to be judged as a writer of ballads, and comparing him to Stephens is like comparing Kipling to Tennyson. What do you think of that ineffable ass our New Poet Laureate and his poem about Jameson's Raid?[24]

I think the Alice Springs blacks only know of the Mole thro' seeing it on the upper *Finke* and their opinions on this beast are more than usually valueless, as even here, where it is comparatively numerous, the Natives know little of nothing of its habits. Still, I think, when all is discovered, Witchetties will be found to form a larger proportion of its diet than ants; tho' no doubt it feeds largely on insects of all sorts as you say.[25]

I cannot for the life of me see that this beast has been modified to feed on Ants. His mouth seems as unsuitable for this purpose as for feeding on Witchetties while his strong claws would enable him to dig the latter out of the soft roots among which he probably builds his nest. Besides the horny extremities are required to protect him while travelling thro' the sand, and the soft thick fur is necessary to Keep him warm—There!

By this mail I am sending you a Couple of Perameles, a worm-like snake, some spiders and a villainous looking Grasshopper, besides the Estheria.

I should have had Urpeela long ago but for the dryness of the Country. We are in a deplorable condition here—no feed anywhere, and only between two and three months water—or rather mud. I'm afraid we are in for it in earnest this time, and we have never been in a worse Position to meet with a big drought. However, there is a slight gleam of light amidst it all, in the advance of W.A. stocks, and I am taking your advice and getting rid of them.

My ass't also arrived about a fortnight ago, but, as he is almost a cripple and an inferior operator, I'm little better off than I was before.[26]

And thus endeth the Jeremiad![27]

Our Elections are all over today and the result goes to show that the Woman Elector is not conservative but rabidly Socialistic and she also seem to have a Penchant for Socialism without brains, rather than with that Commodity, judging from the result of Some of the Elections.[28] But you will hear all about it—from a certain point of view—from Gillen—The only thing I am afraid of is that the rate at which they will want to 'Advance' South Australia will be too much for her weak back and broken Knees and that she will collapse altogether. Our only safeguard is that the Powers that be are such gifted—that in all probability they *will* induce the unsuspecting stranger to put his money into our concerns and so save our own deserving population.

I believe we are going to have a surplus but it *is* derived solely from the advance in Western Australian trade—no mean proportion of it being due to telegrams!

Don't be a bit surprised if you hear of Orangeries at Charlotte Waters before long or that the S.A. Govt purpose breeding rollicking rams in the 'Magnificent Sandhill Country to the Eastward of Charlotte Waters and forming the valley of the famed River Finke!'

I am glad you are coming up again and only wish I could get out with you to George Gill's Range, but I'm afraid it is impossible.[29] Cowle, however, should have no difficulty in getting away, and while you were chasing up the vermin in that direction, I could make a grand raid on the Sandhill Country to the Eastward with an army of old women!

I intend trying to get leave in September (3 months), this would bring me back in December so we might come together, and, if Cowle were here to meet you, you could go on to George Gill's Range, and on return I could run you back to Oodnadatta—that would suit? There is just a bare possibility of my being able to go, as there will be a man here relieving me with whom I might arrange if the High and Mighty Todd approved.

I hope Mrs Spencer is now quite well. Kindest regards.

Yours Ever Sincerely
P.M. Byrne
Professor Baldwin Spencer

Letter 8.4

Charlotte Waters
8th June 1896

Dear Professor,

Bearing in mind that I have such an acute little Critic, I must try and amend the writing and avoid the blots on this occasion.[30] I certainly felt careless and off color when last I wrote, but a few days trip over the delightful Country on the Stephenson, and the Prospect of a holiday in September have restored me to my normal resigned condition.

I was glad to hear about Keartland.[31] He is a genuine worker at all events, and, tho' I don't envy him the appointment and its multifarious duties, the trip, if it includes the country lying west of Barrow and Tennant Creeks, Should be interesting and may result in some good mineral discoveries.

I have just finished reading the Geology and having a look thro' the Botany in Part 3. The Botany, so far as I am capable of judging, seems good, but I cannot see that the Geology adds much to our Previous Knowledge. Since '90 it has been Known that the Main ridges of the McDonnell are Silurian and the ages of the underlying Quartzite Schists may well be left until fossil evidence of their age is forthcoming. A strong unconformability hardly seems sufficient reason for relegating them to the Pre-Cambrian and I am inclined to think that Brown's opinion will prove correct, tho' no doubt he erred with respect to the age of the Post-Silurian Conglomerate.[32]

In describing the Alice Springs Country, Tate gives the usually accepted explanation of the formation of the Gaps etc, but he makes only one mention of a fault, and does not refer at all to the Simpsons Gap Range which should have been of interest. But what amused me in the report was the introduction of Chewings and East.[33] Chewings, no doubt, is now a good man, but when he visited this Country in '91 he knew absolutely nothing about Geology and he learnt little during his sojourn. He thought that the Quartzite was basalt, that the horizontally bedded hills (like Ooramina [sic]) were Tertiary, and that the fossils he discovered were Carboniferous. He was quite jubilant over the Prospect of discovering a Coal field at Alice Springs! When he arrived in Adelaide Tate took him in hand, determined the fossils as <u>Upper Silurian</u>, and between them they brought forth a Pamphlet in which Brown's classification of the Ooraminna Range as Devonian was adopted, and Tennison [sic] Woods' opinion re the Aolian formation of the desert Sandstone put forward as Chewing's.[34] East was a fair mineralogist and had some knowledge of Geology, but he was in the unfortunate Position of having no one to Crib from. He regarded all the rocks to the base of the Silurian, with the exception of those at Horseshoe Bend, as Cretaceous and thought the stony tablelands were the boulder-strewn beds of Ancient rivers which the boulders had protected from denudation, tho' he made no mention of the latter idea in his subsequent report.

Actually, Tate in attacking Chewings' and East is to a great extent demolishing his own earlier views respecting the McDonnells.

The silicification of the Cretaceous rock is certainly a puzzle, but I don't think Tate need have conjured up a land 600 miles long by 200 broad, Pitted with innumerable volcanic vents, vomiting for[th] ashes and bombs, to explain the Phenomenon. The usually mild and inoffensive Finke may have butted the Crown Point Range and Knocked a hole through it—tho I should have thought a Passage thro' the low Country four miles higher up would have been Preferred, but how so many volcanoes could have existed in Post-Cretaceous times and only left bombs to tell the tale is a mystery. The theory covers all the Phenomena no doubt, but it has yet to be proved that the bombs are connected with the Silicification. I am inclined to think that they are derived from outliers of the older rocks, and that the desert sandstone may have derived its silica from sea water, while the lower brecciated hills with Chalcedonic Cappings may represent extinct hot springs. It is hard to believe that the Silicification of the desert sandstone, the lower brecciated hills, and the still lower ironstone Stratum was contemporaneous. If it was it must have occurred yesterday and yet the desert sandstone is much denuded altho' it resists the weather better than the felspathic breccias or ironstone.[35]

When travelling up the Stephenson last week I noticed a number of low hills composed of an impure silicious limestone resembling travertine, and capped with slaggy looking blocks of Chalcedony which in places were cemented to the limestone. These hills are the home of the 'unrolled agate' found between the Stephenson and Bloods Creek but, tho' I searched for some time, I could not find any obsidian in their vicinity. There are also some hills near C.W. capped with large masses (up to 10 tons) of a vesicular Silicious rock, overlying brecciated felspathic rocks, and unaltered argillaceous Sandstone and ironstone but here again there is no obsidian. However, whether the worthy Professor's theory of the contemporaneous Silicification of about 120 000 square miles of Country thro' the Medium of volcanic vents (which broke out like measles on the lower Country instead of Showing along the lines of least resistance)—the ranges is correct or not, he certainly scores over the other Geologists in giving an explanation of those extraordinary features—the claypans[36]—I used to think they were formed thro' the natives corroboreeing on them, and thus pulverising the stones and lowering the level of the ground, but, tho' this view would also explain the hardness of the niggers feet, I suppose I must give it up!

By this mail I am sending you the same old lot of beasts, which I expect you will fervently wish in the Yarra when you receive them, but until rain falls there is no chance of getting either Notoryctes or Urpeela and I am afraid I have worked out the new species about here—in marsupials at any events.

I am also sending specimens of the vesicular rock and the Chalcedony and limestone I mention, besides some Emu Poison bush and a Plant which I would like to know the nature of. It looks like an Euphorbia and is credited with very poisonous properties.[37]

I am glad to hear that you will be able to pay us a good long visit this time, and regret that my departure for town in September will prevent my being here when you arrive. But I will probably see you before you leave, and as I will be back in December we will be able to get the Rain Corroboree Pictures, and any stray beasts that may have been overlooked.

While I am away I expect either Field or my brother Jack will be here,[38] and I know they will be as anxious as myself to assist you in every way.

It is unnecessary to say that it hasn't rained!

With kind regards, and hoping that Mrs Spencer and my captious little critic will have an enjoyable trip.[39]

Yours Ever Sincerely
P.M. Byrne
Professor W Baldwin Spencer

Letter 8.5

Charlotte Waters
21st July '96

Dear Professor,

Many thanks for enquiring about Plant. I should not have sent it but that Several horses have died here lately, and this plant being Euphorbiacous I tho't it was probably the cause.

I quite agree with you that the hot spring theory is quite as bad as the volcanoes, and think in my letter I ascribed the silicification of the Desert Sandstone to deposition from sea water, and only invoked the aid of hot springs to account for some mound-like elevations capped with large masses of Scoriaceous rock, and for the silicification, in places, of the cretaceous ironstone and Kaoline. By this I mean deposition from the Supra-cretaceous Sea coincident with the final upheaval of the Desert Sandstone. But I find that the direct action of hot springs will not account for the Scoriaceous rocks as they (the rocks) are distributed all over the higher tablelands, altho' not in such large masses as on the isolated mounds rising out of the valleys.

The diversity of the formations underlying the Supra-cretaceous at comparatively short distances apart point to denudation of the Cretaceous Prior to the deposition of the Desert Sandstone, and some denudation of the latter may have taken place before its final upheaval and silicification as land and marine conditions appear to have alternated during its deposition. Presuming that the supra-cretaceous formation was thick and arenaceous on the elevations, and thinner and felspathic in the depressions, the silica would penetrate to a greater depth and form a more stable or weather resisting rock combined with the Sand than it would with the clays, and the latter, occupying the depressions, would in time be denuded leaving the Sandstone capped hills isolated.[40] The scoriaceous Chalcedony and allied vesicular masses found on the surface may represent the final deposit of Silica after the underlying rocks were saturated, and as the saturation would occur earlier in the case of the felspathic rocks the surface masses would be larger when found in this conjunction. Their Scoriaceous appearance is probably due to the decomposition of included felspathic and other matter. The coarser felspathic breccias sometimes present a very scoriaceous appearance through the felspars being decomposed and only a network of the cementing silica left. A hill near here is capped with masses of this *scoriaceous* rock underlaid by Desert Sandstone and silicified Cretaceous ironstone and Kaoline. It is noteworthy that where limestone occurs the capping is always Chalcedony. The obsidians must, I think, be derived from the older rocks—probably an examination of the ranges to the westward of here would throw some light on their origin. How they were transported with so little erosion is a mystery unless one inflicts an Ice Age on a Country that has already been roasted and boiled.[41] Still, despite the latitude, such a condition may not have been altogether impossible, tho' I can understand the objection a strict uniformitarian like Tate would have to the introduction of a cause demanding extraordinary conditions.[42]

Your suggestion that the silica was supplied to the sea by hot springs appears probable, as they might represent the second stage of volcanic action, or the accompaniment of such action at a distance. But, tho' a fresh water sea may have existed during tertiary times, I think it could only have covered portions of the Desert Sandstone. To have caused the silicification it would have to be co-extensive. Tate, in the Horn work, is very reticent, merely referring to a basin at Dalhousie Springs and a supposed one at Crown Point. He certainly says that the rainfall was at one time 'vaster' than at Present, but even that condition would not require a rainbow as an assurance of Safety from deluge. In his pamphlet he speaks of the vast <u>lacustrine</u> area which <u>isolated</u> West from Eastern Australia and of the similar fresh water area which continued the isolation into late Tertiary times, but the only evidence adduced in favor of the fresh water sea is the existence of Circumscribed lake basins, extinct rivers, and the remains of Crocodiles and large herbivores. Of course, a Glacial Period in Tertiary times might have occasioned large bodies of fresh water like Lakes Lahoutan and Bonneville in N. America! I agree with your description of the formation of the Gaps, but why should not Crown Point Gorge have been formed in a similar manner? It seems strange that the Finke, which had kept pace with the upheaval of the Silurian and flowed into the supra-cretaceous sea, should, on the upheaval of the Desert-Sandstone, only succeed in cutting a Channel 100 miles in length before the Country was denuded nearly to its present level. It is especially difficult to understand if Tate's theory of Silicification is accepted, for then the Finke would only have to Cut its way through soft sandstone and clays, and the silicification must have taken place while it was wending its way to C Point. Don't you think it more probably that the silicification had already taken place, and that the Finke, on arrival at Crown Point, found a depression between two slight elevations, and, flowing in a broad channel, left a shingle deposit in front, and at the sides, of the elevations. The deposit may have been repeated at different times, and each deposit would be left on the banks as the river Channel became deeper and narrower. With reference to the distribution of the bombs. I know that they are found from Farina to Horseshoe Bend (over 500 miles) and in this vicinity they are found on the tablelands twenty miles East and thirty or forty miles West. Perhaps they are more plentiful in the vicinity of the Peake and here than elsewhere, but I think they come from the West.

Watt's sections are well done, and his account of the Crystal-lisation of the Mica is interesting, but on the whole—tho' I am not at all enamoured with my own opinions—I don't care for the Geology. The Silurian part may be good, but little is added to our knowledge of the Cretaceous. Watt cannot be held responsible for this as the time at his disposal was altogether too short for a detailed examination. I am sending you a few bombs, one of which seems to have taken on its present peculiar form while spinning in the air as it shows no mark of impact with the Ground. It may be a button which his Satanic Majesty dropped when stoking a volcano. I am also sending an Apunga, or bag, and a couple of Troras.[43] Only two Dasyuroides—obtained in time, and one dried Mole have been brought in and I am holding them over till I get enough to fill a tin. I will keep a look out for the Crustacea immediately rain falls and obtain all the information possible about them.

Goodness only knows when we will get a rain. Our waterholes are just dry and I am hard at it getting the stock together and shifting them to the Finke. With this, and inspecting travelling stock for the Queensland bug, I am kept going. The behaviour of this bug is rather difficult to explain according to the doctrine of the Survival of the fittest. Perhaps his mission is to improve the breed of Cattle. It would be sacrilege to suggest that the Country was only suitable for ticks![44]

Gillen must be having a great time amongst the tribes. His whole heart is in the work, and he spares neither himself nor the niggers. One civilized blackboy, whom he had questioned into a state of Semi-imbecility, recently burst out with '—it, Mr Gillen, you know more about these—niggers than I do. Let me alone!'

Cowles suggestion re asking the Comm'r of Police for his assistance is a good one, and there is no doubt the use of the Camels would be gladly granted.[45] If this drought continues it will be impossible for you to do anything without Camels as all the outside waters are dry. Cowle will be pleased to have another trip out with you.

I hope to get away from here about the end of September and will probably be in Melbourne early in October but I can't say exactly until I arrive in Adelaide.

I am glad that I will have at least a week or so with you here when you are returning, when we may solve the Geological problem.[46] I think you will do it—of Course, with the assistance of an eminent Geologist like myself!

Yours Ever Sincerely
P.M. Byrne
Professor W Baldwin Spencer

23rd July
Having finished mustering yesterday I cantered over to the Anderson Range (12 miles West) this morning to have another look at some peculiarities I had noticed there.

I found the Range capped with Shattered Desert Sandstone which in many places was conglomerate from top to base—Both top and base of the Section examined were silicified, but the centre was in many places loose and Crumbling. Imbedded in a section of the Soft Conglomerate I found a grooved and striated siliceous boulder[47]— It projected out of the conglomerate about a foot, and a few inches in from the face it was broken, but the other half or portion was partly visible. On the lower spurs were a few isolated masses of conglomerate, felspathic breccia, and a white vesicular rock which formed the capping—all blended together into a compact mass. In the Conglomerate portions the dark brick red cementing silica was largely in excess of the Quartz inclusions. One boulder of this rock 6 x 6 x 9, weighing say 20 tons, was in an inverted Position, the base presenting a Glazed appearance and the vesicular capping resembling this [drawing]. On a slight saddle there is a smooth space which descends the hill on the North side for twenty or thirty feet and then sweeps East and West, being bordered on both sides (Especially that nearest the hill) by blocks of desert Sandstone Conglomerate.

I had got this far in my examination when I noticed my horse making off in hobbles, and when I got him back to where I had left the saddle it was too late to climb the hill again so I will have to pay it another visit. I send you a rough sketch which doesn't pretend accuracy [Plate 22], and some numbered specimens of rock—No 1 Capping of Conglomerate, No 2 Centre, No 3 underlying felspathic rock; others labelled.

I must apologize for inflicting all this on you, but I won't refer to the subject again, and I promise faithfully not to send any more rocks!

PMB

P.S. Pebbles similar to those in the Conglomerate are distributed over the low hills 9 or 10 miles N of C. Point, and also in a small Creek running out of a hill about 4 miles N of Mt. Squire. [Two drawings of hillside with differently shaded areas of rock, Byrne's annotations follow]:

> *[Shading 1]–10 feet shattered Desert Sandstone conglomerate, varying in mixture and hard-ness*
> *[Shading 2]–12 feet Desert Sandstone conglomerate silicified top and base*
> *[Shading 3]–2 feet of felspathic rock underlying conglomerate*
> *B shingly slopes*
> *S Vesicular capped boulders*
> *R Smooth space*
> *• Striated boulders*

Note. The perspective is Chinese—Height of hill about 200 feet, but top portion is on a large scale to show conglom etc.

Letter 8.6

Charlotte Waters
4th Sept'r '96

Dear Professor,

I am glad to hear that all your arrangements are made for coming up, and only hope that sufficient rain will fall to make your trip a pleasurable and successful one. So far there is not prospect of rain here, and a low barometer only heralds a duststorm.

Do not, on any account, allow my movements to interfere with your Sydney trip, as, owing to my having to assist in floating some Alice Springs Mining Properties, I will probably be detained in Adelaide for some time—How long I won't be able to say until I have seen Winnecke and other shareholders.[48]

Whether I shall go Westwards depends altogether on what the outlook is like when I go down; probably I will go for a short trip and return. So that I may have the pleasure of working out the Geological Problem with you after all.

What you say of Tate's treatment of Brown's work is quite correct, and Brown, when here lately, pointed out some remarks of Tate's that appear to be deliberate misstatements. He (Brown) was too tired after his long trip to listen to my suggestion that he should have a look at the hill to the Westward, but he criticised some Portions of the Horn Geology, especially insisting on the distinct stratification of the Pre-Silurian, in places, and on the unconformability of the Ooramina Sandstones with the underlying limestone. Since he left I have succeeded in unearthing five casts. One resembles Isoarca [sic] and shews teeth on hinge line, the other is *of* a shell about $1\frac{1}{2}$ inches in length, ventricose, with prominent subspiral beaks, equilateral, equivalve, and deeply furrowed concentrically. I think it may be akin to Isocardia [sic]! The casts are not very perfect but Etheridge may be able to determine them. I have also found some more fragments of separate whorled Ammonitile [sic]. The bag I sent was made by a Charlotte Waters blackfellow, and I saw an old man making another in the Camp yesterday. I think, but am not sure, that I have seen similar bags at Alice Springs.[49]

The beast supply has been very limited lately, and I have only succeeded in getting a couple of Antechinomys, and a Larapinta, in addition to a few beasts I am taking down for Winnecke's Museum. I am leaving two Dasyuroides (females with a lot of young ones) a Larapinta and a couple of Antechinomys here for you.[50]

Gillen is still at work with undiminished energy and the wail of the tormented Native is loud in the Land. Cowle has been silent for some time, but I understand that he has had his hair cut so he may intend Paying Crown Point, and possibly C.W. a visit.

Many thanks for information re plant. I must try and get a

flowering specimen as I would like to Know the species. It appears to be very poisonous. Hoping to see you soon.

I am,
Yours Ever Sincerely
P.M. Byrne
Professor W Baldwin Spencer

Letter 8.7

Charlotte Waters
26th March '97

Dear Professor,

Your trip to the Black Spur must have been a very pleasant one. Altho', unless you have the faculty of living in the present only, it must have been somewhat marred by the thought of those coming lectures.

The Photos you sent are perfect, and show the unconformability of the Desert Sandstone and the variation in dip of the underlying rock very distinctly.

David's confirmation of your opinion about the glacial markings should put their Genuiness [sic] beyond question, and no doubt further traces of ice action will be found among the adjacent hills, and northward on the Course of the Finke.[51] With reference to the Yellow Cliff Sandstone. Altho' it is coarser in texture and not so thinly bedded as the Sandstone we examined under the Crown, it agrees well with the Yellowish Sandstone lower down in the Series, and it certainly doesn't resemble an ordinary river deposit any more than the Sandstone underlying Crown Point. Tate, if I remember aright, says that the debacle pushed masses of Sand and Gravel before it 'forming low hills bordering the Finke about four miles South', and possibly he ascribed the 'scratchings' to the grinding together of such masses under great lateral pressure: but, (apart from the improbability of the debacle), in that case the embedded Stones would be scratched, and apparently they are not. Ross procured some of the smaller embedded stones from Yellow Cliff and I am sending them to you by this mail. If I can get a trip north during the winter I will examine the hills to the N and W of the Crown carefully. I would like to go Westward up the Lilla until the older rocks appear, but am afraid the trip would take too long.

Brown has made a new departure in his latest map. The tabletops he marks 'Upper Cretaceous or Tertiary', the claybeds as 'Lower Cretaceous', and the superior Quartzite of the James and Ooramina [sic] Ranges as 'Jurassic'! The central axis of both ranges, and the ranges four miles south of Alice Springs are marked 'Cambrian', and the Lower Silurian is shown as almost completely covered by newer formations along a line from Crown Point to Alice Springs via the Hugh and Ooraminna. He found Cambrian fossils at Alexandra, N.E of Powells Ck, and bases his Cambrian classification of the lower beds of the McD, James, and Ooraminna Ranges on lithological resemblances to other Cambrian areas. I think there can be little doubt that Tate was wrong in saying the Ooraminna Quartzites and Sandstones overlaid the limestone conformably, but whether Brown is right in assigning a Cambrian age to the latter seems an open Question.[52] Eylmann says he found lower Silurian fossils South of Alice Springs, but I haven't heard in what localities or formations.[53] It seems to me that they don't exactly know where they are, and the only way of settling the matter is to make a detailed Survey such as you suggest.

I have not heard from Brown about the fossils I sent him, but he is evidently doubtful about Crioceras or he would have been more positive about the Upper Cretaceous.[54]

Winnecke did not favor me with a letter last mail, but I noticed several copies of the Journal going through. His using the Photo's [sic] come as a surprise but I suppose it is, as you say, that Winnecke is not quite himself when having to do with Horn.

Cowle is right about Eylmann being a close observer. He certainly Kept his eyes about him between here and Oodnadatta, as he noticed everything even to 'Ze croostat vich swim on his back' (apus a), and the obsidian bombs.[55] But *I* don't see how he can do really valuable work without collecting specimens—unless his notes and drawings are exhaustive.

The Wheal Fortune has crushed and been found wanting. The results, being slightly over 4 dwts per ton, just about paid for half the crushing expenses, and, as eighty tons of what I presume is Similar Stone cost us £2,20 for raising alone, I decided to sell out, and did so for £3. The Alice Springs people are still enthusiastic, but it is a tempered enthusiasm as the amount I got for my shares proves.[56]

A large quantity of the Arltunga machinery is still at Oodnadatta, and it will be a least six months before it is erected and ready for crushing. By that time the Government will have expended about £6000, and the cheerful inhabitants will have come to the conclusion that it won't pay to raise stone unless they get a bonus of so much per ton. There is Gold in the Country, but I'm afraid Managers and Miners will have to be imported before it can be made Pay.[57]

The Pontiff was enthusiastic over the Federal Election and was greatly disappointed that the majority of his Sans Culottes did not figure amongst the Chosen.[58] I think Kingston will achieve notoriety at the Convention,[59] as, without being exceptionally clever, he possesses a good deal of cunning and he will probably wait until the majority of the speakers have expressed their views, and then Come in with a carefully prepared speech, which will gladden the hearts of the socialists, and at the same time soothe the Imperialists by referring to the 'Silken bonds', and 'the flag that has braved the battle and the breeze'. Solomon is,[60] I think, our best all round man tho' inferior as a Speaker to Gordon[61] who should divide the honors with Barton[62] and Reid.[63] But the whole affair is vanity and humbug and they are all 'on their own'!

As usual we missed the rain, altho' they had a good fall at Alice Springs and Oodnadatta. The 300 points we had here did not entice the moles out, but I have secured specimens of Crimia and P Minor. The latter appears a full grown male, but the confounded nigger neglected opening him, and he is reminiscent of Dick Palmer's snake.

My side is quite well again and I don't think I ever felt in better form, altho' a little depressed at present thro' having had an overdose of Marie Corelli.[64] Even the consolation of finding that the Devil was a milk and water fraud did not compensate for her treatment of Huxley in the 'Mighty Atom'.

Hoping that you are quite well and that Mrs Spencer has had a safe and pleasant trip.[65]

I am,
Yours Ever Sincerely
P.M.Byrne
Professor W. Baldwin Spencer

Letter 8.8

Charlotte Waters
11th May '97
Dear Professor,

Your account of Tate's interview with David is amusing, and quite bears out what people generally say about him. It seems a pity that a man of his ability should be so unreliable and what makes it worse is that, in South Australia, at all events, he has many disciples.

I don't know what to think of Brown's new map. If he is right there must have been subsidence and elevation east of the Finke which did not affect the country to the Westward. Mt. Watt and Mt. Musgrave are about the same elevation, not very far apart, and yet a wide Gap in their ages. Then the basal parts of Crown Point are shewn as Jurassic while those of Mt. Frank are *marked* 'Upper Cretaceous or Tertiary', and, yet the Sandstone underlying the silicified capping at both places are lithologically alike. However, I suppose, it will be settled some day, but it seems absurd that there should be so many conflicting descriptions of a Country which is not quite as complicated in its Geology as the Scottish Highlands.[66]

Still no sign of rain, and I will be in the throes of shifting to the Finke in a fortnight, unless our Bore strikes water in the meantime. It is now down one hundred feet, through Kaolinite, and blue clay with Gypsum crystals, but the progress is slow and it will take them four or five months to go the seven or eight hundred feet I think they will need to sink before striking water.[67]

Cowle passed here yesterday with a four in hand team of blacks en route for Pt. Augusta.[68] He is lean, but healthy, and looks forward to a 'high old time'. He had a wash here.

Following is from Gillen,[69] 'Vide wanderings Achilpa, column 4. Urachipma is Mt Sonder where, while passing, the Achilpa saw Illuta (big pig-faced rat) man making large wooden Pitchies (uritcha), and named spot Urachipma, which means the place of the Pitchies. Whenever Ariltha was performed special Nurtunja was made all routes. Kowowa always erected, but only used for Engwura'.

I will keep a sharp look out for moles while on the Finke, and may, also, be able to get some more specimens of Urpila [sic] and Ewurra. The trip up Lilla Ck will, I'm afraid, have to wait until the Deity listens to Wragge.[70]

I believe the mines at Alice Springs are more wonderful than ever, but I'm devoting my attention solely to the West which is, I think, on the eve of resurrection. What do Victorians say to the Kalgoorlie output beating that of Ballarat and Bendigo? In another six months the Boulder, Lake View and Ivanhoe, alone will turn out more gold than either of those districts. There!

You can imagine the dearth of anything to write about under existing Circumstances so will close with kindest regards.

Yours Ever Sincerely
P.M. Byrne

Letter 8.9

Charlotte Waters
1st August '97

Dear Professor,

Yours with Nansen's 'Farthest North' received,[71] and I have forwarded the book on to Crown Point after enjoying the Perusal. Reaching 86° was a big feat, but after all there is not a Great deal to show for so much labor and Privation and I think a thorough examination of the Franz Joseph Archipelago,[72] or better still, the Antarctic continent would be more likely to give valuable results.[73] In the latter I have no doubt Primal Man will be found, surrounded by Generalised Polyprotodonts, and lamenting that he had missed the Jubilee junketings!

By the papers I see that the imperialist rash, which broke out so suddenly, is still in evidence, and the pot-bellied little man with the unromantic Countenance who hails from N.S.W. appears to have a bad attack.[74] The other Premiers of Greater Britain have also made magnificent offers of assistance, and I think it was a shabby thing of Goschen to suggest that they should pay for their own fleet.[75] No one but a mercenary Jew would have been capable of such an action, and I should not be surprised if Australia refused to borrow any more money from a country harboring such an individual—

No useful rain of Course, and, with the exception of our attenuated Cristicauda, nothing captured since last I wrote. Six weeks ago we had a light shower which put a fortnights water in some of the crabholes, but, altho I visited them every day, I could not discover any sign of life. When they were just dry I found one thin, white, wormlike, beast, which broke in two when lifted, and a few twigs covered with a viscid substance, all of which I put in spirits. The temperature was max about 70, *min 36 to 40*.

I have the blacks on the look out for S. larapinta, and I suppose the moles will put in an appearance again some day.

Cowle arrived here yesterday looking very stout and well, and he overflows with reminiscences of the tour, which must have been a thoroughly enjoyable one. He intends going into the Photography thoroughly, and I expect he will soon rival the 'Supreme' himself as an artist.[76]

By this mail I am sending you portion of a cast of a cephalopod which shews markings resembling those of the suture. They may give some clue to the species.

With kind regards,
Yours Ever Sincerely
P.M. Byrne
Professor W. Baldwin Spencer

Letter 8.10

Charlotte Waters
1st July '98

Dear Professor,

I was very sorry to hear that you have been unwell, and hope that you are now quite recovered. The anthropological work, in addition to the ordinary routine, was altogether too much, and I am glad that the former is now successfully finished.

Despite the opinion of our veracious English and Colonial Press, I can hardly believe that the U.S. is likely to form an alliance with England. America has always been friendly with Russia, and also owes her independence, in a great measure, to France. In addition, England is, to all intents and purposes, a German appendage and Uncle Sam detests the Gentleman of the mailed fist.[77] As you say it will probably end in a big war—Germany opposes the U.S. in the Phillipines [sic], France mediates between Spain and America—Peace. France, Russia and U.S. attack Triple Alliance. England, if wise, looks on—if not, gets licked. Result—hashed Teuton!! England escaping with the loss of India, and her African possessions, also her fleet, which was lost thro' her Admirals following the example of the late lamented Tryon, and attempting to manoeuvre in smooth waters.[78] Australia invaded by Russians who are horrified at way Govt a/cs [accounts] cooked, and the rottenness of Banks and other institutions, but who are greatly taken with Roundabout Reid! C.A., bravely defended by an army of flies, remains unconquered.[79]

We have had nice rains and the waterholes are full, but there is little feed. Marsupials, with the exception of Larapinta, are scarce. The lubras are now out after moles and bandicoots in the Oodnatchurra country where I believe there is a good deal of water lying about. By mail I am sending some beasts, just captured, which should be in good condition for Sections, also two or three beetles for French.

I saw a notice of a work by Dr. Roth in the Bulletin some time ago, and was much struck with his theory of mimicry as applied to Subincision.[80] I always tho't that the operation on the females was a result of the operation *on* the males, being rendered necessary by the loss of penetrative power in the male organ, but in the LarraKuyah tribe[81] I believe the female is not operated on, and the male is consequently not subincised which proves Roth right.

I will endeavour to get a pouch Echidna, and keep a look out for leaf-piercing ants, but I am afraid the Echidna will be difficult to get as they resemble the moles in hiding until the young are fairly grown.[82]

Our bore is down 1200 feet, water struck about 600 feet.[83] Supply small, rising to within 160 feet of the surface—no increase since. Doubtful when finished as they are continually having accidents and muddling things generally.

Field so far, a ghastly failure. Battery put thro' about 250 tons in five months, Woolcocks salary £35 per month. Cost per ton reckoning W's salary alone 14/-. Rate charged to public about 12/-! Results from battery so far about same as from Huntington Mill viz 12 dwts per ton. Gold on average worth under £3.10 per ounce.[84]

Wheal Fortune and Star of North, under management of Messrs

Gillen and Besley, a great success. Two holes—one twenty, one fifty feet—sunk, and about sixty tons of Stone picked off surface at a cost of £750. Result three Crushings 4 dwts, 10 dwts and 2 dwts. Final result, bankruptcy of Co![85]

I have stuck to W.A. and have been increasing holdings in Kalgurli [sic] Mines. So far have been losing steadily, but if war does not break out, think I will more than recover losses eventually.

Lubra just come in, says old women will be in tonight with moles and other beasts. Mail leaves at 2 p.m. so will not be able to forward for a fortnight.

Yours Ever Sincerely
P.M. Byrne

Letter 8.11

Charlotte Waters
13th Aug '98

Dear Professor,

I am sorry to hear that the last vacation was again given over to work, and that you contemplate devoting the next to the cheerful savages E of Lake Eyre.[86] This will never do. No man can work at high pressure, like you are doing, all the time, and even for the sake of the work a rest would be beneficial.

As one who has cultivated 'Sweet idleness' for years, and who knows its charms, I would strongly recommend spending the next vacation, with the Genial French, in some quiet spot where the 'Gentle Art' can be followed, and where, lying under a shady tree, you can smoke the Pipe of Peace and Content, and watch the clouds going overhead. Only the lightest of literature (carefully selected by French) should be allowed, and all conversation on Scientific subjects strictly prohibited. I really believe a couple of months of this sort of thing would do you a vast amount of good, and that the work would not suffer in the long run.

There seems to be a good deal of truth in what you say about work, and to the real worker the reward, to a great extent, is in the doing. It is useless to say that either Knowledge or Power make men happier when a blackfellow in his Camp is probably more content and free from care than men like Huxley or the Kaiser. Perhaps in the next incarnation the workers become drones and vice versa; but, failing the incarnation, the drones, Provided they own enough dollars, have rather the best of it.

Arltunga is still turning out about half an ounce to the ton, but I'm afraid the stone being put thro' is hardly an average sample, and it is rumoured that some of the gold is of low grade—only worth about 30/- an ounce. An English Syndicate are prospecting in the vicinity of Tennants Creek and I should not be surprised to hear of their striking something good. If they do, plenty of capital will be forthcoming as the Great Zebina Lane is the High Priest of the show.[87]

The country around is looking fairly well—in fact there are several patches of green, the size of a tablecloth, between here and Mt Frank, and a friendly mirage occasionally puts a few lakes on the surrounding tablelands, so that the view from the office door is at times pleasing, if deceptive.

I have been rather busy lately mustering and yard building, and the blacks have been hard at work practising imported Corroborees, which a travelled member of the tribe has brought over from Queensland.[88] Still I have succeeded in getting a few moles, and the lubras are now out after Peragale and Chæropus. Dasyuroides and Phascologale are not about at Present, but they are sure to turn up later on, when the weather gets warmer.

By this mail I am sending you a small tin of beasts, and hope to have Peragale, and some beetles for French, when the expedition returns. The witches <u>will not</u> search for beetles, or if they do they bring a bottle full of one sort—Generally the common green one with the buggy odour!

Things are not looking too bright for England in Cathay, with Russia and France continually encroaching, and 'Divine Right Bill' irritating America and making an ass of himself generally.[89]

It will be a terrible war when it comes, and I don't think it can be far off.

Gillen should be here in two or three weeks en route for Oodnadatta where he leaves Mrs. Gillen and returns to Alice Springs.[90] That is, if he can resist the temptation of a flying visit to Town. The blacks meditate shifting their camp to Oodnatchurra while he is in this vicinity.

I have not heard anything of Eylmann for some time, but I will deliver your message if he turns up.

Yours Ever Sincerely
P.M Byrne

P.S. Don't forget what I say about the next vacation 'From the mouths of babes etc'!

Letter 8.12

Charlotte Waters
25th March '99

Dear Professor,

Your welcome letter and a copy of the Magnum Opus were received by last mail. I was glad to hear that you had a fairly good trip, and your mention of Seeing Snow while passing thro' France came like a cool breeze to temper something over 100 in the shade.[91]

The return to the perpetual grind must be awful and I don't know how you have the courage to face it. I am certain the first lecture would find <u>me</u> missing!

From the Papers I see that Haeckel must have been at Oxford about the time you were in England so I suppose you had some dry and very learned discussions on beast [sic] and other matters.[92]

I have not got thro' the work yet, but I admire it very much and think it should prove a great success.

Gillen starts for the home of the Cousin Jacks next month,[93] and from what I can hear he will have to be circumspect in his new quarters, as the Moontaites are rabidly Wesleyan and Anti-Irish. Just imagine the Pontiff suffering martyrdom for the cause of Home Rule and shouting 'I did it for Ireland', amid yells of 'Kick un Sonny', 'Kick un while un's down'.

Cowle is busily engaged transferring the native population of Tempe Downs to Pt Augusta where, if the tales of their daring and bloodthirstiness are true, they will prove a menace to the Population, and necessitate the presence of the military. Cowle should be down here next month to take charge of the ballot box for that important voting place—Horseshoe Bend.[94]

We are having the same old drought here with just sufficient feed and water to keep the stock alive. Yesterday we had half an inch of rain which will stave off going to the Finke for a couple of months, but the country wants about ten inches of rain to put things right.

The blacks are all congregated here, all outside waters being dry, and the beasts are very scarce. I have a few Antechinomys and one or two moles, but Phascologale, Sminthopsis, Dasyuroides, the Bandicoots and the rodents have evidently sought Greener Pastures and I feel very much like doing the same myself.

With kind regards,
Yours Ever Sincerely
P.M. Byrne
Professor Baldwin Spencer

Letter 8.13

Charlotte Waters
25th July '21,

Dear Sir Baldwin,

I was glad to receive your kind message, and, tho' late, I congratulate you heartily on the well earned honor received in recognition of your services to Science.[95]

I saw Sir Edgworth for only a few minutes when passing, but long enough for me to recognize his courtesy and kindliness, and understand the secret of his popularity. It is a pity he did not have more time at his disposal, but he appeared well satisfied with results, and the knowledge gained should enhance the value of his coming work on Australian Geology. Of later years, I have thought that the Cretaceous rocks north of here rested directly on the Silurian, and that the McDonnell group of ranges, upheaved in the Silurian, were almost completely submerged in the Cretaceous, re-elevated sufficiently during the Tertiary to become glaciated—the glaciation lasting until a recent Tertiary period—and then subsided to their present level.

However, conjectures are futile, as the Easter Islander remarked to the Tasmanian, and Sir Edgworth's work should decide the matter.[96]

During the years since last you saw it, there have been many changes in this country. The rabbits have supplanted the marsupials, and the indigenous plants are gradually giving way to inferior kinds of herbage. A record season, like the present one, may improve matters, but many rabbits survived the last drought, and I think they will soon be as numerous as ever. Many of the old, and some of the young, natives you met about here are dead. Even our form of Administration *has changed* and we now figure as a sort of Police Satrapy. The policemen protects, prosecutes, punishes, and feeds, the Aborigines. He controls their labour, and decides who shall, and who shall not, be permitted to employ them, He rules the Bungalow, and the JPs meekly obey him—in fact he runs Centralia. The result depends on the sort of Policeman we get. It is not an ideal form of rule but is, perhaps, better than that of the mischief making Missionary, or the Sham Philanthropist.[97]

When filling up the Census paper recently, my mind went back to the Census of twenty years ago. Then, in reply to a certain question, poor old Gillen compounded with his conscience, the Cook proclaimed himself a Loman Katlik, and you and I wrote 'Object'. This year, I wrote Pantheist and next time, if I haven't found Conan Doyle's familiars, I suppose I will narrow it to Proto-electromist or something equally trashy!

If the present wave of hatred and discontent subsides, I may visit what was called Civilization some time next year, but I fear there is little chance of a change for the better. My private opinion is that this elderly Sun of ours, not being acquainted with Einstein's 'Relativity', has failed to make enough allowance for leeway, and is dragging us thro' a region of space occupied by ions charged with 'Survival of the fittest' energy. No doubt, the passage of our System thro' such a region of space was, in the Past, the cause of our forefathers clubbing Pithecanthropus and other rivals, and incidentally, losing most of their hair.[98] On the present occasion God, who may be supposed to take a parental interest in us, and who cannot be too well pleased with the *result of the* former experience, was probably steering for a 'survival of the best' region, but Einstein 'bushed' him (those Germans are a bad lot), and now we are faced with a struggle for existence between the Races, which may recur at intervals until only one is left. In this connection, it would be interesting to know how our nearest Anthropoid relatives (the Gorillas for instance) are affected at the present juncture. Anyhow, I believe it will be safer to remain on the tablelands with a secure, if monotonous, present, and mourn for the good old times, 'All gone like snow long, long ago—the times of the Barmecides'![99]

With the best of good wishes,

Yours sincerely
P.M. Byrne.
<u>Sir W Baldwin Spencer F.R.S., K.B.E.</u>[100]
Melbourne.

Letter 8.14

Charlotte Waters
16th Decr '25,

Dear Sir Baldwin,

Another milestone on the road to the 'Dawn of Nothing' is in sight, and with it come memories. Many of the old faces have gone, and the few remaining accentuate the difference between the past and the present, And not only the faces, the manners and the Customs have altered. The Motor, as you foreshadowed, is firmly established, and with some further improvements to the road, and alterations in the Machine, large trucks will be running next year.[101] They will supply all the transport required, and if the Govt builds a railway it will increase its financial difficulties immensely,[102] and, unless Uncle Sam comes to the rescue, land Australia in the Insolvency Court, with railways and water schemes that cannot be made to pay, Irrigation and Soldier supplements that are insolvent and the intelligence of her politicians as her only assets.

I have just read 'The Antiquity of Man', and was pleased to find that the Author had extended the boundaries of the Garden of Eden to the Southern Hemisphere.[103] Still it is a long cry yet to anything approaching finality, whether the Australian was driven here, or merely stranded while on his way elsewhere remains a puzzle. Some day, a relic older than the Talgai skull may be unearthed, and shed some further light on the subject.[104]

Whatever the past hides, the present of the unfortunate Aborigine is sufficiently miserable, Native food of any description is almost non-existent, and under the circumstances, the rations issued to the old natives are insufficient. But for the earnings of the Younger men, who buy food, and the Kindness of some of the older residents, the old blacks would be semi-starved. All these old people have been accustomed to clothes and tobacco, and, now, the amount supplied to them is absurdly small. In addition, our Missionaries undermine their authority, and ridicule their traditions, we take from them everything that makes life worth living, work them until they can work no longer, and then hand them over to the police, whose main endeavour is to work things as cheaply as possible, and thus please a Gov't that has neither Knowledge nor conscience. It is a despicable crime.[105]

There have been a few showers of rain, lately, between Oodnadatta and Alice Springs, but practically the drought is unbroken, and in my opinion, likely to remain unbroken for some time, but, of course, rain in this country is accidental, and accidents will happen!

I hope yourself, Lady Spencer and family are quite well, With the best of good wishes for the New Year.

Yours faithfully
P.M. Byrne
Sir Baldwin Spencer K.C.M.G., F.R.S.

APPENDIX 1

C.E. COWLE LETTERS TO EDWARD STIRLING

The South Australian Museum archives contain two letters written by Cowle to the Director, Edward Stirling. They first met in 1891 when Stirling visited Alice Springs, and contact was renewed during the Horn Expedition. These letters were written following that expedition, when Stirling was compiling his report for the anthropology volume.[1]

Illamurta
16th November 1894

Dear Dr Stirling,

Your letter to hand and I have not forgotten the caste question—some time since I learnt from 'Racehorse' that the distinctions about his part of the Country[2] are as put in the accompanying list but Tempe remains closed to me as yet—the strange thing is how they know the cast [sic] of a lubra or blackfellow of another tribe. At Tempe there is much indiscriminate intermarriage and the Coomarra Pultarra etc is absolutely unknown under these names and yet they know the relationship they

bear to some of our boys who come from away to East of Alice Springs.
When I get hold of an uncivilised one I can get no sense out of him and
when I try one of the others I find they have a smattering of the Finke
Castes picked up from intercourse with blacks from those parts, certainly
at Tempe they are less particular than at any place I have been but yet
I am certain from the fact that they have words expressing Uncle and
Aunt, Father and Mother etc that they must have some divisions.
Racehorse has been here nearly ever since you left the Mission he is a
terrible fool but knows that Country well and I intend going out there
again shortly. You will have a formidable rival in Gillen in anything in
the Aboriginal line, at present he intends discovering the origin of the
tribes from the stones, he reckons he knows more about the Blacks than
any other living man and any yarn he gets into <u>his</u> head is the only correct
solution of anything—now I think from the little you saw up here of
how a/cs vary, you know how difficult it is to really bottom a custom or
determine the real reason of anything, he simply gets hold of a version
and goes straight on and any man holding another is a fool. I came across
a little curio the other day (the owner was absent) which I have kept in
hopes of being able to ascertain its uses but every blackfellow I have
shewn it to is ignorant of it except that 'him come up long way' I am
posting it to you in a separate cover exactly as I got it.[3] Daer is doing
first rate but I am clean off as I am describing in a separate letter
herewith.[4] Our garden is quite a picture and a really fine assortment of
vegetables are growing in it. I hear of another plant of stones towards
Haast's Bluff—Gillen wrote asking me to get him some and I suppose
you could do with some more I don't know when I can get up that way
but I hope to soon. I had a long chase after Arrabi and others for Sheep
and Cattle killing from Mission St'n in August and caught them up South
West of Mareena and last month I was after Meenymurta and several
other young men on the Peterman and Gill's Range for cattle killing but
after putting in about ten days, hard work I got bested and am to go out
again in about a week's time.[5]

Everyone in this part of the World busy just now and nothing
discussed beyond the forthcoming Xmas Races at Alice Spgs I am
not going in if I can get out of it. With best wishes for a prosperous
New Year.

Yours very sincerely
C. Ernest Cowle

The main division of Racehorse's lot are
Tcham-pee-tchimpee corresponding with Coomarra
Tchap-oong-arty
or   *Pultarra*
Gnappoongarty
Tchappoonunga
or   *Purninga*
Gnappoon-unga
Tchap-paroola
or   *Perula*
Gnapparoola
With the same sequence of marriage but now certain ramifications come in such as

> *Gnoon-ar-eye-ee produced by two Tchampee-tchimpee or Tchoon-are-eye-ee Tchung-uller the offspring of Tchampee-tchimpa and Napp-Tchuck-oo murra Uperoola male and Nappoong-unga female-oongarty Uperoola tchuckoomurra male and tchappillcharra female Tchappillcharra-Gnoon-ar-eye-ee male and Nacoom-arrie female Gnacooma-arrie Tchuck-oo-murra male and Gnappoongung female*

I cannot get the hang of these later variations. I thought I had it straight till I tried one more final check today you will observe that most of them are tch or gn I will try and dig to the bottom of this.[6]

Illamurta
16th May 1995

Dear Doctor,

Very many thanks for your kindly expressed sympathy in our great loss[7]. It is the very first time I have been brought close to death in our own circle and as yet I can scarcely realize that I will never see my Mother again in this World. I had made up my mind to go down this year to see all of them again but now can scarcely say when I will get that far. I note what you say re Castes and if you are wrestling harder than I have you must be having a stiff time. I have tried many both male and female out at Tempe and can get nothing lucid. I have asked them what they call <u>their</u> lubras and how they know they are not connected and they reply 'When him see 'em, right one him ketch him' but how they distinguish they can't explain. I asked Coulthard's boy (a half caste) and he did not know but as he talks well I have told him to try and find out. I am almost inclined to be sceptical as to whether these Western tribes are not even a lower type than those on the Finke and are not particular—you need not think I will relax my efforts on this subject not only because I am anxious to oblige you but I am interested and don't like being baffled. My anxiety is chiefly to get the information in time to be of service to you. You certainly have the most difficult task of the Exped'n to work up and one that will not show the real amount of time and labour expended on it[8]. I will write to you next mail again on this subject. I have been getting the names of most parts outwardly of the human body so far I have 40 or 50 which I will send you when properly checked and added to if of any use.

I have been taking 2 tablets a day regularly since I last wrote you without feeling them at all and will start on three tomorrow. I never felt better in my life and those 'chlorate of potash' tabloids worked like a charm.[9]

Daer has been down about Charlotte Waters but writes he will be back before down mail leaves from which I presume he must be doing well—he sent a specimen of his urine to Dr Todd and if he thought it bad I think Daer would have gone right through.[10]

Believe me,
Yours sincerely
C. Ernest Cowle

Appendix 2

C.E. Cowle to R.H. Mathews

R.H. Mathews (1841–1918) was a surveyor who recorded extensive data on Aboriginal social life, customs, languages and material culture. He was a dedicated correspondent, but Baldwin Spencer unfairly considered him to be a plagiarist, thereby influencing his friends to ignore Mathews' queries. This may explain why Cowle evidently wrote him only one letter (see L4.4). Cowle's greater understanding of Aboriginal ethnography may be inferred from comparing this letter of 1900 with those to Stirling five years previously.

Illamurta
16th Feb 1900[1]
R.H. Mathews Esq
Parramatta

Dear Sir,

Yours of 15th Jany with pamphlets, for which many thanks, to hand yesterday. From what I can make out of the Natives of this Country, they have totems connected with practically all animals, birds, foods, reptiles etc and with the various kind of each species but unlike the organization you describe, the totem does not appear to have any influence on marriage relations nor does any totem in particular apply to any one class; for instance a native might be a 'Kumara' 'Bultharra' 'Peroola' or 'Panunga' Green Snake. The totem the Native belongs to is that one pertaining to the place he was born at or perhaps where his mother fancies she conceived him—different localities all over the Country are assigned to different totems & the Native belief is that at these various camping spots of the Natives of such a totem in <u>prehistoric times</u>, spirits of many of them went into the ground & the child born at one of them is the re-incarnation of one of these blacks of that particular totem. I know of a Native Cat man married to a Native Cat woman both of whom were born at the one locality.

Some 200 odd miles South of here, a tribe called the 'Oorabunna'[2] have totems influencing marriage relationships but I do not understand anything about their organisation. I am chiefly amongst the Looritcha Tribe who are distinct from the Arunta but so far have failed to get their systems, the blacks who can talk sufficiently to get anything out of are those who have intermingled with Arunta Blacks and taken their divisions for certain purposes. The less civilized ones do not seem to grip the idea but I live in hopes—the Totems etc in connection with the 'Arunta' and allied tribes have been very fully gone into by Spencer and Gillen and I would advise you to read their work and if I can then answer any further questions for you, I shall be happy to do my best.

I enclose a list of one family I worked out some time ago to show you the Totem of each.

Yours truly
C. Ernest. Cowle
Illamurta
via Charlotte Waters
S.A.

Name	Class	Born at	Totem	Married	Name	Class	Born at	Totem
M Oomah	Coomarra	Stuart's Gap	Wallaby	had issue	Coornta	Bultharra	Idracowra	Possum
	m	'Nukingilka' class Perula.		Born at Bad Crossing married			Totem	Little Bat
F Illyumba	Pernunga had issue	Twatterna	Mulgah seed	& F. 'Lukingeer'		Pernunga had issue	Running Waters	Duck
m 'Enurnbucka'	Coomarra	Twatterna	Mulgah seed	F. 'Algoleeta'	class	Coomarra	Cave Hole	Witchetty Grub
m 'Ittarka'	Coomarra	5 Mile Creek	Oruncha (Devil)	M 'Qualpa'	"	Coomarra	Undiarra	Kangaroo
				M 'Intoochilparka'		Coomarra	Cave Hole	Witchetty Grub
m 'Joeeta'	Coomarra	Hart's Camp	Green Snake & Mulgah Seed as he was conceived at Twatterna					
'Lunkanillyicka'	Coomarra	Stuart's Gap	Wallaby					

See Spencer and Gillen on the subdivision of the classes Coomarra—Pernunga—Perula and Bultharra & also on the sacred or Churina name of each native

APPENDIX 3

OFFICIAL POLICE
CORRESPONDENCE

This important series of letters concerning the whipping of Aboriginal prisoners is reproduced with permission from the South Australian State Records. Their archival reference is GRG 5/2/1894/176.

The series began in response to the journal kept on a patrol by M/C Thomas Daer and submitted to the District Inspector at Port Augusta. Daer and four native police were on patrol from 29 October to 11 November 1893. Cowle was left in charge at Illamurta during this time. Daer's journal for 5 November 1893 simply records: '5th found where 3 Natives had killed a calf, tracked them up and took them to Tempe Downs, where they were whipped by Trackers.'

Inspector B.C. Besley noted in the margin: 'Returned to M/C Daer'. This requires explanation. What magistrate ordered the whipping send full particulars. At present it looks like an unlawful act' 12 Dec 1893. The following letter was Daer's reply.

Illamurta
28 Jan 1894
To B.C. Besley
Inspector of Police Pt Augusta

Sir,

'Native cattle killers whipped by Native Constables.' I have the honor to state that on the 5th November last, when patrolling Tempe Downs Run, I found where a calf had been killed that morning, the Native Constables and myself followed up the offenders tracks and found three full grown Natives carrying the beef away on their heads. On sight of us the Natives dropped the meat and ran for a range close by. I followed one and captured him, the Native Constables catching the other two. I then took the offenders on to Tempe Downs where I ordered the Trackers to whip them, which was done. In explanation I would respectfully point out that I was 140 miles distant from the nearest Magistrate and my reason for having the offenders whipped by the Trackers was to save the Government the expense of taking them to Port Augusta which would have cost a lot of money. I am strongly of opinion that if the Natives were soundly thrashed by the Trackers when caught cattle killing it would have a much better effect than sending them to gaol. Since the boys were whipped in November last, no cattle to our knowledge, have been killed on Tempe Downs by Natives.

I have the honor to be
Sir
Your obedient servant
Thomas Daer 1st C. MC

On back of Daer's letter:

26/2/94 Forwarded to the Commissioner of Police
I have always been of opinion that the whipping of Aboriginals in outlying districts like this for offences is the most salutary way of punishing them but as it is illegal it is my duty to lay the matter before you.
    B.C. Besley
    Inspector 20/2/94

Inspector Besley. Some details of this whipping should be given— with what was it implicated? How many strokes? and what physical affect did it have on them.

[signature indecipherable, but it must be Peterswald, Commissioner of Police] 23/2/94

Returned to M.C. Daer whose attention is drawn to the Commissioner's Minutes above 26/2/94

Respectfully returned to Inspr. Besley. The whipping was inflicted with a horse-whip and consisted of twenty lashes.

The Blacks appeared a little stiff next day and very frightened as I had told them I would repeat the whipping if caught offending again. The moral effect seems to have been excellent.

Thomas Daer 27/3/94

Respectfully returned to the Commissioner of Police with explanation from M.C. Daer endorsed therein.

John Field Sergt.

Respectfully forwarded to the Hon the Chief Secretary.

Peterswald Commissioner 4/5/94

Returned to Commissioner of Police 14/5/94

Illamurta 29 Aug 1894
Recd 20/4/94

Sir,

I have the honour to report leaving here to enquire re Sheep and Cattle killing at the Mission Station on 15th inst. I got the tracks of one party of Offenders and followed same 85 miles when I rounded up a camp and got three—'Mooldurna' 'Nappuppa' and 'Noolgunda', these I flogged and went on another 40 miles and got two more 'Arrabi' and 'Charlkoona' these I also flogged and cautioned.

While tracing these Blacks I found out that another party had killed a beast close to the one reported by Mr Heidenreich—they then met at Arumbera and made a young man after which they split up. I could not trace both parties or get the chief offenders owing to the scrubby and impassable character of the Ranges they got into but I know the names of the principals concerned in both affairs and can get them in time especially if they meet again to corroboree. I was particularly careful to punish only those actually concerned in the killing and all others I fed and gave flour and tobacco to. Since the natives were flogged at Tempe last year, they have behaved well and I feel confident that it has a more lasting effect than any other way of treating them. They received 25 lashes each. I respectfully beg to point out the impossibility of continuing to follow up Blacks in this Country and keeping others in custody with you at the same time.

I have the honour to be
Sir
Your Obedient Servant
C. Ernest Cowle 3C MC
J. Field
Sub Inspector of Police
Pt Augusta

On back of Cowle's letter:
Forwarded to Sub Insper. Field. I am of opinion although the act is illegal that M.C. Cowle did the right thing in this matter, we will get the other offenders and treat them in the same way, they cannot be got in one lot and otherwise the Govnt [sic] would be put to much expense in transporting them to Gaol which does not seem to have a deterrent effect. The offender Arrabi being one of the prisoners recently in Gaol at Port Augusta for a similar offence.
    Thomas Daer 1st C MC
    Illamurta 29/8/94

'Respectfully forwarded to the Commissioner of Police for perusal.'
    John Field
    Sub Inspector 20/9/94

Respectfully forwarded to the Hon the Chief Secretary
    Peterswald Commissioner
    22/9/94
    Commissioner of Police

Punishment without judicial authority can on no account be sanctioned. Police to be cautioned accordingly.

[From Chief Secretary probably dated 1/10/94]

Returned to Sub Inspector Field. I have sent a telegram direct to Alice Springs on this subject. If necessary inform other stations.

[Peterswald] 3–10–94

On cover of this file:

Noted and returned to the Commissioner of Police. I have notified the officers in charge of Illamurta and Barrow Creek, the instruction of the Hon the Attorney General on this subject.

John Field

Sub Inspr. 5/10/94

APPENDIX 4

COST OF ESCORTING PRISONERS

This series of exchanges covers the period July to September 1902 [SAA GRG/5/2/371 (1902)]. The costs involved when Cowle captured eleven prisoners at Hermannsburg and their subsequent sentencing to Port Augusta prison for cattle spearing offences caused concern, as the annual costs for escorts reached £120. The Chief Commissioner of Police requested detailed accounts and sought the opinion of T.A. Bradshaw SM, Gillen's successor at Alice Springs telegraph station. Bradshaw advocated a 'stockade' at Alice Springs, near the telegraph station. It was 1909 before this recommendation was acted upon, but the site selected for a gaol was in Stuart (Alice Springs) township. Only Cowle's correspondence is reproduced here.

Telegram, Cowle to Sub-Inspector J. Field, Port Augusta, 14 July 1902

Ten natives sentenced six months Port Augusta Gaol larceny of beef mission station can you arrange M C Williams take charge of prisoners Charlotte Waters my horses very weak

Expences [sic] in connection with escorting Native prisoners from Mission Station to Alice Sps. for trial and thence to Charlotte Waters [undated]

1902		£. S. D
8 July	To 1 meal each to Natives Mooldurna, Racehorse, Nuctambah, Coota-coota, Mirreeilgna, Cheedeena, Wilkeetanna, Mulgundah, Warmeeterchookeroo, Cunjedai. Chinnapuppa arrested at Mission Station under escort to Alice Sprs. 11 @ 1/-	0. 11. 0
9th 10th 11th 12th July	To 3 meals each p diem to the above 11 aboriginals under escort to Alice Spgs. 4 days each @ 4/- p diem each. 85 miles	8. 16. 0
13th 14th 15th 16th July	To 3 meals each p diem to the above 11 aboriginals at Alice Sps. Awaiting trial and being tried. 2 days each at 2/- per diem each	2. 4. 0
15th 16th July	To 3 meals each per diem to Mooldurna, Racehorse, Nuctambah, Coota-coota, Mirreeilgna, Cheedeena, Wilkeetanna, Mulgundah, Warmeeterchookeroo, Cunjedai, at Alice Sps awaiting escort to Charlotte Waters. Chinnapuppa discharged. 10 for 2 days each at 2/- p. diem each	2. 0. 0
17th to 27th July	To 3 meals each p diem to above ten natives under escort to Charlotte Waters. 11 days each at 4/- p diem each. 239 miles	22. 0. 0
14th July	To 11 shirts for 11 aboriginals @ 4/- each	2. 4. 0
		£37. 15. 0
	C. Ernest Cowle	2C.MC

Also travelling expenses [for himself]

July 7th to Aug 2nd	To 26 days @ 6/- per diem	£7. 16. 0
		£45. 11. 0

M/C Williams submitted an account for £22–12–8 for the cost of escorting these prisoners from Charlotte Waters to Oodnadatta, and his return journey to Charlotte Waters. The prisoners were seven days on the track and waited one further day for the train to Port Augusta.

APPENDIX 5

BYRNE'S KURDAITCHA ARTICLE (1895)

Note on the customs connected with the use of the so-called Kurdaitcha Shoes of central Australia

By P.M. Byrne

Proceedings of the Royal Society of Victoria, 8 (1895), pp. 65–8
[Read 14 November 1895]

The following notes were written in 1892 in response to the request of a correspondent, and are the result of careful inquiries conducted amongst the blacks in the Charlotte Waters district. As they have been gathered at first hand and are somewhat more detailed than any yet published, it has been suggested to me that it would be worthwhile placing them on record.

I have been for many years well acquainted with the natives of this district, but owing to the fact that it is now more than twenty years since the custom was practised, considerable care has to be taken in order to secure authentic information. Any blackfellow will give the inquirer replies to his questions, but it is only after making a great number of inquiries and obtaining corroboration from various sources that it is possible to arrive at conclusion as to what is and what is not reliable information.

There are in this district only two old men who have ever worn the shoes themselves; the younger men only know of the custom from the elders of the tribe, and in a few years it will probably be forgotten. The shoes are now only made to supply the orders of the whites, or perhaps to enable the old men to illustrate the deeds of other days before the half-admiring, half-sceptical members of the younger generation.

The shoes themselves have been previously described. They consist of a sole made of human hair and a great number of intertwined emu feathers, a certain amount of human blood being used as a kind of cementing material. The whole form a large pad, flat above and convex below, with the two ends rounded off so that there is no distinction between them. The upper part is in the form of a net, made of human hair, with a central opening for the foot, across which stretches a cord of hair which serves as a strap for the instep.

The shoes themselves in this district are known by the name of 'Urtathurta', and the occasion on which they were used is spoken of as 'Kurdaitcha luma' (Kurdaitcha—a bad or evil spirit, and luma, to walk).

The wearing of the Urtathurta and going Kurdaitcha luma appears to have been the medium for a form of vendetta, though it was quite distinct from the 'Adninga' or war party which was always despatched to avenge the death of a native supposed to have been killed by spells or to recover a lubra who had been stolen.

When any native threatened the life of a member of a different tribe, the threatened man could await his enemy's attack or take the initiative himself. If he decided upon the latter course the medicine man was consulted and a 'Kurdaitcha luma' arranged. In either case the attacking native was called Kurdaitcha. A medicine man always accompanied the latter, and both were similarly attired.

The head-dress worn consisted of a bunch of feathers in front and a bundle of green leaves behind. As a disguise the face was blackened with charcoal, the whiskers tied back behind the neck and a broad white stripe of powdered gypsum was drawn from the top of the forehead down the nose to the bottom of the chin, while a similar stripe extended across the chest from shoulder to shoulder.

A girdle made from the hair cut from the head of a blackfellow after death was worn round the waist. This special form of hair girdle is supposed to serve the double purpose of increasing the strength of the wearer, his courage, and the accuracy of his aim—it embodied, in fact, all the warlike attributes of the dead warrior—and at the same time it produced inaccuracy of aim in the enemy.

Ordinary hair-string was worn round the legs for the purpose, as the blacks say, of protecting them against snake-bite.

Both medicine man and Kurdaitcha carried a sacred stone, the possession of which is supposed to be even more efficacious than that of the hair girdle.

In addition, the medicine man carried in his girdle a live lizard.

On leaving his camp the Kurdaitcha walked in front, followed at a short distance by the medicine man, both armed with spears, and carrying the Urtathurta, or shoes. When hidden from view of the camp they put on the shoes, and proceeded towards the enemy's camp. The Kurdaitcha always led the way, and every precaution was taken to prevent their advance being seen. On arriving at the camp the Kurdaitcha crept forward alone, holding the sacred stone between his teeth, and (if successful) speared his enemy dead. The medicine man then came up and inserted the head of the lizard which he carried into the wound. The lizard was supposed to drink up the blood, and so to remove evidence of the manner in which the deed had been done. Sometimes the wound was seared to prevent its being recognised as a spear wound. Almost invariably the attack was made at night and, when successful, the Kurdaitcha and medicine man started back at once, halting some distance from their camp to remove and conceal the shoes before going in. If by chance the tracks of the Kurdaitcha were seen they were avoided, and the threatened camp merely kept on the alert. If the Kurdaitcha himself were seen in the vicinity of the camp he was at once attacked and, if possible, killed. The medicine man who accompanied him was, in all cases, allowed to return uninjured to his camp.

When the body of a man murdered by a Kurdaitcha was discovered no attempt was made to track the latter, but the medicine man immediately appointed a relative of the murdered man or, failing a relative, one of the same group (a Kumarra if he were a Kumarra, or a Panunga if he were a Panunga, etc.) to avenge him. This was done by going as a Kurdaitcha in the way described. If the Kurdaitcha were unable to find the particular man he wanted he would spear a man belonging to the same tribe, but this seems to have been of rare occurrence.

Immediately a Kurdaitcha was seen near a camp the man who detected him informed the others of the fact by saying, 'Udnurrah pitchimi' (Udnurrah, a wild dog; pitchimi, is coming). He did not mention the word Kurdaitcha, but his meaning was understood and preparations were made for an attack on the Udnurrah. In this connection one of the head men of the tribe informed me that, when a blackfellow reported 'Udnurrah pitchimi' the medicine man could appoint a Kurdaitcha who had the power of accosting the other Kurdaitcha and of compelling him to return to his camp, but I have been unable to fully corroborate this, though it seems possible that, when the custom prevailed to an abnormal extent, such a course was adopted to prevent excessive bloodshed.

It is usually stated that the object of the curious shape of the shoes was to prevent the tracks of the Kurdaitcha from being recognised. This may have been the case to a certain extent, but at the same time it must be remembered that in certain respects the blacks have a very powerful imagination, and their idea of not being able to track a Kurdaitcha is very possibly an example of this. There is practically little doubt but that if a blackfellow really tried to track a Kurdaitcha he would do so well enough—a stick or a stone turned out of the way or the nature of the impress of the rounded sole in sand would be quite sufficient clue to an expert tracker, such as these natives are, to show him the direction in which the Kurdaitcha had passed. Most probably it is, one might call it, an article of faith that a Kurdaitcha cannot be tracked. There is something mysterious about him—he wears the sacred stone and hair girdle which are supposed to give him special powers; the carrying of a sacred stone when fighting is even supposed to make a man invisible to his enemies, and he commits the deed under the cover of darkness.

It would probably be more correct to say, not that the wearing of the shoes makes it impossible to track the Kurdaitcha, but that the blacks made themselves believe that it does so.

APPENDIX 6

SURVIVING LETTERS FROM BALDWIN SPENCER TO P.M. BYRNE

Despite Spencer's voluminous correspondence with this anthropological collaborators, few of his letters have survived. The following fragments were possibly drafts or unfinished letters which were preserved in the Spencer archive. They are reproduced here because they provide a rare insight into the style and content of Spencer's letters, which evidently sufficed to stimulate the continued interest and involvement of his bush mates.

9th July '95

[. . .] liberty also of asking him, if he will part with them at this price, to send them to you to see about the condition and that I should leave it to your judgement. Do you mind acting as a referee? If he won't part with them at that price and if they are really in good condition I would go to £2 a piece but don't want to.

Judging by the look of your last ones, the breeding season is over. Hang the beasts, they must breed about two or three months before the time at which you sent me down your celebrated female. I am hoping that we will be able to work the beast out in Australia before the wily German gets him and, thanks to your material, I believe that we will.[1]

Leucrura [sic] is the thing I am keenest after just now. It is a strange thing that they don't seem to get any of that pig footed bandicoot.[2]

French tells me that he is still distributing light and elevating literature over the Central region. He had been on the mild bust[3] over the Baron's (i.e. the one and only Baron—von Müller) 70th birthday.[4] The last performance of this celebrated individual is as follows. A leading medical man and his wife go to see the Baron to congratulate him: the top coat is hung up over the only vacant peg. Enter another distinguished visitor who places his top coat on the former one. The lady and gentleman go but can't find the coat. The Baron, in great distress, suggests that 'overcome little mit de emotions avakened mit the extraordinary kindness of his friends' he had probably removed the coat in a fit of abstraction and taken it to his own room. Accordingly he plunges into the latter in the dark and returns in triumph. Exit the distinguished medico with his wife, the former carrying the coat on his arm. 'Why, my dear, what have you got?' remarks the lady, and the medico finds that he has a pair of the barons most ancient and oderiferous [sic] breeches: 'Ach' says the Baron, 'Madame is married so perhaps it will not matter much!'

Someday I trust you will see the Baron: he is a godsend to Melbourne. However I must stop and write a few lines to Cowle.

Yours very sincerely
W. Baldwin Spencer

Kind regards to Giles.[5] Has he got another snake yet. That one is still relegated to a special chamber.

6th Jan '96

[. . .] may see an alliance between England and Russia, though I would prefer, above all, an alliance with Germany; Italy is too bankrupt to be much use.

The U.S. imbroglio is evidently simply a Tammany Hall affair upon which subject I have written to our friend the 'Nation builder'.[6]

Poor S.A. seems to be getting rather into a financial fix—worse than Victoria: indeed we are beginning to improve and are managing to pay off a big lump of interest without raising another loan to do it with.

If only we had a decent railway administrator we should be perfectly right, but with Gillen's friends in power, whose idea is to fund people in land, money and clothes, we stand but a poor chance of having things managed from an ordinary business point of view.

I really hope that when you get anything like a decent chance you will sell out of W.A. I don't a bit believe in the place: for the most part it is a case of booming and unless they can get a change of climate or a much better water supply, plenty of their mines—the majority of which are not worth much really—must really go.

We are getting splendid gold results in Victoria but then, thank Goodness, we are not on the boom so that we don't have flaring paragraphs cabled home to take in the unwary widow and clergyman.

You want to be like W.A.H., one of the original swindlers, to get much or else you want to have so much cash that it doesn't matter if you lose a few thousand.[7] Everything in this world appears to be run on the principle that 'blessed is he that hath, for unto him shall more be given etc.'

Before I go further there is a question to which I want an answer. You sent me down—many thanks for it—a sacred stick which you said 'belonged to the Bulthara class': now what do you mean by that? Do you mean that it is peculiar to some ceremony performed by Bulthara men? May not Kumarra and Purula men see it or what?

You can have no idea of the mass of information which Gillen is getting together on this kind of subject. He must be expending vast quantities of her majesty's baccy and blankets. Now for the sake of corroboration—not that I in the least distrust Gillen's information but that it is always advisable to get the same story from the point of view of two men—can you set to work and find out as much as ever you can about the rain-making ceremony which I believe your C.W. blacks perform. You needn't photograph them! But it would be interesting to see if you would translate their ideas in the same way in which Gillen does, but perhaps you were with him when he was getting his information. If ever you have the chance, could you secure for me a musical instrument with the somewhat ornamented bit of stick. You gave me the two rounded sticks but what I want to get, if possible, is one something like you may remember the one which you sent to French. I am getting a beautiful collection of C.A. things which ornament my study and are associated with most pleasant memories.[8]

The view, as I sit at my study window, out on to green trees and a fence covered with creeping geranium in full flower and a small lawn which, regardless of rates, we manage to keep tolerably green, is very pleasant but I have a kind of hankering after the interior and rather envy you your view over the fertile plains away to the S.W. This time next year I hope to be with you: we must persuade Gillen to come down as I see very little chance in the limited time at my disposal to get as far north as the Alice. I would much prefer, if such a thing were possible, to run across to the S. side of the Levi Range.[9]

Now as to beasts. The lizards were splendid: you could not have got—barring new species—a more valuable lot. Gilleni, eremius and winneckii were especially wanted and still more valuable will be damæus if you can lay hands upon it. I don't mind how many of all these beasts we have as they are still extremely rare. The winneckii set was especially good—it is really a very pretty beast and the reddish variety made me wish that we had had this to figure instead of the bluish one.

As to the new lizards which you tied together. 'Oolamella' as you say is E. whitii and the banded one 'Inakowina' is Egerina fasciolata— the same beast which runs about the house catching flies. It varies a great deal in size and colour. Last mail you sent me down a little beauty with a bright yellowish body—that also is Hinulia fasciolata. The little *longitudinally* banded one which you sent down at the same time is Hinulia lesueuri. Some of these beasts vary very much indeed. There is amongst the lot you sent down this time a whitish beast, smooth and with faint bands *across* its tail but none on the body: this I made sure was a new species but Mr Frost, the lizard man, tells me he thinks it is only a variety of the strongly banded fasciolata. However there is no doubt but that there are a goodly number of new species to be secured around C.W..[10]

I have sent you three tins, one filled with bottles. I didn't put spirits with them for fear of the customs and will send more next mail. I have just run out of them and couldn't get them made in time to send off today. I will send more spirits up soon. As to the long thin Kurdaitcha lizard: Gillen sent me down one last mail and it turns out to be <u>Rhodona bipes</u>—a beast with small limbs and a long body.[11]

[Drawing] There is a small bivalve shelled beast somewhat like this which you will find swimg [swimming] about in muddy pools. I got just a few in a small pool by the side of the Stevenson. If the blacks could find any (make them bring them to you in water so that the soft parts won't be dried up) they would be very welcome.

It is disappointing to think that Notoryctes can't be found. It must be either a little after or just his breeding season and a pouch embryo would be a grand find. I'm not describing the new Peragale as yet but am waiting to see if you can, by good luck, land on one with its plumage fairly intact so as to have a decent type specimen.

Curiously enough Gillen sent me down [. . . letter ends here]

2nd March 1897

My dear Byrne,

The mail has once more come in and I'm busy for a few days over C.A. matters. After reaching Melbourne a fortnight ago I felt somewhat seedy and went off up to the hills for a change before term began, not feeling quite equal to settling down to the eternal grind of lectures once more. Certainly Victoria looked beautifully green and fresh after the parchedness of S.A. generally and it was a great relief to be amongst dense timber and fern gullies with any amount of water. French and myself went up to a place called the Black Spur and much enjoyed ourselves fossicking about quietly for 5 or 6 days.[12] I haven't been able to get through all that I wanted before the mail went off as it was Saturday last before I could settle down to developing the last batch of negatives—the Crown Point ones amongst others. I have printed off two or three and put them inside the Horn Anthropology volume which goes by this post: more shall follow next mail, but there has been such a batch to print off so as to send the Pontiff[13] an anthropological series from my negs, that I have had my hands fully occupied in this line.

It seems an age of a time since I left CW. We had a very comfortable journey down to the head of the line and got through without any mishap and with a day to spare in the metropolis of Oodnadatta which was quite long enough. Luckily for me Kennedy was there and livened up things a bit—how he manages to retain his spirits is a marvel.

Adelaide—'that delightful town' as Gillen styles it in his letter (in contrast to 'dirty, dull, boom-busted Melbourne') looked as uninteresting as usual.

After all I didn't see Winnecke, at least only out of a railway window on my way across at Mt Lofty, so couldn't discuss Hornian matters with him. I daresay he will write you about them. He left me a copy of Horn's letter to the Premier to look at and his reply thereto. The former was very short and simple, the latter in the best Winneckian vein and must have made the minister smile as it did me. The funniest part of it was a sentence in which he stated that many things in the 'narrative' were taken out of his journal, which is a remarkable statement in consideration of the fact that I had only once had a short glance through the said journal in manuscript in his office and knew practically nothing whatever of its contents.[14]

I suppose that before this you will have had a copy of it. It is much like the usual run of such things—'started in the morning on a bearing 107°30' altered this to 105°20'' and so forth and doesn't strike me as being particularly interesting or as containing much in the way of valuable observations. If Ernest Cowle Esq is not attracted by the par on page 45 I shall be surprised. 'Mr Cowle whose leave of absence has long since expired, <u>now asked to be permitted to</u> [. . .]'

I don't know how far this is private on second thought, so please regard it as such unless, which I think he is pretty sure to do, W. writes to you.

[letter ends here]

Melbourne
11th April '99

My dear Byrne,

Many thanks for your letter. As you surmise I simply detest the usual grind which has begun again and leaves one no time from lectures and Committee meetings. The first lecture I always just go in and take a look at the men and tell them what to get in the way of books and apparatus so as to kind of break the ice. Once in the work it is not so bad and it is wonderful with what rapidity the weeks slip away.

With the working off of the opus magnum I had hoped for a little spare time but one thing after another comes up.

This year it is the Aust. Ass. Adv. Sci. which will keep me busy. We are holding the meeting here in January next and it means a lot of work for the Secretaries.[15] If you could, by any chance, get over I am sure you would enjoy it as a lot of the Geological people will be here. Which reminds me that I saw David the other day and asked him why they had not sent any copies of the Crown Point glacial account. He promised me to see after it. At present he is head over ears in the Funafuti, the results of which ought to be of great interest. Very soon he goes home to England to see people there about it as the core is being examined in London under the auspices of the Royal Soc.[16]

We are having any amount of reviews of the opus—most of the leading English papers giving us a column or two: they are all, so far as they are anything, favourable—some very much so.[17]

I hear indirectly that the Bulletin is going to review us unfavourably but why for I can't quite think after their laudation of Roth: perhaps it is on a question of style. It certainly is somewhat heavy but one can't write up the organisation in the style of the Bulletin. Cowle has kindly promised me a 'review' in his next letter so doubtless he is busily engaged thinking out something particularly scathing. 'Grimms fairy tales up to date' is all that he remarks about it so far.[18] I can imagine him using language and tearing his hair over one or two things in the introduction. At the present rate of proceedings he is rapidly leaving himself no work to do or niggers to look after.

The only excitement that we have here is the illness of Sir F. McCoy (our prof. of Geology), he has been delivering the same lectures for 37 years past and in his absence we are to have a substitute and so may perhaps for an interim have a little geology taught in the University.[19]

Added to this we have some mild excitement owing to the fact that the Gov. is opening its purse to a slight extent. We are getting about £10000 at the University for metalurgical [sic], pathological and Physiological labs, and some £15000 at the Public Library, some of which (£7000) is to go to the national Museum for building so that as you may see things are going up in the Colony.[20] What about W.A.?

I'm sorry for Forrest whose time must be nearly over now that bad times have come.

I hope you'll get a good rain: we have had a grand season down here and things are looking splendid. I hope you are well.

Yours very sincerely
W Baldwin Spencer

P.S. When, if ever, you get the chance, could you get me one or two death-adders. I saw Boulenger, the great snake man at the Brit. Mus., and he is confident—in opposite to Lucas and Frost—that the C.A. beast is a distinct species from ours and I want two or three to see if it be anything more than a variety.[21] *What about P.leucrura [sic]?*

NOTES

Preface

1 Mulvaney, D.J. and Calaby, J.H. 1985 *'So Much That is New': Baldwin Spencer 1860–1929*. Melbourne: Melbourne University Press.
2 Mulvaney, J., Morphy, H. and Petch, A. 1997 *'My Dear Spencer': The letters of F.J. Gillen to Baldwin Spencer*. South Melbourne: Hyland House.

Introduction: Correspondents on a Frontier

1 Documentation of most matters raised in this chapter is contained in Chapters 1 and 6. For the Horn Expedition, M&M, 1996, and for details of the Overland Telegraph and the Gillen–Spencer partnership, MDS, 1997.
2 see Morphy, in M&M, 1996.
3 cited from Stocking, *After Tylor* 1996, p. 21.
4 ibid.
5 for a full biography see M&C 1985.
6 Morphy, Spencer and Gillen in Durkheim 1998.
7 Hiatt, *Arguments about Aborigines* 1996.
8 Mulvaney, Morphy and Petch 1997.
9 e.g. Geertz, *Interpretation of Cultures*, 1975, p. 34.

Chapter 1: Cowle of Illamurta

1 Baldwin Spencer, *Wanderings in Wild Australia*. London, 1928, p. 157.
2 C. Winnecke, *Journal of HE*, 1897, p. 44.
3 Birth cert. no. 892—births in the district of Launceston 1862. Much family information has been supplied by Mrs Elizabeth Dyer, grandniece of C.E. Cowle, as the result of painstaking research on family records on our behalf; also from the late Robin Hadrill, Tasmania. Further family history: *The North-West Post*, 12 May 1894; S. Schnackenberg, *Kate Weindorfer*, 1995, pp. 1–2 (Kate Weindorfer was the daughter of T.P. Cowle II); *Courier*, 7 Nov. 1846, p. 1, col. 5.
4 Chief Archivist, Westpac Group Archives and Records, Homebush Bay, to Mrs E. Dyer, 17 May 1994. Board Minutes, 28 Nov. 1854.
5 Register of marriages, Ballarat, 4 Mar. 1856, no. 76.
6 Information on the Lewers family tree kindly supplied by Mrs E. Dyer and Emeritus Professor A.G.L. Shaw.
7 Testimonial, signed by regimental officers, in possession of a grand-nephew, Charles Symon, Jamestown, SA, dated 6 Mar. 1865.
8 Bank of NSW service details Westpac Archives; Felix Cowle birth cert. registered Maldon, 16 Sept. 1865.
9 Certificate owned by C. Symon, Jamestown, SA.
10 ANZ Bank Archivist to Mrs E. Dyer, Mar. 1994, supplied details of C.T. Cowle's career in the E.S. & A. Chartered Bank.
11 *The St Peter's College Magazine* 1878 and 1879, 1894, p. 257; *The Advertiser* (Adelaide), 28 Dec. 1878, 20 Dec. 1879. The assistance of Mr R.W. Fisher, the College archivist, is acknowledged. On the status of St Peter's College as educators of sons of the gentry, see Rickards, *Flinders History*, 1986, pp. 362–3.
12 ADB 12, pp. 156–7.
13 *The Advertiser*, 21 Mar. 1922, p. 4; pers. comm. Mrs E. Dyer.
14 Felix graduated in law from the University of Melbourne; Gerald became an electrical engineer.
15 Pers. comm. Mrs E. Dyer, 21 Nov.1995; Emeritus Professor A.G.L. Shaw, 23 July 1996.
16 The two previous paragraphs derived from *Historic Homesteads*, Australian Council of National Trusts, vol. 2, 1992, pp. 472–91; Cockburn, *Pastoral Pioneers*, vol. 1, pp. 27, 74–5; Anon., *Elder Smith*, p. 63; Farwell's reflection, *Ghost Towns*, p. 80.
17 Beltana Pastoral Company papers, Mortlock Lib. S.A., BRG 133, series 37, vol. 1, 1883–1886, including pp. 11, 22, 23, 34, 38; H. Pearce, *Homesteads of the Stony Desert*, 1978, p. 31.
18 *Wanderings*, p. 157.
19 e.g. *South Australian Register*, 1 Apr. 1890: a deputation from the Tempe Downs Pastoral Co. requested increased police protection. The most comprehensive study of race relations in the region is an unpublished doctoral thesis by M.C. Hartwig, 'The progress of white settlement . . .' 1965.

20 On Willshire: see Mulvaney in ADB, 12, p. 515; Mulvaney, *Encounters in Place*, 1989, pp. 123–30; R. Clyne 1987, *Colonial Blue*, p. 188; SAA, GRG/5/2/359, 28 Apr. 1890.

21 Willshire, *The Land of the Dawning*, 1896, pp. 40–1. For an evaluation of Aboriginal death by violence in central Australia, see R. Kimber, *Genocide or Not?*, 1997.

22 Dee Brown, *Bury My Heart at Wounded Knee*, 1981, pp. 414–18.

23 Clyne, *Colonial Blue*, pp. 188–9. The assistance of the South Australian Police Historical Society Inc. is acknowledged, especially letters to DJM from R. Clyne, 24 Mar. 1994, and R.J. Potts, 30 Mar. 1995.

24 The Tempe Downs incident: Mulvaney, *Encounters in Place*, 1989, pp. 129–30; Strehlow 1969, *Journey to Horseshoe Bend*, pp. 38–49; M.C. Hartwig, 'The progress of white settlement . . .'; Reid, *Picnic with the Natives*, pp. 122–7.

25 Some letters from Cowle to Stirling are preserved in the South Australian Museum. (See Appendix 1.)

26 E.C. Stirling, *Journal of a Journey across Australia with the Earl of Kintore*. SA Museum AD43, 9 May 1891.

27 On the background to Gillen's partnership with Spencer, M & C, 1985.

28 Clyne, *Colonial Blue*, p. 188; Mulvaney, ADB 12, p. 515.

29 Inspector Besley to Peterswald, SAA GRG 5/2/304, 6 Mar. 1893.

30 Willshire to Inspector R. Saunders, SAA GRG 5/2/304, 22 Feb. 1893.

31 Cowle's service record notes his transfer on 1 Apr. 1893; a fine map with Aboriginal place names is included in Strehlow 1971, *Songs of Central Australia*.

32 SAA GRG 5/2/684, 7 Aug., 7 Sept. 1893.

33 HE, vol. 1, p. 62.

34 J.F. Field to W.B. Spencer, 30 Jan. 1896. Spencer coll., PRM.

35 P. B. Thorley, Pleistocene settlement, *Antiquity* 72 (1998) pp. 34–45.

36 HE, vol. 4, p. 8.

37 SAA GRG 5/2/371.

38 SAA GRG 5/2/949 Cowle to Field, 24 Nov. 1898.

39 SAA GRG 5/2/1984/176. Besley's comment 12 Dec. 1893; Clyne, *Colonial Blue*, pp. 188–9.

40 ibid., 29 Aug. 1894.

41 Larry, a native police trooper, was reported to have been involved by some sources. Naimi, Larry's father, had been killed previously by the two men who were shot during the Willshire raid, Willshire exploiting the reprisal theme to justify the attack. Reid, *Picnic*, p. 123.

42 F.W. Belt to Spencer, 5 and 29 Oct. 1894. ML MSS 29/5 vol. 1.

43 FJG to WBS, 10 July 1898, MDS, p. 236.

44 *Wanderings*, p. 157.

45 FJG to WBS, 30 May 1900, MDS, p. 276, see also p. 300.

46 MDS, H. 177, 179.

47 SAA GRG 5/2/655, 3, 6, 11 Aug. 1896.

48 Gillen's correspondence has been edited by Howard Morphy, Alison Petch and John Mulvaney (MDS).

49 FJG to WBS, 9 Feb. 1897, MDS, p. 148.

50 FJG to WBS, 18 June, 30 July, 3 Dec. 1897, 28 May 1898; J.F. Field to WBS, 18 Feb. 1902.

51 Symon Papers, NLA ms 1736, ser. 1/889, p. 409, 22 Dec. 1898.

52 Gillen's Diary, 31 Mar. 1901, pp. 16, 82.

53 FJG to WBS, 23 Mar. 1903, MDS, p. 441.

54 ibid.

55 *Wanderings*, p. 157.

56 FJG to WBS, 3 Dec 1897, MDS, p. 198.

57 *Gillen's Diary*, pp. 17, 82.

58 MDS, p. 338.

59 WBS to P. Byrne, 11 Apr. 1899.

60 FJG to WBS, 6 May 1897, MDS, p. 160; Cowle's police file was endorsed on 21 July 1897; following his promotion on 1 Jan. 1897.

61 *Register* (Adelaide), 24 Mar. 1902, p. 104.

62 *Gillen's Diary*, p. 16, 31 Mar. 1901.

63 Cowle to WBS, 16 May 1895; to Stirling, 16 May 1895, SAM. archives.

64 F.W. Belt to WBS, 29 Oct. 1894, ML MSS 29/5, vol. 1.

65 FJG to WBS, 25 Jan. 1901, MDS, p. 313; *Gillen's Diary*, 2 Apr. 1901, p. 18.

66 Pers. comm. Mrs Barbara Brummitt, Stirling, SA, the grandniece of Ruth Moulden; Brummitt, *The Moulden Family*, pp. 214–16.

67 FJG to WBS, 28 May 1898, MDS, p. 226.

68 ibid.

69 FJG to WBS, 10 July 1898, MDS, p. 236.

70 FJG to WBS, 13 Nov. 1898, MDS, p. 246.

71 Details of police postings and other career details are contained on their official records of service, kindly supplied by The South Australian Police Historical Society, courtesy of Robert Clyne and R.J. Potts.

72 Compiled from CEC to WBS, 10 June 1899, 30 Sept. 1900, 17 Feb. 1901; FJG to WBS, 21 June 1900.

73 Compiled from CEC to WBS, 28 May, 31 Aug., 30 Sept. 1900; 12 Apr. 1902; 21 Jan., 17 Feb., 17 June 1903; FJG to WBS, 23 Mar. 1903; J.F. Field to WBS, 10 Feb. 1902; 29 Mar. 1903.

74 As was the explanation of his condition by Gillen to WBS, 23 Mar. 1903. Spencer, *Wanderings*, p. 157, also agreed that Cowle's lifestyle 'helped, at least, to bring on the illness'.

75 *Black's Medical Dictionary*, London, 1943, pp. 561–2; *The Merck Manual*, edn 16, Rahway: New Jersey, pp. 262–3.

76 This information is contained in Strehlow's 'Family Trees' VI, 3, September 1960. The assistance of David Hugo, Research Director, Strehlow Research Centre, Alice Springs, is gratefully acknowledged; thanks also to Dick Kimber.

77 R.B. Plowman, *Camel Pads*; *NT Dictionary of Biography* vol. 2, pp. 164–7; R.B. Plowman's journals simply record where he travelled, those Europeans he met and religious services he conducted. NLA ms 5374 Box 167, visit to Illamurta and Tempe Downs 13–15 Sept. 1915, 5–6 June 1917.

78 FJG to WBS, 7, 28 Sept. 1903, MDS, pp. 469, 471; J.F. Field to WBS, 2 Oct. 1903.
79 FJG to WBS, 28 Sept., 28 Oct. 1903, MDS, pp. 471, 475.
80 Symon Papers NLA ms 1736, Ser 1/1277, 1536.
81 See n. 75 and Mulvaney, *Encounters* 1989, p. 191.
82 Symon Papers, NLA ms 1736, Ser 10/853.
83 Symon Papers, NLA ms 1736, Ser 1/1074, 1276–7, 1473, 1526–7, 1687, 2019.
84 Copy of poem, dated Belair 12 May 1913, supplied by Charles Symon, Jamestown, SA.
85 Walter Hutley (1858–1931) was the secretary of the Liberal Union in 1913, and was the chief executive officer in its establishment. *The Advertiser*, 14 Feb. 1931, p. 8
86 The Will is dated 26 July 1920, No. 37357. Proved in the Supreme Court SA, 20 Apr. 1922. Mrs Perdita Eldridge, Cowle's grandniece, provided a copy of the Will.
87 NLA ms 1736, Ser 1/2540, 18 Apr. 1922.
88 ADB 12, p. 158; NLA Australian Inland Mission Papers, ms 5574, box 93/1 and 3.
89 *Adelaide Chronicle*, 4 June 1942, p. 24.
90 DJM interview with Eily and Mary Kathleen Gillen, 16 Nov. 1971; pers.comm. Mrs E. Dyer, who interviewed (the late) Jocelyn Evans, Ernest's niece.
91 *Wanderings*, p. 157.
92 *The Advertiser*, 21 Mar. 1922, p. 4.
93 pers. comm. Rev. P. A. Scherer; B. Henson, *A Straight-out Man*, 1992, p. 90. This could be the site of the Horn Expedition's camp 35 (Winnecke, p. 37).

Chapter 2: Home at Illamurta

1 Honey ants: the sweet nectar in the swollen abdomen is a useful Aboriginal food source. On Cowle's collecting see HE, vol. 1, p. 88; vol. 2, pp. 387–92. He evidently dug through the galleries of two different kinds of ants, both new species. The bigger ant with large mandibles is the major worker of *Camponotus midas*. The smaller ant with yellow abdomen is the minor worker of *C. midas*, but this species is *not* a honey ant. The honey ant is described in HE (vol. 12, pp. 387–9) as *Camponotus cowlei* (now *Melophorus cowlei*). From other collections made by Cowle, the winged adults of both sexes of the honey ant *Camponotus inflatus* were described (HE vol. 2, pp. 389–90).
2 Charlotte Waters was an OT Repeater Station on the track north from the Oodnadatta railhead. Only archaeological traces remain today.
3 (Sir) Edward Stirling CMG, FRS (1849–1919), the anthropologist on the HE, was professor of physiology, University of Adelaide, and the Director of the South Australian Museum (ADB 6, pp. 200–1).

4 J.A. Watt (1868–1958), a HE member, recently graduated, University of Sydney mineralogist. Following study in London in 1895 he joined the NSW Geological Survey; he later became a medical practitioner (Branigan, 1996).

5 F.W. Belt (1862–1938), a member of HE and W.A. Horn's brother-in-law. He was an Adelaide barrister and solicitor, a big-game hunter, later soldier and naval officer (ADB 7, pp. 260–1); the pub was the Stuart (Alice Springs).

6 G.A. Keartland (1848–1926), HE member, Melbourne ornithologist and journalist (ADB 9, p. 540). The finch eggs could be only those of the zebra finch (*Taeniopygia guttata*), common in this region. This is confirmed by L2.5, where he refers to the bird as the chestnut-eared finch, the common name for the bird at that time.

7 Cowle always signed with a full stop after Ernest.

8 Spencer sent regular consignments of collecting bottles and preservative spirits to several voluntary specimen collectors.

9 The lizards were of the genus *Lerista* (called *Rhodona* by Lucas and Frost in HE vol. 2, pp. 142–3), but there is insufficient evidence to be certain of the species. *Lerista* spp have reduced limbs and some species lack any forelimbs.

10 The 'rats' were species of hopping mice (*Notomys*).

11 The Alice Springs Races were a celebrated annual late-year event.

12 F.J. Gillen SM, JP (1855–1912), Alice Springs post and telegraph station-master 1891–99 (MDS, 1997).

13 Charles Winnecke (1857–1902), surveyor, explorer, entrepreneur and HE member.

14 Cowle escorted a HE party—Spencer, Belt and Watt—to Ayers Rock, across the salt pans of Lake Amadeus.

15 Arrabi (Arabi, Arabi Bey) was a young Luritja man who had been imprisoned at Port Augusta for cattle spearing, and would later return there. He also had a brief career as a police tracker at Barrow Creek, following the official policy of employing Aboriginal police outside their traditional context. As Arabi Bey he had guided the HE (Winnecke, 1896, pp. 26, 37, 45). Mennamurta, as Winnecke called him (p. 45), also was a guide.

16 C. Pritchard was an Arltunga prospector attached to the HE; for this 'digging' episode see HE vol. 1, p. 63.

17 Professor Ralph Tate (1840–1901) was Elder Professor of Natural Science, University of Adelaide; an HE member (ADB 6, pp. 243–4).

18 J.F. Field (1864–1926), telegraph operator on OT Line, then at Alice Srings and later Tennant Creek. He was Amelia Gillen's cousin.

19 The nurse from Hergott Springs (Marree) employed for Amelia Gillen's confinement was described by Gillen as a dominating 'Sarey Gamp' personality (MDS, p. 64).

20 Gillen's nickname.

21 A brand of whiskey.

22 These 'rats' were the marsupial *Dasycercus cristicauda*, confirmed by Spencer's note on the letter. The meaning of 'Ulmatum' is unknown.

23 Kathleen and Reedy Hole were permanent water sources in the George Gill Range, east of Kings Canyon, visited by the HE. They are still significant places for Aboriginal people.

24 The grass trees were *Xanthorrhea thorntonii*, named in honour of Thornton of Tempe Downs.

25 M/C T. Daer (1853–95) was at that time officer-in-charge at Illamurta, having arrived in central Australia in 1879.

26 A.E. Martin was manager of Tempe Downs.

27 W.H.J. Carr-Boyd (1852–1925), Western Australian prospector and raconteur, renowned as a spinner of yarns (ADB 3, p. 357).

28 Henbury station was the closest cattle station southeast of Illamurta.

29 The gecko *Nephrurus levis*.

30 The 'piss-ant' was not identified in the HE report, but probably was a small species of *Iridomyrmex*.

31 The honey ant *Melophorus cowlei*.

32 This bulldog ant was probably *Myrmecia nigriceps*.

33 Redbank Creek is a tributary of the Finke near Mt Sonder. The HE visited it at the time Cowle was accompanying it. Five fish species were collected (HE, vol. 2, pp. 176–80).

34 *Nature*, vol. 50 (1894), p. 528 credited Edward Stirling with the discovery of a new marsupial species, a 'marsupial rat' then termed *Phascologale*, now known as *Pseudantechinus macdonnellensis*. It had actually been caught by M/C South's cat in Alice Springs, South rescued it and gave it to Spencer to describe. Spencer wrote a correction to *Nature*, vol. 51 (1895), p. 222, to which Cowle refers.

35 A few of Cowle's letters to Stirling exist at the South Australian Museum (see Appendix 1).

36 The Euro is the hill kangaroo *Macropus robustus*.

37 The little button-quail is common in the area, so it probably was *Turnix velox*.

38 Hermannsburg Lutheran Mission (now Ntaria).

39 J.A. Watt

40 *Moloch horridus*, the thorny devil lizard.

41 P. M. Byrne (1856–1932) was stationed for decades at Charlotte Waters OT station. Step-brother to Amelia Gillen, he was Spencer's chief source of marsupial specimens (see Calaby 1996).

42 Barcoo rot: scurvy.

43 C.W.: telegraphic code for Charlotte Waters.

44 Cowle refers to the new scientific names he has heard, including *Sminthopsis psammophila*, the Sandhill Dunnart.

45 Aljalbi, a spring a few kilometres east of Haast Bluff was evidently so frequented by Cowle that it was known as 'Cowles Soak' (pers. comm. Rev. P. A. Scherer).

46 Cowle mentions his experiment wth salting small mammal specimens (see also L2.7). Under their field and transport conditions it was difficult to preserve specimens so that they reached Melbourne in a good state; eggs were another problem.

47 Most Australian native rodents have only four teats, in the inguinal region, but the genus *Rattus* has more (six to twelve) along the belly up to the chest.

48 Charles French, assistant Victorian Government Entomologist and Spencer's close friend.

49 *Polytelis alexandrae*, the Princess Alexandra's parrot, is a rare arid zone inhabitant, but at this period it appeared periodically in numbers.

50 Presumably Dick Palmer, referred to by Pat Byrne in his letter of 15 March 1895 as travelling with Spencer.

51 Cowle cynically implied that, because Gillen had easy access to government rations, he used them to influence Aborigines to provide him with artefacts and fauna. There is no doubt, however, that these rations did assist his ethnological and zoological activities.

52 Louis Becke 1894, *By Reef and Palm*. London.

53 Spencer made a visit to Charlotte Waters in 1895 to collect faunal specimens and to experience their habitats. Byrne arranged the details and numerous Aboriginal people were involved in collecting. Spencer's photograph of a naked woman was referred to by Belt and Winnecke as the 'dusky venus' (M&C, p. 121).

54 C.T. Cowle retired as General Manager of the E.S.&A. Chartered Bank, King William Street, Adelaide, in 1895.

55 The 'Jerboa species' refers to the genus *Notomys*. *Leporillus apicalis*, the Lesser Stick-nest Rat (see Calaby 1996, p. 199) is the only species found in central Australia. Blanchewater and Montecollina cattle stations appear on an 1883 map (Litchfield, p. 13) in the vicinity of Lakes Blanchewater and Callabonna; Strzelecki Creek is to the northeast. This comment indicates Cowle's familiarity with the region, during the 1880s. Also, his reference to the Stick-nest Rats in that area could have been either the same species or *Leporillus conditor*.

56 These bats are unidentifiable because no characteristics are mentioned.

57 The Irish patriot Michael Davitt visited South Australia in 1895. As a founder of the Irish Land League, he praised the village settlement scheme along the Murray River, promoted by Gillen's brother, Peter Paul Gillen (1858–96), S.A. Commissioner of Lands. The settlement named 'Gillen' failed (MDS, p. 23). Cowle was making typically cynical remarks concerning F.J. Gillen.

58 'Norwest' was the geographic term colonists used to describe northern South Australia and central Australia, then controlled by South Australia.

59 (Sir) George Turner (1851–1916) was elected Victorian Premier and Treasurer in late 1894. His 1895 budget attempted to grapple with the serious economic Depression, slashing public works and education funding (ADB vol. 12, p. 293).

60 'crayfish': to retract or 'back down' in a cowardly manner (AND).

61 Margaret Cowle (neé Lewers) died from combined diabetes and pneumonia on 22 Apr. 1895. As a daughter, Florence Anderson, lived in Melbourne, the parents intended to retire there. (Death Cert. 6254, District of East Melbourne, 1895).

62 M/C W.H. Willshire (1852–1925), the 'disperser' around Alice Springs, then the Victoria River District. He and Cowle were stationed at Alice Springs in 1889 (ADB 12, p. 515).

63 Pastors Carl Strehlow and J.M. Bogner arrived in late 1894 at Hermanns-burg, some 50 km northeast of Illamurta, on the Finke River.

64 Tempe Downs was in the area named the Vale of Tempe by Ernest Giles in 1872; cattle were depastured there in 1885. Martin succeeded Thorn-ton as manager, then R. Coulthard who ran cattle in the Alice Springs area, later leased Tempe Downs and Glen Helen station.

65 Gillen.

66 This incident probably occurred at Mt Sonder on 27 June 1894. HE member Belt and Cowle ascended, evidently to collect plant specimens. The following day 'Harry the black boy' was sent back to obtain better specimens of heather (*Epacris*) than those already collected, so possibly Harry was 'Belt's friend' (Winnecke 1896, pp. 45–6).

67 'shirroccoed': presumably sirocco, a hot African wind, used also to describe Australian desert wind (AND). In this context refers to Arrabi who had 'blown through', or rapidly absented himself.

68 *Notomys* sp. (hopping mouse). Spencer previously wrongly identified a specimen as *Hapalotis mitchellii*, a species not found in central Australia, hence Cowle's reference (Calaby 1996, p. 200).

69 P. J. Squire and Field were both OT operators at Alice Springs; Squire collected Crustacea, Field collected a few species of rodents.

70 Mrs J.F.C. (Florence) Anderson.

71 Referring to an offer to transfer to the NT division of the SA police, presumably resulting from Willshire's recommendation.

72 The lure of the newly opened Western Australian goldfields. Presumably the party would prospect *en route* to Kalgoorlie. Had it eventuated, they may have beaten Lasseter to his notorious mythical reef!

73 *Notomys* sp.

74 House mouse (*Mus domesticus*). This is the first recorded mouse plague in the NT.

75 As Commissioner of Crown Lands 1892–96, P. P. Gillen sponsored village settlements along the Murray River for unemployed people.

76 Telegraphic code for Alice Springs.

77 Conlon's Lagoon was an expansive clay pan whose impermeable clay retained shallow water. Cowle erroneously wrote Condon.

78 Gillen was on leave with his family at Mt Gambier, and he also visited Melbourne.

79 The local black cockatoo is the red-tailed *Calyptorhynchus banksii*.

80 W.A. Horn (1841–1922), mining and pastoral magnate, who sponsored the H.E. During his absence in England Horn raised numerous difficulties over publishing the report, which Spencer was editing (M&C, pp. 132–5).

81 Lord Rosebery succeeded Gladstone as British Prime Minister in 1894, but his government was defeated at the 1895 election. Gillen was a staunch Liberal supporter, largely because of Gladstone's support for Irish Home Rule.

82 Before Federation each colony imposed customs duties. Possibly the most improbable revenue post was Charlotte Waters, where Patrick Byrne combined the duties of customs officer with other station activities. As he was Amelia Gillen's step-brother and Gillen's long time mate, it was improbable that Gillen paid duty on the green female blouses which he brought back, which provide an amused and intermittent theme in Gillen's and Cowle's correspondence.

83 This removal of sacred incised wooden tywerrenge (churingas) was made before their full ritual significance was known. The symbolic designs prompted Egyptological parallels. Even though Cowle was ignorant of their meaning, it is evident that he was aware of the dangers of their theft for his Aboriginal guide. Chambers Pillar featured prominently in Arrernte Dreaming stories (see Mulvaney 1989, pp. 113–16).

84 It is ironic that Cowle's racially slanted double standards prompted him to condemn European horse thieves, while recounting his own deception and theft of artefacts.

85 At this point in the letter there is a drawing, presumably of the brand he is describing: WG 77.

86 There is insufficient detail to identify this animal.

87 'Hallux' is the inner digit on the foot (the human great toe); 'crassated' is fat. Byrne was the best-informed collector of fauna in central Australia.

88 M/C T. Daer suffered from diabetes, from which he died in Adelaide on 12 Nov. 1895.

89 *NT Times*, 1 Nov. 1895, p. 2. 'New Butchery! New Bakery! Byrne and Palmer. Smith St, Palmerston, in Old Exchange Building opposite E.S.&A. Bank. Opening next week. Shipping supplied at shortest notice'.

90 J. Ruskin, 1887. *Sesame and Lilies: Two Lectures*. Orpington: G. Allen.

91 This species, the Mulgara, is known today as *Dasycercus cristicauda*.

92 M/C W.B. Kean was stationed at Illamurta from 24 Dec. 1894 to 17 June 1898.

93 The Aborigines presumably were firing porcupine grass (spinifex).

94 Richard Lydekker, English naturalist and geologist, published several natural history volumes between 1889 and 1900. This was *A Handbook to the Marsupialia and Monotremata*, London: W.H. Allen, 1894. The 1896 edition was published by Edward Lloyd Ltd; it contained data from the 1896 HE report, vol. 3, pp. 293–8.

95 The 'ittootoonee' is the honey ant *Melophorus cowlei*.

96 M/C A Kelly (c1852–1932) was stationed at Alice Springs 1895–98; at his retirement he was an Inspector.

97 Probably ceremonial boards, tywerrenge.

98 BK was telegraphic code for Barrow Creek.

99 This incident shows how rapidly Aboriginal craftsmen adapted to the market for tywerrenge, which may be said to have begun largely with the HE, only eighteen months previously. The possibility that many tywerrenge in museum collections were manufactured for the market merits consideration.

100 'Home': Britain. The crisis of December 1895 concerned a boundary dispute between British Guiana and Venezuela, in which the US President became involved.

101 Fountain pens only became popular overseas during the 1880s, so it was a novelty to possess one at Illamurta.

102 HE vol. 2 (Zoology).

103 The SA Chief Commissioner of Police.

104 Coolada (Goyder) Springs are 40 km southwest of Erldunda and 130 km south of Illamurta. Cowle refers to marsupials and rodents.

105 The Stick-nest Rats were *Leporillus apicalis*, a species extinct today. *Hapalotis conditor* is the Greater Stick-nest Rat, now *Leporillus conditor*, a species which does not occur in central Australia.

106 Reference to the marsupial *Pseudantechinus macdonnellensis*, also 'discovered' by a cat (see n. 34). This is a pointer to the ecological impact of domestic cats.

107 The crimson chat *Epthianura tricolor*.

108 Baldwin and Lillie Spencer's son was born on 5 Feb. 1896, but died the same day.

109 Reference to the Turkish–Armenian dispute, during which Britain, France and Russia exerted pressure on the Turkish sultan. Their collaborative opposition failed and, in August 1896, 6000 Armenians were massacred with impunity in Constantinople.

110 P. P. Gillen.

111 Rabbits had various introductions into Australia, but their release near Geelong in 1859 proved critical. Cowle records their arrival near Illamurta by 1896. Byrne reported them on the Finke River at Henbury in 1895 (Calaby 1996, p. 201).

112 A bandicoot, probably *Isoodon auratus*, the golden bandicoot (Calaby 1986, p. 194).

113 The ghost bat, now known as *Macroderma gigas*, but today extinct in this region.

114 R.E. Warburton, Erldunda station, 85 km southeast of Illamurta.

115 Patrick Byrne.

116 Spencer had ideas of revisiting the George Gill Range at the end of the year to study the fauna, so Cowle was making plans. In the event, drought barred the way, so Spencer went to Alce Springs to work with Gillen, resulting in *NT*.

117 Stirling and Winnecke. Because of a vituperative dispute between Horn and Winnecke, Horn was refused permission to include Winnecke's excellent map in the HE report. Horn retaliated by rejecting Winnecke's detailed journal of the expedition, which the latter published separately, thereby involving further disputes (M&C, pp. 132–5).

118 See n. 1. The ants were described in HE Report, vol. 2, pp. 387–91.

119 *Pseudantechinus macdonnellensis*.

120 Jado collected faunal specimens for Cowle.

121 Gillen and Strehlow were the only JPs in central Australia at this time. Martin of Tempe Downs later was sworn in as a JP, in which case he may have sentenced Aborigines for spearing his own cattle.

122 C.C. Kingston, the Premier, was Gillen's friend. A current controversy involved the Board of the Adelaide Hospital. (See Glass, *C.C. Kingston*, pp. 107–30.)

123 HE Report, vol. 3.

124 Keartland was a member of the 1896 Calvert Scientific Exploring Expedition to northwest Australia.

125 See n. 89.

126 Gillen, Byrne; George Gill Range.

127 A photograph of the crowd at the Alice Springs races around 1896 contains images of at least 58 men and no women, reproduced MDS, p. 238.

128 Spencer's request for the services of M/C Cowle for the duration of his proposed visit was granted by the Chief Commissioner of Police on 3 Aug. 1896 (SAA, GRG 5/2/655).

129 'bouilli': boiled or stewed meat (OED), in this context presumably tinned bully beef.

130 central Australia.

131 The western native cat or western quoll (*Dasyurus geoffroii*).

132 Rabbit bandicoot *Macrotis lagotis*, called *Peragale lagotis* by Spencer.

133 Yelka: *Cyperus bulbosus*, small edible corms abundant on creek banks or moist areas, extracted by Aboriginal women using digging sticks. Witchetty grubs (family *Hepialidae*) are nutritious larvae of large moths; in popular usage also the larvae of ghost moths (family *Cossidae*).

134 Golconda: a term for a 'mine of wealth' (OED); Cowle was being sarcastic.

135 For Gillen's version of this incident, MDS, pp. 132–3.

136 HE vol. 4—Anthropology.

137 *Macrozamia macdonnellii.*

138 *The Native Tribes of central Australia* (1899).

139 Police Commissioner W.J. von Peterswald died on 30 Aug. 1896; Peter Paul Gillen died on 22 Sept. 1896.

140 Eleanor Cowle, wife of (Sir) Josiah Symon, barrister, SA parliamentarian and federal Senator.

141 HE Report, vol. 1. Spencer wrote the Narrative; Cowle praised Pls 9, 10.

142 Referring to prospecting at Arltunga, east of Alice Springs.

Chapter 3: People and Environment

1 Gaff: to gamble (AND)—possibly a lucky gamble.

2 Crown Point is a striking feature on the Finke River, where Alec Ross then had a cattle station. Jane was the partner of Sargeant who maintained an expensive shanty store at Horseshoe Bend.

3 Fred Warman was a stockman who had accompanied Winnecke (1897, pp. 17–18).

4 Presumably the man was killed because he gave Cowle sacred objects. His name is unknown, but it cannot be Racehorse, who had revealed the site of a sacred storehouse to the HE, because he was alive at later times.

5 Nat was an Aboriginal tracker at Illamurta; Kean was to collect personal hair adornments.

6 Parinthi: parenti lizard (*Varanus giganteus*).

7 Nurtunja: a decorated pole used in sacred ceremonies and emblematic of the plant or animal which gives its name with which the ceremony is concerned. The Arrernte term is Atnartentye.

8 Ungoora: probably the WBS & FJG term Engwura, a series of ceremonies associated with male initiation. The Arrernte term is Ingkwere.

9 E.W. Parke, lessee of Henbury station.

10 Jackawarra: Jackamarra or Tjakamarra is an important subsection name today in the Papunya area.

11 WBS & FJG claimed that the Engwura ceremony which they described in *NT* was one of the last held. Cowle correctly points out that traditional ceremonies were performed elsewhere (and subsequently until the present).

12 Erhard Eylmann, a German geologist and ethnographer spent over a year in the NT, publishing work on birdlife and a major ethnographic study, *Die Eingeborener der Kolonie Südaustralien*. Berlin, 1908.

13 Cowle was promoted to M/C Second Class following HE commendation.

14 Sleever: a tall beer glass (AND).

15 The Ilchillya presumably was the gecko *Nephrurus levis*. *Amphibolurus maculata*, the dragon lizard, now called *Ctenophorous maculata*. Cowle's Hinulia Lesueri [sic] was called *Hinulia lesuerii* in HE, vol. 2, p. 140. Today this is known as a skink of the genus *Ctenotis*, probably *C. leonhardii*, a common species in the area. *Varanus eremius* is a small goanna, discovered by the HE. The two marsupials are known today as *Pseudantechinus macdonnellens*is and *Macrotis lagotis* (Calaby, 1996).

16 John Bailes, an artesian bore contractor, must have driven Spencer from Charlotte Waters to Oodnadatta (O.D.).

17 C. Beattie managed Glen Helen station. As he later was killed by Aborigines, it may have involved payback for some serious offence.

18 Dart: a favoured locality (AND).

19 *Hinulia fasciolata*, a skink described in HE, vol. 2, p. 142, is now called *Eremiascincus fasciolata*. The dragon lizard Amphib's Mac's is *Ctenophorous maculata*. *Egernia* is a genus of skinks, of which a number of species inhabit this region. 'Ruficaudata' was a skink discovered on the HE and Lucas and Frost (HE, vol. 2, p. 144) called it *Ablepharus lineo-ocellatus* var. *ruficauda*, now called *Morethia ruficauda*; 'ocellat' presumably refers to *Ablepharus lineoocellatus*, now called *Morethia lineoocellata*; 'Jew lizards' refers to small dragon lizards of the genus *Ctenophorus*.

20 'Aloota': Cowle's spelling of the Aboriginal name of the central rock-rat *Zyzomys pedunculatus* (see Calaby 1996, p. 199, and also for discussion of 'Con's conditor').

21 Boggy Hole (Alitera) was site of M/C Willshire's police post on the Finke River, downstream from Hermannsburg.

22 These are not ticks, but a species of louse *Piagetiella australis*, found only in the bill pouches of pelicans.

23 Eight months later, Gillen described Cowle as 'clean shaved and looks like a variety actor' (MDS, p. 198).

24 *Bulletin*, 9 Jan. 1897, p. 13, praised Gillen, who was writing a 'monumental book'.

25 Cowle's reward was for arresting Beattie's attackers at Glen Helen. He attended their trial at Port Augusta. His reward suggests that there was a premium when a white man was the victim.

26 Hammerdene may be a misspelling by Cowle of the name of Spencer's home in Alma Rd. St Kilda—Hammerdale; presumably Cowle had visited him there—he has the name wrong.

27 Keartland was a member of the disastrous 1896 Calvert Scientific Exploring Expedition during which two members died. Following the retrieval of their remains, Keartland arranged for their transport from Derby, on 10 June 1897, for burial in Adelaide.

28 '. . . there was a little store kept by a well-known Territorian named "Sargent of the Bend"' (*Wanderings*, p. 52).

29 'Boomerang leg': an anterior curvature of the shin bone (*Wanderings*, p. 194).

30 Sandford's store at Blood's Creek, north of Oodnadatta, must have been a colourful place.

31 'Hammerdale' had grounds sufficiently spacious to have a rose garden and a paddock to graze a cow, which the gardener milked.

32 'On the wallaby': on the move (AND).

33 *Moloch horridus*, the thorny devil lizard.

34 M/C A. Kelly left Alice Springs in June 1898 and was replaced by M/C C.E. Brookes.

35 Kingston attended Queen Victoria's diamond jubilee celebrations in London.

36 An example of long-distance transfer of artefacts involving ceremonial exchange rituals. Cowle's description suggests that it may have been a bifacially flaked point from the Kimberley region.

37 In common with current ethnographic opinion, Cowle considered the substitution and adaptation of European materials as 'degenerate' technology. In this case, more efficient metal was replacing stone, so it represented an intelligent 'progressive' move.

38 The installation of the OT duplex system allowed simultaneous two-way transmission.

39 Today, the scenic Palm Valley, a refuge for cycads (*Macrozamia macdonnellii*) and palms (*Livistona mariae*), is a tourist venue.

40 Meaning that Gillen would make an appropriate Chief Protector of Aborigines for SA.

41 Strehlow adhered strictly to a policy of allowing only 'civilised' converts at Hermannsburg, maintaining a segregation from more traditionally oriented people. He refused to view any ceremonies, even though he wrote major studies of traditional society. Cowle was correct, because Mission dwellers attended ceremonies, of which Strehlow apparently remained ignorant. His dislike of Cowle's policies and lifestyle may have led him to complain to authorities (see L5.3). Cowle's attitude seems equally critical (L2.16).

42 The western bower bird, *Chlamydera guttata*.

43 'Tiliqua': blue-tongued lizards (skinks). Two species inhabit the area: *Tiliqua multifasciata* and *T. occipitalis*.

44 The pudding posted by Cowle's sister was heavier than the acceptable postage rate, so Cowle was charged six shillings extra by Sargent. Cowle seems amused by 'Honest Ted's' financial account.

45 Cowle shows awareness of the potential environmental impact of overgrazing during the drought.

46 The Federal Convention met in Melbourne on 20 Jan. 1898 for an important session. Josiah Symon was a SA delegate, while Ernest's brother Felix, a barrister at Cue on the WA goldfields, also attended.

47 *The Native Tribes of central Australia*, 1899.
48 Possibly a euphemism for being shot in the leg.
49 The Princess Alexandra parakeet, now *Polytelis alexandrae*.
50 Nickname for Charles French.
51 J. Breaden, Owen Springs station.
52 The Referendum concerning Federation was held in all colonies; the South Australian electorate voted two to one in favour of Federation on 3 June 1898.
53 S&G, Notes on certain of the initiation ceremonies of the Arunta tribe, central Australia. (*Proc. Royal. Soc. Victoria* 10(1898) pp. 142–74).
54 A special term of relationship applied to the woman by a man to whom her daughter has been specially allotted. In Arrernte, Urtaltye is a man's mother-in-law, while a woman's son-in-law is Mwere, the terms being synonymous. Perhaps compounding these synonyms is a means of signifying a man's 'true' mother-in-law as opposed to classificatory mothers-in-law.
55 Spencer reviewed W.E. Roth, *Ethnological Studies* . . . , in the *Australasian*, 18 Dec. 1897, p. 1354. The *Bulletin* reviewed it a week later. That Cowle read them six months later reflects the cultural time lag in the bush. Langshan is a breed of black fowl from China.
56 That an intelligent man such as Cowle could even consider this nonsense surely testifies to the depth of popular racial prejudices.
57 M/C Kean never returned to Illamurta.
58 Wells held the Oodnadatta—Alice Spring mail contract, though Cowle identified the postal service with Sir Charles Todd.
59 Sir Charles Ryan (1853–1926), a prominent surgeon and president of the Australian Ornithologists' Union 1905–07 (ADB 11, p. 491).
60 Cowle's date erred. Two columns by W.H. Hardy appeared in the *Adelaide Observer* on 16 July 1898. They contain stereotypical comments on Aboriginal society. The significant admission was that 'nearly every white has his young lubra' at Arltunga.
61 Hergott Springs was renamed Marree during World War I.
62 Foot Constable J.R. Barlow was stationed at Illamurta from 10 June 1898 to 29 May 1900.
63 On this implicit threat of flogging, see discussion in Ch. 1.
64 Cowle sent eggs to French which broke. He declined to urge Pat Byrne to write in case he became uncooperative ('snaky'), because he allowed overweight postal items past Charlotte Waters.
65 Insectibane: a popular commercial insecticide, with an active ingredient of finely crushed pyrethrum flowers.
66 W.E. Gladstone died on 19 May 1898.
67 In late October 1898 Spencer voyaged to England ostensibly to discuss publication of *NT* with Macmillan, but largely to test his prospects of appointment to Oxford's Chair of Biology (M&C, pp. 184–7).
68 Gillen lectured in Adelaide on 23 Sept. 1898, meeting the Acting-Governor, Sir Samuel Way. He subsequently lectured frequently in the Moonta region, all his lectures being written by Spencer.
69 HHE: Horn Expedition campsite. Beattie was killed by a former Hermannsburg resident. See MDS, p. 247, *Gillen's Diary*, p. 107.

70 This describes the police station under M/C C.E. Brookes, who remained there until May 1905, when he was transferred (demoted?) to Illamurta.

71 As Price Maurice had died in 1894, the visitor was his third son, Richard Thelwall Maurice, a minor explorer, pastoralist and amateur ethnographer; he was C. Winnecke's partner.

72 Alfred Gibson, a member of the Ernest Giles expedition in 1874, perished in the region Giles named the Gibson Desert.

73 F.J. Gillen departed for Moonta post office on 30 Apr. 1899, having arrived in Alice Springs in 1875.

74 Rev. F.J. Jervis-Smith, FRS (1848–1911) was Millard Lecturer in Experimental Mechanics and Engineering at Trinity College, Oxford. He invented several forms of dynamometer. Possibly he wished to test the mechanics of Aboriginal weapons.

75 As the snake was on the bough roof, it probably was a harmless python.

76 WBS & FJG eventually visited the Arabana region near Lake Eyre in 1903.

77 *Piraungaru*: institutionalised wife-sharing practices claimed for the Diyeri people by A.W. Howitt, and by WBS & FJG for the Arabana. Nupa: term applied by a man to certain women who stood to him in the relationship of *nupa*, to whom he lawfully may have sexual access.

78 NT, p. 50, Figs 4–6, 13–14.

79 Standard practice was to neck-chain prisoners together in addition to handcuffs; Arabi also must have been chained to a tree.

80 Obviously Europeans carried firearms. How to prove, therefore, whether Martin shot only in self-defence? This was the conventional explanation.

81 Amelia Gillen and children had gone to her family home in Mt Gambier, until Gillen took up his Moonta post.

82 Alatunga: Alatunja, the headman of a local totemic group. Presumably Gillen's 'observations' were the set meteorological recordings.

83 Kingston's party was re-elected in the SA election.

84 T.A. Bradshaw was Gillen's successor at Alice Springs 1899–1908.

85 Charlotte Waters was the Customs frontier post, so possibly Bradshaw's buggy was ceremonially pushed across the border of central Australia with South Australia.

86 Gillen was to deliver the presidential address to the Anthropology Section at the forthcoming Australasian Association for the Advancement of Science congress in Melbourne.

Chapter 4: After Gillen

1 *Bulletin*, 15 Apr. 1899, criticised *NT* on its red page, describing its style as 'almost tedious'.

2 Harry Stockdale (c1841–1919), a friend of Adam Lindsay Gordon, led an expedition to the Kimberley in 1885, collecting Aboriginal artefacts. Enlarging his collection in northern Australia, around 1900 he became a dealer in artefacts at Botany, NSW; he also contributed to the *Bulletin*.

3 Influenced by his work with Edward Tylor at Oxford, when transferring to the Pitt Rivers Museum the ethnographic collections of evolutionary conscious General Pitt-Rivers, Spencer accepted explanations of technological evolution from simple to complex forms. His 1901 *Guide to the Australian Ethnographic Collection in the National Museum of Victoria* explained that the boomerangs exhibited illustrated the evolutionary model 'in the possible development from a straight stick' (pp. 24–5). Cowle rightly saw the weakness of the scheme when faced with reality.

4 Any profits were small because Macmillan printed only 1500 copies of *NT*.

5 Mrs 'Myers' was wife of Alice Springs saddler, Charles Meyers. She would have gone to Hermannsburg so that the women there would assist her confinement (Blackwell and Lockwood, *Alice on the Line*, p. 112).

6 Another example where Cowle assumes that people living distant from Europeans retained their 'pure' culture. By implication these were the only people worth studying. Spencer's views were similar when he queried the validity of A.W. Howitt's research in Victoria (M&C, p. 393).

7 Gillen left Alice Springs for transfer to Moonta, and leave, on 30 Apr. 1899.

8 Inapertwa: 'Echidna men—embryonic human beings which inhabited the earth's surface as a number of amorphous 'chains' at the beginning of the Dreaming' (Morton 1985, p. 683). From Arrernte: Inape: (echidna), Artwe (men).

9 Undiara: an important site where kangaroo totem ceremonies were performed (Arrernte name: Inteyerre).

10 M/C H. Chance (1856–1911) stationed at Alice Springs 1893–1898 was transferred to Beltana. Like Gillen, he was posted to Moonta in 1899; he accompanied S&G on their 1901–2 expedition.

11 Racehorse, who revealed the location of a sacred storehouse to the HE was still alive in 1899, despite Spencer's claim that he was killed (*Arunta*, vol. 1, p. 101, n 4). See also n. 25.

12 Spencer was appointed honorary director of the National Museum of Victoria in May 1899. By December he had supervised the removal of the entire collections from the university to its city site in Swanston Street (M&C, p. 245).

13 Cowle's description of the incised decoration on this sacred board is characteristic of Western Australian style; rather than stolen, it possibly was exchanged along a ceremonial route.

14 Gillen returned to Moonta from the AAAS congress.

15 WBS & FJG used the word Udnirringita for the Arrernte word Utnerrengayte: 'an edible grub found on the emu bush'. These are larvae of grubs which feed on emu bush (*Eremophila longifolia*). Many current landscape features in the Alice Springs region were created by the movements of caterpillar ancestors during the Dreaming.

16 Incharlka: WBS & FJG called it Unchalka. The Arrernte term is Ntyarlke, another caterpillar (the elephant grub).

17 Cowle meant that five cattle were speared.

18 Pastor Bogner did not return to Hermannsburg.

19 R.H. Mathews (1841–1918), a NSW surveyor and ethnographer, publish-
    ed numerous papers of value today. Spencer unfortunately judged him
    to be a plagiarist and influenced his friends against assisting him (M&C,
    pp. 195, 220). Evidently that is what happened in this case. The
    R.H. Mathews papers in the NLA (ms 8006 Ser 2/4) contain a letter to
    Mathews from Cowle, dated 16 Feb. 1900, responding to a request of
    15 Jan. 1900. It is an informative reply concerning totemism, concluding
    with the advice to read NT first, 'and if I can then answer any further
    questions for you, I shall be happy to do my best'. As there are no
    further letters in the Mathews papers, presumably Spencer's response to
    Cowle's April request was negative (see Appendix 2).

20 Afghan was the term applied to all Cameleers from the Indian subcon-
    tinent, mainly from Baluchistan.

21 Presumably the 1899 Border Exploration Syndicate led by H.W. Wills.
    Their camels travelled east from Menzies, WA, through the Warburton,
    Rawlinson, Peterman and Musgrave Ranges to Oodnadatta. C.Norton
    was fatally speared in the Rawlinson Range and the cameleer, Shannawiz
    was shot (M. Terry *Untold Miles*, p. 274).

22 F.W. Belt enlisted in 1899 as a trooper in the 2nd South Australian
    (Mounted Rifles) contingent and saw action in the Boer War (ADB 7,
    p. 260).

23 'Time by the wool': not in AND or OED.

24 Kamaran's Well, north of Lake Amadeus, was visited by the HE party
    in 1894, when it proved to be putrid. Kamaran was a cameleer on
    W.E. Gosse's party to Uluru in 1873.

25 Meenamurtyna obviously must have been known to Spencer, so he was
    the 'Meenamurtyna' (with Arabi Bey), described by Winnecke *Report on
    Work of HE*, p. 45, as 'two of my black boys' as HE guides. From the
    context of Winnecke's journal, the party knew him as Racehorse. That
    Racehorse was alive in 1900 is important, because T.G.H. Strehlow
    inferred that he had been killed for betraying the location of a sacred
    depository to HE members (Winnecke, *Report*, pp. 40–3) Strehlow, *Tote-
    mic Landscape* 1970, p. 120 quoted Spencer, *The Arunta* 1927, p. 101 n. 4
    as evidence for Racehorse's death. It seems probable that Spencer's recall
    telescoped the HE events with information received by Gillen during
    1897 that a man was killed for divulging secret information to Cowle.
    It is relevant that Gillen made no reference to the death of Racehorse,
    but was deeply upset by the news that Cowle's informant was killed
    (MDS p. 178).

26 The palm was *Livistona mariae*; 'Tecoma Australis' is now known as
    Pandorea doratoxylon; the cycad is *Macrozamia macdonnellii*. *Tribulus* is a
    genus of herb with several species, at least two of which have prickly
    seeds.

27 Such testimony concerning Aboriginal attachment to the landscape and
    the significance of individual, small places is highly relevant to modern
    disputes concerning Aboriginal land rights for two reasons: Cowle is an
    otherwise critical witness, and this evidence is a century old.

28 These are all Arrernte words: Erlia (Arleye) is the name of an important totemic group; Achilpa (Atyelpe) refers to the wild cat totem (*Dasyurus geoffroii*); Lallira (Lalira) are large flaked quartzite knife blades; Nanja is a term applied to a natural object, such as a tree or a stone, which arose to mark the spot were a Dreaming ancestor went into the ground. The tree or stone is the Nanja of that spirit. Ullakupera (Alekapere), the collared sparrowhawk, is another important totem.

29 Baron von Münchhausen, an eighteenth century German soldier, the teller of greatly exaggerated tales. A book of stories attributed to him was published in 1785 and subsequently embellished.

30 Cowle was unaware that Mafeking had been relieved by British troops on 17 May; Field Marshall Lord Roberts had assumed the South African command in 1899.

31 Even so, Cowle's brother-in-law, Josiah Symon, who evidently invested on his behalf, reported a profit of £94 in 1898, on an investment of £110 (NLA mss 1736, 22 Dec. 1898).

32 Gillen delivered several lectures (written by Spencer) in Moonta, Wallaroo and Kadina.

33 Iloota: (Arrernte Illuta) the central rock-rat (*Zyzomys pedunculatus*).

34 Possibly *Santalum lanceolatum*, the wild plum or plum bush.

35 The National Museum of Victoria purchased Gillen's ethnographic collection for £300 in 1899 (M&C, p. 249).

36 Attnyum-eeta: perhaps Arrernte, Atnyemayte—witchetty grub, or Idnimita—grub of longicorn beetle (a totem).

37 (Sir) Josiah Symon stoutly defended the cause of Western Australia joining the Federation, supporting C.C. Kingston. Yet during 1896 he conducted a vituperative campaign in the press against Kingston, concerning the hospital scandal. An 1898 cartoon depicted Symon and Kingston in bed as 'strange bedfellows' (Glass, *C.C. Kingston*, p. 148).

38 Spencer was elected to the Fellowship of the Royal Society and of the Anthropological Society in 1900 (CMG, 1904). He unsuccessfully attempted to obtain some official recognition for Gillen (M&C, p. 220).

39 Actually *Ptilotus*, of which numerous species exist of this genus of small shrubs or herbs. The flower heads are 'feathery' and usually pink. Their variety of common names include foxtail, silvertail and mulla mulla.

40 The quandong is *Santalum acuminatum*.

41 M/C F.J. Ockenden, whose stay was 4 July–3 Nov. 1900.

42 In several letters to Spencer, Gillen reported that relations between Cowle and Yorkshireman Martin were strained.

43 The churinga (tywerrenge) symbolises *Melanodryas bicolor* (now *M. cucullata*), the hooded robin, and the cuckoo shrike, a species of the genus *Coracina* of which there are a number. Eaglehawk is the wedgetailed eagle (*Aquila audax*); 'blue crane' is the white-faced heron (*Ardea novaehollandiae*). The majority of witchetty grubs are the larvae of the large moth *Xyleutes biarpiti* collected from the roots of witchetty bush *Acacia kempeana*.

44 Cowle's interest in the anthropological and symbolic significance of tywerrenge had been aroused. From random collecting, he began to realise that there werespecific species, totemic and place associations to the objects he collected. While it is considered morally wrong today to have amassed these sacred items, unlike many collectors, Cowle was seriously documenting their association of species with place across the country; many tywerrenge were given freely to him.

45 Cowle gave many specimens to the National Museum of Victoria, as reported by Spencer in the Report of the Trustees of the Public Library, Museums and National Gallery of Victoria, *Victorian Parliamentary Papers*, vol. 2 (1900), pp. 4, 21–3; 1901, pp. 38–9; 1903, p. 25.

46 *Amphibolurus maculata* (now *Ctenophorus maculata*), a dragon lizard.

47 Note that domestic cat had then reached a remote area, and that it had already been adapted into traditional resource use.

48 Another reference to the common ethnographic collectors' belief that when European materials were incorporated into traditional technology they were 'contaminated' and hardly worth collecting. Even though, as in this case, it rendered the adze (tula chisel) more effective.

49 Spencer initiated a proposal that he and Gillen be granted a year's leave to undertake fieldwork, writing to Gillen in May 1900 to ascertain his concurrence. Meantime Lorimer Fison, his Melbourne friend, communicated the idea to James Frazer in Cambridge. Frazer then told Spencer that he was arranging for a petition to be sent to the governments of Victoria and South Australia. As Spencer received this response in July, he must have informed Cowle. By late July Frazer had the signatures of 77 influential men (M&C, pp. 188– 90).

50 'Dodder' raises problems for central Australia. J.H. Maiden the Sydney authority on economic botany and Australian plants, probably referred to the poisonous species in NSW, *Cuscuta campestris*, a parasitic leafless creeper over other plants, an introduced American plant. As it is un-recorded otherwise in central Australia, the only possibility is that it was introduced in horse feed from the south and subsequently died out. More likely is its identification with the genus *Cassytha*, dooder or dooder laurel, also a leafless creeper on other plants, of which two species grow in the area. Yet there are no records of stock poisoning from this plant, while Aboriginal people eat the fruit.

51 Jimmy Governor (1875–1901) was a part-Aboriginal born at Gulgong, NSW, who served as a police tracker 1896–97. In July 1900 he and others murdered five women and children, then rampaging across country he and his brother Joe killed four more people before their capture in October. Joe was shot and Jimmy was hanged (ADB 9, pp. 62).

52 M/C F.J. Ockenden left Illamurta with Aboriginal prisoners in September and resigned from the force on 3 Nov. 1900.

53 (Sir) Sidney Kidman (1857–1935), 'the cattle king', developed a vast pastoral empire from 1886, when be bought Owen Springs station. He specialised in purchasing cattle and moving them across his chains of properties to grassland or market. He purchased the Tempe Downs stock,

but not the lease. Much of his stock was moved to Broken Hill, where his brother conducted a large butchery (ADB 9, p. 584).

54 The Victorian Premier agreed in Sept. 1900 to fund a teaching replacement for Spencer, and the university council granted him a year's leave, following Frazer's petition (M&C, p. 191). No funds were provided by the prestigious signatories.

55 Back blocks: a colloquial term for a tract of land in the remote interior (AND).

56 The staff quarters at the Post and Telegraph Station were built around a narrow quadrangle with a rear entrance which could be closed in the case of a feared (but non-existent) Aboriginal attack.

57 This is the blue pincushion (*Brunonia australis*).

58 Presumably a large spinifex clump.

59 Cowle refers to the tight schedule of the 1894 HE party, when they rode from Tempe Downs to Uluru and Katatjuta (Mt Olga), reaching Glen Helen on return within twelve days.

60 Pitchi: a hollowed wooden container with multi-uses ranging from winnowing seeds and scooping soil to carrying water or babies.

61 An early clue that European demand may have stimulated tywerrenge production (see P. G. Jones, 1996, Ch. 10).

62 An oblique reference to his long-standing engagement to Ruth Moulden Moulden, which was terminated when she announced her intention to marry. She married Edward Johns, a senior railway officer in Burma, in Rangoon on 22 Nov. 1900 (Brummitt 1986, pp. 214–16).

Chapter 5: Bush Ethnography

1 The Bailes family contracted to sink bores in the Alice Springs district.

2 In *Sandhurst and Echuca Districts' Residence, Trade, and Mining Directory.* Sandhurst: Burrows & Co, 1881, the Knight Brothers are listed as follows: Gardeners, p. 94; Seedsmen, p. 100; J.E. Knight, Florist, p. 53. Palms were in vogue in late nineteenth century gardens, so this relatively new species discovery offered commercial attraction.

3 David Syme contributed £1500 to the S&G expedition, in return for 26 articles and numerous photographs which Spencer contributed to *The Leader*, an *Age* newspaper (M&C, p. 193). The articles were published as *Across Australia* in 1912.

4 Gillen was indeed 'riled' by 'Cropless farmer' (MDS, p. 299, 1 Nov. 1900).

5 George Hablett was a handyman and stockman at Alice Springs OT station for 33 years. M/C H. Chance was stationed at Moonta.

6 Earl Kitchener, commander-in-chief of British forces in the Boer War 1900–02.

7 William Hayes (c1827–1913) contracted to sink dams around Alice Springs in the 1880s. He took up Deep Well lease in the 1890s before moving to Mt Burrell. W. Coulthard shifted to Tempe Downs and Glen Helen (*NT Dictionary* 1990, p. 140).

8 Lewis Alexander Bromfield (1870–1914), pastoralist and horse breeder, worked on Henbury and Todmorden from 1887 until 1906 (*NT Dictionary*, 1990, p. 24).

9 see Ch. 4, n. 62.

10 Sir Charles Todd was aged 74. Although the Commonwealth was to assume control of all postal departments, Todd did not retire until 1905.

11 Cowle refers to the expected arrival of an Afghan camel train returning unloaded, probably bound for Oodnadatta, and travelling fast.

12 Another example of Cowle's acceptance of the close identification of Aboriginal 'owners' with specific sites and traditions; he was attempting seriously to comprehend Aboriginal beliefs.

13 Lillie Spencer returned to England while Spencer was on the 1901 expedition.

14 P. M. Byrne would have attended the inquest as the local JP.

15 Ockenden.

16 Hallam, Lord Tennyson, was the SA governor. Possibly the author of this letter was pastor Carl Strehlow, whom Cowle found was antagonistic (see L3.5). Carl's grandson, John Strehlow, informed DJM that in preparing a biography of his grandparents, some comments in Strehlow's papers suggest his dislike of Cowle.

17 T. Bradshaw, JP, OT stationmaster.

18 R.T. Maurice, pastoralist, ethnographic collector and C. Winnecke's partner.

19 Cowle hoped that the S&G expedition and his paths may cross, which they did at Charlotte Waters and Alice Springs.

20 Fred Raggett (Raggart) owned a store in Alice Springs and transported goods from Oodnadatta.

21 Like L5.1, this letter represents Cowle's most thoughtful attempt to present systematic information, probably informed by possession of a copy of *NT*. He named his three informants by his version of their southern Arrernte names, reported the Dreaming stories associated with the tywerrenge, and related them to their social classes. He noted that they were associated with known places, which provided elders with permanent visiual testimony to ancestral events.

22 Panunga, one of the Arrernte sub-classes according to S&G. The contemporary word is Penangke. This is one of the eight subsection or 'skin' names as known locally. The other seven names are: Peltharre, Kemarre, Ampetyane, Pengarte, Kngwarrge, Angate and Perrurle.

23 Bultharra is the modern Peltharre. The term was assigned by Spencer.

24 Possibly the Pengarte sub-section.

25 Reference to the Hugh R., Jay and Temple Bar creeks.

26 WBS & FJG returned in March 1902 from their enforced wet season isolation at Borroloola.

27 Following Spencer's Honorary Directorship of the National Museum of Victoria in 1899, he arranged ethnographic exhibits following the functional/technological classification of Oxford's Pitt Rivers Museum. Cowle would have consulted Spencer's 1901 *Guide to the Australian Ethnographical Collections in the National Museum of Victoria*, Melbourne: Government Printer.

28 Harry Rickards (1843–1911), music hall proprietor who built up the Tivoli circuit during the 1890s (ADB 11, pp. 387–8).

29 *Register* (Adelaide), 24 March 1902. Cowle travelled almost 1000 km, largely through dry, sandy country, during this search for a youth, Graham Wells, and his companion.

30 The lurid and false Maria Monk, *Awful disclosures of Maria Monk, a narrative of her sufferings in the Hôtel Dieu Nunnery at Montreal.* London, 1836.

31 Gillen and Spencer both delivered public lectures, although Spencer wrote Gillen's. Any revenues Spencer diverted to the university, but returns from Gillen's Adelaide lectures were minimal, so although intended for Aboriginal welfare in central Australia, little was achieved (MDS, p. 375).

32 Cowle correctly refers to problems posed by rationing, which encouraged people to congregate, but he overlooks the reality that access to waterholes and freedom to hunt were restricted by pastoralists (see Rowse 1996).

33 The abandoned Tempe Downs station, where Willshire cremated Aboriginal bodies, is now a pile of rubble, eroded by the Walker River (Mulvaney 1989, pp. 136–8).

34 W. Bennett was the policeman at Barrow Creek and F.R.W. Scott was the OT stationmaster at Tennant Creek.

35 M/C Chance was stationed at the remote Diamantina post upon his return from the WBS & FJG expedition.

36 Charles Winnecke died in September 1902, aged 45.

37 Spencer and Gillen were marooned at Borroloola at the end of their 1901–2 expedition until rescued by a Queensland naval launch and then travelled south via Normanton and Thursday Island.

38 Spencer's family had moved from their St Kilda home to a house on the university campus, designed by Spencer's architect friend, Anketell Henderson.

39 *The Northern Tribes of central Australia* (1904).

40 The Melbourne Cup horse race held on the first Tuesday in November.

41 Jerboa rat is a species of *Notomys* (hopping mouse).

42 Spencer identified this bandicoot species as *Perameles obesula*, a species that does not occur in central Australia. It was *P. aurata*, now known as *Isoodon auratus* (golden bandicoot).

43 Raspberry vinegar was a common rural cordial, raspberry in colour and flavour, and excessively sweet.

44 See Ch. 2, n. 133.

45 The fortunes of the Arltunga gold field had been boosted, but without justification.

46 Simoon, or Simoom: a hot, dry suffocating sand-wind which sweeps across African or Asian deserts (OED).

47 There was a short-lived gold mining episode from 1890 at Tarcoola in the remote west of S.A. on the railway to Perth (Richardson 1925, pp. 144–52).

48 In 1902 the South Australian government passed the *Transcontinental Railway Act* to extend the line from Oodnadatta to Pine Creek. The commercial incentive was a land grant system, with a bonus of almost 80 million acres in fee simple. That is an estate of inheritance in the land. Cowle assumes that the railway company would receive treatment

similar to the United States, where absolute ownership was granted, not simply leases. He anticipated problems with Aboriginal rights to land a century before this became a major political issue. Although a contract to construct the line was almost agreed, negotiations broke down chiefly because of federal government restrictions on the employment of Asian labour (Litchfield *Marree*, pp. 15–16).

49 Locomotor ataxia is a progressive degeneration of the nervous system, one manifestation of tertiary syphilis. Cowle's symptoms described in L5.8 accord, as the disease produces muscular uncoordination, unsteadiness, double-vision and a stamping gait (*The Merck Manual*, edn 16, pp. 262–3).

50 Dr R. Humphrey Marten was a leading Adelaide specialist and a pioneer of neuro-surgery. He owned an artefact collection made by Cowle and was a Fellow of the Anthropological Institute of London.

51 Manfield is mentioned in the caption to a photo in the Elder Coll., Mortlock Library BRG 133/41/1: 'J.W. Manfield's Store and Camels at Innamincka', so he probably ran a camel transport agency.

52 Patrick Byrne, Charlotte Waters.

53 H.N. Hutchinson, J.W. Gregory and R. Lydekker, *Living Races of Mankind*. London: Hutchinson, [1903?]

54 M/C A. Kelly, late of Alice Springs, was stationed west of Gawler, at Two Wells.

55 OT employees J. Field and F.R.W. Scott were partners in Banka Banka station as an investment. It was 100 km north of Tennant Creek and was managed and part-owned by the colourful Territorian Tom Nugent, also known as Holmes (MDS, p. 425).

56 H.Y.L. Brown (1844–1928), SA government geologist, well known in central Australia.

57 M/C R.J. White was stationed at Illamurta from 11 May 1903 until July 1905.

58 The Black Spur, in the mountains near Healesville, was the location of J.W. Lindt's celebrated society guest house, the Hermitage, Spencer's favourite retreat (M&C, pp. 177, 182, 341).

59 *Australasian*.

60 For four years following his retirement from the university in 1919, Spencer lived at Ferntree Gully in the Dandenong Ranges, near Melbourne.

61 Kathleen Mabel Hughes was described in Cowle's will as 'my friend and housekeeper'. He bequeathed her £800 and sufficient of his household furniture and effects to furnish two roooms (S.A. Will registration no. 37357, dated 26 July 1920). He left an estate valued at £3990.

62 William Thorold Grant led an expedition which traversed the eastern MacDonnell Range and into Western Australia.

63 A Royal Commission on the NT administration was held in 1919–20.

64 Jack Gillen (1895–1934), F.J. Gillen's second son, graduated in medicine at the University of Adelaide.

65 Stuart's Range opal field, west of Lake Eyre, was discovered in 1915 and is known today as Coober Pedy. The wolfram field probably was at Hatches Creek, SW of Tennant Creek, discovered in 1902 by A.A. Davidson.

66 Alfred Kelly, by then an Inspector, retired from the police force in 1917.
67 Both L. and E.H. McTaggart witnessed Cowle's Will. J.D. McTaggart held large properties west of Port Augusta, so the family was connected with the *Norwest* (Richardson, 1925, p. 21).
68 His nephew, Neville Anderson, who died at Gallipoli, was the younger son of his sister Florence.
69 James Frederick Downer (1874–1942), later Chairman of Directors Elder Smith and Co and Advertiser Newspapers.
70 Edward, Prince of Wales, commenced a three-month tour on the day Cowle wrote, 26 May 1920.
71 At the conclusion of Spencer's fieldwork at Alice Springs in 1896, Cowle escorted him to Charlotte Waters, the subject of the following notes in this final letter taken from his 1897 diary.
72 Senior Constable A. Kelly and M/C second class H. Chance were stationed at Alice Springs.
73 The Staff of the OT station, Alice Springs. A.G. was the telegraphic code for that station.
74 Gunter was an Alice Springs publican. M/C W.G. South should have been at Mt Gambier this date according to his official police record.
75 Undiarra (Inteyerre) was an Aboriginal ceremonial cave associated with the kangaroo totem.
76 The cyanide plant was at Arltunga; *Tiliqua occipitalis*: blue tongue lizard.

Chapter 6: Pado Byrne of Charlotte Waters

1 P. M. Byrne record of service. Service Book. At the time of this research, in the archives of the Public Relations Department, GPO, Adelaide.
2 *Wanderings* 1928, p. xviii.
3 John Besley and Catherine Byrne marriage cert., 30 Oct. 1865, Adelaide District cert. 1796, St Patrick's Church, Adelaide. Information derived from obituaries for John Besley, *Southern Cross*, 7 July 1916, p. 532; *The Border Watch*, 5 July 1916. The family tradition recorded by D.J. Mulvaney on 19 Nov. 1971 in an interview with Frank and Amelia Gillen's daughters, Eily and Kathleen. Death notice of Catherine Besley, *Southeastern Star*–died 10 Oct. 1892.
4 A fuller family summary MDS, pp. 10–11. The statement made there that possibly Catherine Byrne was Monsignor Byrne's sister-in-law is erroneous.
5 *Gillen's Diary*, 30 Mar. 1901, p. 22.
6 P. M. Byrne record of service.
7 Donovan, *A Land Full*, p. 122.
8 P. M. Byrne record of service.
9 *NT Times*, 10 Mar., 8 May 1875.
10 *NT Times*, 25 Dec. 1875; the attack occurred on 17 December.
11 *NT Times*, 18 Nov. 1876.
12 *NT Times*, 10 Mar. 1877.
13 Donovan, *A Land Full*, p. 199.

14 *Gillen's Diary*, p. 14; pers. comm. Dr Luise Hercus.
15 D.J. Mulvaney is indebted to R.G. Kimber, Alice Springs, for information; Williams, *Pastoral History*, p. 36; *SAPP* 1884, vol. 4, paper 191, pp. 151–2; *Wanderings*, p. 358. For technology involved in repeater station, Taylor, *End to Silence*, pp. 171–80, *Gillen's Diary*, p. 68.
16 *Wanderings*, p. 39.
17 Gillen's Diary, p. 14.
18 W. Littlejohn, oral tape transcript, NT Archives, TS 263 (1977).
19 Blackwell and Lockwood, *Alice on the Line*, p. 39.
20 Curr, *Australian Race*, vol. 1, pp. 416–19.
21 S.A. Directory, 1893, list of JPs. Byrne's name appears as a JP intermittently in Directories until 1919.
22 T. Rowse, in M&M, p. 107; pers. comm. R.G. Kimber.
23 SAPP 1884, vol. 4, paper 191, pp. 151–2; pers. comm. R.G. Kimber.
24 MDS, p. 189.
25 SAPP 1899, vol. 1, paper 2, p. 85.
26 Donovan, pp. 4, 197; Bauer, pp. 42–3.
27 Preserved in AA NT D 2613/8.
28 Litchfield, *Marree*, p. 5.
29 AA A3/1 NT 1915/4262.
30 *Gillen's Diary*, p. 16; see Byrne L8.10.
31 AA A3/1 NT 1920/3954, 15 Oct. 1920.
32 AA A3/1 NT 1915/5996, 3 July 1915.
33 Grant, *Camel Train*, p. 96.
34 All documents included in file, AA A3/1 NT 1915/5996, 3 July 1915.
35 AA A3/1 NT 1918/2202.
36 Grant, *Camel Train*, p. 96.
37 Report by Senior Inspector G.L. Dix on Charlotte Waters, 19 June 1930–AA SA B37/2963; oral tape transcript Constable W. Littlejohn (1977), NT archives TS 263.
38 Pers. comm. R.G. Kimber.
39 SA Registrar of Births, Deaths and Marriages, District of Frome, no. 17, entered on 15 February 1932; *Advertiser*, 5 Feb. 1932, p. 18.
40 Grant, *Camel Train*, p. 193.
41 ibid., p. 96.
42 MDS, p. 244, 30 Oct. 1898.
43 *Gillen's Diary*, p. 15.
44 ibid., pp. 13–14.
45 Winnecke, *Journal*, p. 8.
46 Eylmann, p. 8.
47 R.B. Plowman, Journal, 11 Apr. 1916 (NLA Ms 5574, Box 167).
48 Cowle, L5.10, 17 June 1903.
49 MDS, p. 203, 13 Jan. 1898; *Gillen's Diary*, p. 15.
50 Cowle, L3.10, 1 Sep. 1898.
51 MDS, p. 192, 22 Oct. 1897.
52 MDS, p. 203, 13 Jan. 1898.
53 J.F. Field to WBS, 10 Feb. 1902–Spencer coll. Pitt Rivers Museum.
54 Cowle, L5.6, 20 Sep. 1902.
55 Eily and Kathleen Gillen, interview with D.J. Mulvaney, 19 Nov. 1971.

56 Pers. comm., R.G. Kimber, 18 Dec. 1998.

57 MDS, p. 315, 18 Feb. 1901.

58 *Wanderings*, pp. 406–7, 586–7; *Across Australia*, pp. 491–2; *NTCA*, p. viii; *Gillen's Diary*, pp. 28, 75–6, 102–52, 233, 306; Kimber, in *NT Dictionary of Biography*, vol. 1, pp. 92–3.

59 AA A3/1 NT 1922/831, contains three documents 1920–21; Sayers, *Aboriginal Artists*, pp. 78–9, 116.

60 Carment, *History and Landscape*, p. 16.

61 SAPP 1884, vol. 4, paper 191, pp. 151–2. For the role of C.W. in OT construction, Taylor, *End to Silence*.

62 *Gillen's Diary*, pp. 15, 18–19; *Wanderings*, pp. 359–60.

63 M&M, p. 205.

64 *Wanderings*, pp. 406–7; *Gillen's Diary*, p. 152.

65 MDS, p. 192, 22 Oct. 1897.

66 Cowle, L2.5, 18 Feb. 1895.

Chapter 7: Correspondence 1894–95

1 Spencer farewelled Byrne at Charlotte Waters on 12 August 1894, so he lost little time in writing to him; he evidently immediately commenced collecting data.

2 This letter describes the ritualised process of an avenger who wore emu feather footwear to kill an individual accused of injuring a person by magical means. The term Urtathurta was the Southern Arrernte term for those shoes, while the person involved was the Coordaitcha (Kurdaitcha; modern Kwertatye). Spencer rewrote Byrne's version with his permission (L7.13) and read it at a meeting of the Royal Society of Victoria on 14 November 1895 (Byrne 1895; reproduced in Appendix 5). He wrote the word as Kurdaitcha (see MDS, p. 500). With some elaboration by Gillen it formed the basis of E.C. Stirling's version in HE, vol. 4, pp. 109–11, and *NT*, pp. 476–85.

3 If Byrne was correct that the last Kurdaitcha incident occurred before 1874, it indicates the rapidity of cultural change since Stuart's expedition passed here in 1860. Note that Byrne stated that by 1894 feather shoes were made to order for sale to Europeans (L7.11).

4 Spencer and Gillen use the term *Atninga* for this avenging party (NTCA, p. 747).

5 Spencer and Gillen (*NT*, p. 481) identify this reptile as a skink *Rhodona Bipes* (*Lerista bipes*). See also Ch. 2, n. 9.

6 Gascon: a braggard, boaster.

7 Bleak House: the nickname for Charlotte Waters telegraph station (MDS, p. 327).

8 Amperta: the Mulgara, marsupial mouse (*Dasycercus cristicauda*). Unfortunately for Byrne, Spencer found that it had been described previously by Krefft in 1867 from a single poor specimen (see Calaby, M&M, pp. 191–2).

9 A reference to the so-called 'barking spider', whose 'bark' was produced by birds. Spencer (HE, vol. 4, pp. 412–15) described it as *Phlogius*

(*Phrictus*) *crassipes*. H.R. Hogg (1901) named it as a new species, *Selenoc-mia stirlingi*. Presumably the 'old Professor' was R. Tate.

10 Bernard Joseph Giles was a C.W. telegraphist. To judge from Byrne's comment, the lizard was *Moloch horridus*.

11 Nitrate of silver was a solution for developing photographic plates.

12 J.F. Field (1864–1926): telegraph operator at Alice Springs and Tennant Creek, a cousin of Amelia Gillen, Byrne's half-sister.

13 Perchloride: a compound of mercury with the maximum proportion of chlorine. As arsenic also was used, preserving biological specimens was a dangerous pastime.

14 A request for Spencer's photographs taken during his visit in June.

15 *Notoryctes typhlops*, marsupial mole. Byrne sent Spencer the first of over 40 specimens on 15 Nov. 1895.

16 Reference to 'rats' probably concerns species of Dunnart, marsupial mice (*Sminthopsis*) of which some species have fattened carrot-shaped tails. The fat is stored for survival in arid times. *Nephrurus platyurus* (now *Nephrurus levis*) is a gecko.

17 From Byrne's comments in L7.4, probably W.H. Hudson, *Idle Days in Patagonia*. London, 1893.

18 *Dasycercus cristicauda* (mulgara, crest-tailed marsupial mouse).

19 Probably later recognised as *Dasyuroides byrnei* (Kowani, Byrne's pouched mouse); Calaby, in M&M, p. 190.

20 That 150 people depended upon the Finke River well, some 13 km from C.W. telegraph station, indicates the extent of population concentration due to the availability of rations during drought. The well was named Illunga. (AA NT1915/4262, 16 Sep. 1914)

21 Quotation from C.S. Calverley's (1831–84) poem *Disaster*.

22 J.E. Talmage (1862–1931), geologist and Mormon theologian and spokesman on relations between science and theology. He was president of Latter-day Saints College, Salt Lake City 1888–93, and president of the University of Utah 1894–97. As a mining geologist who used 'his talents to justify and defend Mormonism', he would have offended Byrne (*Dictionary of American Biography* 9, p. 286).

23 Peridotite: a class of ultrabasic rock consisting mainly of olivine. Kimber-lite is a brecciated peridotite containing mica. Evidently prospectors ventured west of the MacDonnell Ranges, prompted by the Coolgardie discoveries in 1892.

24 The final cost of the four HE volumes (1000 copies) was almost £1100 (M&C, p. 135).

25 The nor'west was the South Australian term for central Australia. M/C C.E. Cowle was stationed to the northwest, at Illamurta.

26 As Spencer visited C.W. during Feb. 1895, Byrne refers to his return journey to the Oodnadatta railhead, travelling in a two-wheeled spring carriage (or trap, gig).

27 Further adverse comments on Dick Palmer were made by Cowle (L2.6, 11 April 1895).

28 Charles Winnecke (1856–1902), a member of HE as surveyor. Princess

Alexandra parakeets (*Polytelis alexandrae*) were sent from Alice Springs by Gillen to Spencer, via Winnecke (MDS, pp. 63, 74).

29 W.A. Horn (1841–1922) financed the HE and the publication of results. Spencer volunteered to edit the volumes, published in 1896, but in 1895 Horn threatened to edit and publish them in England because of friction with some expedition members (M&C, pp. 132–5).

30 *Antechinomys laniger* (Kultarr): long-legged marsupial mouse; *Sminthopsis crassicaudata* (Fat-tailed Dunnart—also a marsupial mouse), a species not referred to again in Byrne's correspondence. Probably it was another *Sminthopsis* species (Calaby, in M&M, p. 193). Harry was the name of a native policeman at C.W. who accompanied the HE and supplied Spencer with information.

31 *Peragale leucura* (now *Macrotis leucura*), the Lesser Bilby, or rabbit-eared bandicoot. Oodnatchura was to the northeast.

32 On these photographs of the native 'Venus' see M&C, p. 121.

33 J.A. Watt (1868–1958), geologist and mineralogist on HE.

34 M. Doolan was a labourer at C.W.

35 Sir Charles Todd, SA Postmaster-General, also issued meteorological bulletins.

36 H.Y.L. Brown (1844–1928), SA government geologist, was nicknamed Mica Schist by Centralians.

37 In modern terminology *Dasyuroides byrnei* (pouched mouse) and *Diplodactylus byrnei* (a gecko).

38 *Ceramodactylus damaeus* (= *Lucasium damaeum*) a gecko (Calaby, in M&M, p. 202).

39 As Spencer sent copies of 'Venus' images to his Indigenous female subjects, they evidently were not intended only for male voyeurs.

40 A further indication of the important faunal collecting role of Aboriginal women.

41 See n.29; 'at home': England.

42 (Sir) Edward Stirling (1848–1919) University of Adelaide professor of physiology and South Australian Museum Director, was official anthropologist on HE. He depended upon Gillen for much data; Gillen eventually contributed a chapter to HE, vol. 4. A.G. was the telegraphic code for Alice Springs.

43 *Notoryctes typhlops*, marsupial mole (Calaby, in M&M, pp. 196–7).

44 *Dasyuroides byrnei*, Byrne's pouched mouse, Kowani (Calaby, in M&M, p. 190).

45 Fossorial: burrowing.

46 Henry Grattan (1746–1820) Irish orator and statesman; David O'Connell (1775–1847) Irish patriot. Gillen ardently supported Irish Home Rule, although Irish born, Byrne never seemed to espouse the Irish cause, despite his republican sympathy.

47 Gillen's eldest son, Brian, was born in 1893.

48 Gillen admired Henry George's Single tax (on land) theory. The land grant practice refers to providing incentive to a railway building company by generous land grants along the route.

49 Reference to the dispute between Winnecke and Horn concerning HE

publication of reports, which led Winnecke to publish his journal separately in 1897.

50 Gillen was a poultry fancier and later bred poultry at Moonta, where he judged poultry at shows.

51 This is an important ecological observation, proving that rabbits took fewer than 35 years to reach C.W. from Victoria's Geelong district. Cowle reported them further west of Haast Bluff in March 1896.

52 The Overland Telegraph originally consisted chiefly of wooden poles, but they were replaced with Oppenheimer metal poles, so presumably these were spare poles (illustrated, Taylor, *End of Silence*, p. 165).

53 *Antechinomys laniger*, long-legged hopping mouse, was found in a box with the lizard *Moloch horridus*.

54 Spencer failed to publish this data, but handed it to his distinguished student, Georgina Sweet, who wrote her doctoral thesis on the marsupial mole. By that time, Byrne had supplied over 40 specimens (M&C, p. 160).

55 Spencer was an early biologist to utilise the new techniques in microscopy (M&C, pp. 38–43).

56 Tom Hanley was a senior linesman on the Overland Telegraph.

57 *Macrotis leucura*, lesser rabbit-eared bandicoot; *Macrotis lagotis*, bilby, common rabbit bandicoot (Calaby, in M&M, pp. 195–6).

58 Spencer, as editor of the HE Report, visited Adelaide during May 1895 in an attempt to ensure that some antagonistic members submitted their reports (M&C, pp. 132–3).

59 H.Y.L. Brown, SA Government Geologist, travelled from north to south in the NT in 1894, mapping the country. He offered minimal prospects for mining (ADB, 7, p. 439).

60 Presumably the Norwegian naturalist Knut Dahl and the taxidermist I. Holm, who worked in the NT from June 1894 to September 1895. However they did not make faunal collections south of Katherine and the Victoria River (Dahl 1926).

61 Critics hinted that William Austin Horn expected a knighthood for sponsoring the HE, but Byrne reduced the award to a Companion of the Order of St Michael and St John. Horn never received an honour (M&C, p. 134).

62 Ralph Tate (1840–1901) professor of natural science at the University of Adelaide, and a member of HE.

63 Gillen was travelling south on leave.

64 Reference to Gillen's chapter for HE, vol. IV. The colourful names refer to species of gecko and lizards.

65 T.A. Magarey published a paper on Aboriginal smoke signals in 1893 with which Spencer and Gillen disagreed (MDS, p. 111). T. Worsnop, the Adelaide Town Clerk, was author of a rather uncritical book, *The Prehistoric Arts, Manufacture, Works, Weapons, etc. of the Aborigines of Australia* (Adelaide, 1897).

66 The founder of the Salvation Army, General William Booth.

67 Probably the stripe-faced Dunnart, *Sminthopsis larapinti* (now within *froggatti*).

68 Charles French (1868–1950), a close friend of Spencer; appointed Victorian government entomologist in 1896.

69 *Diplodactylus byrnei* (gecko); *Apus* (now *Triops*) *australiensis* (tadpole-shrimp).

70 Niall was an Irish King around the early fifth century. St Patrick came as a slave to Ireland during his rule. His exploits are told in the Books of Leinster and Ballymote. The Irish phrase is possibly wrongly spelled, but a free translation may read 'young men celebrating'.

71 The four HE volumes were all published between February and September 1896, the Zoology one first.

72 The marsupial mole (*Notoryctes typlops*) was described by Edward Stirling in 1889. He now agreed to collaborate with Spencer to describe aspects of the animal's anatomy. Neither man published, however, although Spencer passed his data to Georgina Sweet to research (Calaby, in M&M, p. 197).

73 Alfred Russell Wallace, *Darwinism*, 1889. See also n. 79.

74 Byrne's discussion reflects Lamarkian theory, that environmental and other external factors influence the inheritance of acquired characteristics, an influential belief around this period (Stocking, pp. 242–5).

75 After Gillen reached Adelaide, he was diagnosed by E. Stirling to have suffered from typhoid fever (MDS, p. 83).

76 The 'jerboa' was a species of *Notomys* (hopping-mouse), but insufficient detail is provided here to identify it further (Calaby, in M&M, p. 200).

77 See Calaby, in M&M, p. 191.

78 *Ceramodactylus damaeus* (= *Lucasium damaeum*), a skink, first collected on HE (vol. 2, pp. 119–20). Previously it was known only from Arabia and Iran, hence Spencer's marginal note on Byrne's letter (Calaby, in M&M, p. 202).

79 A.R. Wallace, 1889, *Darwinism*, London: Macmillan. Byrne's reasoned criticism relates to Wallace's discussion, pp. 431–3. Spencer evidently adopted Byrne's case in *Across Australia*, pp. 79–80.

80 Presumably the dragon lizards *Amphibolurus maculatus* (now *Ctenophorus maculata*) and *Amphibolurus pictus*, described HE, vol. 2, pp. 126–7, 129 and finely illustrated in colour by Spencer pls IX(4) and X(1).

81 Presumably *Sminthopsis larapinta* (now within *S. froggatti*), HE vol. 2, pp. 33–4 (Calaby, in M&M, p. 193).

82 Classed within the family Dasyuridae, as also is *Sarcophilus harrisii* (Tasmanian Devil), hence Byrne's wry comment.

83 Refer back to L7.8.

84 J. McKay, telegraph operator, Barrow Creek; French was an entomologist.

85 Varanus gilleni and *V. eremius* were new goanna species collected on the HE. This consignment included four marsupial moles, Kultarr the long-legged marsupial mouse, a short-tailed hopping mouse, and 'assorted' Dunnarts and lizards.

86 *Macrotis leucura* (lesser Bilby); as predicted in HE, vol. 2, p. 13, *Macropus isobellinus* is within *M. robustus* (red kangaroo); *Chaeropus ecaudatus* (pig-footed bandicoot). This collecting area was 40 miles northeast of C.W. in sandhill country.

87 Richard Lydekker (1849–1915), English naturalist. *A Hand-book to the Marsupialia and Monotremata*. London, 1894.

88 Jackaroo was the local name for the Pied butcherbird, *Cracticus nigrogularis* (Calaby, in M&M, p. 197).

89 Andrew Hewish was a station hand on the Overland Telegraph and had a cartage business at Oodnadatta.

90 Totem stones: tjurunga; *Phascogole calura* (red-tailed phascogale); *Hapalotis* was probably *Notomys alexis* (spinifex hopping-mouse), (Calaby, in M&M, pp. 199–200, 348, 350).

91 E'wurra: *Perameles eremiana* (desert bandicoot), (Calaby, in M&M, p. 195).

92 Possibly the fawn hopping-mouse (*Notomys cervinus*) was a misidentification, though *Notomys* is correct (Calaby, in M&M, pp. 199–200).

93 Gillen's family lived at Clare. While on leave he visited them. Then he went to Melbourne, where he met the anthropologists Fison and Howitt (MDS, p. 77).

94 That Spencer paid £20 for this consignment alone is an indication of the extent of his personal investment in zoological research. His annual university salary was £800.

95 Byrne's observations were substantially reproduced by Spencer in his description of the marsupial mole, HE, vol. 2, p. 44.

96 In the bitter dispute between Horn and Winnecke over publication rights and ownership, Winnecke refused to allow publication of his useful map in the Horn volumes, while he published his HE journal separately as a Parliamentary Paper (*SAPP* 2(1896) paper 19).

97 The Spencer family home in 1895 was in Walsh St, South Yarra. As it was a year before they moved to 'Hammerdale' in Alma Rd, St Kilda, this reference may be to redecoration at Walsh St (M&C, p. 88).

98 Byrne refers to *Dasycercus cristicauda* (Mulgara) and *Sminthopsis crassicaudata* (Dunnart).

99 *Notomys cervinus*, fawn-coloured hopping-mouse.

100 Tubaija—pig-footed bandicoot; e-wurra-bandicoot; ur-peela (urpila)—lesser Bilby. This sandhill country was named elsewhere as Oodnatchurra.

101 Possibly 'Joe Blake', rhyming slang for snake (AND).

102 Kurdaitcha shoes and an edge-ground axe were being made for sale, presumably years after their use in traditional activities.

103 Colour pls 1, 2, 3 in HE, vol. 2 were drawn by Spencer. *Dasyuroides byrnei* (pl.3) received a full plate. That Spencer sent proof pages to Byrne reflects his respect and gratitude for their collaboration.

104 Ugartah, *Macrotis lagotis*, bilby; Ur-peela, *M. leucura*, lesser bilby.

105 Handsel: gratuity.

106 *Dasyurus geoffroii*, western quoll, native cat (Calaby, in M&M, p. 192).

107 Spencer, HE, vol. 2, p. 40, described the dentition. Presumably 'stapalotis' refers to large beetles (Coleoptera).

108 Between 1885 and 1891 Melbourne constructed a tramway service that 'was amongst the most extensive in the world' (Davison, pp. 14, 163–4).

109 Gillen and Spencer feared that Stirling would appropriate Gillen's ethnographic data for his anthropology chapter in HE, vol. 4. They now decided to collaborate and keep further evidence to themselves. In the end, however, Stirling was generous in his praise of Gillen, while Gillen contributed a separate chapter (MDS, pp. 76–8).

110 Published under Byrne's name by Spencer in *Proceedings of the Royal Society of Victoria*, 8(1895), pp. 65–8 (see Appendix 5).

111 O.D.: telegraphic code for Oodnadatta.

112 Presumably a reference to the recent arrival of both the Governors of South Australia and Victoria, although the comments on their ancestry is obscure. Sir Thomas Buxton arrived in Adelaide on 29 Oct. 1895; Earl Thomas Brassey reached Melbourne on 25 October 1895 (ADB, vol. 7, pp. 392, 515).

113 David Syme, editor of Melbourne's *The Age*, was a trenchant critic of many causes.

114 During Gillen's Adelaide visit during September 1895, he was present in the operating theatre to observe Stirling performing an operation for cancer (MDS, p. 79).

115 C.C. Kingston, SA Premier.

116 When Gillen's brother, Peter Paul Gillen, a member of the SA Legislative Assembly died suddenly in 1896, Frank Gillen was asked to stand for that seat (MDS, pp. 142–3).

117 Captain Samuel Grau Hübbe (1848–1900) was killed in action in the Boer War. He had worked as a valuer in the department of Crown Lands. In 1896–97 he led an expedition from Oodnadatta to Kalgoorlie, then to Fowler's Bay, vainly seeking a stock route to the goldfields (*Advertiser*, 15 September 1900, pp. 6, 8). W.H.J. Carr-Boyd (1852–1925), explorer, prospector and raconteur, between May and August 1895 led a party from Kalgoorlie through the Warburton Ranges to Warrina, south of Oodnadatta, so Byrne made a topical observation (ADB, 4, p. 357).

118 Jupiter Pluvius: a common Australian colloquialism involving the Roman sky god, but unusual in ancient times (see MDS, p. 194n).

119 M/C T. Daer (1853–95) was stationed at Illamurta from 1893, but he had spent some years at C.W. before then.

120 B.J. Giles, telegraphist at C.W.

121 Pultara: Peltharra, one of the eight Arrernte subsection or 'skin' names.

122 R. Lydekker, 1894, *A Hand-book to the Marsupialia and Montremata*. London: W.H. Allen.

123 *Varanus gilleni* and *V. eremius* (goannas); *Amphibolurus maculatus* and *Diporophora winnecki* (lizards: HE, vol. 2, pp. 125, 132); *Ceramodactylus damaeus* (gecko: HE, vol. 2, p. 123).

124 Another example of the way in which the control of rations impacted upon traditional culture.

125 Byrne explains that the reptile involved in the Kurdaitcha ritual resembled a gecko species (*Heternota bynoei*), or a skink (*Egernia whitii*) (HE, vol. 2, pp. 120, 138).

126 Horn's introduction, containing many insensitive racial comments, was included.

127 As editor of the HE report, Spencer had to deal diplomatically with recalcitrant authors who objected to Horn's authoritarian methods. His visit to Adelaide ensured Tate's contribution, but Winnecke refused to be associated and published independently (M&C, p. 134).

128 Presumably the Arltunga goldfield, where Byrne, Cowle and Gillen invested in mines. This was the period when Coolgardie and Kalgoorlie were at their prospecting peak.

129 Armenia was the focus of world attention. As part of the Ottoman empire it was subjected to repression in 1894 by the Turkish sultan. Britain and France were concerned to prevent Russian expansion and intervened diplomatically to ensure Turkish reforms. In 1895, however, 80 000 Armenians were massacred.

130 These specimens probably were a new species of crustacean *Apus* (now *Triops*) *australiensis* (tadpole-shrimp).

Chapter 8: The Mail 1896–1925

1 The alliance of Germany, Austria–Hungary and Italy.

2 Byrne's estimate of German Emperor Wilhelm II and his military power was proved wrong in 1914. Napoleon defeated the Prussian army at Jena in 1806.

3 L.S. Jameson, friend and agent of Cecil Rhodes, invaded the Transvaal from Bechuanaland on 29 Dec. 1895. The raid was a fiasco. *Nolens volens*: willy-nilly.

4 President S.G. Cleveland (1837–1908) evoked the Monroe Doctrine in 1895, during the Venezuela boundary dispute with Great Britain.

5 The water problem was solved partially in 1903, with the pipeline to Kalgoorlie from the Mundaring weir.

6 F.R.W. Scott, Tennant Creek Overland Telegraph stationmaster. T.K.: telegraphic code for Tennant Creek. See MDS, pp. 109, 141.

7 Byrne inferred correctly that the system of gestures was used ritually by women silently mourning the death of an actual or classificatory spouse, particularly among Warlpiri and Warramungu people (*Encyclopaedia of Aboriginal Australia*, p. 989).

8 Refers to Spencer's drawing of *Ceramodactylus damaeus*, HE vol. 2, pl IX(2).

9 Crown Point station staff hoped to enter into a commercial collecting proposition with the British Museum, but apparently nothing eventuated.

10 I steal by lawns and grassy plots,
    I slide by hazel covers;
    I move the sweet forget-me-nots
    That grow for happy lovers.
    Alfred Tennyson, *The Brook*, verse 10.

11 Alec Ross, son of John Ross, Overland Telegraph explorer and pastoralist, was manager of Crown Point cattle station. His hospitality and cool garden were praised by Spencer (*Wanderings*, p. 51).

12 On 5 February 1896 Lillie Spencer gave birth to a son who died within a few hours. It affected her future health. The Spencers had two daughters, born previously (M&C, pp. 88–9).

13 The HE Report, vol. 2 (Zoology) was published in February 1896, followed in that year by three further volumes.

14 Byrne cynically contrasted Horn's minimal time spent with the HE (he returned from Horseshoe Bend) with his reputed tales about his experiences. Except for brief visits to Australia, Horn spent the remainder of his life in England.

15 The tadpole-shrimp *Apus australiensis*, now *Triops australiensis*.

16 Aroondah: Arunta, modern Arrernte.

17 An interesting aspect of contemporary anthropology. The influential European determined when, where, and which ceremonial activities would be performed, whether or not it was culturally appropriate.

18 The report on the few crustacean species collected on the HE was written by Spencer. Byrne refers to HE vol. 2, pp. 234–9.

19 R. Tate was the HE member chiefly covering geology and botany.

20 A.B. (Banjo) Paterson (1864–1941), poet, journalist.

21 Victor Daley (1858–1905), Irish born poet.

22 Henry Lawson (1867–1922), poet, short story writer.

23 A.G. Stephens (1865–1933), literary editor.

24 Alfred Austin (1835–1913) succeeded Tennyson as Poet Laureate in 1896. His first official duty was some inept verses on the Jameson raid, which attracted much ridicule.

25 Byrne's observations on the food habits of the marsupial mole remained the most detailed until recent times. Even in 1970, Ride (p. 132) observed that 'little is known about the Marsupial-mole in the wild'.

26 H.O. Kearnan, who served at C.W. 1896–1918, becoming stationmaster when Byrne left in 1909. Kearnan was appointed on 1 May 1896 (*SAPP*. 1899, vol. 1, paper 2, p. 85).

27 Jeremiad: tirade of complaint.

28 Women voted in an Australian election for the first time at this SA election on 25 Apr. 1896. Byrne's anti-feminist views were well known on the Overland Telegraph (Blackwell and Lockwood, *Alice on the Line*, p. 39).

29 Spencer and Cowle proposed this expedition during August–September 1896, but drought forced its cancellation.

30 Either Dorothy, born Feb. 1888, or more probably Spencer's second daughter, Alline, born Feb. 1891.

31 G.A. Keartland (1848–1926) ornithologist on HE and a member of the disastrous Calvert Expedition to northwestern Australia 1896–97.

32 Byrne correctly inferred that H.Y.L. Brown's work was able to withstand Tate's and Watt's criticisms. Yet he judged their work too harshly, as the studies by Branagan (1996) and Murray (1996) demonstrate. They examine their results in detail, Branagan (p. 50) concluding: 'In general the geological reports . . . have stood the test of time. They remained the basic information until the 1930s, and were still essential reading when the detailed mapping . . . began in the 1950s'. Generally, Byrne ignored Watt's work, attributing it all to Tate.

33 Charles Chewings and J.J. East had published papers in the *Transactions of the Royal Society of South Australia* between 1889 and 1894 (Branagan, pp. 56–7). Again, Byrne is over-critical of their work.

34 J.E. Tenison-Woods, SA Catholic priest, educationist and geologist. The Ooraminna Sandstone is Devonian in age, as H.Y.L. Brown had believed, and not Ordovician as Tate claimed (HE, vol. 3, p. 57).

35 The puzzle confronting Tate was how to explain the dominant feature then termed Desert Sandstone, occurring over vast areas and presumed contemporaneous. He invoked impossible volcanic activity (HE, vol. 3,

pp. 65–71). The concept of Desert Sandstone has been abandoned. Today this extensive and often thick rock capping is termed silcrete duricrust. It was formed on a level weathering soil surface by the deposition of silica, iron oxides or calcium carbonate during long weathering periods in wet and warm climates. Byrne invoked sea water, but the varying chemistry of the artesian water along its zone of discharge could provide the relevant factor.

Tate argued that obsidian bombs and agates resulted from volcanic action. Presumably the smaller 'bombs' were tektites, splash material from meteorite impact, although larger pieces may have been chemically formed concretions. The agate breccias were derived from chalcedonous caprocks on mesas. Byrne's criticisms indicate that he thought carefully about the published interpretations (Murray and Branagan in M&M, pp. 158–60, 52; Mabbutt, p. 156; Thompson, p. 45).

36 Tate (HE, vol. 3, pp. 22–3) reasonably related the formation of claypans to lack of drainage gradient and continual evaporation processes.

37 'emu poison bush' may refer to a species of *Eremophila*, with a chief suspect being *Eremophila latrobei* ('emu bush'), a silvery leafed shrub with some toxicity to stock.

Euphorbiaceae embraces some 47 genera and 290 species across Australia. In central Australia they include semi-succulent herbs or small shrubs with milky latex. A likely candidate is *Euphorbia drummondii* (mat spurge, caustic or milk weed), a branchy prostrate herb with thick tap root. It was used medicinally by Aborigines and is reported as toxic to stock. An alternative, *Phyllanthus fuernrohrii* (sand spurge) grows on sandy flats and at the foot of dunes, also is suspected of poisoning stock (Jessop, *Flora*, pp. 186, 191; Everist, *Poisonous Plants*, pp. 265–6, 532). Spencer (*Across Australia*, p. 79) refers to 'poisonous' *Euphorbia* in this region.

38 Jack Besley, Byrne's step-brother.

39 In mid–1896 Lillie Spencer and her two children voyaged to England, returning around March 1897 following Spencer's return from fieldwork.

40 See n. 35. The explanation is that from 60 to 20 million years ago, the warm humid conditions resulted in water penetrating the rock, dissolving or altering materials. Dissolved silica in the ground-water rose to the surface through capillary action and was deposited as silcrete, or duricrust (Thompson, pp. 47–8).

41 The 'obsidians' were the tektites, which showered the region following the meteorite impact.

42 Uniformitarianism: one who attributes geological processes and phenomena to forces operating continuously and uniformly (OED). Presumably Byrne was unaware that Tate previously had recognised glacial evidence at Hallett Cove, SA.

43 Troras: Byrne's name for wooden chopping sticks (HE, vol. 1, p. 73).

44 In 1895 Byrne was appointed as a Customs Officer, supplementing his postal salary of £180 by a further £12. This was not as curious an appointment as it seems, because the inspection of stock travelling south was its chief objective. Tick fever, or 'redwater disease' produced by the

cattle tick (*Boophilus microplus*) probably was introduced at Darwin in 1872. During the 1890s it spread rapidly in Queensland. From 1894 quarantine areas were declared, and in 1895 Queensland north of 21° latitude was declared quarantined (Bauer 1959, pp. 42–3). C.W. was located about 27°S.

45 Spencer requested Cowle's assistance during the proposed George Gill Range visit. Permission was granted by the Chief Commissioner of Police on 11 August (SAA, GRG 5/2/655).

46 Their subsequent geological excursion was described and illustrated by Spencer, *Across Australia*, pp. 84–5, and *Wanderings*, pp. 50–1.

47 Striations: sub-parallel scratch marks or shallow grooves produced through the slow movement of ice. This deposit dates from the phase of Permian glaciation (290–250 M.Y.A.) and this discovery proves Byrne's abilities as a field geologist (Thompson, p. 81).

48 Probably refers to investment in mining at Arltunga, involving at least, Byrne, Winnecke, Gillen, Cowle and Besley (MDS, pp. 138, 156).

49 Byrne had collected Ordovician fossils.

50 Respectively, *Antechinomys laniger* (Kultarr), *Sminthopsis* (now *frogatti*) (Dunnart), *Dasyurus geoffroii* (Western Quoll).

51 Professor T. Edgeworth David (1858–1934), University of Sydney, was Australia's best known geologist. In 1924 David and W. Howchin reported on 'Glacial research on deposits at Yellow Cliff central Australia'. *AAAS* 16(1924), pp. 74–94.

52 Byrne's evaluation seems sound (cf. Murray, in M&M, p. 156). Brown's fieldwork observations suffered from his minimal published reports, as they were open to misinterpretation (pers. comm., D. Branagan).

53 Erhard Eylmann, a German scientist and ethnographer, spent two years in the NT during the years 1896–99, publishing an important ethnographic study in 1908.

54 Byrne obtained silicified casts of this fossil and a coral, which Tate and Watt dated to the Upper Cretaceous (HE, vol. 3, p. 69).

55 Tadpole-shrimps and tektites.

56 Wheal Fortune was one of two mines invested in by the Gillen-Byrne and friends syndicate (see MDS, pp. 138, 156).

57 The Arltunga stamper mill and cyanide treatment plant was declared open by Gillen in 1898. Byrne correctly predicted that Arltunga would never prove a good investment.

58 Sans culottes: without knee-breeches, literally working class who wore trousers.

59 The election of delegates to the second Federal Convention was held in Adelaide during March–April 1897. C.C. Kingston played a prominent role.

60 V.L. Solomon (1853–1908) was elected to the SA House of Assembly in 1890. Leader of the conservative Opposition, he defeated Kingston to become premier briefly in 1899.

61 Sir John Gordon (1850–1923), SA Chief Secretary and Attorney-General.

62 Sir Edmund Barton (1849–1920) NSW politician and first Prime Minister in 1901.

63 Sir George Reid (1845–1918) NSW politician and Prime Minister 1904–5.

64 Marie Corelli (1855–1924) English author, popular for her sentimental and melodramatic expression of Victorian morality. *The Mighty Atom* (London: Henderson) was published in 1896, indicating that Byrne was able to acquire recent publications.

65 Lillie Spencer and children had returned after an absence in England of some nine months.

66 The Permian glacial Crown Point Formation unconformably overlies older sandstone, so Brown's map erred. Byrne's comparison with Scotland overlooked the very different weathering processes over immense time periods in central Australia which so complicated reading its geology.

67 The kaolinite deposits some 3 kilometres west of C.W. telegraph station occur near the surface and were quarried by post-contact Aborigines for carving ornaments and pipes for sale to Europeans. Erlikilyika, Jim Kite (c. 1865–1930) produced many items (Sayers 1994, pp. 78–9; *NT Dictionary of Biography*, pp. 92 3). He also accompanied Spencer and Gillen on their 1901–2 cross-continental expedition. The commercial prospects of the kaolinite deposits for pipe clay resulted in a professional examination of the area and laboratory analysis during 1920–21. The report found that it 'has no value as a pottery material, nor for the manufacture of ceramic ware' (AA, A3 NT 1922/831).

68 Cowle escorted four neck-chained prisoners for trial at Port Augusta, presumably arrested for spearing pastoralist Beattie on Glen Helen station (Cowle L3.2, 3.3; MDS, p. 223).

69 Presumably a supplement to MDS, p. 159.

70 C.L. Wragge (1852–1922) was the Queensland meteorologist, formerly Australia's most authoritative meteorologist. Sir Charles Todd also conducted a SA meteorological service.

71 Fridtjof Nansen (1861–1930) Norwegian explorer, drifted the ice-locked Fram to 85°55'N between 1893 and 1896. Using dog sleds he reached 86°14'N, and published his account, *Farthest North*, 2 vols, in 1897.

72 Franz Josef Land (Zemlya Frantsa Iosifa) consists of islands in the Barents Sea, Russia. Byrne probably knew of current Australian interest in Antarctica.

73 In 1893 Spencer's name was submitted to Sweden as a potential member of a proposed Swedish-Australian expedition (M&C, pp. 110–13). 1897 was Queen Victoria's sixtieth jubilee year.

74 George Reid.

75 Viscount Goschen, British First Lord of the Admiralty 1895–99.

76 A sarcastic reference to Gillen.

77 Presumably German Chancellor Otto von Bismarck (1815–98).

78 Admiral Sir George Tryon (1832–93), Commander-in-chief Mediterranean fleet, rammed his flagship into another warship and he and most of the crew perished.

79 central Australia.

80 W.E. Roth (1861–1933), Spencer's Oxford classmate, in 1897 published *Ethnological Studies among the North West Central Queensland Aborigines*, reviewed in *The Bulletin*, 25 Dec. 1897.

81 The Darwin area tribal group, the Larrakia.

82 The HE collected an echidna specimen near C.W., but evidently Byrne never succeeded in collecting any (HE, vol. 2, p. 51; Calaby in M&M, p. 197).

83 Water supply remained a problem. The bore water was analysed in 1920 and found 'not suitable for drinking purposes . . . and quite unsuitable without treatment for use in steam boilers or for domestic purposes' (AA A3/1 NT 1920/3954).

84 The Arltunga stamper battery was now in use, managed by J.G. Woolcock, but the returns were disappointing.

85 On these mines and photographs, M&C, p. 165, pls 31, 32.

86 Spencer and Gillen only visited the Dieri people east of Lake Eyre in 1903, because their 1901–2 expedition intervened.

87 Zebina B. Lane (1856–1912) mining engineer, was then based in WA. No significant discoveries resulted from this venture.

88 Almost certainly the Mudlunga (Molonga) ceremony which travelled from northwestern Queensland through the 1890s. It was performed in Alice Springs around Mar. 1898 (MDS, p. 206.).

89 During 1895–98, European powers were on the brink of war. In various disputes, the British Prime Minister, Lord Salisbury, was deeply involved, including the Armenian massacres, Jameson's filibustering Transvaal excursion, British occupation of Egypt and Sudan, the Cretan revolt and Turkey's defeat of Greece, the United States intervention in a border dispute between British Guiana and Venezuela. In China ('Cathay') Russia seized Port Arthur. The Boer War commenced in 1899.

90 Gillen was transferred to Moonta from 1899. His family left Alice Springs on 23 Aug. 1898 to vacation with their Mt Gambier relatives before going to Moonta (MDS, p. 241; for Byrne, p. 244).

91 Spencer sent Byrne a copy of *NT* upon his return from a hurried voyage to England.

92 E.H. Haeckel (1834–1919), prominent evolutionary biologist, whom Spencer had met in Jena in 1893 (M&C, p. 106).

93 Australian nickname for Cornishmen (AND).

94 The final SA referendum approving of Federation.

95 Spencer was President of the AAAS Congress held in Melbourne in 1921, the first postwar meeting.

96 Sir Edgeworth David conducted extensive fieldwork during 1921 and afterwards, gathering data for a proposed major book on Australian geology, but he died before it was completed.

97 Sergeant Robert Stott (1858–1928) controlled Alice Springs police station at this time. He was known as the 'uncrowned king of Alice Springs' and had been at Borroloola when Spencer and Gillen were there in 1902 (M&C, pp. 211–12, 378–9).

98 Pithecanthropus (Java Man): now *Homo erectus*.

99 Barmecidal: illusory, unreal.

100 Spencer received a knighthood in 1916: KCMG, not KBE.

101 In 1912 Spencer accompanied Administrator J.A. Gilruth on a car trial of some 600 miles from Darwin to (unsuccessfully) establish the credentials

of road travel (M&C, pp. 296–9). On his 1923 visit to the Centre, Spencer urged further road construction (M&C, p. 378).

102 The railway was extended from Oodnadatta to Alice Springs 1927–29.
103 Sir Arthur Keith, *The Antiquity of Man*. London, 1925.
104 The Talgai cranium was discovered on the Darling Downs, Queensland, in 1886, but was not made public until 1914. It is now known to be late Pleistocene in age, but younger than the Lake Mungo burials.
105 A percipient summary of the consequences of pastoralism, issuing rations and other misdirected 'welfare' policies. Byrne's racial attitude seems considerably more sympathetic than that of most of his contempories.

Appendix 1: C.E. Cowle Letters to Edward Stirling

1 S.A.M. AA 298 acc. no. Stirling presumably sought information for his section of the HE Report.
2 Racehorse was the HE guide who was browbeaten by Stirling and Winnecke to reveal the location of a sacred storehouse north of Haast Bluff, so he presumably belonged to this area well to the north of Tempe Downs.
3 Presumably an object transferred a long distance through ceremonial exchange.
4 It must be inferred from the following letter that Cowle sought Stirling's medical advice on his state of health.
5 Arrabi (or Arabi Bey as Winnecke termed him in his *Journal* 1897, p. 45) and Meenymurta (or Mennamurta) were attached to the Illamurta station in 1894 and acted a guides to the HE. They subsequently speared cattle and served sentences in Port Augusta prison.
6 Before Cowle gained experience through Spencer's urging, it is clear that he lacked understanding of the social system.
7 The death of Cowle's mother on 22 Apr. 1895.
8 Spencer was editing the four HE volumes.
9 Presumably he suffered from indigestion and Stirling had prescribed the tablets.
10 M/C Daer had diabetes; he died in Nov. 1895.

Appendix 2: C.E. Cowle to R.H. Mathews

1 R.H. Mathews collection, NLA, ms 8006, series 2/4.
2 Arabana.

Appendix 6: Surviving Letters from Baldwin Spencer to P.M. Byrne

1 The 'wily German' must refer to the Norwegian Knut Dahl (see chapter 7, n. 60). The German scientist Erhard Eylmann had not arrived in the NT at this date.

2 *Macrotis leucura*, the lesser Bilby; *Chaeropus ecaudatus*, the pig-footed bandicoot.

3 bust: to squander (money).

4 Baron Sir Ferdinand von Mueller (1825–96), botanist and explorer. Government Botanist, Victoria, from 1853. Following his death, Spencer sponsored and designed the Mueller Medal, awarded by the Australian and New Zealand Association for the Advancement of Science (M&C, pp. 109–10).

5 B.J. Giles, then a telegraphist at C.W. repeater station.

6 For Gillen's fiery response, see MDS, pp. 93–4.

7 W.A. Horn.

8 This offers rare insight into how Spencer checked information supplied to him.

9 Spencer's proposed visit to the western ranges was arranged by Cowle, but drought forced its cancellation; consequently Spencer undertook extended fieldwork at Alice Springs with Gillen during the 1896–97 summer months.

10 These lizards were described in HE, vol. 2, pp. 138–42, by A.H.S. Lucas and C. Frost.

11 For Gillen's letter of 7 November 1895, see MDS, p. 87. The lizard was *Rhodona bipes*, a sandy spinifex country species which lacks front legs, while its small hind legs ensure snake-like movement.

12 The Hermitage, Black Spur, near Healesville, was a 'society' guest house run by J.W. Lindt, ethnographic photographer and Spencer's friend. Dame Nellie Melba vacationed at this guest house (M&C, p. 177).

13 The Pontiff: Gillen.

14 Winnecke's report on HE was published in S.A.P. P., vol. 2, paper 19, 1896. As it was ordered to be printed on 29 October 1996, Horn's correspondence presumably was related to this. Spencer wrote the 'Narrative' in HE, vol. 1.

15 The 8th AAAS congress, for which Spencer acted as congress secretary and editor of its *Handbook to Melbourne* (1900). Spencer's influence is indicated by contributors to this handbook: Howitt, Fison, Keartland and French; Gillen served as anthropology section president. Two students from Spencer's department were the first females to deliver congress papers (M&C, pp. 181–2).

16 Edgeworth David examined rock specimens collected by Byrne and Spencer, pronouncing them glacially striated (*AAAS* 7[1898], p. 109). During 1897–98, David directed a project to core through coral on Funafuti, an atoll in the Ellice Islands, to a depth of 340 metres (*ADB 8, p. 219*).

17 NT was published by Macmillan in January 1899.

18 Cowle, L3.11, *The Bulletin* review (15 Apr. 1899) described NT as 'almost tedious'.

19 Sir Frederick McCoy (1827–99) was a Creationist, who held multiple science chairs at the university and directed the National Museum of Victoria (M&C, pp. 78–9).

20 In 1899, Spencer succeeded McCoy as Hon. Director of the museum, so he supervised the planning and design of the additions to the museum which opened in Russell Street, Melbourne, in 1906.

21 In HE Report, vol. II, p. 150, Lucas and Frost attributed a C.W. death-adder to *Acanthophis antarctica*. In describing another central Australian specimen, Boulenger (1898) assigned it to a new species *Acanthophis pyrrhus*, and concluded that the HE specimen 'will no doubt prove to belong to the new species'. This new attribution was never challenged (Calaby, in M&M, pp. 202–3).

BIBLIOGRAPHY

Anon 1940 *Elder, Smith & Co Limited*. Adelaide: Advertiser Printing Office.

Australian Council of National Trusts 1982 *Historic Homesteads*. Heritage Reprints vol. 2. Canberra: Beltana, pp. 472–91.

Bauer, F.H. 1959 *Historical Geographic Survey of Part of Northern Australia*, Part 1. Canberra: CSIRO, Division of Land Research and Regional Survey.

Blackwell, D. and Lockwood, D. 1965 *Alice on the Line*. Sydney: Angus & Robertson.

Boulenger, G.A. 1898 Description of new Death-Adder (*Acanthophis*) from central Australia. *Annals and Magazine of Natural History* 2(7):75.

Branagan, D.F. 1996 John Alexander Watt: Geologist on the Horn Expedition. In S.R. Morton and D.J. Mulvaney (eds) *Exploring Central Australia: Society and Environment and the 1894 Horn Expedition*, pp. 42–58.

Brown, Dee 1981 *Bury My Heart at Wounded Knee*. New York: Washington Square Press.

Brummitt, B. n.d. *The Moulden Family*. Adelaide: Lutheran Publishing House.

Byrne, P. M. 1895 Notes on the customs connected with the use of the so-called Kurdaitcha Shoes of Central Australia. *Proceedings of the Royal Society of Victoria* 8, pp. 65–8.

Calaby, J.H. 1996 Baldwin Spencer's post-Horn Expedition collectors in central Australia. In S.R. Morton and D.J. Mulvaney (eds) *Exploring Central Australia: Society and Environment and the 1894 Horn Expedition*, pp. 188–208.

Carment, D. 1991 *History and Landscape in Central Australia*. Darwin: North Australian Research Unit.

Clyne, R. 1987 *Colonial Blue: A History of the South Australian Police Force 1836–1916*. Netley: Wakefield Press.

Cockburn, R. 1927 *Pastoral Pioneers of South Australia*. Adelaide: Lutheran Publishing House, (reprint and index).

Curr, E.M. 1886 *The Australian Race*, 4 vols. Melbourne: Government Printer.

Dahl, K. 1926 *In Savage Australia*. London: Philip Allan.

Davison, G. 1978 *The Rise and Fall of Marvellous Melbourne*. Melbourne: Melbourne University Press.

Donovan, P. F. 1981 *A Land Full of Possibilities*. St Lucia: University of Queensland Press.

Durkheim, E. 1971 *The Elementary Form of Religious Life* [translated by J. Ward Swan]. Melbourne: Allen & Unwin.

Everist, S.L. 1981 *Poisonous Plants of Australia*. Sydney: Angus & Robertson.

Eylmann, E. 1908 *Die Eingeborenen der Kolonie Südaustralien*. Berlin: Dietrich Reimer.

Farwell, G. 1965 *Ghost Towns of Australia*. Hong Kong: Rigby.

Geertz, C. 1975 *The Interpretation of Cultures*. New York: Basic Books.

Gillen, F.J. 1968 *Gillen's Diary. The Camp Jottings of F.J. Gillen*. Adelaide: Libraries Board of SA.

Glass, M. 1997 *Charles Cameron Kingston*. Carlton: Melbourne University Press.

Grant, A. 1989 *Camel Train & Aeroplane: The Story of Skipper Partridge*. Erskineville: Frontier Publishing.

Hartwig, M.C. 1965 The Progress of White Settlement in the Alice Spring District and its Effects upon the Aboriginal Population 1860–1894. PhD thesis, University of Adelaide.

Henson, B. 1992 *A Straight-out Man: F.W. Albrecht and Central Australian Aborigines*. Melbourne: Melbourne University Press.

Hiatt, L.R. 1996 *Arguments about Aborigines*. Cambridge: Cambridge University Press.

Jessop, J. (ed.) 1981 *Flora of Central Australia*. Sydney: Reed.

Jones, P. G. 1996 'A Box of Native Things': Ethnographic collectors and the South Australian Museum, 1830s–1930s. PhD thesis, University of Adelaide.

Kimber, R. 1997 Genocide or Not? The Situation in Central Australia, 1860–1895. *Genocide Perspectives 1. Essays in Comparative Genocide*. Sydney: Centre for Comparative Genocide Studies.

Litchfield, L. 1983 *Marree*. Adelaide: Privately printed.

Mabbutt, J.A. 1967 Denudation Chronology in Central Australia. In J.N. Jennings and J.A. Mabbutt (eds) *Landform Studies from Australia and New Guinea*, pp. 144–81. Canberra: ANU Press.

Morphy, H. 1996 'More than Mere Facts: Positioning Spencer and Gillen in the History of Anthropology'. In S.R. Morton and D.J. Mulvaney (eds) *Exploring Central Australia: Society and Environment and the 1894 Horn Expedition*, pp. 135–49. Sydney: Surrey Beatty and Sons.

——1998 'Spencer and Gillen in Durkheim: The Theoretical Construction of Ethnography'. In N. Allen, W. Pickering and W. Watts Miller (eds) *On Durkheim's Elementary Forms of Religious Life*. London: Routledge.

Morton, J. 1985 Sustaining Desire: A Structuralist Interpretation of Myth and Male Cult in Central Australia. PhD thesis, The Australian National University, Canberra.

Morton, S.R. and Mulvaney, D.J. (eds) 1996 *Exploring Central Australia: Society, the Environment and the 1894 Horn Expedition*. Sydney: Surrey Beatty.

Mulvaney, D.J. 1989 *Encounters in Place: Outsiders and Aboriginal Australians 1606–1985*. St Lucia: University of Queensland Press.

Mulvaney, D.J. and Calaby, J.H. 1985 *'So Much that is New' Baldwin Spencer 1860–1929*. Melbourne: Melbourne University Press.

Mulvaney. J., Morphy, H. and Petch, A. 1997 *'My Dear Spencer' The Letters of F.J. Gillen to Baldwin Spencer*. South Melbourne: Hyland House.

Murray, P. J. 1996 Tate's Palaeontological Observations with Reference to the Geological Work of the Horn Expedition. In S.R. Morton and D.J. Mulvaney (eds) *Exploring Central Australia: Society, the Environment and the 1894 Horn Expedition*, pp. 150–67. Sydney: Surrey Beatty.

Northern Territory Dictionary of Biography, vol. 1 1990. Darwin: Northern Territory University.

Pearce, H. 1978 *Homesteads of the Sandy Desert*. Adelaide: Rigby.

Plowman, R.B. 1933 *Camel Pads*. Sydney: Angus & Robertson.

Reid, G. 1990 *A Picnic with the Natives*. Melbourne: Melbourne University Press.

Richards, E. (ed.) 1986 *The Flinders History of South Australia. Social History*. Netley: Wakefield Press.

Richardson, N.A. 1925 *The Pioneers of the North-West of South Australia 1856 to 1914*. Adelaide: W.K. Thomas and Co.

Ride, W.D.L. 1970 *A Guide to the Native Mammals of Australia*. Melbourne: Oxford University Press.

Rowse, T. 1996 Rationing the Inexplicable. In S.R. Morton and D.J. Mulvaney (eds) *Exploring Central Australia: Society and Environment and the 1894 Horn Expedition*, pp. 104–13.

Sayers, A. 1994 *Aboriginal Artists of the Nineteenth Century*. South Melbourne: Oxford University Press.

Schnackenberg, S. 1995 *Kate Weindorfer The Woman Behind the Man and the Mountain*. Launceston: Regal Publications.

Spencer, W.B. (ed.) 1896 *Horn Expedition Report Parts 1 [Narrative] 2 [Zoology] 3 [Geology and Botany] and 4 [Anthropology]*. London: Dulau and Co.

——1928 *Wanderings in Wild Australia*. London: Macmillan.

Spencer, W.B. and Gillen, F.J. 1899 *The Native Tribes of Central Australia*. London: Macmillan.

——1904 *The Northern Tribes of Central Australia*. London: Macmillan.

——1912 *Across Australia* (vols I and II). London: Macmillan.

——1927 *The Arunta*. 2 vols. London: Macmillan.

Stocking, G. 1996 *After Tylor: British Social Anthropology 1888–1951*. London: Athlone Press.

Strehlow, T.G.H. 1969 *Journey to Horseshoe Bend*. Sydney: Angus & Robertson.

——1970 Geography and the Totemic Landscape in Australia. In R.M. Berndt (ed.) *Australian Aboriginal Anthropology*, pp. 92–140. Nedlands: University of Western Australia Press.

——1971 *Songs of Central Australia*. Sydney: Angus & Robertson.

Taylor, P. 1980 *An End to Silence*. Sydney: Methuen.

Terry, M. n.d. *Untold Miles*. London: Selwyn and Blount.

Thompson, R.B. 1991 *A Guide to the Geology and Landforms of Central Australia.* Alice Springs: NT Government.

Thorley, P. B. 1998 Pleistocene Settlement in the Australian Arid Zone. *Antiquity* 72:34–45.

Williams, E.A. 1992 *The Postal History of the Northern Territory, 1824–1988.* Melbourne: Royal Philatelic Society of Victoria.

Willshire, W.H. 1896 *The Land of the Dawning.* Adelaide: W.K. Thomas and Co.

Winnecke, C. 1897 *Journal of the Horn Scientific Exploring Expedition 1894 with Maps and Plans and a Report on the Physical Geography of Central Australia by Professor R. Tate and J.A. Watt.* Adelaide: Government Printer.

INDEX